To Andy
Who matters so much.

To Anne, Jack, and Maddie
Me ke aloha.

PREFACE to the SECOND EDITION

It is difficult to believe that the first edition of *The Capability Problem* has been in print for twenty-six years. The book hardly seems that old. Most of the cases featured in the original edition are still taught in first-year Contracts courses. And the insights to be gleaned from the materials still seem useful and important to us.

In particular, the book's emphasis on the practical problems confronted by lawyers and courts – on capability problems – is more relevant now than ever. Law teaching increasingly focuses on skills these days, as law faculties have grown increasingly troubled that law graduates don't know how to read a record, or interview a witness, or conduct a cross-examination. Reflecting this concern, the ABA may soon require accredited law schools to oblige all students to take courses designed to develop lawyering skills.

The book has also held up well as a work of scholarship. Indeed, *The Capability Problem* helped inspire a new brand of scholarship, sometimes referred to as "legal archaeology," that seeks to uncover the social and factual complexities undergirding familiar cases. The result has been a wide variety of fascinating studies of capability problems not just in contract law, but in other areas as well.

Still, while *The Capability Problem* has thrived over the years, it has become apparent that a new edition is in order. We have deleted one case and replaced it with three new ones. We have also made many revisions and corrections, most of them minor, to the materials carried forward from the original edition. In addition, we have added an index. More information on the content and organization of this edition can be found in the new Introduction, immediately following the Table of Contents.

We would like to take this opportunity to thank all of those who have supported us in making this second edition a reality. In particular, we express our gratitude to Dean William Fox, Associate Dean Lucia Silecchia, Professor Heidi Schooner, and Sabrina Hilliard of The Catholic University of America Columbus School of Law; Dean Mike Young, Associate Dean Roger Trangsrud, and Professor Steve Schooner of George Washington University Law School; Professor Phil Schrag of Georgetown Law School; Associate Dean Kellye Testy and Professors Jan Ainsworth and Sid DeLong of Seattle University Law School; and Professor George Cohen of the University of Virginia School of Law. We are also grateful to our publisher, Steve Errick, for persistently pointing out the value of a new edition and then vigorously supporting the project.

The cover image of Hedy Lamarr is TM/©2004 Hedy Lamarr by CMG Worldwide. The photo of Hedy Lamarr is ©CinemaPhoto/Corbis. The image is reproduced with permission. The cropped images of the mill, the sick person, and the lumber are hosted at the website of the Library of Congress and are apparently in the public domain; we thank the Library for making them available to the public. The images of the brain and the melting ice were developed by Anne Lawrence based on clipart purchased by her. The image of the ax is based on a photo by Edward J. Watson and Saydean Zeldin. The images of the pipe and pleadings in *Webb v. McGowin* are based on photos by Geoffrey R. Watson. Anne Lawrence and Geoffrey R. Watson designed the cover in conjunction with Richard Danzig. Geoffrey R. Watson set the text in Adobe InDesign with the very helpful advice of Kathleen Tinkel.

We owe special thanks to the many faculty members of the University of Wisconsin Law School who have been such ardent supporters of *The Capability Problem* over the years, including Professors Marc Galanter, Kathy Hendley, John Kidwell, Stewart Macaulay, Gordon Smith, Joe Thome, and Bill Whitford. We are, finally, especially indebted to Professor Lisa Lerman of Catholic University Law School who, by introducing us, took the critical step toward making this second edition a reality.

RICHARD DANZIG
GEOFFREY R. WATSON

Washington, D.C.
May, 2004

ACKNOWLEDGEMENTS
for the FIRST EDITION

The intellectual lineage of this book is varied, and my debts to many people and institutions are great. My interest in contract law was sparked by two wonderful teachers at Yale Law School, Ellen Peters and Friedrich Kessler. They offered what every student needs in the beginning: role models worthy of emulation, a kindness which made me think that emulation was possible, and an enthusiasm for their (and now my) subject matter.

The American Bar Foundation, the Society of Fellows at Harvard University, and the Rockefeller Foundation offered another kind of support: each extended a grant which permitted study and writing of one or another of the essays in this volume. I am grateful to these institutions; without their generosity this work would not have been done.

I am yet more grateful to friends and colleagues on the faculties of the Stanford, Wisconsin and Harvard Law Schools. At Harvard I was generously housed for two years. While there I learned a good deal while teaching in the Law and Humanities Program and from extended conversations with both faculty and visitors (of whom I must note Jan Vetter and Fred Konefsky). Members of the faculty at Wisconsin did me an even greater service by teaching with these and other of my materials. Stewart Macaulay of that law school has contributed an essay to this volume. John Kidwell co-authored another of the essays with me, and Bill Whitford has consistently offered useful advice and encouragement from the very beginning of this enterprise.

Above all I owe a debt to Stanford Law School. Teaching at Stanford is a delight because it is that rarest of institutions: a place where the whole is greater than the sum of its parts; where junior and senior faculty are both truly supported in the exploration of their interests and the development of their own perspectives.

To friends there, including the faithful women of the xerox room, my secretaries B. Fahr, Greta Hall, and Gloria Thomas, students too numerous to mention, research assistants (of whom Jim Liebman, Larry Robinson, and Ann Bailey must be mentioned), past and present Deans (Tom Erlich and Charlie Meyers) and my colleagues, I offer thanks.

RICHARD DANZIG

Washington, D.C.
May, 1978

TABLE OF CONTENTS

INTRODUCTION

About any legal dispute a judge, a lawyer, or a student of the law must ask three quite distinct questions. What rights do each of the parties enjoy? To what extent has a litigant (or a potential litigant) been deprived of a right or rights? What, if anything, will society do to redress the deprivation of these rights?

The answer a legal system gives to these questions consciously or unconsciously, but indubitably, reflects the values of the people who control that system. Equally significant, the constantly articulated, repeatedly implemented answers to these questions shape the values of all who are affected by that system. This is true whether the issues are stark or mundane. Ask: What right does a master have in a runaway slave? What remedies do we allow the master against the slave or against the abolitionist who hid the slave? Or ask: What are the respective rights of Harpo and Groucho when Harpo reneges on a promise to work for (or to sell tomatoes to) Groucho? Whose right do we give a greater priority, Harpo's right to change his mind or Groucho's right to his expectation? The resolution of either bundle of issues says much about the society which resolves them.

Issues of value are becoming increasingly salient in the modern law curriculum. We have tried to give them center stage in our own teaching. In this short book we want, however, to focus on a different cluster of problems, on a set of less noticed, less easily documented, and therefore less often discussed companions to value questions. We shall call these capability problems. By this we mean the cluster of problems that impede and distort efforts to further preferred values through a legal system. If values are the quiet engines of our legal system, the capability problems are the frictions, the ruts and the biases of the road. The machinery of Justice responds as much to the road as to the engine. This book is about the road.

1

The capability problems discussed here may be summarized as arising before, during and after trial.

BEFORE TRIAL. Not all people know the law or have the means for contacting people who know it; fewer still have the means, time, energy, and skills to litigate or to get others to litigate for them; not all issues are worth litigating; few issues outlive the delay that precedes any modern trial. Some conduct will be affected by the law quite apart from these impediments.* Litigative incapacity makes it certain, however, that the join between law and society will be imperfect; that, as Karl Llewellyn once put it, the law in action will be different from the law on the books.

DURING TRIAL. The law may command witnesses to speak "the truth, the whole truth, and nothing but the truth," but it is clear that a judge or jury does not even come close to receiving such verity. Testimony is typically confused, mistaken and biased. When it escapes these three failings it normally encounters a fourth: it is contradicted. The uninitiated might expect that documents often would provide "proof," but in amazing proportions these are incomplete, inconclusive, unavailable or impeachable. On top of these difficulties, the forms of question and answer and the rules of evidence exclude much that is relevant to "the whole truth." Then the tensions of the courtroom and the differential capacities of litigants to perform credibly on the witness stand further flaw the process. Finally, all the confused and confusing "evidence" is filtered through the idiosyncratic perceptual lenses of jurors or judges. One thinks about the truth-finding capabilities of such a system rather as Dr. Johnson thought about the performing dog: to question its quality seems superfluous, the remarkable thing is that it performs at all.

AFTER TRIAL. Save for the rare instances where psychological satisfaction is sought or where a desired remedy is ministerial (e. g. the alteration of a recorded deed), a favorable judicial decision does not itself give litigants anything they desire. Most often the judiciary orders others to do things: to perform services,

---

*Laws will sometimes have no effect on conduct at which they are aimed. Often they will have intermittent and imperfectly predictable, unintended, effects. It is important to note that these effects will not always be randomly distributed. Laws become weapons used by those with brains, energy and funds against others who lack these assets.

to tender goods, to pay money. At this point the same difficulties that impede the operation of the law before and during trial recur with a vengeance. The court has little capacity to compel the performance of complicated acts and less capacity to determine whether in fact those acts have been performed. Cash payments can be coerced and supervised more readily, but the expense of the process preempts much that might be gained, resources are frequently hidden or exhausted, and, even when obtainable, dollar compensation is frequently difficult to measure and inadequate regardless of amount.

These are the capability problems. They now matter some and ought to matter more to legislators, judges, practicing lawyers and litigants. They are, however, issues that are rarely discussed in the course of law school training. In large measure, we think, this is because that staple of traditional teaching materials, the appellate opinion, does not lend itself to this inquiry. The appellate opinion gives no insight into what precedes litigation and what is not litigated; perforce it pays even less attention to what happens after litigation. Moreover, the appellate decision is predicated on "found" or presumed facts; it assumes many of the issues that are flagged here.

This collection of readings is designed to provide teachers and students with supplementary material that will make capability problems more visible and thus more subject to analysis and discussion. Throughout, we hope that readers will try to reconcile the issues raised here with those provoked by the regular reading of appellate decisions in contract law.

The structure of the book is straightforward. We first present three essays on remedies cases – *Sullivan v. O'Connor, Hadley v. Baxendale,* and *Jacob & Youngs v. Kent.* The essay on *Sullivan* was co-authored by Professor John Kidwell and Richard Danzig; the essays on *Hadley* and *Kent* were written by Danzig alone. Although there are cross-references between the essays, each can be read alone, and teachers and students ought not to feel compelled to follow the order of our presentation.

Each of these three chapters reprints the appellate opinion in the case. The reader is invited to study this opinion and to reflect both on the general issues of doctrine and value it raises and on the particular capability problems that affect the decision. To aid in these reflections, we have provided a set of "First Questions." The essay that follows is designed to take the reader behind the scenes so as to enhance an understanding of the events that underlay and succeeded the appellate opinion. "Further Questions" then seek to sharpen an appreciation of the capability problems involved and of their implications for the substantive law of contracts.

Next, we present three cases on formation and the doctrine of consideration: *Mills v. Wyman, Webb v. McGowin*, and *Harrington v. Taylor*. These materials, written by Geoff Watson, are new to this edition. The chapters on *Mills* and *Webb* follow the pattern of the first three chapters, whereas the chapter on *Harrington* presents transcripts and other primary-source material in lieu of an essay. All three chapters include First Questions and Further Questions.

The final three chapters present cases on public policy and defenses to contractual obligation. Professor Stewart Macaulay's essay on *Fullerton Lumber v. Torborg*, which involves a covenant not to compete, remains as topical as ever. Richard Danzig's chapter on *Ortelere v. Retirement Board*, which involves capacity doctrine, was one of the most widely-used chapters in the first edition. Like the chapter on *Harrington*, this chapter reprints trial transcripts in order to shed light on capability problems.

The chapter on *Allen v. Quality Furniture*, also prepared by Danzig, takes a different tack. It reviews a case that never gave rise to an appellate opinion. The data in this case are presented by reprinting a simulated interview between lawyer and client. The First Questions focus on the ways in which the lawyer-client relationship gives rise to capability problems. The subsequent essay describes what happened in this litigation as one very talented lawyer, Professor Philip Schrag (now at Georgetown Law School), pursued the matter. The questions after Professor Schrag's account emphasize the innumerable capability problems that must be hurdled before a case even gives rise to an appellate opinion.

Whether used alongside more traditional contracts casebooks or read independently, we hope that this book will make up for a real shortfall in the average student's education not just about contracts, but about the law in general.

I. ALICE SULLIVAN v. JAMES H. O'CONNOR[*]

SULLIVAN v. O'CONNOR
Supreme Judicial Court of Massachusetts, 1973.
363 Mass. 579, 296 N.E.2d 183.

KAPLAN, JUSTICE.

The plaintiff patient secured a jury verdict of $13,500 against the defendant surgeon for breach of contract in respect to an operation upon the plaintiff's nose. The substituted consolidated bill of exceptions presents questions about the correctness of the judge's instructions on the issue of damages.

The declaration was in two counts. In the first count, the plaintiff alleged that she, as patient, entered into a contract with the defendant, a surgeon, wherein the defendant promised to perform plastic surgery on her nose and thereby to enhance her beauty and improve her appearance; that he performed the surgery but failed to achieve the promised result; rather the result of the surgery was to disfigure and deform her nose, to cause her pain in body and mind, and to subject her to other damage and expense. The second count, based on the same transaction, was in the conventional form for malpractice, charging that the defendant had been guilty of negligence in performing the surgery. Answering, the defendant entered a general denial.

On the plaintiff's demand, the case was tried by jury. At the close of the evidence, the judge put to the jury, as special questions, the issues of liability under the two counts, and instructed them accordingly. The jury returned a verdict for the plaintiff on the contract count, and for the defendant on the negligence count. The judge then instructed the jury on the issue of damages.

---

[*]Our footnotes appear as asterisks or other symbols. Numbered footnotes appeared in the original. Some numbered footnotes are omitted.—RD/GW.

As background to the instructions and the parties' exceptions, we mention certain facts as the jury could find them. The plaintiff was a professional entertainer, and this was known to the defendant. The agreement was as alleged in the declaration. More particularly, judging from exhibits, the plaintiff's nose had been straight, but long and prominent; the defendant undertook by two operations to reduce its prominence and somewhat to shorten it, thus making it more pleasing in relation to the plaintiff's other features. Actually the plaintiff was obliged to undergo three operations, and her appearance was worsened. Her nose now had a concave line to about the midpoint, at which it became bulbous; viewed frontally, the nose from bridge to midpoint was flattened and broadened, and the two sides of the tip had lost symmetry. This configuration evidently could not be improved by further surgery. The plaintiff did not demonstrate, however, that her change of appearance had resulted in loss of employment. Payments by the plaintiff covering the defendant's fee and hospital expenses were stipulated at $622.65.

The judge instructed the jury, first, that the plaintiff was entitled to recover her out-of-pocket expenses incident to the operations. Second, she could recover the damages flowing directly, naturally, proximately, and foreseeably from the defendant's breach of promise. These would comprehend damages for any disfigurement of the plaintiff's nose – that is, any change of appearance for the worse – including the effects of the consciousness of such disfigurement on the plaintiff's mind, and in this connection the jury should consider the nature of the plaintiff's profession. Also consequent upon the defendant's breach, and compensable, were the pain and suffering involved in the third operation, but not in the first two. As there was no proof that any loss of earnings by the plaintiff resulted from the breach, that element should not enter into the calculation of damages.

By his exceptions the defendant contends that the judge erred in allowing the jury to take into account anything but the plaintiff's out-of-pocket expenses (presumably at the stipulated amount). The defendant excepted to the judge's refusal of his request for a general charge to that effect, and, more specifically, to the judge's refusal of a charge that the plaintiff could not recover for pain and suffering connected with the third operation or for impairment of the plaintiff's appearance and associated mental distress.[1]

The plaintiff on her part excepted to the judge's refusal of a request to charge that the plaintiff could recover the difference in value between the nose as promised and the nose as it appeared after the operations. However, the plaintiff in her brief expressly waives this exception and others made by her in case this court overrules the defendant's exceptions; thus she would be content to hold the jury's verdict in her favor.

We conclude that the defendant's exceptions should be overruled.

It has been suggested on occasion that agreements between patients and physicians by which the physician undertakes to effect a cure or to bring about a given result should be declared unenforceable on grounds of public policy. See Guilmet v. Campbell, 385 Mich. 57, 76, 188 N.W.2d 601 (dissenting opinion). But there are many decisions recognizing and enforcing such contracts, see annotation, 43 A.L.R.3d 1221, 1225, 1229-1233, and the law of Massachusetts has treated them as valid, although we have had no decision meeting head on the contention that they should be denied legal sanction. Small v. Howard, 128 Mass. 131; Gabrunas v. Miniter, 289 Mass. 20, 193 N.E. 551; Forman v. Wolfson, 327 Mass. 341, 98 N.E.2d 615. These causes of action are, however, considered a little suspect, and thus we find courts straining sometimes to read the pleadings as sounding only in tort for negligence, and not in contract for breach of promise, despite sedulous efforts by the pleaders to pursue the latter theory. See Gault v. Sideman, 42 Ill.App.2d 96, 191 N.E.2d 436; annotation, supra, at 1225, 1238-1244.

It is not hard to see why the courts should be unenthusiastic or skeptical about the contract theory. Considering the uncertainties of medical science and the variations in the physical and psychological conditions of individual patients, doctors can seldom in good faith promise specific results. Therefore it is unlikely that physicians of even average integrity will in fact make such promises. Statements of opinion by the physician with some optimistic col-

---

1. The defendant also excepted to the judge's refusal to direct a verdict in his favor, but this exception is not pressed and could not be sustained.

oring are a different thing, and may indeed have therapeutic value. But patients may transform such statements into firm promises in their own minds, especially when they have been disappointed in the event, and testify in that sense to sympathetic juries.[2] If actions for breach of promise can be readily maintained, doctors, so it is said, will be frightened into practising "defensive medicine." On the other hand, if these actions were outlawed, leaving only the possibility of suits for malpractice, there is fear that the public might be exposed to the enticements of charlatans, and confidence in the profession might ultimately be shaken. See Miller, The Contractual Liability of Physicians and Surgeons, 1953 Wash.L.Q. 413, 416-423. The law has taken the middle of the road position of allowing actions based on alleged contract, but insisting on clear proof. Instructions to the jury may well stress this requirement and point to tests of truth, such as the complexity or difficulty of an operation as bearing on the probability that a given result was promised. See annotation, 43 A.L.R.3d 1225, 1225-1227.

If an action on the basis of contract is allowed, we have next the question of the measure of damages to be applied where liability is found. Some cases have taken the simple view that the promise by the physician is to be treated like an ordinary commercial promise, and accordingly that the successful plaintiff is entitled to a standard measure of recovery for breach of contract – "compensatory" ("expectancy") damages, an amount intended to put the plaintiff in the position he would be in if the contract had been performed, or, presumably, at the plaintiff's election, "restitution" damages, an amount corresponding to any benefit conferred by the plaintiff upon the defendant in the performance of the contract disrupted by the defendant's breach. See Restatement: Contracts § 329 and comment a, §§ 347, 384(1). Thus in Hawkins v. McGee, 84 N.H. 114, 146 A. 641, the defendant doctor was taken to have promised the plaintiff to convert his damaged hand by means of an operation into a good or perfect hand, but the doctor so operated as

---

2. Judicial skepticism about whether a promise was in fact made derives also from the possibility that the truth has been tortured to give the plaintiff the advantage of the longer period of limitations sometimes available for actions on contract as distinguished from those in tort or for malpractice. See Lillich, The Malpractice Statute of Limitations in New York and Other Jurisdictions, 47 Cornell L.Q. 339; annotation, 80 A.L.R.2d 368.

to damage the hand still further. The court, following the usual expectancy formula, would have asked the jury to estimate and award to the plaintiff the difference between the value of a good or perfect hand, as promised, and the value of the hand after the operation. (The same formula would apply, although the dollar result would be less, if the operation had neither worsened nor improved the condition of the hand.) If the plaintiff had not yet paid the doctor his fee, that amount would be deducted from the recovery. There could be no recovery for the pain and suffering of the operation, since that detriment would have been incurred even if the operation had been successful; one can say that this detriment was not "caused" by the breach. But where the plaintiff by reason of the operation was put to more pain that* he would have had to endure, had the doctor performed as promised, he should be compensated for that difference as a proper part of his expectancy recovery. It may be noted that on an alternative count for malpractice the plaintiff in the *Hawkins* case had been nonsuited; but on ordinary principles this could not affect the contract claim, for it is hardly a defence to a breach of contract that the promisor acted innocently and without negligence. The New Hampshire court further refined the *Hawkins* analysis in McQuaid v. Michou, 85 N.H. 299, 157 A. 881, all in the direction of treating the patient-physician cases on the ordinary footing of expectancy. See McGee v. United States Fid. & Guar. Co., 53 F.2d 953 (1st Cir.) (later development in the *Hawkins* case); Cloutier v. Kasheta, 105 N.H. 262, 197 A.2d 627; Lakeman v. LaFrance, 102 N.H. 300, 305, 156 A.2d 123.

Other cases, including a number in New York, without distinctly repudiating the *Hawkins* type of analysis, have indicated that a different and generally more lenient measure of damages is to be applied in patient-physician actions based on breach of alleged special agreements to effect a cure, attain a stated result, or employ a given medical method. This measure is expressed in somewhat variant ways, but the substance is that the plaintiff is to recover any expenditures made by him and for other detriment (usually not specifically described in the opinions) following proximately and foreseeably upon the defendant's failure to carry out his promise. Robins v. Finestone, 308 N.Y. 543, 546, 127 N.E.2d 330; Frankel

---

* [*Sic.*] Justice Kaplan must mean "than."

v. Wolper, 181 App.Div. 485, 488, 169 N.Y.S. 15, affd., 228 N.Y. 582,
127 N.E. 913; Frank v. Maliniak, 232 App.Div. 278, 280, 249 N.Y.S.
514; Colvin v. Smith, 276 App.Div. 9, 10, 92 N.Y.S.2d 794; Stewart
v. Rudner, 349 Mich. 459, 465-473, 84 N.W.2d 816. Cf. Carpenter
v. Moore, 51 Wash.2d 795, 322 P.2d 125. This, be it noted, is not
a "restitution" measure, for it is not limited to restoration of the
benefit conferred on the defendant (the fee paid) but includes other
expenditures, for example, amounts paid for medicine and nurses;
so also it would seem according to its logic to take in damages for
any worsening of the plaintiff's condition due to the breach. Nor is
it an "expectancy" measure, for it does not appear to contemplate
recovery of the whole difference in value between the condition as
promised and the condition actually resulting from the treatment.
Rather the tendency of the formulation is to put the plaintiff back
in the position he occupied just before the parties entered upon the
agreement, to compensate him for the detriments he suffered in
reliance upon the agreement. This kind of intermediate pattern of
recovery for breach of contract is discussed in the suggestive article
by Fuller and Perdue, The Reliance Interest in Contract Damages,
46 Yale L.J. 52, 373, where the authors show that, although not
attaining the currency of the standard measures, a "reliance" measure has for special reasons been applied by the courts in a variety
of settings, including noncommercial settings. See 46 Yale L.J. at
396-401.[4]

For breach of the patient-physician agreements under consideration, a recovery limited to restitution seems plainly too meager,
if the agreements are to be enforced at all. On the other hand, an
expectancy recovery may well be excessive. The factors, already
mentioned, which have made the cause of action somewhat suspect, also suggest moderation as to the breadth of the recovery
that should be permitted. Where, as in the case at bar and in a
number of the reported cases, the doctor has been absolved of negligence by the trier, an expectancy measure may be thought harsh.

---

4. Some of the exceptional situations mentioned where reliance may be preferred to expectancy are those in which the latter measure would be hard to apply or would impose too great a burden; performance was interfered with by
external circumstances; the contract was indefinite. See 46 Yale L.J. at 373-386;
394-396.

We should recall here that the fee paid by the patient to the doctor for the alleged promise would usually be quite disproportionate to the putative expectancy recovery. To attempt, moreover, to put a value on the condition that would or might have resulted, had the treatment succeeded as promised, may sometimes put an exceptional strain on the imagination of the fact finder. As a general consideration, Fuller and Perdue argue that the reasons for granting damages for broken promises to the extent of the expectancy are at their strongest when the promises are made in a business context, when they have to do with the production or distribution of goods or the allocation of functions in the market place; they become weaker as the context shifts from a commercial to a noncommercial field. 46 Yale L.J. at 60-63.

There is much to be said, then, for applying a reliance measure to the present facts, and we have only to add that our cases are not unreceptive to the use of that formula in special situations. We have, however, had no previous occasion to apply it to patient-physician cases.[5]

5. In Mt. Pleasant Stable Co. v. Steinberg, 238 Mass. 567, 131 N.E. 295, the plaintiff company agreed to supply teams of horses at agreed rates as required from day to day by the defendant for his business. To prepare itself to fulfill the contract and in reliance on it, the plaintiff bought two "Cliest" horses at a certain price. When the defendant repudiated the contract, the plaintiff sold the horses at a loss and in its action for breach claimed the loss as an element of damages. The court properly held that the plaintiff was not entitled to this item as it was also claiming (and recovering) its lost profits (expectancy) on the contract as a whole. Cf. Noble v. Ames Mfg. Co., 112 Mass. 492. (The loss on sale of the horses is analogous to the pain and suffering for which the patient would be disallowed a recovery in Hawkins v. McGee, 84 N.H. 114, 146 A. 641, because he was claiming and recovering expectancy damages.) The court in the Mt. Pleasant case referred, however, to Pond v. Harris, 113 Mass. 114, as a contrasting situation where the expectancy could not be fairly determined. There the defendant had wrongfully revoked an agreement to arbitrate a dispute with the plaintiff (this was before such agreements were made specifically enforceable). In an action for the breach, the plaintiff was held entitled to recover for his preparations for the arbitration which had been rendered useless and a waste, including the plaintiff's time and trouble and his expenditures for counsel and witnesses. The context apparently was commercial but reliance elements were held compensable when there was no fair way of estimating an expectancy. See, generally, annotation, 17 A.L. R.2d 1300. A noncommercial example is Smith v. Sherman, 4 Cush. 408, 413-414, suggesting that a conventional recovery for breach of promise of marriage included a recompense for various efforts and expenditures by the plaintiff preparatory to

The question of recovery on a reliance basis for pain and suffering or mental distress requires further attention. We find expressions in the decisions that pain and suffering (or the like) are simply not compensable in actions for breach of contract. The defendant seemingly espouses this proposition in the present case. True, if the buyer under a contract for the purchase of a lot of merchandise, in suing for the seller's breach, should claim damages for mental anguish caused by his disappointment in the transaction, he would not succeed; he would be told, perhaps, that the asserted psychological injury was not fairly foreseeable by the defendant as a probable consequence of the breach of such a business contract. See Restatement: Contracts, § 341, and comment a. But there is no general rule barring such items of damage in actions for breach of contract. It is all a question of the subject matter and background of the contract, and when the contract calls for an operation on the person of the plaintiff, psychological as well as physical injury may be expected to figure somewhere in the recovery, depending on the particular circumstances. The point is explained in Stewart v. Rudner, 349 Mich. 459, 469, 84 N.W.2d 816. Cf. Frewen v. Page, 238 Mass. 499, 131 N.E. 475; McClean v. University Club, 327 Mass. 68, 97 N.E.2d 174. Again, it is said in a few of the New York cases, concerned with the classification of actions for statute of limitations purposes, that the absence of allegations demanding recovery for pain and suffering is characteristic of a contract claim by a patient against a physician, that such allegations rather belong in a claim for malpractice. See Robins v. Finestone, 308 N.Y. 543, 547, 127 N.E.2d 330; Budoff v. Kessler, 2 A.D.2d 760, 153 N.Y.S.2d 654. These remarks seem unduly sweeping. Suffering or distress resulting from the breach going beyond that which was envisaged by the treatment as agreed, should be compensable on the same ground as the worsening of the patient's condition because of the breach. Indeed it can be argued that the very suffering or distress "contracted for" – that which would have been incurred

---

the promised wedding. See Garfield & Proctor Coal Co. v. Pennsylvania Coal & Coke Co., 199 Mass. 22, 43, 84 N.E. 1020; Narragansett Amusement Co. v. Riverside Park Amusement Co., 260 Mass. 265, 279-281, 157 N.E. 532. Cf. Johnson v. Arnold, 2 Cush. 46, 47; Greany v. McCormick, 273 Mass. 250, 253, 173 N.E. 411. But cf. Irwin v. Worcester Paper Box Co., 246 Mass. 453, 141 N.E. 286.

if the treatment achieved the promised result – should also be compensable on the theory underlying the New York cases. For that suffering is "wasted" if the treatment fails. Otherwise stated, compensation for this waste is arguably required in order to complete the restoration of the status quo ante.[6]

In the light of the foregoing discussion, all the defendant's exceptions fail: the plaintiff was not confined to the recovery of her out-of-pocket expenditures; she was entitled to recover also for the worsening of her condition,[7] and for the pain and suffering and mental distress involved in the third operation. These items were compensable on either an expectancy or a reliance view. We might have been required to elect between the two views if the pain and suffering connected with the first two operations contemplated by the agreement, or the whole difference in value between the present and the promised conditions, were being claimed as elements of damage. But the plaintiff waives her possible claim to the former element, and to so much of the latter as represents the difference in value between the promised condition and the condition before the operations.

Plaintiff's exceptions waived.

Defendant's exceptions overruled.

---

6. Recovery on a reliance basis for breach of the physician's promise tends to equate with the usual recovery for malpractice, since the latter also looks in general to restoration of the condition before the injury. But this is not paradoxical, especially when it is noted that the origins of contract lie in tort. See Farnsworth, The Past of Promise: An Historical Introduction to Contract, 69 Col. L.Rev. 576, 594-596; Breitel, J. in Stella Flour & Feed Corp. v. National City Bank, 285 App. Div. 182, 189, 136 N.Y.S.2d 139 (dissenting opinion). A few cases have considered possible recovery for breach by a physician of a promise to sterilize a patient, resulting in birth of a child to the patient and spouse. If such an action is held maintainable, the reliance and expectancy measures would, we think, tend to equate, because the promised condition was preservation of the family status quo. [Citations omitted.]

It would, however, be a mistake to think in terms of strict "formulas." For example, a jurisdiction which would apply a reliance measure to the present facts might impose a more severe damage sanction for the wilful use by the physician of a method of operation that he undertook not to employ.

7. That condition involves a mental element and appraisal of it properly called for consideration of the fact that the plaintiff was an entertainer. Cf. McQuaid v. Michou, 85 N.H. 299, 303-304, 157 A. 881 (discussion of continuing condition resulting from physician's breach).

FIRST QUESTIONS

1. One way of sharpening an appreciation of the capability problems inherent in an opinion is to force yourself to retell the story of what happened in a case in as much detail as possible. Begin with the relationship between Mrs. Sullivan and Dr. O'Connor. How did they come to their agreement? Was it written or oral? In what words and in what setting do you imagine that Dr. O'Connor promised Ms. Sullivan that he would, as Justice Kaplan put it, "enhance her beauty and improve her appearance"? What happened in the course of the parties' dealings with each other? What happened in the litigation process? Answering these questions should underscore what you do not know about this litigation. Do you think Justice Kaplan knew what you do not know? Would you want to know any of what you must speculate about before deciding what rule of law to adopt in this case?

2. One sign of the modernity of *Sullivan v. O'Connor* is the "realism" of the opinion. The legal realists, a loosely allied group of legal academics among whom Karl Llewellyn was perhaps most eminent, had a major impact on American jurisprudence from the late 1920's onward. Realists argue that law does not and cannot work merely as a matter of formal logic, as a system of dispassionate reasoning resolving cases only by deduction and analogy. From this several different deductions have been made. As one author put a major viewpoint early in the Realist revolution: "Creative legal thought will more and more . . . appraise . . . the social values at stake in any choice between two precedents. 'Social policy' will be comprehended not as an emergency factor in legal argument, but rather as a gravitational field that gives weight to any rule or precedent, whether it be in constitutional law, in the law of trademarks, or in the most technical details of legal procedure." Felix Cohen, Transcendental Nonsense and the Functional Approach, 35 Cal.L.Rev. 809, 833-34 (1935). Realists of this persuasion thus believe in explicitly instrumental decision-making, in courts doing "social-engineering." Another group advocated a less activist stance. It argued for basing decisions on a sensitive ad hoc assessment of the facts in a particular case, rather than on legal formalities. Still another group of realists offered a third view that tended to undermine the first two to the degree it was taken seriously.

This group emphasized the need for skepticism about fact and rule determinations. Its proponents see rules as often in conflict or laden with ambiguity. Facts are said to be similarly difficult to discern, contradictory and ambiguous. Thus, judges are left with a good deal of leeway. At the same time, they need to be conscious of the difficulties of the material with which they work.

Justice Kaplan was a student of Karl Llewellyn's. Pinpoint at least two examples of "realism" in his opinion. Which strand or strands of realism does he manifest? What capability problems does he appear to recognize? Which does he overlook?

3. Note the language used in this opinion. Justice Kaplan rarely takes responsibility for, endorses, or in the words of contemporary psychology, "owns" any assertion he advances. What phrases does he use to avoid the appearance of himself choosing or making law? How does his linguistic posture relate to his realism?

4. Why have appellate review at all in cases like this? Why not simply have the trial judge instruct the jurors to "do Justice" in the case before them, and leave the entire matter to their discretion? Suppose it were argued that in effect this is what we do, that the jury's discretion is unconfined and even unchanneled. How would you respond?

5. What role, if any, did gender play in the opinion in *Sullivan*? How might it have influenced the jurors, judges, and other actors in the case? Recall the male jurors who talked about "women they had gone out with who had big noses," and one juror's belief that this talk was "intended to intimidate the women on the jury and perhaps make for an atmosphere less sympathetic to Mrs. Sullivan." Would an all-female jury have decided the case any differently? An all-male jury? If you believe that these outcomes would be different, does that argue for eliminating juries or giving them less leeway? Those interested in these questions may wish to read Mary Jo Frug, Re-Reading Contracts: A Feminist Analysis Of A Contracts Casebook, 34 Am. U.L. Rev. 1065 (commenting on gender bias in a contracts casebook and (at p. 1100) on *Sullivan* in particular).

SUPPLEMENTARY COMMENTS*

The following accounts, based on interviews done six years after the trial in *Sullivan v. O'Connor*, try to capture how the different participants saw the litigation. As you read them try to reflect on what, if any, capability problems they raise.

Mrs. Sullivan's Trial Lawyer

Mrs. Sullivan arrived in Francis Newton's[†] office asking him to represent her against Dr. O'Connor. It quickly became apparent to Newton that she had begun litigation using the services of another Boston Attorney, Frank Goode, but that her relationship with Goode had deteriorated to the point where she had snatched his files and come running to Newton. She came to Newton because she had met him when she was working as a librarian for a Boston hospital and he had on several occasions subpoenaed records. Newton took the basic details of Sullivan's case. He then called Goode, who was an acquaintance of his, and discovered that Goode was representing an entertainer and friend of Mrs. Sullivan's in another suit against O'Connor. Goode thought that his relationship with Mrs. Sullivan had reached a point where it was advisable for Newton to take over the case. Goode kept the friend's case, and ultimately secured a verdict for her. Newton proceeded to represent Mrs. Sullivan, working from a complaint that had already been drafted and filed by Goode.

Newton recalls that he was surprised by Goode's drafting of the contract count of the complaint. At the time it was customary in Massachusetts to include a claim that the doctor impliedly promised to do the work with customary skill. But this claim was functionally identical to a negligence claim (since the duty was the same). These implied contract claims were almost always dropped before or during trial for fear of confusing the jury. Newton thinks

---

*The essay was researched and written by Richard Danzig and by Professor John Kidwell of the University of Wisconsin Law School. Both authors are grateful to Professor Sally Neely of Harvard Law School who was involved in the early stages of the work and interviewed Dr. O'Connor's lawyers.

[†]A graduate of Amherst College, Mr. Newton obtained his law degree from Boston University in 1952. In 1966 he formed his own law firm specializing in medical malpractice work, both plaintiff and defendant.

that he would not have included the express contract claim had he drafted the complaint. He considered dropping the express contract claim but decided that the negligence claim was "not overwhelming" and that the evidence of a pre-operative picture of Mrs. Sullivan with a line drawn on it showing a shorter nose, gave some credibility to an express warranty theory. He recalls being concerned that Dr. O'Connor's insurance policy might not cover breach of contract. Had the insurance company disclaimed contract liability it would have made life more difficult, since it was a better defendant than the doctor for purposes of collection.

Newton also remembers having second thoughts about the contract claim once the trial judge proposed to split the verdict. He recalls objecting to the judge's proposed course of action because a recovery based on contract, particularly one which followed a novel instruction on the measure of damages, made a risky appeal all but certain. He thinks this risk may have been avoidable, because if the negligence claim had stood alone the jury would have found for his client on it. The damages, he notes, were in the range he would have expected on a negligence theory. He thinks the contract option simply gave the jury an easy means of deciding the case without "embarrassing" the doctor.

The jury's refusal to find negligence created additional difficulties for Newton. Alice Sullivan was firmly convinced that O'Connor was guilty of negligence and he was never able to persuade her that technical problems with the claim posed legitimate obstacles to recovery. He recalls that she felt strongly that she should have received a larger sum of money as damages.

Newton does not have a vivid memory of the oral argument on appeal. He recalls that the threshold policy question of whether to permit express contract claims against doctors was not raised by the defendant's brief, but was raised during oral argument in the Supreme Judicial Court. Newton says that other lawyers have reported that they find the Supreme Judicial Court opinion difficult to understand. He also says that it is much more common now in Massachusetts to include an express contract allegation in the complaint in a malpractice case.

Mrs. Sullivan's First Lawyer

Francis X. Goode,* Alice Sullivan's lawyer before she gave the case to Mr. Newton, recalls that Mrs. Sullivan came to him upon the recommendation of an acquaintance, Branca Lord, who was also suing Dr. O'Connor following cosmetic surgery. He remembers Mrs. Sullivan as a woman who appeared to be in her forties [she was in fact born in 1916] and who "must have been extremely attractive when she was younger." He characterizes her as "a demanding client. She was the kind who would call at least once a week . . . . She was very emotional."

He recalls the circumstances under which Newton acquired the case in the following way:

> She left me and went to Fran Newton because she thought I was pushing Lord's case harder. I was, in fact, because I thought I could win the Lord case and then force a settlement in Sullivan's case. I had a doctor who would testify in the Lord case . . . . The Lord case was stronger than the Sullivan case. I could have won the Sullivan case for the defendant . . . . It is very hard to win a malpractice case against a doctor in Massachusetts. It isn't like California. Here the jurors have a lot of respect for doctors. You really have to show the doctor to have been very bad to win.

Why did Mr. Goode include an express contract claim in the complaint on Mrs. Sullivan's behalf?

> I always put a contract claim in. A lot of lawyers thought you could only get damages for the amount of the fee. I know Finnerty thought so. But I always assumed you could get all the damages flowing from the breach.

In conclusion, Mr. Goode, asked whether clients generally want things other than money from law suits, responds: "Most of them just want the money."

---

*Mr. Goode attended Boston University and Portia Law School before joining the Massachusetts Bar in 1953.

Dr. O'Connor's Lawyer

As part of its policy coverage Dr. O'Connor's insurance company undertook to defend O'Connor against claims arising from his medical practice. John Finnerty* did not regularly handle the work of Dr. O'Connor's insurance company, but he thinks that the insurance company sent the O'Connor case to him because he had recently "saved them about a million dollars." At about the same time, the insurance company also retained him as counsel for Dr. O'Connor in another malpractice action filed by Miss Branca Lord.

Mr. Finnerty did not originally consider the contract count in Mrs. Sullivan's declaration seriously. It was unusual in Massachusetts at that time to include a contracts claim in a medical case (he did not know of any prior case in which it had been done), and he thought plaintiff's counsel had thrown it in as an afterthought. Nevertheless, the insurance company asked for his advice as to its potential exposure on this aspect of the claims. Therefore as part of the 88 pre-trial hours he spent "working up" the case he devoted "substantial research" to the contracts damage issue. This research turned up the cases he later cited in the defendant's brief on appeal and convinced him that liability on that count would be limited to Mrs. Sullivan's medical expenses. He so advised the insurance company. He also advised the company that, under its policy, it could disclaim liability for any judgment on the contract count, but the company chose not to do so.

Mrs. Sullivan did not seem to have a strong case on malpractice. There was not much difference in her looks before and after the operation, and there was not much evidence of negligence. Because of that, the unconventionality of the contract claim, and the limited liability which apparently flowed from it, no settlement offer was made or considered by the insurance company.

Mr. Finnerty's biggest concern was that Dr. O'Connor was "aggressive" and "obnoxious . . . a lousy witness." Finnerty thought

*Mr. Finnerty received his law degree from the Boston College School of Law in 1947. He was a solo practitioner until 1971, when his son John Jr. joined his practice. His work centered on insurance defense including medical malpractice. According to the firm's website, Mr. Finnerty was portrayed in the film *The Verdict*, presumably by the James Mason character. Mr. Finnerty died in 1994.

that the jury would not be sympathetic to the doctor. By contrast, Mrs. Sullivan was "a pretty good witness." Therefore, Mr. Finnerty was delighted when the judge decided to split the jury's verdict. In fact, he thinks he may have suggested that tactic because he was confident about liability on the tort count, and believed that damages on the contract count would be limited to Mrs. Sullivan's medical expenses. He was somewhat surprised that the Judge refused to limit the jury to an award of medical expenses on the contract count.

However, Mr. Finnerty felt that the jury's award of $13,500 was about what he would have expected had Mrs. Sullivan prevailed on her tort/malpractice claim. He was relatively sure that the Supreme Judicial Court would reverse the verdict based on error in Judge Brogna's instructions. He felt confident about the brief he had filed, which was actually written by his son (and law partner) and he thought that oral argument had gone well. Mr. Finnerty was shocked by the decision of the S.J.C.

The Trial Judge

Judge Vincent Brogna, a Yale College and 1937 Harvard Law School graduate, had a general trial practice (not including malpractice cases) before he became a judge of the Massachusetts Superior Court in 1960.

As was typical in such matters, he "came cold" to *Sullivan v. O'Connor*, knowing nothing about the case before it came on for trial. He began, as he does "all the time," by summoning the lawyers to "the lobby" (his chambers) to discuss settlement possibilities. At the settlement discussion "we discussed the case informally . . . talking the way lawyers talk."

Despite apparent good will between the lawyers and some pressure from Brogna ("Have you thought about settling?"; "Make the plaintiff your best offer"; "You will not get another bite at the apple on a motion for a new trial in this court, even if the verdict seems to you to be out of line."), no serious settlement offers were forthcoming. The trial began immediately.

Brogna reports that he became concerned about the contract claim during the first day of the proceedings. Realizing that he would have to charge the jury and that he had no informed sense of the measure of damages on this as compared to the normal mal-

practice count, he summoned the lawyers to another lobby conference at the end of the first day of trial.

As he recollects it, neither lawyer had thought about the problem. The three of them, Brogna, Finnerty and Newton, parted
with each committed to researching the matter. For his part Judge
Brogna retired to the Suffolk County Law Library. (At this time
Superior Court Judges had no clerks to provide research support.)
Beginning at around 4:30 in the afternoon, the Judge spent about
an hour in the library, much of it devoted to reading a "textbook"
on contract damages. The "textbook" gave Judge Brogna a citation
to *Hawkins v. McGee*. He had "never heard of it before," but read it
and recognized it as a leading case relevant to his concern.

On the next morning his researches were not significantly
augmented by the lawyers. Judge Brogna recalls only that the
plaintiff's lawyer, Finnerty, presented him with a photostat of a
page from a handbook for defense attorneys. The page dealt with
damages for breach of contract. During the second day of the trial,
the Judge decided that if possible he would finesse the problem by
taking the unusual (but not unprecedented) step of asking the jury
to render separate verdicts on liability for the contract claim and
for the malpractice claim.* Only if liability were found on the first
count would he proceed to instruct on the contract damages. "My
hope," he recalls, "was that the jury would take me off the hook on
the contract claim."

The jury, however, found for the plaintiff only on the contract
count.[†] Now faced with delivering the charge he did not wish to
give, Brogna thought about his instructions on damages, "probably
for about a half an hour." He thinks he again consulted *Hawkins
v. McGee*. He did not consult any reference book, nor did he talk
to any judges about the question. He has no recollection of ever
having thought about this issue before, and certainly nothing in

---

*The judge did not reflect on whether O'Connor's insurance company would
cover a contract judgment as well as a malpractice judgment.

[†]Brogna himself thought that if he had been sitting without a jury he would
have found for the plaintiff on the malpractice claim (he was impressed by the
testimony of the plaintiff's expert witness). However, Judge Brogna speculates
that the jury may have acted differently because "malpractice suits were not too
common at the time, and the jury might have thought that to find malpractice
would unnecessarily stigmatize the doctor."

his law school training particularly prepared him to think about it. It was not until Justice Kaplan's opinion came down that he ever had occasion to hear reference to a "reliance interest" in contract cases. Certainly that was not how he conceptualized the issue as he thought about his charge.

Though Judge Brogna assumed that the charge would be appealed, he had no inkling of how the Supreme Judicial Court of Massachusetts would resolve the matter. He also decided to give the charge, as he gives all charges, without the aid of a written text. Judge Brogna, like most trial judges, has little contact with the appellate court. Until recently the trial judge was not even sent a copy of the Supreme Judicial Court opinion reversing or upholding one of his decisions. Often a trial judge would not read what an appellate judge had to say about his cases.

Four Jurors[*]

At the time of the trial, Arthur B. was 58 years old. An accounting clerk who once attended college at night but then dropped out, he has been on juries since 1937.

This juror has little recollection of the case and offers only a laconic, matter of fact commentary on it. "The doctor was a pretty good doctor in his line. But he didn't live up to the expectations. He showed her a photograph and said her nose would be like this photograph but it was different. So we permitted a recovery." His own experience with doctors has been good. "I think that every

---

[*]In April of 1977, six jurors were traced after research from the original jury list, phone books, etc. Two declined to be interviewed. The comments of the remaining four were elicited through unstructured telephone interviews in which they were first asked to simply tell what they remembered about the case and then questioned about specific points. Their comments are here reorganized and sometimes paraphrased to present reasonably abbreviated and coherent accounts. An effort has been made, however, to keep the stress where these individuals themselves placed it.

Those interested in utilizing the technique of questioning jurors will want to read ABA Model Rule of Professional Conduct 3.5; see also the ABA Model Code of Professional Responsibility, D.R. 7-108 (D). A federal court invalidated an earlier version of Model Rule 3.5 as a violation of the First Amendment because it restricted juror interviews in unconstitutionally vague terms. Rapp v. Disciplinary Bd., 916 F. Supp. 1525 (D. Hawaii 1996). A new paragraph 3.5(c), approved by the ABA in 2002, is intended to cure this defect. It provides that a lawyer may not communicate with a juror after discharge of the jury if "prohibited by law or court order."

doctor probably does his job as well as could be expected." He doesn't remember the deliberations in the jury room except that some people changed their votes. He doesn't remember how the magnitude of the recovery was determined. Asked about insurance, he responds "insurance never entered my mind."

* * *

At the time of the trial, Esau B. was a forty-two year old post office worker. This was his first time as a member of a jury pool. During his time in the pool he sat on three murder trials, on *Sullivan v. O'Connor* and then on two land fraud cases. He has a keen recollection of *Sullivan v. O'Connor*.

As Mr. B. remembers it, Mrs. Sullivan was represented by the District Attorney who took this as a private case on the side, presumably being paid a portion of her recovery. Why did Mr. B. think the attorney was a D.A.? Because "I saw him in the District Attorney's box in the jury pool room." Did other jurors think Mrs. Sullivan's attorney was a D.A.? "I think some called him that in the jury room." The doctor was represented by a private lawyer. The "District Attorney" seemed "much better" than his adversary: he asked more questions and the doctor's lawyer seemed to let a lot of irrelevancies in without objection. What made it seem that some questions were irrelevant? "My previous experience sitting on the murder trial."

What impressions did he have of the other persons involved in the trial? "The doctor [defendant] seemed proficient at shorthand; he only answered questions after writing the question or perhaps his answer on paper."* When instructed by the court not to write, that the court stenographer would keep the record, the doctor seemed "in a huff about that." Also, "by looking at the doctor he looked like he had a hostile personality against the woman for bringing him to court." B. imagines that the doctor was hostile to Mrs. Sullivan when she repeatedly telephoned him about postoperative procedures.

Mrs. Sullivan made less of an impression. He remembers that she looked angry and hurt when the verdict of acquittal was re-

---

*The trial transcript indeed shows Dr. O'Connor being reprimanded for taking notes while on the witness stand.

turned on the first count of the negligence claim, but then seemed joyous and grateful when the verdict on the contract claim was read. It seemed as if she wanted to shake hands with the members of the jury and thank them personally. She gave a "sort of bow" to the jury. A couple of the older men on the jury, "unmarried, lewd guys," told B. they thought she had winked at them and would be a good date. B. is not inclined to credit this but thinks Mrs. Sullivan "would have gone into hysterics" if she did not receive a favorable verdict.

The "most amazing part of the jury experience" for B. was the judge's neutrality. "I always wondered how judges could sleep at night. Now I see that they just tell the law to the jury and let the jury decide." He has no idea how Judge Brogna would have decided the case. He does not remember having been particularly affected by the "little talk that they give you about the law" before you go into the jury room.

In the jury room, everyone sat quietly at first looking at the pictures of the plaintiff. All the jurors pretty quickly agreed that there was no negligence. B. recalls that "I voted no negligence because there was no criminal act . . . The doctor did the operation. After the operation, who knows what she did? It looks like she didn't follow the post-operative procedures. There was a picture of her in an evening gown after the operation. Someone [on the jury] pointed out that if she went out to a nightclub in that dress so soon after the operation, perhaps she got bumped and injured her nose. Who knows? I couldn't find negligence." Quite apart from the picture B. thinks it probable that Sullivan "went out too early." After all, "she had something nice to show everybody." He thinks the other jurors reasoned similarly, and recalls that the doctor said on the stand that she hadn't followed the proper post-operative procedures and that his attorney had reiterated this point.*

---

*The trial transcript shows Judge Brogna interrupting his charge to the jury to ask: "There is no question, is there, Mr. Finnerty, about any contributory negligence on the part of the plaintiff?" To which Mr. Finnerty replied: "None at all, your Honor."

In their mammoth study of juries in criminal cases, Kalven and Zeisel report that juries often introduce notions of contributory fault by the victim, though the criminal law theoretically holds such variables irrelevant. G. Kalven and H. Zeisel, The American Jury 242-257 (1966).

The vote on the breach of contract issue was divided. B. sees the judgment on this count as in some respects a credit to the women on the jury. During breaks in the trial a couple of the older single men had talked about "women they had gone out with who had big noses." B. thought this was intended to intimidate the women on the jury and perhaps make for an atmosphere less sympathetic to Mrs. Sullivan. He recalls that it was these men who first voted against Sullivan's recovery on the contracts claim. But the women and most of the men, including B., definitely came down the other way. B. had no trouble making up his mind. Six years later he re-membered quite vividly that "she was supposed to have a nose like Hedy Lamarr. If he'd never said that there wouldn't have been a breach of contract." He felt that it was clear that she had not re-ceived a "Hedy Lamarr nose." There was "a definite hump on the bridge of her nose." After some discussion and three or four votes, with a nay changing to an aye on each vote, the jury unanimously agreed that there was a breach of promise.

The jurors then turned to the issue of damages. B. remembered that the discussion started with a relatively low figure (he recalls it as eleven or twelve thousand dollars) and then drifted upward (he recalls towards twenty thousand dollars). The figure mounted as different jurors at different times argued that "we should give her more because of this or that." Some suggested that she might want a job in a nightclub or in movie-making and be handicapped by her nose. The old men who had opposed her recovery now made remarks about how "she might have a hard time trying to meet a guy." B. felt that their implication was that she would be picking up a guy for pay.

As the figure for Sullivan's recovery went up, someone raised a question about the doctor's ability to pay. One or two people said they knew that the doctor had a large Cambridge clinic and thought he was opening another. There was general agreement, however, that this and other knowledge which came from outside the courtroom should not be considered. Then someone com-mented "Hey — he's got malpractice insurance." B. says that he then thought that perhaps malpractice insurance would not cover a breach of promise as distinguished from negligence, but he did not say anything about this at the time. Retrospectively, he thinks this insight may have been due to his exposure to a business law class he was then taking at night.

* * *

William C. was thirty-five years old at the time of the trial. He is a high school graduate and a truck driver for a paper company. This was his first time in a jury pool. Before this case he sat on a rape trial.

The key fact was that "her nose was really messed up. She was an older woman, but still that didn't make any difference. Her nose was really messed up. Like she had been hit by a shovel . . . . If it was me, I would have shot [the doctor]." Did the doctor promise her a particular type of nose? "I just don't know or care. It wouldn't have mattered to me if he had or hadn't promised her the moon. Besides common sense suggests that he had to promise her something. Why else would she have the operation?"

There was an acquittal on negligence because "it is next to impossible to get a doctor on negligence. Next to impossible to convict him on that. The proof has to be enormous to get him on negligence." This doctor "didn't show any remorse . . . . Even his own records weren't complete like I thought they should be. Of course a doctor doesn't have to answer like others. He's a professional. They can get away with anything . . . . I just don't like doctors, they think they're God." Mr. C. has not had any experience of his own which he recalls as contributing to his opinion of doctors, but he has heard of unhappy experiences from people "in general."

The only real issue was "just how much" Mrs. Sullivan was entitled to. Mr. C. doesn't remember how this was decided or how much ultimately was given. He recalls only two points about the discussion. One is that the older people talked too much. "Being on the jury is like a hobby to them. They draw it out." The other is that some people said Mrs. Sullivan shouldn't get too much in damages because she was vain and didn't need the operation in the first place. As he remembers it, someone said, "Why did she even have it done? She's no chicken to begin with."

* * *

David R. is a Scottish born, trade school educated, ship welder, who at the time of the trial was in his mid-sixties and working as a bank security guard because a ship welding job was unattainable. Mr. R. had served in two jury pools before this one, sitting on murder cases, a personal injury case, etc. He recalled:

> The operation was not successful .... You hated to pass the decision against the doctor for operating, but wanted to give some remuneration to the woman for what she had gone through .... The doctor wasn't negligent by any means. We wanted to give her compensation for what she'd been through ... at the same time we didn't want to testify against the doctor because of negligence. That wouldn't be fair either. We wanted to keep his record clean .... He performed the duty, you know. He looked like a professional man. (His wife and child were with him in court. He wasn't too happy to be in court, you could see it in his face. Rather worried looking.) To say that he was negligent, that wouldn't have been fair. There was no evidence to show that he was negligent, but there was evidence to show he didn't give her a Hedy Lamarr nose. You could see that.

How did he know that the doctor had promised to give her a Hedi LaMarr nose? "We took her [Sullivan's] word." Why? "Well, after the operation she was pretty sick." On further questioning, Mr. R. also says that the jury was influenced by the marked x-ray from the doctor's files.

Besides the failure to give Mrs. Sullivan a nose "like that movie star," two other factors recurred in Mr. R.'s comments. One was that in contrast to Mrs. Sullivan's expert witness, "a prominent Harvard doctor who was in a special field, hard to get into, which required special degrees," Dr. O'Connor "wasn't qualified to do that type of work." In doing this operation he was "out of his line." The expert was a member of "a select group of surgeons. The [defendant] doctor didn't belong."

> The doctor probably was ... of course we're not qualified to say whether the operation was correct. But it was clear that he was going out of his field. That was the main point. For that particular operation you're supposed to have some kind of degree. He admitted that he didn't have the degree.

The other point that bulked large for Mr. R. was that Mrs. Sullivan, "got pretty sick" for a while. "It was hard to say whether he was or was not negligent, but she seemed entitled to money for what she had gone through." The jury probably "had some sympathy with the woman and against the doctor." Everyone realized that the doctor would be covered by insurance and that "the insurance company has the money."

Mr. R. does not remember any "real disagreement" in the jury room. He has been on juries where the women see the case very differently from the men, but does not recollect this as being such a case. "Everyone seemed in favor of giving her compensation for what she had gone through. The point was what would she get. She got a few thousand dollars. I can't remember how we arrived at the figure . . . . She was out of work for quite a while I think."

The Plaintiff

Alice Sullivan lived in Boston and was unemployed when interviewed. Twelve years after the surgery performed by Dr. O'Connor and nearly five years after the final disposition of the case by the Supreme Court of Massachusetts she spoke with fierce emotion about "my case" and at times had difficulty maintaining her composure as she recalled aspects of her trial. Her precarious health (in part due to an ulcer condition that pre-existed her cosmetic surgery) made prolonged interviewing impossible. What follows was culled from a telephone conversation.

Mrs. Sullivan regards her suit as "not successful." She is dissatisfied with the amount awarded her. (She reports that her lawyer received a third of the award but that interest due brought her own recovery to $11,000 or $12,000.) But the size of the verdict is not the only, or perhaps even the principal, basis for her dissatisfaction. She feels that she was not permitted to tell her story in court. She mentions being constantly interrupted by a host of objections. She also feels that her attorney did not keep her sufficiently informed of the progress of her case. She points out that she was not invited to participate in deciding who should be on the jury, even though the members of the jury were going to sit in judgment on her and on her case. She recalls that an acquaintance had taken an interest in her case but was not able to attend. She thinks this was because of her attorney's failure to notify him.

Moreover, Newton failed to return her phone calls and didn't seem to be interested in talking with her about the case. Her dissatisfaction with Newton compounds the frustration she had already felt with Mr. Goode, her first attorney, whom she recalls discharging because "he wasn't prosecuting" with enough vigor: "It had been three years and he hadn't done anything." Mrs. Sullivan expresses surprise that the interviewer has read a transcript of the case: "I didn't even get one, and it was my case." She repeats several times that "You probably know more about my case than I do."

Mrs. Sullivan mentions several times that after the second operation she began bleeding profusely, her blood pressure dropped to half of normal, and she was administered the Last Rites of the Roman Catholic Church. She vividly recalls that "I nearly died." To the extent that one can, by conversation, identify one incident of many that is critical to Alice Sullivan's perception of herself as a victim, and as being injured by the doctor's neglect, the post-operative shock incident is such an event.

Mrs. Sullivan is bitter about the jury's failure to "punish" the doctor sufficiently. For her the trial was a "whitewash." The doctor got away "scot-free." She thinks that her attorney had evidence at his disposal which could have been used to brand the defendant's testimony as false, but this evidence was not used. Worst of all, though the doctor was the wrongdoer, she feels as if she were the accused. Why? Well, for example, she did not feel that she had the sympathy of the judge. ("At the end of the trial the judge turned to the jury and practically told them they couldn't give me anything.") Moreover, an acquaintance of hers knew someone on the jury. The acquaintance told her that two jurors resisted awarding her anything at all. She remains deeply hurt by their attitude. Her memories of the surgery and trial, merged by now into one painful episode, remain vivid; it is the lack of compassion that she senses accompanying both that, it appears, injured her most deeply, not just her disappointment that the cosmetic surgery was not successful, and not even the considerable physical pain that accompanied the surgery.

The Defendant

When interviewed six years after the trial in which he appeared as the defendant, Dr. O'Connor was a first year law student in the evening division of a Southern California law school. He practiced medicine during the day.

Dr. O'Connor recalls *Sullivan v. O'Connor* as a part of a larger pattern of events which led to profound changes in his life. Dr. O'Connor graduated from Tufts Medical School in 1948 and for the next nine years served on the staffs of various hospitals while developing a specialization in "general surgery." In 1958 he "purchased" the Cambridge Clinic. Within a decade he had built it into "an operation with assets of a quarter of a million dollars. Working with nurses (but no other doctors) I had thirteen examining rooms and could see as many as a hundred patients a day."

As Doctor O'Connor relates it, "emotional storms" filled the decade between 1964 (when he first saw Alice Sullivan) and the spring of 1973 (when, coincidentally, the *Sullivan v. O'Connor* litigation ended in the Supreme Judicial Court opinion reproduced supra). In April of 1964 his wife gave birth to a fourth child whom Dr. O'Connor describes as having chromosome deficiencies leading to his intermittent institutionalization. Dr. O'Connor thought then (and thinks now) that this was not his child, but rather the product of an illicit affair. Over the next several years Dr. O'Connor's marriage deteriorated and finally ended in divorce in 1969. Dr. O'Connor thinks that some of the strain of those years led to an operation for an inflamed colon in 1968. Nor did the 1969 divorce end his difficulties. Custody and alimony disputes led to further litigation which culminated in an alimony order which Dr. O'Connor claimed he could not pay. In March of 1971 he was jailed for several days and his clinic was placed in receivership to satisfy his former wife's claims. On being released from jail Dr. O'Connor fled the state "with three suitcases, my [second] wife and a new baby. An arrest warrant is still out for me in Massachusetts."

Difficulties with Mrs. Sullivan were at least temporarily interwoven with these marital troubles. The child with congenital abnormalities was born in April of 1964; Mrs. Sullivan first came to the clinic in November of 1964. Dr. O'Connor claims that she and Branca Lord (a contemporaneous patient) were the first patients ever to sue him for malpractice.

The 1971 trial of *Sullivan v. O'Connor* immediately preceded the climax of Dr. O'Connor's alimony litigation with his wife. Compared to the controversy with his ex-wife he regarded Mrs.

Sullivan's claim as a relatively small matter: the insurance company was paying, they had selected the lawyer, much more was at stake (indeed the whole of the clinic was at stake) in the alimony case. Dr. O'Connor remarks that his wife's lawyer was in the courtroom through the Sullivan litigation. He was most concerned that the allegations in the Sullivan case might be introduced into the alimony litigation as evidence of his incapacity. This "very much" affected his answers. "I could see down the road for the rest of my life."

When O'Connor left Massachusetts he largely forgot about Sullivan, and was surprised to find that the case had been appealed.* As to the actual merits of Mrs. Sullivan's claim, Dr. O'Connor concedes that the operation did not go well. "It was one of the poorest results I've had." However,

> It was not my fault. I tried to do it well, but she had a tremendous nose — the biggest nose I've ever seen in my whole life. We made her a smaller nose — not a great nose, but the best that could be done under the circumstances .... I was friendly with her. She thought I was some kind of a miracle worker. She was on the dark side of forty. She was getting desperate. She thought that I would give her a nose that would make her look like a movie actress. Of course I couldn't do that.

He never promised any particular results. "She stole the picture, took a rule, and drew a straight line." She and Branca Lord pursued the litigation because they saw money in it.

Dr. O'Connor is unhappy with his recollections of the litigative process. "I had a feeling of helplessness. My lawyer was just sitting there while I was questioned. He was asleep." He thinks his lawyer was under-prepared for the trial, most particularly because "he only spent a half an hour with me before we went to trial. . . . Lawyers have a tendency to use curbstone conversations as a way

---

*The practical impact of the litigation on his licensing in California is nil. The licensing authorities only inquire about disciplinary proceedings, and Dr. O'Connor was never disciplined by the Massachusetts Board of Licensing and Discipline.

to prepare for trial. Doctors spend hours with their patients . . . going over problems. I have never met a lawyer who does this."

Dr. O'Connor has no memory of the jury, but thinks their decision understandable in the light of the inferences he thinks they would draw from the "forged photograph." Judge Brogna "didn't attract my attention. He was very fair."

The malpractice suits joined with the divorce litigation apparently catalyzed Dr. O'Connor's desire to go to law school. He recalls that he had been admitted to Harvard Law School in the late forties, but decided to pursue a medical career instead. At the time he was interviewed for this article, however, he had become involved in much litigation. He said he was involved in forty-two suits, among them one against a drug company for marketing, and a psychiatrist for employing, a "mind control drug" by means of which the psychiatrist has poisoned the mind of Dr. O'Connor's second wife. Dr. O'Connor said he hoped law school would better equip him to deal with these and related legal problems. "I went through life trying to be a nice guy . . . Leo Durocher said it first . . . nice guys finish last."

The Testimony in Sullivan v. O'Connor

A summary of four aspects of the several hundred pages of transcript arising from this six day trial should suggest some of the capability problems raised by the jury's difficulties as fact-finders and by the disparities in perception between those trained in the law and those not so trained.

1. The Witnesses' Demeanor

On behalf of Mrs. Sullivan Mr. Newton called as witnesses Dr. O'Connor, Mrs. Sullivan, a friend of Mrs. Sullivan's who cared for her after the operations, and, as an expert witness, a local plastic surgeon who was a graduate of Harvard Medical School. The defense recalled Dr. O'Connor, called an expert witness of its own, and otherwise contented itself with cross-examining the plaintiff's witnesses. By far the most significant witnesses, in terms of time on the stand, information revealed about the contracts claim, and emotional intensity were Mrs. Sullivan and Dr. O'Connor.

Dr. O'Connor's attitude throughout could fairly be described as belligerent. He repeatedly nit-picked at plaintiff's attorney's questions, asked to have questions and answers read back, and sneered at questions. On the second day of his testimony, the trial judge interrupted:

THE COURT: Doctor, perhaps its about time I explained a few things to you in small words.

For three hundred years our system has been operating very, very well. The lawyers ask the questions and the witnesses answer them. If the opposing lawyer thinks that the question is improper or illegal, he can object. And I will rule on it.

The witness does not argue with an attorney. And, unlike in the medical profession, I run the courtroom.

Do you understand?

O'CONNOR: Excuse me if I have offended you, Your Honor.

THE COURT: You haven't offended me. I've got very thick skin, believe me. What I am afraid of is that you may be creating a very poor impression on the jury.

Now, just answer the questions.

Appearing as the second witness, Miss Sullivan also had difficulty, as the following excerpts may suggest:

SULLIVAN: I hope I answered correctly; but show business is funny.

FINNERTY: I object to all this.

SULLIVAN: I am going to continue. I am going to explain.

NEWTON: You can't explain.

THE COURT: You can't explain here, Mrs. Sullivan. He asked you, had you an opinion. You can answer that, yes or no.

* * *

MR. NEWTON: What did [Dr. O'Connor] do for you [between the first and second operations] . . .?

MRS. SULLIVAN: Yes. Just checking, you know, waiting for the next operation.

MR. FINNERTY: I object to that last statement.

THE COURT: The last statement, after 'just checking' may be stricken.

Will you please just answer the question asked?

MRS. SULLIVAN: I'm sorry . . . .

MR. NEWTON: Now, was there any discussion during this period of time about when the second operation was going to take place between you and Dr. O'Connor?

MRS. SULLIVAN: Yes, there was.

MR. NEWTON: When did that occur and what was the discussion?

MRS. SULLIVAN: Well, we thought — I'm afraid to say anything.

2. Difficulties with the Documentary Evidence

There was a great deal of conflicting testimony and confusion about the documentary evidence used to try to reconstruct the course of Mrs. Sullivan's treatment. Dr. O'Connor accused Mrs. Sullivan of stealing pre-operative photographs from his files, of drawing a line on them to create the appearance that he promised a nose of particular dimensions, and of forging memoranda on Cambridge clinic stationery to indicate that she had an inflated number of operations. Mrs. Sullivan hotly denied these accusations. Neither side's view was ever convincingly rebutted or supported.

Difficulties were compounded by the fact that Dr. O'Connor's written records were designed only to attend to his financial relations with his patients. Office visits were billed, but the records did not show their purpose. Moreover, though hospital operating room regulations required that a doctor describe any surgery he performed, only one of the three operations performed on Mrs. Sullivan's nose was performed in a hospital and the account of that operation was irretrievably garbled, apparently by the hospital typist, at a key point. (The account is reproduced below.)

3. Conflicting Accounts of Promises Made and Broken

The testimony of Mrs. Sullivan and Dr. O'Connor was rarely congruent as to the details of their professional relationship. They could neither agree on what they had said to each other, nor on how many times Mrs. Sullivan saw Dr. O'Connor, nor on what happened during those visits and during the three operations which were performed. In reading excepts from their testimony it may be helpful to bear in mind the following list of dates relevant to operations by Dr. O'Connor on Mrs. Sullivan:

Nov. 16, 1964	Mrs. Sullivan's first visit to Dr. O'Connor's clinic.
Nov. 23, 1964	First operation, removed ½ inch of cartilage on tip of nose under local anesthesia at the clinic.
Feb. 2, 1965	Dr. O'Connor sent Mrs. Sullivan a note suggesting a second operation.
Feb. 25, 1965	Second operation performed in Somerville Hospital. Bone removed.
May 20, 1965	Third operation (in the clinic) partially performed.

a. Testimony About Promises Before the First Operation

Dr. O'Connor's Account

NEWTON: Do you recall having a discussion with Mrs. Sullivan before her first operation, in which you showed her the picture and drew a line on the picture, to show how her nose would look after you had finished reconstructive surgery on it?

O'CONNOR: No.

NEWTON: You had no such discussion?

O'CONNOR: I don't recall any such.

NEWTON: You don't remember any such discussion?

O'CONNOR: No. I do remember a discussion with the woman.

Mrs. Sullivan's Account

NEWTON (after having established that O'Connor had taken a photograph of plaintiff's face): Now, at the time that he took that photograph did he draw a line on your nose as indicated on this present photograph?

SULLIVAN: Yes, he drew that line.

NEWTON: He drew this particular line?

SULLIVAN: Yes.

NEWTON: And this is the photograph that he took.

SULLIVAN: Yes.

* * *

Dr. O'Connor's Account

NEWTON: Well, you did tell her, didn't you, doctor, what you intended to do to her nose? Isn't that correct?

O'CONNOR: No.

NEWTON: You never told her? She did ask you, didn't she, doctor, at some time, on either her first, second, or third visit, whether you could or felt it wise or warranted to perform reconstructive surgery on her nose? She did ask you that, didn't she?

O'CONNOR: No.

*   *   *

(a bit later)

NEWTON: And did you describe to her how her nose would look after you had performed the procedure?

O'CONNOR: No.

NEWTON: I'm sorry. I didn't hear that.

O'CONNOR: No.

NEWTON: No?

O'CONNOR: No.

NEWTON: So that your conversation was limited merely to the fact that you could operate on her nose but it did not include what the nose would look like after you had finished with the procedure?

O'CONNOR: That is correct.

NEWTON: Is that right?

O'CONNOR: That is correct.

Mrs. Sullivan's Account

NEWTON: Tell us what he said, concerning that line.

SULLIVAN: When he drew the line he said that it would look more or less like that when he finished, you know.

b. Testimony About Promises Before the Second Operation

| Dr. O'Connor's Account | Mrs. Sullivan's Account |

Dr. O'Connor's Account

(After testifying in several different, apparently contradictory ways, Dr. O'Connor testified that he told Mrs. Sullivan at the outset that more than one operation on her nose might or might not be necessary, "One can never predict.")

NEWTON: Did you at any time . . . from the time you first saw Mrs. Sullivan up to December 4, tell her that you would perform a second operation on her nose two weeks after you performed the first operation?

O'CONNER: No. I never told her any such thing. That is absurd.

NEWTON: May that last go out, Your Honor?

THE COURT: Yes.

You don't have to editorialize. That's what you've got a lawyer for. Just answer the questions.

O'CONNOR: . . . I was rather satisfied with the results of the first operation . . . since Miss Sullivan's complaint was more or less about the length of her nose, not the size of it. It was a rather large nose as noses go.

And she had given me a history of having considerable psychological difficulty as a child because the other kids in the neighborhood called her Pinocchio. And I thought that shortening her nose was enough.

She, however, prevailed on me, in between November 23rd and February 23rd, to make the nose

Mrs. Sullivan's Account

FINNERTY: So you agreed at the outset to have it (the operation) done in two stages, is that right?

SULLIVAN: Yes sir.

He said it would be done in two operations.

* * *

NEWTON: And did he tell you how long after the first stage, or the first operation, he was going to perform the second operation?

SULLIVAN: Yes, he did. . . . I asked him that because I was concerned about losing work.

FINNERTY: I object.

THE COURT: Just what did he tell you?

SULLIVAN: He said it would be two weeks in between the operations.

NEWTON: After the first operation did you have any discussion concerning a second operation . . . ?

SULLIVAN: Well it was supposed to be sooner —

THE COURT: No. The question is comparatively simple. If you can't remember, just say you can't remember.

SULLIVAN: It's hard to say just, yes or no, Your Honor.

THE COURT: . . . It's very simple.

SULLIVAN: Yes, I did.

* * *

Dr. O'Connor's Account	Mrs. Sullivan's Account
smaller. So that the purpose of the second operation was to work on the nasal bone. . . .	NEWTON: And what was that discussion? SULLIVAN: Well, every week he'd say 'Don't book any work this weekend because you're going in the hospital soon.' So I wouldn't book any work. And then something would happen: The hospital was filled up and I couldn't get in. And this went on for several weeks.

c. Testimony About Promises Before the Third Operation

Dr. O'Connor's Account	Mrs. Sullivan's Account
O'CONNOR: [After the second operation] she was on the phone all the time. NEWTON: And was she complaining about something? O'CONNOR: Well, some of the time she'd want to complain, some of the time she'd want to chat and so on and so forth. She made dozens of phone calls to my office. NEWTON: And what type of complaint did she make? O'CONNOR: Well it ranged from things that have nothing to do with the nose whatsoever, other physical complaints of her body. But she wanted to know if they were related to the operation.	FINNERTY: When you went to see Dr. O'Connor [for the first time] did you have any newspaper clippings with you? SULLIVAN: No, I didn't. FINNERTY: Didn't you have a picture of Hedy Lamarr in your pocketbook? SULLIVAN: No I didn't. * * * FINNERTY: And is it your testimony before this Court and jury that Dr. O'Connor told you he would create for you a nose like Hedy Lamarr's? SULLIVAN: No. He said he gave me one like that afterwards.

Dr. O'Connor's Account

And at some period of time she started a line of questioning, wanting to know if she was going to look like Hedy Lamarr when all this was finished. . . .

FINNERTY: Now Dr. O'Connor, did you ever, as she's testified, say, after you had completed surgery, 'I have given you a Hedy Lamarr nose?

O'CONNOR: No.

FINNERTY: Did you make any promises with respect to a result in this case?

O'CONNOR: Certainly not. One can never guarantee results, Mr. Finnerty. . . .

. . . O'CONNOR: ". . . [S]ome time after the second operation I realized that there was some more to this situation than I had originally thought.

Miss Sullivan started bringing in pictures of Hedy Lamarr to me and kept —

FINNERTY: Was this the first time she kept bringing in Hedi LaMarr's pictures?

O'CONNOR: Yes . . . And I realized at that time that there was more to this situation than I had originally realized. So that we were also getting some spreading postoperative and some shading of the nasal bones. And this is something that sometimes happens . . . She had what I considered a little bit too much convexity of the tip of her nose to suit me. So that we scheduled her for a third procedure on May 20th.

Mrs. Sullivan's Account

FINNERTY: He said he had already given you one?

SULLIVAN: This was after the operation. [Apparently the second operation.]

4. On the Question of Damages

The jury awarded $13,500 to Mrs. Sullivan. How did it arrive at this figure? The only dollar figures mentioned at trial referred to $622.65 as Mrs. Sullivan's medical costs and to $150 to $175 as the average pay that would be earned each week by an entertainer doing the sort of work that Mrs. Sullivan did. Mrs. Sullivan also testified that she had appeared in over fifty clubs in the period 1947-1964. She admitted that after her operations she had sung for five months in a Boston club. The jurors were explicitly instructed that the evidence was insufficient to award damages for loss of employment. The jurors were instructed that they could compensate Mrs. Sullivan for her suffering for the third, but only the third operation. Samples of the principal parts of her and Dr. O'Connor's testimony insofar as it touched on her "suffering" in all the operations are here provided.

a. Dr. O'Connor's Testimony

NEWTON: . . . what did you do for Mrs. Sullivan on the 25th during the [second] operation? What was your procedure?

O'CONNOR: The procedure was a second-stage rhinoplasty.

NEWTON: What is a second stage rhinoplasty, doctor?

O'CONNOR: Merely a second operation. . . .

THE COURT: . . . What did you do? . . .

O'CONNOR: I'll read you my operative description of the procedure. . . . You asked me what I did. I'll read it to you.

"Under satisfactory ten percent cocaine packs and two percent xylocaine — this is a local anesthesia — incisions were made over the upper lateral cartilage and the entire skin of the nose was dissected free from the underlying structures from the columella.

"The upper lateral nasal cartilages were shortened. The extensive sub-mucous resection of the nasal septum — an extensive submucous resection of the nasal septum was carried out, to correct the deviation of the septum to the right at the lower end of the nose.

"The septum at the close of the operation seemed to be almost perpendicular. In the correction of the septum the bony floor of the nasal passage was chiseled away in some places. Medial lateral lower cartilages were reshaped and repositioned at the tip of the nose which had shown a large deviation to the right pre-opera-tively.

Multiple 5 0 nylon sutures were used to attach the columella to the septum. A plaster face mask was applied and the patient returned to the ward in good condition."

NEWTON: So that in effect, doctor, what you did was chisel away some bone on the bridge of her nose, isn't that right? You removed some bone?

O'CONNOR: Yes. We took some bone away from the bridge of her nose and from the base of the nasal septum, where it was deviated.

[Dr. O'Connor's account of Mrs. Sullivan's recovery was that she did not "get into . . . serious difficulty" after the op-eration. She "fainted" and vomited blood, and experienced wide fluctuations in her blood pressure, but "So far as I was concerned it was a very minor matter. This sort of thing happens all the time. . . . She was operated on Thursday morning; by Friday afternoon she was perfectly all right. She was released on a telephone order Saturday morning, in accordance with normal check-out hours of the hospi-tal."]

*   *   *

O'CONNOR: . . . [W]e scheduled her for a third procedure [to be conducted in the clinic] on May 20. Unfortunately, on that date we weren't able to accomplish what we set out to do because Miss [*sic*] Sullivan wasn't in a psychological condition to accept the procedure.

*   *   *

THE COURT: . . . Do I now understand you to say that on May 20th that you did not carry out a third procedure or operation?

O'CONNOR: We only got about as far as the anesthesia in that case, Your Honor. The operation was not completed . . . an incision was made, Your Honor, but we couldn't proceed to the finish of this operation. One stitch was used to close the incision.

*   *   *

b. Mrs. Sullivan's Testimony

NEWTON: . . . [W]ere you awake during the surgery?

SULLIVAN: Yes, most of the time.

*   *   *

NEWTON: Would you describe to us what took place [in the second operation] . . . ?

SULLIVAN: Well, I remember, it was a very small room that we were in and there was a nurse and Dr. O'Connor; and that is about it. And I was lying on the table and I was talking to them at the time. And I remember at one point he was, like, as I looked up, he was on this side of me and the nurse was on this side of me. And I think he had a saw. And she had a chisel and a hammer. And I heard him say to the nurse, "Hit it a few more times."

So she's hammering the chisel, breaking my bones, which I don't think should have been done.

FINNERTY: I move that be stricken.

THE COURT: It isn't a question as to whether you think it should be done; that's up to the jury.

You heard him say to the nurse, "Hit it a few more times?"

SULLIVAN: Yes.

THE COURT: Everything after that the jury can ignore.

[Mrs. Sullivan continued, explaining that at the end of the operation a plaster hood was placed completely over her head. It left no opening for her eyes and only small openings for her nose and mouth. Then she was brought back to a hospital bedroom and given three pills by a nurse.]

SULLIVAN: . . . So I took one pill and then another pill. And immediately after I took the third pill, it wasn't vomiting, it was just like my mouth opened up and something gushed right out of my mouth, three times, like, boom, boom boom, you know. And I heard somebody say, "Oh, my God, its all blood." . . .

[Mrs. Sullivan passed out. When she came to, she heard a number of voices. Though she could not see through the hood she recognized one of the voices as that of Dr. O'Connor.]

SULLIVAN: I heard him say, my blood pressure was like a yo-yo. It was going down to forty then to a hundred and ten, and then to forty again. . . . I had the Last Rites of the Church.

[After several days Mrs. Sullivan left the hospital and spent three weeks being cared for at a friend's house. During the first week she remained in the plaster cast. Her testimony continued:]

Well, I was at her house and I didn't feel good. I went right to bed. And she had to do everything for me, lead me around. If I had to go to the bathroom she'd bring me to the door and put me in and leave me.

She had to wash me, feed me. My upper lip was swollen about this much below my teeth, so that I couldn't talk good or eat good, or anything. And every night I'd get so hysterical and crying and couldn't breathe under the mask, because I had all blood clots from my nose to my throat. . . .

NEWTON: How could you describe any physical result that you observed or felt from the mask being on your head, the case?

SULLIVAN: Well, for one thing, I couldn't see. I couldn't breathe at all, hardly, except from my mouth and lips were all grey from breathing from my mouth.

And, naturally, being confined it makes you nervous, you know. You feel as if you're smothering. And I was sick. I didn't eat much and my lip was swollen.

*   *   *

[Mrs. Sullivan did not testify to any significant extent about the third operation. She certainly provided no account of suffering during or because of this operation. Her only comments relevant to this operation were as follows:]

NEWTON: Now the last time you saw him was there any suggestion on his part that you return for further treatment or did he discharge you from treatment?

SULLIVAN: Yes, there was. . . . He said he wanted to operate on me again. And I said, "What would you do?"

And he said, "I'd like to take a piece of flesh out of your ear and put it up your nose, to fill up the hole up here."

NEWTON: And what did you tell him?

SULLIVAN: I said, "You aren't going to operate on me any more. I'm not a guinea pig."

And he told me to shut up.

* * *

FINNERTY: Now, you do agree, do you not, that your nose, now, is a lot better than it ever was, don't you?

SULLIVAN: It's smaller, but it's distorted, though.

FINNERTY: Remember my asking you this question [while taking your pretrial deposition]? Let me ask you this question in all seriousness, "You agree that it's a lot better than it ever was?"

And your answer: "Yes, but there is a lot wrong with it, too. It isn't what I was supposed to get."

Remember that answer.

* * *

FURTHER QUESTIONS

1. Justice Kaplan says "the law has taken the middle of the road position of allowing actions [against doctors] based on alleged contract, but insisting on clear proof." In light of the background materials on this case and your reflections thus far on the capability problem, do you think this standard can be maintained? Was it met here? If the proof is less than completely clear, does that appear to be taken into account in computing damages? Should it be?

2. Several states have enacted legislation making guarantees of cure enforceable only if they are in writing. See generally Comment, An Analysis of State Legislative Responses to the Medical Malpractice Crisis 1975 Duke L.J. 1417, 1450-51 (1975), endorsing this approach. As a legislator how would you vote if such a provision were proposed?

3. An observer might be justified in believing that Mrs. Sullivan had better than average counsel, an impartial judge, and an impartial jury. Her case was aired in six days of precious trial time at considerable cost to the state as well as to the litigants. Moreover, she secured about the then normal range of recovery for a plaintiff positioned as she was. Yet one cannot deny the reality of her feelings about the process, nor escape noticing the analogy between her dissatisfaction with her lawyers and her dissatisfaction with her doctor. It appears that the trial stands in her memory as a part of a long and painful experience. The trial was not a resolution of her bad experience, but rather an extension of it.

In light of these reactions, criticize Judge Brogna's statement that "[f]or three hundred years our system has been operating very, very well. The lawyers ask the questions and the witnesses answer them." How, if at all, might the system be improved to reduce the frequency of feelings like Mrs. Sullivan's?

4. In his interview, the trial judge described the attorneys in this case as both "able lawyers." Both, however, made noteworthy mistakes (as all lawyers do some of the time and some lawyers do most of the time). At times also the transcript reveals them in the exercise of significant skills.

Prof. Louis Brown of the University of Southern California Law Center has suggested that law students ought to engage in

a "legal autopsy" of past cases, examining them for clues to successful and unsuccessful practice. Do a legal autopsy on this case.
Insofar as these unfortunately but necessarily heavily edited materials permit you to draw conclusions, what lessons do you draw
from them that might be relevant to your performance as an attorney? What capability problems arise as a result of the variance
in lawyers' skills?

5. Justice Kaplan contrasts the position of the New York courts,
which award a reliance recovery, with that of the New Hampshire
courts, which award an expectation recovery. How, if at all, do you
think the differences in measure might affect the performances
of:

(a) juries? (How was this jury instructed, on a reliance or an
expectation measure? What measure does it appear that it used?)

(b) lawyers trying cases or attempting to settle them?

(c) judges trying cases without juries?

(d) doctors?

6. Essau B., the second juror interviewed, reported that the
jurors would not consider Dr. O'Connor's personal finances because they had not been submitted into evidence. Without sense
of contradiction he went on to report a juror's comment that he
presumed Dr. O'Connor was insured. He apparently took this as
an appropriate point, though it too was not discussed in court.
For his part, the first juror interviewed, Arthur B., said he never
thought about insurance.

Is insurance a relevant variable? Courtroom comment on it
is prohibited, but aren't some jurors implicitly considering the
doctor's ability to pay? Can you keep jurors from considering it?
Should factors affecting ability to pay be made more explicit for
the jury?

7. If you were law clerk to Justice Kaplan and had whatever
insight these interviews provide into the jury process, how would
you advise him about the relevance of that insight to the position
he adopts?

8. Suppose someone asked you: (a) whether Alice Sullivan
"won" this case? (b) why $13,500 was awarded, assuming that
there was a breach of contract? (c) whether the lawyers in this
case were "good"? (d) whether the appellate opinion was "right"?

How would you answer? Do your four answers connect with one another?

9. "In light of these interviews Justice Kaplan appears to be engaging in an over-subtle, pedantic, meaningless exercise. It is sadly ironic that a legal realist should be operating at such distance from reality." Is this comment well-taken? If not, why not? If so, isn't most of your law school education an "over-subtle, pedantic, meaningless exercise"? If Justice Kaplan suffers from an inbreeding of the twin perspectives of a law professor and an appellate judge, don't you similarly suffer from being raised on the opinions of appellate judges, as selected and taught by law professors?

II. HADLEY AND ANOTHER v. BAXENDALE AND OTHERS

HADLEY AND ANOTHER v. BAXENDALE AND OTHERS
9 Ex. 341, 156 Eng.Rep. 145, 1854.

[As with most old English appellate cases the account begins with a "headnote" by the Court Reporter describing
the "facts" as they are revealed by the pleadings, and sum-
marizing proceedings in the lower court.]

... At the trial before Crompton, J., at the last Gloucester Assizes, it appeared that the plaintiffs carried on an extensive business as millers at Gloucester; and that, on the 11th of May, their
mill was stopped by a breakage of the crank shaft by which the
mill was worked. The steam-engine was manufactured by Messrs.
Joyce & Co., the engineers, at Greenwich, and it became necessary
to send the shaft as a pattern for a new one to Greenwich. The
fracture was discovered on the 12th, and on the 13th the plaintiffs
sent one of their servants to the office of the defendants, who are
the well-known carriers trading under the name of Pickford &
Co., for the purpose of having the shaft carried to Greenwich. The
plaintiffs' servant told the clerk that the mill was stopped, and that
the shaft must be sent immediately; and in answer to the inquiry
when the shaft would be taken, the answer was, that if it was sent
up by twelve o'clock any day, it would be delivered at Greenwich
on the following day. On the following day the shaft was taken by
the defendants, before noon, for the purpose of being conveyed
to Greenwich, and the sum of £2 4s. was paid for its carriage for
the whole distance; at the same time the defendants' clerk was
told that a special entry, if required, should be made to hasten its
delivery. The delivery of the shaft at Greenwich was delayed by

some neglect; and the consequence was, that the plaintiffs did not receive the new shaft for several days after they would otherwise have done, and the working of their mill was thereby delayed, and they thereby lost the profits they would otherwise have received.

On the part of the defendants, it was objected that these damages were too remote, and that the defendants were not liable with respect to them. The learned Judge left the case generally to the jury, who found a verdict with £25 damages beyond the amount paid into Court.

Whateley, in last Michaelmas Term, obtained a rule nisi for a new trial, on the ground of misdirection.

[The official report of the case now proceeds with a summary of the arguments of the appellants (that is the Hadleys).]

Keating and Dowdeswell shewed cause. The plaintiffs are entitled to the amount awarded by the jury as damages. These damages are not too remote, for they are not only the natural and necessary consequence of the defendants' default, but they are the only loss which the plaintiffs have actually sustained. The principle upon which damages are assessed is founded upon that of rendering compensation to the injured party. . . . The authorities are in the plaintiffs' favour upon the general ground. In Nurse v. Barns (1 Sir T. Raym. 77), which was an action for the breach of an agreement for the letting of certain iron mills, the plaintiff was held entitled to a sum of £500, awarded by reason of loss of stock laid in, although he had only paid £10 by way of consideration. In Borradaile v. Brunton (8 Taunt. 535, 2 B.Moo. 582), which was an action for the breach of the warranty of a chain cable that it should last two years as a substitute for a rope cable of sixteen inches, the plaintiff was held entitled to recover for the loss of the anchor, which was occasioned by the breaking of the cable within the specified time. . . .

[Here the Three "Barons" who sat as Judges in this case intruded in the argument with a discussion of their own:]

Alderson, B. Why should not the defendant have been liable for the loss of the ship? Parke, B. Sedgwick doubts the correctness of that report. Martin, B. Take the case of the non-delivery

by a carrier of a delicate piece of machinery, whereby the whole of
an extensive mill is thrown out of work for a considerable time; if
the carrier is to be liable for the loss in that case, he might incur
damages to the extent of £10,000. Parke, B., referred to Everard v.
Hopkins (2 Bulst. 332).

[The Hadleys' counsel resumed:]

These extreme cases, and the difficulty which consequently exists in the estimation of the true amount of damages, supports the
view for which the plaintiffs contend, that the question is properly for the decision of a jury, and therefore that this matter could
not properly have been withdrawn from their consideration. In
Ingram v. Lawson (6 Bing.N.C. 212) the true principle was acted
upon. That was an action for a libel upon the plaintiff, who was
the owner and master of a ship, which he advertised to take passengers to the East Indies; and the libel imputed that the vessel
was not seaworthy, and that Jews had purchased her to take out
convicts. The Court held, that evidence shewing that the plaintiff's
profits after the publication of the libel were £1500 below the usual average, was admissible, to enable the jury to form an opinion
as to the nature of the plaintiff's business, and of his general rate of
profit. Here, also, the plaintiffs have not sustained any loss beyond
that which was submitted to the jury. . . . The recent decision of
this Court, in Waters v. Towers (8 Ex. 401), seems to be strongly in
the plaintiffs' favour. The defendants there had agreed to fit up the
plaintiffs' mill within a reasonable time, but had not completed
their contract within such time; and it was held that the plaintiffs
were entitled to recover, by way of damages, the loss of profit upon
a contract they had entered into with third parties, and which
they were unable to fulfil by reason of the defendants' breach of
contract. [Parke, B. The defendants there must of necessity have
known that the consequence of their not completing their contract
would be to stop the working of the mill. But how could the defendants here know that any such result would follow?] There was
ample evidence that the defendants knew the purpose for which
this shaft was sent, and that the result of its nondelivery in due
time would be the stoppage of the mill; for the defendants' agent,
at their place of business, was told that the mill was then stopped,
that the shaft must be delivered immediately, and that if a special

entry was necessary to hasten its delivery, such an entry should be made. The defendants must, therefore, be held to have contemplated at the time what in fact did follow, as the necessary and natural result of their wrongful act.

[The official report now summarizes the arguments of Baxendale's counsel.]

Whateley, Willes, and Phipson, in support of the rule. It has been contended, on the part of the plaintiffs, that the damages found by the jury are a matter fit for their consideration; but still the question remains, in what way ought the jury to have been directed? It has been also urged, that, in awarding damages, the law gives compensation to the injured individual. But it is clear that complete compensation is not to be awarded.... Sedgwick says (page 38), "In regard to the quantum of damages, instead of adhering to the term compensation, it would be far more accurate to say, in the language of Domat, which we have cited above, 'that the object is to discriminate between that portion of the loss which must be borne by the offending party and that which must be borne by the sufferer.' The law in fact aims not at the satisfaction but at a division of the loss." And the learned author also cites the following passage from Broom's Legal Maxims: "Every defendant," says Mr. Broom, "against whom an action is brought experiences some injury or inconvenience beyond what the costs will compensate him for." Again, at page 78, after referring to the case of Flureau v. Thornhill (2 W. Blac. 1078), he says, "Both the English and American Courts have generally adhered to this denial of profits as any part of the damages to be compensated and that whether in cases of contract or of tort. So, in a case of illegal capture, Mr. Justice Story rejected the item of profits on the voyage, and held this general language: 'Independent, however, of all authority, I am satisfied upon principle, that an allowance of damages upon the basis of a calculation of profits is inadmissible. The rule would be in the highest degree unfavourable to the interests of the community. The subject would be involved in utter uncertainty. The calculation would proceed upon contingencies, and would require a knowledge of foreign markets to an exactness, in point of time and value, which would sometimes present embarrassing obstacles; much would depend upon the length of the voyage, and the season of arrival, much upon the vigilance and activity of the master, and much upon the momentary demand. After all, it would be a calculation upon conjectures, and not upon facts; such a rule therefore has been rejected by Courts of law in ordinary cases, and instead of deciding upon the gains or losses of parties in particular cases, a uniform interest has been applied as the measure of damages for the detention of property.' "There is much force in that admirably constructed passage. We ought to pay all due homage in this country to the decisions of the American Courts upon this important subject, to which they appear to have given much careful consideration. The damages here are too remote. Several of the cases which were principally relied upon by the plaintiffs are distinguishable. In Waters v. Towers (1 Exch. 401) there was a special contract to do the work in a particular time, and the damage occasioned by the non-completion of the contract was that to which the plaintiffs were held to be entitled. In Borradale v. Brunton (8 Taunt. 535) there was a direct engagement that the cable should hold the anchor. So, in the case of taking away a workman's tools, the natural and necessary consequence is the loss of employment: Bodley v. Reynolds (8 Q.B. 779). Here the declaration is founded upon the defendants' duty as common carriers, and indeed there is no pretence for saying that they entered into a special contract to bear all the consequences of the non-delivery of the article in question. They were merely bound to carry it safely, and to deliver it within a reasonable time. The duty of the clerk, who was in attendance at the defendants' office, was to enter the article, and to take the amount of the carriage; but a mere notice to him, such as was here given, could not make the defendants, as carriers, liable as upon a special contract. Such matters, therefore, must be rejected from the consideration of the question. If carriers are to be liable in such a case as this, the exercise of a sound judgment would not suffice, but they ought to be gifted also with a spirit of prophecy. "I have always understood," said Patteson, J., in Kelly v. Partington (5 B. & Ad. 651), "that the special damage must be the natural result of the thing done." That sentence presents the true test. The Court of Queen's Bench acted upon that rule in Foxall v. Barnett (2 E. & B. 928). This therefore is a question of law, and the jury ought to have been told that these damages were too remote; and that, in the absence of the proof of any other damage, the plaintiffs were entitled to nominal damages only. . . . If the defendants should be held responsible for the damages awarded by the jury, they would be in a better position if they confined their business to the conveyance of gold. They cannot be responsible for results which, at the time the goods are delivered for carriage, are beyond all human foresight. Suppose a manufacturer were to contract with a coal merchant or mine owner for the delivery of a boat load of coals, no intimation being given that the coals were required for immediate use, the vendor in that case would not be liable for the stoppage of the vendee's business for want of the article which he had failed to deliver: for the vendor has no knowledge that the goods are not to go to the vendee's general stock. Where the contracting party is shewn to be acquainted with all the consequences that must of necessity follow from a breach on his part of the contract, it may be reasonable to say that he takes the risk of such consequences. . . .

Cur. adv. vult.

The judgment of the Court was now delivered by

ALDERSON, B. We think that there ought to be a new trial in this case; but, in so doing, we deem it to be expedient and necessary to state explicitly the rule which the Judge, at the next trial, ought, in our opinion, to direct the jury to be governed by when they estimate the damages.

It is, indeed, of the last importance that we should do this; for, if the jury are left without any definite rule to guide them, it will, in such cases as these, manifestly lead to the greatest injustice. . . .

Now we think the proper rule in such a case as the present is this: — Where two parties have made a contract which one of them has broken, the damages which the other party ought to receive in respect of such breach of contract should be such as may fairly and reasonably be considered either arising naturally, i. e., according to the usual course of things, from such breach of contract itself, or such as may reasonably be supposed to have been in the contemplation of both parties, at the time they made the contract, as the probable result of the breach of it. Now, if the special circumstances under which the contract was actually made were communicated by the plaintiffs to the defendants, and thus known to both parties, the damages resulting from the breach of such a contract, which they would reasonably contemplate, would be the amount of injury which would ordinarily follow from a breach of contract under these special circumstances so known and communicated. But, on the other hand, if these special circumstances were wholly unknown to the party breaking the contract, he, at the most, could only be supposed to have had in his contemplation the amount of injury which would arise generally, and in the great multitude of cases not affected by any special circumstances, from such a breach of contract. For, had the special circumstances been known the parties might have specially provided for the breach of contract by special terms as to the damages in that case; and of this advantage it would be very unjust to deprive them. Now the above principles are those by which we think the jury ought to be guided in estimating the damages arising out of any breach of contract. . . . Now, in the present case, if we are to apply the principles above laid down, we find that the only circumstances here communicated by the plaintiffs to the defendants at the time the contract was made, were, that the article to be carried was the broken shaft of a mill, and that the plaintiffs were the millers of that mill. But how do these circumstances shew reasonably that the profits of the mill must be stopped by an unreasonable delay in the delivery of the broken shaft by the carrier to the third person? Suppose the plaintiffs had another shaft in their possession put up or putting up at the time, and that they only wished to send back the broken shaft to the engineer who made it; it is clear that this would be quite consistent with the above circumstances, and yet the unreasonable delay in the delivery would have no effect upon the intermediate profits of the mill. Or, again, suppose that, at the time of the delivery to the carrier, the machinery of the mill had been in other respects defective, then, also, the same results would follow. Here it is true that the shaft was actually sent back to serve as a model for a new one, and that the want of a new one was the only cause of the stoppage of the mill, and that the loss of profits really arose from not sending down the new shaft in proper time, and that this arose from the delay in delivering the broken one to serve as a model. But it is obvious that, in the great multitude of cases of millers sending off broken shafts to third persons by a carrier under ordinary circumstances, such consequences would not, in all probability, have occurred; and these special circumstances were here never communicated by the plaintiffs to the defendants. It follows, therefore, that the loss of profits here cannot reasonably be considered such a consequence of the breach of contract as could have been fairly and reasonably contemplated by both the parties when they made this contract. For such loss would neither have flowed naturally from the breach of this contract in the great multitude of such cases occurring under ordinary circumstances, nor were the special circumstances, which, perhaps, would have made it a reasonable and natural consequence of such breach of contract, communicated to or known by the defendants. The Judge ought, therefore, to have told the jury, that, upon the facts then before them, they ought not to take the loss of profits into consideration at all in estimating the damages. There must therefore be a new trial in this case.

Rule absolute.

FIRST QUESTIONS

1. Try to tell the story of *Hadley v. Baxendale* as you tried to tell the story of *Sullivan v. O'Connor* — from the beginning and in great detail. Who said what to whom and what happened thereafter? What don't you know that you need to know in order reasonably to recount the story? Does the appellate court seem to know more than you do? On what factual assumptions does it proceed? What basis, if any, is there for these assumptions?

2. Recall what was written about the jury in *Sullivan v. O'Connor*. Do you think the jury in *Hadley v. Baxendale* functioned differently from that in *Sullivan*? Did it face different capability problems? Judge Crompton is said to have "left the case generally to the jury." Is the argument for doing that in this instance better or worse than the argument for taking that tack in *Sullivan v. O'Connor*?

3. The defendant's barrister quotes Judge Story to the effect that because profits are an "utter uncertainty" they ought not to be awarded to a plaintiff. Is this an idiosyncratic view, based on the peculiar case before Story? Is it an antiquated view, a reflection of an age in which concepts of accounting, of markets, and of profits were immature? Or is it still a strong argument today? How would you compute the profits forgone by the Hadleys if they were entitled to them? Do the possibilities of perjury suggested by Justice Kaplan in *Sullivan v. O'Connor* come into play here?

4. What are the capability problems inherent in Baron Alderson's holding?

5. The decision in *Hadley v. Baxendale* has stood for over 150 years. (Note that there has been some modification of the decision in the language of the Uniform Commercial Code, Section 2-715.) To what extent does the *Hadley v. Baxendale* rule seem to you to be outdated? Make an argument that it is a product of the age in which it was created and, among other things, assumes capabilities which are unachievable in the context of a modern economy. Then consider the following essay.

SUPPLEMENTARY COMMENTS[*]

Hadley v. Baxendale is still, and presumably always will be, a fixed star in the jurisprudential firmament.
— Grant Gilmore, The Death of Contract 83 (1974)

Of the many thousands of students who graduate from American law schools every year, probably all save a few hundred are required to read the 1854 English Exchequer case of *Hadley v. Baxendale*.[1] It is, indeed, one of a startlingly small number of opinions to which graduates from law school will almost assuredly have been exposed even if they attended different institutions, used a variety of textbooks, and opted for disparate electives.[2] The exceptional pedagogical centrality of the case is further underscored by the similarly widespread attention the case receives in the curricula of all Commonwealth law schools.

But if the case is unusually widely read, it is typically narrowly studied. In the first-year law curriculum, where the opinion usually appears, cases are normally treated like doctrinal fruits on a conceptual tree: some bulk large, some are almost insignificant; some display a wondrous perfection of development, others are shown to be rotten at the core; some are further out along conceptual branches than others; but all are quite erroneously treated as though they blossomed at the same time, and for the same harvest.

This ahistorical view may have some didactic advantages, but it overlooks much that is important. Cases are of different vintages; they arise in different settings. It matters that *Hadley v. Baxendale* was decided in 1854 in England, and not in 1974 in California. Without reflecting on the ramifications of these facts of timing

---

[*]These comments originally appeared as Danzig, *Hadley v. Baxendale*: A Study in the Industrialization of the Law, 4 Jrnl. of Leg. Studies 249 (1975). Some footnotes are omitted.

1. 9 Ex. 341, 156 Eng.Rep. 145 (1854).

2. Thus, for example, the authors of the leading hornbook on the Uniform Commercial Code remark that knowledge of "The Rule" in *Hadley v. Baxendale* "has become a sine qua non to second-year standing in law school." J. White & R. Summers, Handbook of the Law Under the Uniform Commercial Code 314 (1972).

and setting, perhaps teachers and students can understand black letter law as it now is, but neither can comprehend the processes of doctrinal innovation, growth, and decay.

By focusing on one central case in its historical setting I hope in this article to provide an experiential supplement to the legal reader's steady diet of logic.[3] My theme is that *Hadley v. Baxendale* can usefully be analyzed as a judicial invention in an age of industrial invention. After describing the facts and the holding of *Hadley v. Baxendale* in the first section that follows, my concern in succeeding sections is to discuss why the "rule of the case" was invented in its particular form and in this particular case, to assess the relationship between this judicial invention and the existing legal and economic technology, to underscore the impact of the rule in effecting a specialization of judicial labor and a standardization, centralization, and mass production of judicial products, and to demonstrate that the rule of the case became widely known and generally accepted because, as with other successful inventions, it was well advertised and marketed. I shall conclude by suggesting that although this invention was useful for the age in which it was created, it is very possible that it is now of limited significance and in need of modernization.

I.

In Gloucester, England, on Thursday, May 12, 1853, the engine shaft at City Flour Mills[4] broke, preventing the further milling of corn. On May 13, the mill proprietors, Joseph and Jonah Hadley, dispatched an employee to Pickford and Co., "common carriers," to

---

3. It should be emphasized that I do not purport to offer a perfect or a certain understanding of *Hadley v. Baxendale* in its historical context. Much of what follows is speculative both because scholarly inquiry into nineteenth-century British legal history has been limited and because widespread inquiries have yielded only a minimum of primary source material relevant to the case. . . . Manuscript collections reflecting the thought of the principals either were never collected, no longer survive, or proved valueless. Company records were destroyed, some of them as recently as a few years ago.

4. The enterprise is described in the official reports as City Steam Mills, but contemporary commercial directories list Joseph and Jonah Hadley as proprietors of "City Flour Mills." See Slater's Royal National Commercial Directory and Topography of Gloucester and Hereford 195 (1858-1859), and the Gloucester Post Office Directory 296 (1856).

inquire as to the fastest means of conveying the shaft to W. Joyce and Co., Greenwich, where it would serve as a model for the crafting of a new shaft. A Pickfords employee, Mr. Perrett, represented that it would be delivered "on the second day after the day of . . . delivery" to Pickfords.

The shaft was delivered to Pickfords on Saturday, May 14, but it did not, in fact, reach W. Joyce and Co. until the 21st, because at the last stage of the voyage the shaft was shipped with a consignment of iron bound for Joyce and Co. by canal[5] rather than by rail. In consequence, the Hadleys calculated that the steam mill stoppage was prolonged an unnecessary five days, at a cost in lost profits of £300. When Pickfords refused to make good these losses, the Hadleys brought suit before the Queen's judges, sitting in the Assize Court for Gloucester, naming Joseph Baxendale, the London-based managing director of Pickfords, as the defendant. (Baxendale was personally liable for the failings of his unincorporated business.) Baxendale paid £25 into court as a settlement offer, but this was spurned, and the case went to trial before a "special jury" (about which more later) in August, three months after the alleged damages were inflicted. The Hadleys, now claiming "near £200" damages,[7] presented witnesses to show the nature of their understanding with Pickford and the magnitude of the damages they incurred as a result of the delay. (It developed that the witnesses testified to only £120 damages.) The well-known barrister, Sir Henry Singer Keating, then summarized the plaintiff's case:

> The issue they (the jury) had to try was extremely simple, and peculiarly fitted for them to decide, namely, whether what he could not help designating the paltry sum of £25 was sufficient to compensate them [the Hadleys] . . . . The defendants Messrs. Pickford and Co., were common carriers, and as such possessed certain rights, and took upon themselves certain obligations.

5. ". . . [I]nstead of being forwarded by wagon immediately, it was kept for several days in London, and was at length forwarded by water on the 20th, along with many tons of iron goods which had been consigned to the same parties." Assize Report, The Times (London), Aug. 8, 1853, at 10, col. 1.

7. Gloucester Journal, Supplement August 13, 1853, at 1, col. 4.

Against this the defendants argued that the damages incurred were "too remote."

Sir Roger Crompton, the new but by all accounts careful and competent Assize judge, instructed the jury

> to consider what, under the circumstances was a reasonable time for delivering the shaft; and next, what was the damages caused to the Plaintiffs by the delay in the delivery. . . . They should give their damages for the natural consequences of the defendant's breach of contract, and with that view they would have to consider whether the stoppages of the Plaintiff's works was one of the probable and natural consequences of that breach of contract, and then, looking to all the circumstances of the case and the position of the parties, to say what was the amount of the damages occasioned by the stoppage of the works.

So instructed, the jury retired for about a half an hour and returned with a compromise verdict: damages were assessed at £50.[12]

Baxendale promptly appealed. The case was heard in the Exchequer on February 1 and 2, by Barons Alderson, Parke and Martin, and then, after "great pains were bestowed upon" the question,[13] Baron Alderson delivered an opinion on February 23, 1854. This opinion, the only one rendered in *Hadley v. Baxendale* (for no further appeal was taken), refashioned the substantive law of contract damages by effecting a subtle but significant change in the contemporary understanding of the rule that damages be awarded only for the "natural consequences" of a breach. Other judges, and indeed, this same Exchequer bench at other times, read the limitation as a simple rule tending by the criterion of "naturalness" to exclude that portion of damages which the plaintiff had himself exacerbated (and thus unnaturally sustained), and by the criterion

12. The decision was a compromise in every respect. The Gloucester Journal reported: "The jury retired to consider the amount of damages, and after an absence of more than half an hour returned into court, when it appeared that eleven, out of the twelve had agreed to put it at £45, while one considered it ought to be £75. It was ultimately agreed to take the damages at £50." Gloucester Journal, supra note 7, at 1, col. 4.

13. Chief Baron Pollock later remarked: "The argument took place several weeks before the judgment was given, and I know that great pains were bestowed upon it." Wilson v. Newport Dock Co., 35 L.J.Ex. 97, 103 (1866).

of "consequence" to exclude those injuries which could not, in fact, be causally related to the breach. In contrast, Baron Alderson here read the phrase "natural consequences" as though it meant normal consequences and thus predictable consequences — obviously a more rigorous standard. In the most critical sentence of the opinion, he said:

> Where two parties have made a contract which one of them has broken, the damages which the other party ought to receive in respect of such breach of contract should be such as may fairly and reasonably be considered either arising naturally, i. e., according to the usual course of things, from such breach of contract itself, or such as may reasonably be supposed to have been in the contemplation of both parties, at the time they made the contract, as the probable result of the breach of it.

Not content with simply ordering a new trial after the articulation of the standard, Baron Alderson went on to "apply the principles above laid down" to the case at hand, and advanced three rather remarkable propositions. First, he asserted that "the only circumstances here communicated by the plaintiffs to the defendants" at the time the contract was made were that they were millers whose mill shaft was broken. According to Baron Alderson, there was no notice of the "special circumstances" that the mill was stopped and profits would be lost as a result of delay in the delivery of the shaft. Thus, the Baron concluded that damages for lost profits could not be awarded under the contemplation branch of the rule.

Second, Baron Alderson held that "it is obvious that in the great multitude of cases of millers sending off broken shafts to third persons by a carrier under ordinary circumstances" the mill would not be idle and profits lost during the period of shipment. Millers, he held, ordinarily would have spare shafts or, at any rate, if their mills were stopped it would usually be a consequence of other difficulties as well. Thus, there could be no recovery for lost profits under the "usual course of things" branch of the rule.

Third, Baron Alderson held "that the Judge ought, therefore, to have told the jury, upon the facts before them, they ought not to take the loss of profits into consideration at all in estimating the damages."

The first of these propositions is remarkable because it flies in the face of what the reporter of Baron Alderson's decision apparently thought was established by the record. The reporter's headnote says unequivocally that the defendant's clerk "was told that the mill was stopped, that the shaft must be delivered immediately, and that a special entry, if necessary, must be made to hasten its delivery. . . ."

The second and third propositions are remarkable because they hold that the trial judge, and in case of his error, the appellate judge, ought to preempt a local jury in determining commercial error, even though the issue appears to be one of fact and not one of law. These latter propositions serve to underscore an important, although generally less noticed, procedural innovation corresponding to the substantive change effected by *Hadley v. Baxendale*: the case not only modifies instructions to juries, it also directs judges to keep some issues from the jury.

II.

The novelty of the changes effected in procedural and substantive law by *Hadley v. Baxendale* suggests that the opinion may be examined as an invention. The innovation effected in the law is here unusually stark. Baron Alderson, in support of the central proposition he advanced, cited no precedent and invoked no British legislative or academic authority in favor of the rule he articulated. Nor was this due to oversight. The opinion broke new ground by establishing a rule for decision by judges in an area of law — the calculation of damages in contracts suits — which had previously been left to almost entirely unstructured decision by English juries.

Chitty's preeminent 1826 treatise on contracts, for example, even in its 771 page 1850 edition, had allocated only 13 of its pages to the subject of damages, and virtually all of those pages concerned issues associated with penalty clauses. As to damages in the normal run of cases, Chitty had only one comment to offer:

> When the parties have not furnished the criterion of damages by stipulating for a liquidated sum to be paid as such,

it is, in general, entirely the province of the jury to assess the amount, with reference to all the circumstances of the case.

Similarly, *Smith's Treatise on Contracts*, prominent in the same period, mentioned damages not at all, and *Smith's* general collection of leading law cases touched on damages only in the context of tort. Thus, the Hadleys' counsel seems to have fairly summarized the state of prior thinking on the subject when he argued "the difficulty which . . . exists in the estimation of the true amount of damages, supports the view . . . that the question is properly for the decision of a jury" without elaborate instruction or review.

The strikingly novel nature of the innovation in English law effected by *Hadley v. Baxendale* must have been particularly apparent to the participants in the case because among the cases outmoded by this opinion, one decided seven years earlier involved this same Baxendale and these same judges.[26] In *Black v. Baxendale*, Pickfords was two days late in the delivery of "five bundles of haycloths" thus causing Black's employee to incur both wasted time (valued at £1/1/0 per day) and an otherwise unnecessary "removal cost" of 10 shillings. At trial, Chief Baron Pollock "directed the jury that they were at liberty to give these expenses as damages if they should think fit." Inexplicably the jury awarded £10 damages — apparently more than the amount the most generous calculation of damages would have justified. Baron Martin, who was to sit on the panel that decided *Hadley v. Baxendale*, argued the case on appeal for Baxendale, claiming, inter alia, that the jury verdict should be overturned because Pickfords "had no notice for what purpose the goods were sent" or what expenses would en-

---

26. Black v. Baxendale, 1 Ex. 410, 154 Eng.Rep. 174 (1847). It is not so improbable as it may seem that the earlier case on point also involved Baxendale. An historian who has studied Pickfords has remarked about Baxendale: "he was a formidable litigant and fought stubbornly for his rights as he saw them. . . . A note in Pickford's records relates that from 1 January 1858 to 25 May 1863, 34 actions were brought [by Baxendale] against railroad companies." G. Turnbull, Pickfords 1750-1920: A Study in the Development of Transportation (unpublished Ph.D. dissertation, Univ. of Glasgow, Scotland). I note, in the period of concern here, Hart v. Baxendale, 6 Ex. 769, 155 Eng.Rep. 755 (1851), and Hudson v. Baxendale, 2 H & H 574, 27 L.T.Ex. 93, 157 Eng.Rep. 237 (1857), as well as the litigation involving Black and the Hadleys.

sue on failure to deliver. Neither Baron Parke nor Baron Alderson, both later to sit with Baron Martin in *Hadley v. Baxendale*, would accept this argument. Baron Parke said, "The defendants are responsible only for reasonable consequences of their breach of contract. It was a question for the jury whether [the expenses were] . . . reasonable." And Baron Alderson added, "[w]hether these expenses were reasonable was entirely a question for the jury." Had the sum been larger both judges would have reversed on grounds of miscalculation of the expenses, but both (joined by the rest of the court) agreed that the type and limit of the liability incurred was exclusively a matter for the jury. This view, of course, was what *Hadley v. Baxendale* rejected.

In a lecture given at the Seldon Society while this article was in draft, Professor A. W. B. Simpson of the University of Kent pointed out that both Pothier's treatise on the French Civil Code (translated into English in 1806) and Sedgwick's American treatise in its first and second editions of 1847 and 1852 argued for rules of contract liability essentially like that adopted by the Court in *Hadley v. Baxendale*. Further, Professor Simpson noted that Baron Parke remarked in the course of the argument in *Hadley v. Baxendale* that he thought that "[T]he sensible rule appears to be that which has been laid down in France . . . and which is . . . translated by Sedgwick. . . ." From this Professor Simpson concludes that "the moving spirit behind *Hadley v. Baxendale* was surely Baron Parke" and argues, more generally, that this illustrates a proposition advanced in his lecture: that innovation in the law in the nineteenth century was largely prompted by the quiet absorption of the observations of treatise writers, particularly treatise writers influenced by the civil law, into the decisions of English common law judges.

There is much to be said for this position. But Professor Simpson's otherwise admirable discussion seems insufficient in two ways. First, in looking to Baron Parke as the animating force behind the decision, Simpson neglects to consider the role of Baxendale's counsel, Sir James Shaw Willes. As we shall see, the fact that Willes was a principal actor in the case was of no small significance in effecting the spread of the rule.

Contemporary descriptions convey a portrait of Willes as extraordinary on three counts, all of which must have operated to his advantage in this litigation. He was reputed to the ablest commercial lawyer of his time, he was co-editor of the most prominent, annotated volume of British legal cases, and he was remarkably cosmopolitan. It was said of Willes that he spoke seven languages, many of them so fluently that when, for example, he was accused in Spain of having murdered a coachman who fell under the horses of a carriage in which Sir James was riding, Sir James successfully defended himself before the Spanish Court without assistance. It seems clear that his commercial interests combined with his academic orientation and his cosmopolitan outlook caused Willes to be thoroughly familiar with the French Civil Code's provision on damages and with the similar views of Sedgwick, then the outstanding American commentator on the subject. Indeed, the official report of the arguments before the appellate bench makes it clear that the counsel on both sides came to court well primed on Pothier and Sedgwick and that they cited them to the judges more often than vice versa.

I shall return to Willes' influence later. Obviously, the fact that Willes had read Pothier and especially Sedgwick only reinforces Mr. Simpson's point as to the influence of treatise writers. Two years after the case was decided, when Willes had occasion to comment on it in his next edition of *Smith's Leading Cases*, he underscored Sedgwick's influence:

> [T]he subject is discussed at length in the very learned work of Mr. Theodore Sedgwick "On the Measure of Damages" Ch. 3 . . . . The suggestion of Mr. Sedgwick . . . seems to agree in substance with the decision of the Court of Exchequer in the case of *Hadley v. Baxendale* and others.

However — and this is the second, more significant regard in which Professor Simpson's discussion can be faulted — if an understanding of the rule in *Hadley v. Baxendale* must begin with some recognition of the influence of foreign models on British thinkers, it need not end there. As Friedman and Ladinsky note in another context, an interest in foreign ideas may be prompted by "dissatisfaction" with existing law. "A foreign model here sharpens discussion and provides a ready made plan. Yet the felt need for such [a law change] has domestic origins." Why was there a felt need for an innovation in the law of damages at the time of *Hadley v. Baxendale*? The search for a more satisfactory answer than that provided by reference to foreign treatise writers requires us to look further.

III.

To understand the origins and the limitations of the rule in *Hadley v. Baxendale* we must appreciate the industrial and legal world out of which it came and for which it was designed. In 1854 Great Britain was in a state of extraordinary flux. Between 1801 and 1851 its population rose from 10.6 to 20.9 million people and its gross national product increased from £232.0 to £523.3 million. By 1861 its population was 23.2 million and its GNP £668.0 million. Contemporaries saw the magnitude of this change and were aware of its impact on the law. As one writer, surveying the scene in 1863, put it:

> What our Law was then [in 1828], it is not now; and what it is now, can best be understood by seeing what it was, then. It is like the comparison between England under former, and present, systems of transit, for persons, property, and intelligence: between the days of lumbering wagons, stage coaches, and a creeping post — and of swift, luxurious railroads and lightening telegraphs. All is altered: material, inducing corresponding moral and social changes.

Arising squarely in the middle of the "industrial revolution" and directly in the midst of the "Great Boom" of 1842-1874, *Hadley v. Baxendale* was a product of these times. The case was shaped by the increasing sophistication of the economy and the law — and equally significantly by the gaps, the naiveté, and the crudeness of the contemporary system.

The raw facts of the case should alert the reader to the half-matured and unevenly developing nature of the economy in which the decision was rendered. For example, the Hadley mill was steam-powered. While it was not hand-run, animal-driven, wind-powered, or water-powered, as in an earlier age, it was also not powered by electricity as it would be in the next century. So with the now famous broken shaft. It was a complicated piece of machinery, manufactured by a specialized company on the other side of England. But it was neither a standardized nor a mass-produced machine. It was handcrafted. Thus, the transaction in

Hadley v. Baxendale: the old shaft had to be brought to eastern England as the "model" for the new one.

The circumstances of the breach similarly reflect a half-way modernized society. The breach occurred because the shaft was sent by canal, the early industrial transport form, rather than by rail, the mature industrial transport form. That both co-existed as significant means of shipment suggests the transitional nature of the period. The ready acceptance of the notion that delay gave rise to damages, that time meant money, suggests the affinity of the modes of thought of this age to our own. But the units of account for measuring time in *Hadley v. Baxendale* suggest the distance between our period and this one: speed for a trip across England was measured in days, not hours.

If the facts of the case offer us a glimpse of an economic world in transition, what of the legal system which had to deal with that transition? This system was also modernizing, but, at the time of *Hadley v. Baxendale*, it was still strikingly underdeveloped. The case itself indicates the rudimentary and uneven development of the commercial law of the period. *Hadley v. Baxendale* is frequently described as a case involving a claim for damages consequent on a breach of a negotiated contract for especially quick delivery of a consigned package; but in fact, although this was the first of two counts on which the Hadleys initially pressed their suit, both the official and the contemporary press reports make it clear that before going to trial against Baxendale they abandoned all claim to damages based on a specific contract. Instead their pleadings claimed damages arising as a consequence of Pickford's failure to effect delivery "within a reasonable time" as it was obliged to do because of its status as a common carrier. If, as Maine posited ten years after *Hadley v. Baxendale*, the process of modernization involves a movement from status to contract, this most famed of modern contract cases is peculiarly antiquarian!

The pleadings' emphasis on status rather than contract appears to have been related to the underdeveloped nature of the law of agency in England at the time. The Gloucester Journal report of the Assize trial comments:

> The declaration had originally contained two counts; the
> first charging the defendants with having contracted to de-

liver the crank within the space of two days, which they did
in truth do, but there was a doubt how far Mr. Perrett, the
agent of the defendants, had authority to bind them by any
special contract which would vary their ordinary liability.
It was therefore thought not prudent to proceed upon that
count, but upon the count of not delivering within a reasonable time.

The Hadleys' counsel apparently reasoned that a jury verdict
against Baxendale predicated on what was said to or by the Pickfords' clerk might be upset by an appellate court on a theory that
personal liability could not be imputed to Baxendale through comment to or by an agent. The situation was summarized by Baxendale's counsel in the argument on appeal:

> Here the declaration is founded upon the defendants' duty
> as common carriers, and indeed there is no pretense for
> saying that they entered into a special contract to bear all
> the consequences of the non-delivery of the article in ques-
> tion. They were merely bound to carry it safely, and to de-
> liver it within a reasonable time. The duty of the clerk, who
> was in attendance at the defendants' office, was to enter
> the article, and to take the amount of the carriage; but a
> mere notice to him, such as was here given, could not make
> the defendants, as carriers, liable as upon a special con-
> tract. Such matters, therefore, must be rejected from the
> consideration of the question.

Baxendale's counsel here overstates the case, but at the least it
appears that there was an uncertainty in the rudimentary law of
agency as it existed at the time.

This uncertainty may explain Baron Alderson's surprising assertion that the Hadleys failed to serve notice that the mill operations were dependent on the quick return of the shaft. It may be
that as a factual matter the Hadleys never served notice on the
Pickfords' clerk of their extreme dependence on the shaft, and that
the Court reporter simply erred in asserting that notice had been

served to this effect.[53] But it is also possible that Baron Alderson saw the case as the Pickfords' counsel urged: ". . . a mere notice . . . was here given . . . [but it] could not make the defendants liable . . . [and therefore it was to] be rejected from the consideration of the question."

This agency problem underscores the fact that the case is *Hadley v. Baxendale*, not *Hadley v. Pickfords' Moving Co.*; in other words, that the opinion was handed down at a time and in a situa-

---

53. Lord Asquith took this position ("the headnote is definitely misleading") in Victoria Laundry v. Newman Indus. Ltd., 2 K.B. 528, 537 (1949). The best available account of the Assize trial supports this view. It reports the Hadleys' counsel as saying only:

> On the morning of the 12th of May, it was discovered that the shaft of the steam-mill was broken, rendering it necessary to forward it to Messrs. Joyce. . . . A clerk of the plaintiffs was therefore dispatched on Friday, the 13th of May, to the office of Messrs. Pickford and Co., where he saw their agent, Mr. Perrett, to whom he stated what had occurred and that the plaintiffs were anxious that the crank should be delivered to Messrs. Joyce and Co. as soon as possible . . . . The shaft was not [promptly] received by Messrs. Joyce. Meanwhile the mills of the plaintiff were stopped.

Gloucester Journal, supra, note 11, at 1, col. 3. A contemporary newspaper report of the Exchequer proceedings, moreover, paraphrases Baxendale's counsel as saying, "there was no special contract, and the defendants had no knowledge of the inconvenience to which the plaintiff was subject by the delay." 7 Cty.Cts.Chron. 133 (June 1854).

On the other hand, two remarks in the course of argument strongly suggest that notice of the stoppage was in fact given to Pickfords' clerk. Baron Parke attempted to distinguish Waters v. Towers, 8 Ex. 401, 155 Eng.Rep. 1404 (1853) by saying that "[t]he defendants there must of necessity have known that the consequence of their not covmpleting their contract would be to stop the working of the mill. But how could the defendants here know that any such result would follow?" 9 Ex. 341, 349, 156 Eng.Rep. 145, 149 (1854). To this the Hadleys' counsel is reported as having answered flatly: "There was ample evidence that the defendants knew the purpose for which this shaft was sent, and that the result of its non-delivery in due time would be the stoppage of the mill; for the defendants' agent, at their place of business, was told that the mill was then stopped, that the shaft must be delivered immediately, and that if a special entry was necessary to hasten its delivery, such an entry should be made." Ibid.

The comment of Baxendale's counsel which I have quoted in the text is even more striking. The argument is that "a mere notice [to the clerk], *such as was here given,* could not make the defendants, as carriers, liable as upon a special contract. Such matters, therefore, must be rejected from the consideration of the question." 9 Ex. 341, 352, 156 Eng.Rep. 145, 150 (1854) (emphasis added).

tion in which principals were personally liable for the misfeasance
of their companies. Although the principle of limited liability was
already recognized in England for exceptional "chartered" companies, it was not until 1855 that Parliament extended the right to
ordinary entrepreneurs, and it was not until 1901 that Pickfords
(and many other companies) incorporated. In 1854 the desirability
of limiting personal liability for corporate debts was a major item
of parliamentary debate and the legal world's most hotly disputed
subject. This contemporary ferment was fed by, and in turn reinforced, related areas of concern about the run of liability: a Royal
Commission was meeting in 1854 to consider expanding the right
to petition for bankruptcy; the right to limit liability for torts by
means of a prior contract was being pondered in the courts; and
the alleged right of common carriers to limit liability for property
loss by mere prior notification was being keenly debated.

Under these conditions the concept of a severe restriction on
the scope of damages in contract actions must have seemed both
less alien than it would have appeared to a judge a decade earlier, and more important than it would have seemed to a judge a
decade later. For in 1854 judges were, at one and the same time,
confronted with a growing acceptance of the idea of limited liability and yet with a situation of unlimited personal liability for commercial misfeasance. This was a time, moreover, when commercial interactions involved increasing agglomerations of capital and
a pyramiding and interlocking of transactions, so that any error
might lead to damages that could significantly diminish annual
profits or even destroy the personal fortunes of those sharing in
thinly financed ventures.

Two particular aspects of the incomplete evolution of ideas
about limited liability appear to be especially intertwined with the
litigation in *Hadley v. Baxendale*. A quarter of a century before
the litigation, Parliament had addressed the question of substantial claims against coach and canal carriers for loss of sealed boxes
which contained jewels, currency and the like, but whose exceptional value was not superficially apparent and which were consequently carried for regular fees and with no more than regular
care. Parliament's solution in the Common Carriers Act of 1830,
was to declare that shippers of "articles of great value in small

compass" were required to give notice of that value or otherwise have their right of recovery limited to £10.

That the Act did not control *Hadley v. Baxendale* — a case involving a bulky object — must have been evident. But it is doubtful that the Act was irrelevant to *Hadley v. Baxendale*. If the Hadley's agent went out of his way to assert that the mill's operations depended on the speedy return of the shaft, it may have been because of the pattern established by the Act's notice requirement. It is yet more probable that by the time of litigation the lawyers involved had turned to the Act as the first legislative referent in cases involving loss by a common carrier such as Pickfords. Further, it is worth noting that Baron Parke, a member of the *Hadley v. Baxendale* panel, was the author of the authoritative opinion on the 1830 Act. Given this familiarity, it seems reasonable to suggest that in their emphasis on the interplay between notice and liability and in their ready acceptance of the notion of the desirability of limiting damages for cases which are not signaled as (if the pun will be forgiven) more than run-of-the-mill affairs the *Hadley v. Baxendale* judges followed patterns already established by Parliament.

Viewed from this perspective, the common law innovation promulgated in *Hadley v. Baxendale* may be seen as a technical adaptation of an older idea to new circumstances. The Act of 1830 may have been sensibly phrased given the state of carriers' and shippers' businesses when it was enacted, but by mid-century commerce was more complicated. Bulk shipments had increased with the advent of the railroad, and it may reasonably be supposed that this increase was not so much the product of increases in shipments of horses, cows, produce and other things easily recognized and valued, as it was a consequence of more shipments of machinery which — like the Hadleys' mill shaft — performed complex functions and was of uncertain worth and importance. By 1854 it must have been strikingly apparent that an item did not have to be of "small compass" to be "of uncertain value."

If from one vantage point *Hadley v. Baxendale* simply effected a judicial extension of the Act of 1830, from another vantage point *Hadley v. Baxendale* stands as an example of a tension between Parliament and the judiciary. This tension grew from an ambiguity in section 6 of the Act of 1830. That section was open to the interpretation that by posting notice carriers could limit their liability for loss or injury to £10. The consequent railroad practice of limiting liability by published handbills or printed notice on tickets or bills of lading aroused much public anger. A modern British legal historian has summarized the situation:

> . . . while it could be said that many carriers had the check of competition to oblige them to take an accommodating line with dissatisfied customers, the railways could afford to face claims for loss and injury with the disdainful wave of an exemption clause. By the early 1850's there had been a number of well publicized refusals to pay which made the railways extremely unpopular with the press and in Parliament.

In 1852, the Exchequer, in an opinion by Baron Parke in *Carr's Case*, held effective the practice of limiting liability by notice as within the meaning of the 1830 Act. By the time of *Hadley v. Baxendale*, a year and a half later, it was clear that this would not be allowed to continue. "The effect of nineteenth century parliamentary reform was to compel the parties to have competitive legislative programmes on every subject," and this issue was no exception. In December of 1852 a Parliamentary Select Committee was charged with considering revision of the 1830 Act, and by July 1853 it had held hearings and submitted five reports, urging revision of the 1830 Common Carriers Act. Although the Committee had not focused on Carr's case, and the bill effecting reversal of the case was not passed until April of 1854, as *Hadley v. Baxendale* was being argued and decided in January and February of 1854 it must have seemed very probable that this legislation was coming. Seen in this light *Hadley v. Baxendale* effected a judge-made limitation on damages as a matter of public law just as Parliament was about to inhibit severely carriers' capacities to limit their liability as a matter of private law.

Other more comprehensive studies of Victorian judges and legislators will have to explore this tension between Parliamentary and judicial dispositions toward the entrepreneur,[70] and particularly the common carrier, but insofar as a case study can shed any light on the matter, it is worth noting that the predisposition of this panel seems clear. Two of the three Exchequer judges were tied to Pickfords in contexts likely to make them sympathetic to the company. Baron Martin had represented Pickfords before ascending to the bench,[71] and Baron Parke's brother had been the managing director of the company before Baxendale.[72]

The opinion in *Hadley v. Baxendale* is written in general terms and has had a broad impact on the law of contracts for 120 years. But at the time of its conception it was probably seen and shaped by its authors in the context of uncertainties about the law of agency and conflicts about the shape of the law of liability — particularly common carriers' liability — which are now generally forgotten.

70. The interaction of Parliamentary and judicial law-making becomes of particular interest in this period, as the propensity for legislation rose dramatically. See generally Alan Harding. A Social History of English Law 355 (1966), quoting Pollock: "Our modern law of real property is simply founded on judicial evasions of Acts of Parliament."

I do not mean to imply by this discussion that one can simplistically say that the courts were sympathetic to the nationwide entrepreneur and Parliament antithetic to him. . . .

71. ". . . [T]o a barrister Pickford's custom must be worth having, as most of Pickford's standing counsel have found their way to the bench — the present Chief Baron and Mr. Baron Martin, among others." H. Mayhew, The Shops and Companies of London 50 (1865).

As a barrister before his appointment to the bench, Baron Martin argued Black v. Baxendale. See the case report at 1 Ex. 410, 154 Eng.Rep. 174 (1847).

72. See Evidence of Joseph Baxendale, Select Committee on Railroads, Gt. Brit., Parl. Papers, H.C. 1844, Vol. XI, at 249, Q. 3402, remarking that his predecessor as manager was "the brother of Mr. Baron Parke, Major Parke." That this web of relationships seems to have been not uncommon or thought improper at the time provides yet another indication of the distance between this period and our own age. The idea of impersonalization of business relationships, which the "rule" of this case both reflected and encouraged, had not yet been applied, it appears, to relations between those on the bench and those before them. These personal involvements may go some way, it should be noted, to explaining Baron Alderson's activism in asserting what he took to be common practice when mill shafts were shipped.

IV.

An understanding of the relationship of the rule in *Hadley v. Baxendale* to the contemporary law affecting common carriers may be a predicate to comprehending the impulse behind the rule and its form, but standing alone it tells only a part of the story. I think the rule in *Hadley v. Baxendale* may have had its most significant contemporary effects not for the entrepreneurs powering a modernizing economy, but rather for the judges caught up in their own problems of modernization.

By the middle of the nineteenth century Parliament had acted to modernize the judicial system in a number of important ways. Successive law revision commissions and ensuing enactments had effected changes in the substantive laws of tort, debt, criminal law and, as we have seen, contractual liability. Antiquated aspects of pleading and procedure were similarly remodeled. But the size and case disposition capacity of the common law courts remained remarkably stagnant.

In 1854 the entire national judiciary[73] of Britain and Wales sitting in courts of general jurisdiction numbered fifteen. These judges, distributed equally between three benches — the Court of Common Pleas, the Queen's Bench and the Exchequer — sat individually to hear all cases in London and at Assize (court held in major provincial towns) for two terms of about four weeks each year. They convened as panels of three or four to hear appeals in London at other times. They sat in panels usually numbering seven (confusingly denominated as the Exchequer Chamber) to hear appeals from the panels of three or four. Only appeals from the panels of seven would be heard by another body of men: The House of Lords.

A quarter of a century earlier, in a famous speech in the House of Commons, Lord Brougham had asked: "How can it be expected that twelve judges can go through the increased and increasing business now, when the affairs of men are so extended and multiplied in every direction, the same twelve, and at one time

---

73. The following discussion makes no reference to the chancery, ecclesiastical, admiralty or other specialized courts of the time. For an unusually lucid and comprehensive overview of the judicial systems of this period see Bowen, Progress in the Administration of Justice During the Victorian Period, in 1 Select Essays in Anglo-American Legal History 518-48 (1907).

fifteen, having not been much more than sufficient for the comparatively trifling number of causes tried two or three centuries ago?" Brougham's call for more judges was answered in 1830 by the addition of one judge to each court. But even with this improvement, it was apparent that there was a severe limitation on the number and intricacy of the trials and appeals that these judges could process. Indeed over the fifty years surrounding the decision in *Hadley v. Baxendale* the number of cases brought to trial in the common law courts each year remained remarkably stable and low (around 2400 cases) despite the extraordinary increase in commercial transactions over the period. Although the modern observer is likely to approach this situation with his view colored by images of the endless, enervating litigation described in Dickens' *Bleak House* (published in 1853), this stability in case processing apparently was not achieved by allowing a case backlog to accumulate. Extant docket sheets show that at any given Assize no more than half a dozen cases would typically be held for later sittings. The *Hadley v. Baxendale* litigation is suggestive of this speed in disposition. The Hadleys suffered their injury in May; they brought their suit and received prompt jury trial and judgment in August. Baxendale appealed on the fifth of November, had the appeal argued on the first of February, and received a favorable decision by the end of the month.

Probably the most critical factor in enabling the Courts at Common Law to operate on so intimate a basis was the reconstruction, by act of Parliament in 1846, of the haphazardly functioning local "Courts of Requests" into an extensive and competent court system capable of handling a large volume of cases. This system of "county courts" was rendered inferior to the Common Law Courts (which began being called "Superior Courts") by permitting appeal from County Court judgments to a Common Law Court and by limiting county court claims to sums less than £20. Further, the intent of the legislature to effect a transfer of minor cases away from the Superior Courts was manifested by the enactment of a statute assessing costs against even a victorious plaintiff in Superior Court if his recovery in a contract case amounted to no more than £20, or in a tort case to £5.

After their creation in 1846, the County Courts immediately became the journeyman carriers of the judicial workload. Within their first year of operation they reported receiving 429,215 cases. In 1857 they dealt with 744,652 "plaints." We are properly cautioned to discriminate between substantial judicial business and routine administrative debt collection cases in assessing the significance of case loads over this period. This advice is particularly apt because the County Courts were initially conceived as debtor-creditor courts and always drew the bulk of their business from this context. But it seems clear that the County Courts also quickly began handling a substantial number of more substantial lawsuits and this development was strongly reinforced by an Act of Parliament in 1850 which expanded County Court jurisdiction to encompass claims of up to £50. By the time of *Hadley v. Baxendale* the County Courts were very probably handling many times the number of tort, contract, and other non-debt cases then being processed by the Superior Court judges at Assizes.

Against this backdrop the rule in *Hadley v. Baxendale* can be seen to have had significant contemporary implications which are normally invisible to the modern observer. The bifurcation of the County and Superior Court systems effected a specialization of labor insofar as it tended to discriminate between unimportant and important cases at least on the basis of the amount of recovery they involved. This division of labor was perfectly sensible so long as County Court work was almost exclusively concerned with debts, because in that form of litigation the amount likely to be awarded can be ascertained with great certainty. But by 1854 the events I have sketched probably prompted an increase in contract litigation in the County Courts. If brought in Superior Courts these cases were pressed at the peril of securing only minor recovery and then having that success washed out by the burden of costs. Under such conditions it is not surprising that previously ignored questions of the calculation of damages in contracts cases began to receive attention, not so much because these rules were considered important as matters of substantive law as because they were important as rules of jurisdiction. By identifying the criteria by which damages were to be assessed, the *Hadley v. Baxendale* court enhanced the predictability of damages and therefore the correct allocation of cases between the systems. Moreover, since the rule of the case coupled this enhanced predictability with an assertion of limitations on recovery, it tended to shunt cases from the Superior Courts toward the County Courts and thus to protect the smaller system from at least a portion of the workload that if untrammeled would overwhelm it.

Some standardization of court decisions was implicit in these developments. But this standardization afforded more advantages than simply those associated with caseload allocation and (because of enhanced predictability of outcome) caseload reduction through settlement. Standardization was a means by which the Superior Courts could enhance their authority over County Courts at the very moment they were yielding primary jurisdiction to them.

In 1854 it must have been apparent to the fifteen judges who composed the national judicial system that they had no hope of reviewing half a million cases or even that fraction of them which dealt with genuinely contested issues. Moreover the relatively small stakes involved in County Court cases left all but a miniscule proportion of litigants disinclined to incur the costs of appeal. Under these conditions it is not surprising that ad hoc review gave way to attempts at a crystallized delineation of instructions for dispute resolution which more closely resembled legislation than they did prior common law adjudication.

In its centralization of control, the judicial invention here examined paralleled the industrial developments of the age. The importance of the centralization of control is particularly evident when the rule is put back into the context in which it was promulgated: in terms of judges' control over juries. Told at its simplest level, *Hadley v. Baxendale* is the tale of a litigation contest between two local merchants and a London-based entrepreneur in which the local jury decided for the local merchants and the London judges asserted the priority of their judgment for the national entrepreneur. The tension inherent in the conflict of perspectives between the two decision-making centers — local juries and appellate judges — is underscored when one focuses on the particular decision-makers in this case. It was a special jury that rendered a verdict for the Hadleys. Special juries were drawn, at the request of a party (probably on assertion of unusual complication in the litigation) from a limited list of property owners. At the Baxendale trial nine of the twelve jurors were designated "merchants." Three were labeled simply "Esquire." If life in the mid-nineteenth century was anything like life in our times, the jury members, themselves local merchants who must have suffered frustration or injury from the then frequent occurrence of carrier error, probably sympathized much more readily with the Hadleys than with Baxendale.[99] In contrast, the panel which heard the case on appeal was "special" in a way quite different from the jury. Two of the panel's members had experienced the difficulties and adopted the perspective of Pickfords at one time or another. Under these conditions the invention of the case must have seemed particularly appealing to its promulgators. It led not simply to a resolution of this case for Baxendale, but also, more generally, to a rule of procedure and review which shifted power from more parochial to more cosmopolitan decision-makers. As Baron Alderson put the matter, "we deem it to be expedient and necessary to state explicitly the rule which . . . the jury [ought] to be governed by . . . for if the jury are left without any definite rule to guide them, it will, in such cases as these, manifestly lead to the greatest injustice."

From a less personal perspective the invention also effected a modernization by enhancing efficiency as a result of taking matters out of the hands of the jurors. Whatever its other characteristics, jury justice is hand-crafted justice. Each case is mulled on an ad hoc basis with reference to little more than, as Chitty put it, "the circumstances of the case." In an age of rapidly increasing numbers of transactions and amounts of litigation, a hand-crafted system of justice had as little durability as the hand-crafted system of tool production on which the Hadleys relied for their mill parts.

---

99. A speech of Viscount Midleton's some twenty years later gives us a sense of the performance of these local juries.

> . . . take the case where the parents of a young man at the University refused to pay for things supplied, on the ground that they were such things as no tradesman ought to supply to youths under age, the creditor brought an action in local or other Courts, where a jury of his own class had to decide the question whether the goods were "necessaries" or not, and they seldom had any difficulty in arriving at the conclusion that they were necessaries. He would mention two or three cases in illustration of his meaning. An Oxford jury held that champagne and wild ducks were necessaries for an undergraduate; another jury of the same place found that studs of emeralds set in diamonds came within the same category; and a third jury found that expensive prints — proofs before letters — were necessary furniture for the rooms of an undergraduate of moderate expectations.

Speech in Support of the Infants' Contracts Bill, 219 Parl.Deb. (3rd ser.) 1225 (1874).

By moving matters from a special jury — which cost £24, untold time to assemble, and a half hour to decide — to a judge, the rule in *Hadley v. Baxendale* facilitated the production of the judicial product.[103] And by standardizing the rule which a judge employed, the decision compounded the gain — a point of particular importance in relation to the County Courts where juries were rarely called.

Thus, the judicial advantages of *Hadley v. Baxendale* can be summarized: after the opinion the outcome of a claim for damages for breach of contract could be more readily predicted (and would therefore be less often litigated) than before; when litigated the more appropriate court could more often be chosen; the costs and biases of a jury could more often be avoided; and County Court judges and juries alike could be more readily confined in the exercise of their discretion. Clearly the rule invented in the case offered substantial rewards to the judges who promulgated it and in later years reaffirmed it.[105]

V.

How does an opinion whose primary functions seem to correlate with a quarrel over an 1830 transport act and with the needs of a judicial system in the 1850's come to be viewed as "a fixed star in the jurisprudential firmament" 120 years later?[106]

103. It is doubtful that the parties to the decision in *Hadley v. Baxendale* were insensitive to this phenomenon. In the early 1850's Sir James Shaw Willes and Baron Martin were principal members of the Common Law Commission, whose second report decried the inefficiencies associated with jury trial.

105. I suspect there is far more opportunity for study of the relationship between judges' caseloads and their articulation of rules of law than researchers have thus far demonstrated. On this point we have only a few suggestive remarks by academics (e. g., Llewellyn: "The whole history of the English Constitution could be written in terms of pressure of work," quoted in William Twining, Karl Llewellyn and the Realist Movement 116 (1973); and Posner: "models of the firm that stress personal utility maximization by the executives may be relevant" to the Supreme Court of the United States, Richard A. Posner, Economic Analysis of the Law 326 (1972)); an occasional hint from a sitting judge (see, e. g., the remarks of Mr. Justice White, Supreme Court Review of Agency Decisions, 26 Ad.Law Rev. 107, 109 (1974)); and the very brief reflections of one legal historian (see John Dawson, A History of Law Judges 278-80 (1960), comparing the small number of national judges in the English system from the 13th to 17th centuries with the much larger numbers in France and Germany during this time, and suggesting a possible effect of this difference on the nature of appellate review).

106. Grant Gilmore, The Death of Contract 49 (1974).

The fame and widespread acceptance of the innovation effected by this case seems particularly remarkable when we remember that this was a decision of one of three equal intermediate courts. Other Exchequer opinions were vulnerable to rejection or recasting by Queens Bench and Common Pleas judges sitting either in their appellate capacity as the Exchequer Chamber, or within their own systems as Assize and *nisi prius* judges. Why did this case escape overruling and anonymity? The theme of invention suggests an answer. For an invention to be widely employed it must not only fill a need and be well fabricated; it must also be marketed. In mid-nineteenth century England it was perhaps easier than ever before for a judge-created rule to take hold and influence other judges and lay conduct. Prompt press reporting of opinions and an expanding bar served to transmit at least the gist of commercial opinions to those likely to be affected by them. More important, an increasing professionalization of the system of court reporting made the then common tactic of "doubting" the accuracy of an adverse reported opinion[108] more difficult, and thus enhanced the power of precedent.

There was another factor at play which has been lost sight of by modern observers. Sir James Shaw Willes, overlooked by Professor Simpson but to whom I have ascribed much of the responsibility for the invention in the case, appears to have been remarkably situated to effect the marketing of the invention by virtue of his position as co-editor of the foremost legal textbook of the time: *Smith's Leading Cases*. Yet more remarkably — and this underscores the already mentioned intimacy of the mid-century British legal world — Willes' opposing counsel on appeal (and the counsel for the Hadleys at trial), Sir Henry Singer Keating, was the other editor of *Smith's*.

---

108. The argument in *Hadley v. Baxendale* itself provides an example of this practice. When counsel for the Hadleys cited Borradaile v. Brunton, 8 Taunt. 535, 2 B.Moo. 582 (1818), the official reports record Baron Parke as remarking that "Sedgwick doubts the correctness of that report," and the reporter adds the footnoted observation that "the learned Judge has frequently observed of late that the 8th Taunton is of but doubtful authority, as the cases were not reported by Mr. Taunton himself." 9 Ex. 341 at 347, 156 Eng.Rep. 145, 148 (1854). (22 Law Times Reports 69 (1854) attributes the remark to Baron Alderson in the form: "I should very much doubt that case, both in law and in fact.")

The two "editors" wasted no time in converting their litigation arguments into an academic analysis, so that a primary difference between the 1852 edition of *Smith's Leading Cases* and the 1856 edition was a lengthy description of and commentary on *Hadley v. Baxendale*. The impact of such notoriety cannot, of course, be precisely ascertained, but it seems fair to surmise that it was substantial. The breadth of *Smith's* readership and the respect with which it was regarded can be inferred in part from the frequency with which it is noted as referred to by judges in the official reports. Our rudimentary sources, moreover, show *Smith's* note on *Hadley* quoted by litigants in cases where the *Hadley* rule might apply and in public discussion of the rule.

Nor did Sir Henry and Sir James end their association with *Hadley v. Baxendale* upon enshrining the opinion in *Smith's*. Both culminated illustrious careers by elevation to the Superior Courts; and Sir James, in particular, in his capacity as an appellate judge had frequent occasion to endorse and expound on the opinion in *Hadley v. Baxendale*. Within a year of arguing for Baxendale he was one of three judges offering an opinion in the case in which the Court of Common Pleas accepted the Exchequer rule. Over the next decade Willes established himself as the outstanding commercial law judge of the latter half of the century. He then crafted the most significant nineteenth century opinion interpreting and endorsing *Hadley v. Baxendale*, and followed it, four years later, with the next most often cited elaboration of the rule — in this instance in an opinion reviewed and sustained by the Exchequer Chamber.

In sum, Sir James was a central actor in the importation, spread and interpretation of the rule of *Hadley v. Baxendale*; and he contributed toward these ends as an academic, as a litigator and as an esteemed appellate judge. If the common law is thought to be some "brooding omnipresence" working itself pure, it obviously acquired some substantial human assistance in this instance.

VI.

But if we have some idea of the first causes of the spread of the invention, what explains its staying power? Here, I think, the histories of industrial and legal inventions part company. As a rule industrial inventions are prized in proportion to their use. If, like the model T Ford, some inventions remain valued long after they have lost their general utility, it is only because some aficionados treasure them as acknowledged antiques. The present curricular predominance and asserted intellectual centrality of *Hadley v. Baxendale* suggests that this is not so in the law. For as presently taught and ensconced in the Uniform Commercial Code, the rule is almost as irrelevant to the modern age as are those artifacts — the Hadley hand-crafted shaft and the Baxendale canal barge — which provided the occasion for its articulation.

I have suggested that the rule's utility for nineteenth-century judges and entrepreneurs was as a control mechanism. It tended to make damages both predictable and limited by constraining them to the bounds of the normal, in the absence of special notice leading to advance contemplation of an abnormal state of affairs. In another context Professor Posner suggests that the rule is of societal advantage because it increases the chances of optimization of precaution-taking. He describes the "general principle" of the case as "that where a risk of loss is known to only one party to the contract, the other party is not liable for the loss if it occurs," and then suggests that this principle "induces the party with knowledge of the risk either to take any appropriate precautions himself or, if he believes that the other party might be the more efficient loss avoider, to disclose the risk to that party."[118]

He illustrates this advantage by the following hypothetical:

A commercial photographer purchases a roll of film to take pictures of the Himalayas for a magazine. The cost of development of the film by the manufacturer is included in the purchase price. The photographer incurs heavy expenses (including the hire of an airplane) to complete the assignment. He mails the film to the manufacturer but it is mislaid in the developing room and never found.

---

118. Richard A. Posner, supra note 105, at 61. See also John H. Barton, The Economic Basis of Damages for Breach of Contract, 1 J. Leg. Studies 277, 296 (1972), and Lawrence Friedman, Contract Law in America 126 (1965) ("avoidable consequences must be abided by those with power to avoid them; it would distort the market system to allow an offender against this principle to cast his losses upon another party. . . .").

Compare the incentive effects of allowing the photographer to recover his full losses and of limiting him to recovery of the price of the film. The first alternative creates little incentive to avoid similar losses in the future. The photographer will take no precautions. He is indifferent as between successful completion of his assignment and the receipt of adequate compensation for its failure. The manufacturer of the film will probably not take additional precautions either; the aggregate costs of such freak losses are probably too small to justify substantial efforts to prevent them. The second alternative in contrast, should induce the photographer to take precautions that turn out to be at once inexpensive and effective: using two rolls of film or requesting special handling when he sends the roll in for development.

It should be obvious that the rule's achievement of the advantages Professor Posner describes or the benefits I have noted earlier has been and continues to be premised on the viability of its underlying concepts of normalcy and notification. Yet the manner in which these concepts were pressed into service by the Exchequer panel is characteristic of the half-way industrialized period in which the case arose.

On the one hand, the panel helped to bring the law in phase with the industrializing economy. By its presumption of normalcy the rule invented in the case eroded the prior legal deference to idiosyncrasy and opened the prospect of a standardization of damages as a concomitant of the standardization of transactions effected by mass production. Moreover, in its emphasis on contemplation as the only alternative to natural damages, the rule signaled an evolution away from the pre-industrial emphasis on status and towards the more modern volitional concepts of contract. On the other hand, as developed in *Hadley v. Baxendale*, these concepts were tainted by anachronism, and as they were applied over the following years their antique aspects became more salient.

Consider, first, the notification or "contemplation" branch of the rule. Willes and some others — in America, most notably Holmes — interpreted this as requiring at least a tacit agreement or assumption of risk as a prerequisite to recovery of abnormal consequential damages. This interpretation of the rule, has, however, been rejected both in England and America. It is now almost universally recognized that, in the words of the Uniform Commercial Code, if at the time of the making of the contract the seller has "reason to know" of possible consequential damages, that is enough to make him liable for recovery of those damages.

Whether viewed as a simple "notice" or a more exacting "contemplation" requirement, however, this portion of the rule in *Hadley v. Baxendale* runs counter to the tide of an industrializing economy. It was already somewhat out of date when expressed in the Exchequer opinion. For in *Hadley v. Baxendale* the court spoke as though entrepreneurs were universally flexible enough and enterprises small enough for individuals to be able to serve "notice" over the counter of specialized needs calling for unusual arrangements. But in mass-transaction situations a seller cannot plausibly engage in an individualized "contemplation" of the consequences of breach and a subsequent tailoring of a transaction. In the course of his conversion of a family business into a modern industrial enterprise, Baxendale made Pickfords itself into an operation where the contemplation branch of the rule in *Hadley v. Baxendale* was no longer viable. Even in the 1820s the Pickfords' operations were "highly complex."

> The bulk of Pickfords' traffic was of an intermediate kind, which came on to the main north-south route from east and west. This was directed to certain staging points, sorted, and thence dispatched to its destination. Cross-traffic of this kind was tricky to organize, and required very clear methods of procedure. According to Joseph Baxendale, then a senior partner in Pickfords, a cargo of 15 tons might involve up to 150 consignees and thus the same number of invoices.

By 1865 the business had grown to the point where it left that contemporary chronicler of industry, Henry Mayhew, without words to "convey . . . to the reader's mind a fair impression of the gigantic scale upon which the operations of the firm are conducted." This was "an enormous mercantile establishment with a huge staff of busy clerks, messengers and porters. . . . It is divided into innumerable departments, the employees in each of which find it as much as they can comfortably do to master its details without troubling themselves about any other."

A century later most enterprises fragment and standardize operations in just this way. This development — and the law's recognition of it — makes it self-evidently impossible to serve legally cognizable notice on, for example, an airline that a scheduled flight is of special importance[129] or on the telephone company that uninterrupted service is particularly vital at a particular point in a firm's business cycle.

In its comments about "normal" damages the Exchequer panel speaks in terms which again seem singularly antique. Businesses are assumed to be so straightforward as to admit of a rule of damages which characterizes a single mode of operation as "normal" and one set of consequences as "predictable." This leads the panel to announce, apparently on the basis of nothing more than its a priori impressions, that it "is obvious that . . . millers sending off broken shafts to third persons" would not normally be dependent on the prompt return of these shafts for the operation of their mills. Further, the panel implies that if millers were normally dependent on the return of shafts, then one could readily assess the run of damages which would normally follow from delay.

Contemporary British cases indicate that this approach was freighted with enormous difficulties at the time it was conceived. A survey of the most recent American cases brings home the fact that as the economy has become more diverse and complex, the rule has become less viable.[131] Elements of standardization in the

---

129. It is notable that the Civil Aeronautics Board, while appearing to maintain the option of utilizing the *Hadley v. Baxendale* rule, now grants airline passengers who are victims of overbooking the alternative right to recovery of the price of a ticket over and above their normal refund. 14 CFR § 250.1-.10 (1973). See Ian Macneil, Cases and Materials on Contracts 22 (1971). This obviates any need for notice of special consequential damages within the range of the extra payment (not less than $25 nor more than $200) authorized by the statute.

131. See, e. g., Lewis v. Mobile Oil Corp., 438 F.2d 500 (8th Cir. 1971), a case as much like *Hadley v. Baxendale* as any likely to arise in modern times. There a federal court held a supplier who provided the wrong fuel to a sawmill liable for all profits lost while the mill was stopped because of the improper oil. It premised this conclusion on its assertion (quite contrary to the intuition of the *Hadley v. Baxendale* court) that "Where a seller provides goods to a manufacturing enterprise with knowledge that they are to be used in the manufacturing process, it

modern economy produce some regularities in dealing, but by and large the normalcy rule does not now function so as to afford anything like the certainty that would optimize risk planning or render litigation unnecessary because outcomes were predictable.

The inadequacies of the rule are masked by still more fundamental phenomena which render the case of very limited relevance to the present economy. At least in mass-transaction situations, the modern enterprise manager is not concerned with his corporation's liability as it arises from a particular transaction, but rather with liability when averaged over the full run of transactions of a given type. In the mass-production situation the run of these transactions will average his consequential-damages payout in a way far more predictable than a jury's guesses about the pay-out. In other words, for this type of entrepreneur — a type already emerging at the time of *Hadley v. Baxendale,* and far more prevalent today — there is no need for the law to provide protection from the aberrational customer; his own market and self-insurance capacities are great enough to do the job.

Another modern development has yet further displaced *Hadley v. Baxendale.* Though the right to limit liability by agreement was disputed at the time of the case, the entrepreneur now has the undoubted capacity to set a ceiling on his liability by a contract clause. Almost without exception large-scale entrepreneurs now avail themselves of that privilege. In consequence, they limit as well as normalize damages on their own initiative.

Even Posner's hypothetical is belied by the ubiquitous limitation-of-liability clause. For when a case approximating this hypothetical arose in the real world, the developer (Kodak) apparently readily conceded the magnitude of the consequential damages due

---

is reasonable to assume that he should know that defective goods will cause a disruption of production, and loss of profits is a natural consequence of such disruption." Id. at 510 (interpreting Arkansas law). After finding liability, however, the court had immense difficulty in reviewing the jury's assessment of damages. In remanding for a new trial on the damage question the court said: "Plaintiff's recovery for a loss of profits must take into account these different market conditions, his actual production capacity, his type of operation, its efficiency and any and all other relevant factors that would have a bearing upon and that would influence the amount of profits during the period that profits are recoverable as well as the years used for comparative purposes." Id. at 513.

(the cost of retaking photographs in Alaska) and rested its case instead on the scope of its limitation-of-liability clause.

It is only for small-volume sellers, those who deal in custom-made transactions or with a small number of customers — i.e., for those transactions most like early nineteenth century commerce — that the rule invented in *Hadley v. Baxendale* is arguably of commercial significance. These sellers also, of course, may limit their liability by contract or cushion their liability by insurance, but since their sales transactions are less routinized (and also often less professionalized) they are more likely to miscarry and their miscarriage is less likely to have been provided for through economic precautions such as insurance, or legal precautions effected as a result of consulting farsighted counsel. As unexpected difficulties arise these small volume sellers may therefore be most likely to feel the impact of the residual common law of contracts, and thus of the *Hadley v. Baxendale* rule.[134]

Even within this realm, however, it can be doubted that the rule much affects economic life. It is doubtful that it affects information flow at the time of the making of the contract, because by hypothesis the parties are not very accurate or self-conscious planners. A more sophisticated rationale for the rule in this context might focus on its effect on a seller not at the time of his entering a contract, but rather at the time of his deciding whether to voluntarily breach or to risk breaching. Only at that time and only where an option exists as to whether to breach or to increase the risk of breach, does it seem likely that a seller who has not opted for a limitation of liability clause will consult a lawyer, and consequently be affected by the legal rules. It can be argued that the societal gain from the rule in *Hadley v. Baxendale* stems from its improvement of the seller's calculus about whether to breach in this situation.

To put this observation in context, consider the position of a truck owner, A, who has a contract to sell his truck to B, and assume that B would suffer a "normal" net loss of $200 if the truck were not made available as scheduled. If C arrives on the scene

---

134. They are also more likely, however, to resolve difficulties by negotiation which bears little if any relation to formal contract law doctrine. See S. Macaulay, Non-Contractual Relations in Business: A Preliminary Study, 28 Am.Soc.Rev. 55 (1963).

and bids to preempt the truck for an urgent need, A can estimate the damages he will "normally" owe B. He will presumably sell to C only if the new sale price will exceed the old sale price plus $200 in damages. If C is willing to buy for such a high price, it is to everybody's advantage to let him do so. C benefits because he values the truck more highly than he values the money he is paying for it; B benefits because he receives his expected profits by way of damages; A benefits because he makes more money, even after paying damages than he would have made had the truck not been sold to C. Society benefits because one party, C, has gained while no other party has lost. If B were in an abnormal situation and so expected to suffer greater damages than $200, the rule of *Hadley v. Baxendale* would coerce him into signaling these higher damages, so that the proper damage calculation and subsequent truck allocation would be made. Thus, in theory, by facilitating an accurate calculus of breach, the rule optimizes resource allocation.

But if this is its modern rationale, it is apparent that considerable thought ought to be given to restructuring the rule. Resting the seller's liability on whether the type of damages incurred was "normal" (or, in the UCC's words, whether it was a type of damage of which the seller had "reason to know"), seems undesirable because it lets an all-or-nothing decision ride on an indicator about which many sellers cannot, at the time of breach, speculate with confidence. Further, if the recoverability of a type of damages is established, a seller may often have no reasonable basis for determining the magnitude of the damages involved. On this dimension — obviously critical to any calculus of the care warranted to avoid breach — the rule has nothing to say. Lastly, if the rule were truly finely geared to optimizing the allocation of resources, it would place its emphasis on the damage known to the seller at the time of breach, rather than at the time of contract, at least where the breach was voluntary. When the rule was framed stress had to be placed on communication at the time of the making of a contract because that was the only occasion on which information exchange could be coerced without fear of imposing enormous transaction costs. Now the telephone and vastly improved telegraphic facilities make it possible to mandate discussion at the time of breach. Would it be desirable to move the focus of the rule to this point? On this question, some empirical evidence would be desirable. Do the average transaction costs associated with information exchange at the time of the contract multiplied by the number of instances in which such information is exchanged exceed the average transaction costs of information exchange at the time of voluntary breach multiplied by the number of occasions when breach is seriously considered? If so, there is much to be said for a revision in the rule.

Of course the rule may be defended on purely equitable grounds. Even if its economic repercussions are trivial or counterproductive, when the parties do not prospectively or retrospectively agree on damages, this may be the fairest means of assessing them. But is it? Why should the courts look exclusively to whether a defendant could foresee a type of damages (e. g., lost profits from the stoppage of a manufacturing enterprise), but not attend to whether he could foresee their magnitude? Does the recovery of tens of thousands of dollars, where most parties would have anticipated hundreds of dollars, comport with our sense of fairness? Conversely, is the analysis of fairness so well developed in contract law that we can say with confidence why, in the above hypothetical, A rather than B ought, on equitable grounds, to obtain the special profits from dealing with C?

This brief discussion of the functioning of *Hadley v. Baxendale* in the modern world is not intended to resolve arguments about how UCC 2-715(2) or the common law consequential-damages rule ought to be phrased or interpreted. Rather, it is intended to provoke such arguments. I do not think anyone can explain why we should now accord this mid-nineteenth century rule such curricular predominance, much less how it functions, and still less how it ought to function, in the modern world. Yet it retains its place because it seems as though it has always held this place. It seems, as one English judge at the time of *Hadley v. Baxendale* wryly commented in another context, that when "a rule is well established by decisions, it is not necessary to give any reasons in its support, or to say anything to show it to be a good and useful one."

VII.

My aim in this article has been to supplement the 120 years of doctrinal explication lavished on the text of *Hadley v. Baxendale* with a sufficient understanding of context to afford some insights — albeit speculative ones — into the process of law-change. I would hope that this discussion would serve as a counterpoise to the tendency to regard some rules of law as "fixed stars" in our legal system. Judicial rules are more like inventions, designed to serve particular functions in particular settings. I have tried to demonstrate that an analysis of the original setting and functions of one particular rule will enhance an understanding of that rule even when it has long outlived that setting and those functions. Further, I have sought to suggest that if a rule is to be regarded as an invention, then it ought to be subject to review, lest we make too big an investment in it even as it is becoming outmoded.

FURTHER QUESTIONS

1. As described in this essay the rule in *Hadley v. Baxendale* was provoked in part by the perception of an acute capability problem: the courts needed a rule of decision which would enable them to cope with a much larger number of cases than they could otherwise handle. As noted in footnote 105, Karl Llewellyn, the principal drafter of Article II of the Uniform Commercial Code, once said that "[t]he whole history of the English constitution could be written in terms of the pressure of work."* Examine some of the provisions of Article II of the Code in light of this observation. Are they drafted so as to alleviate the "pressure of work" on trial and appellate courts? Consider, for example, the UCC's phrasing of the rule in *Hadley v. Baxendale* in terms of a seller's "reason to know" of consequential damages, rather than in terms of the more subjective standard of a seller's actual knowledge. Will this rule alleviate the "pressure of work" for the courts? Compare, as an instance of another type of phrasing in Article II of the UCC, § 2-313 which states that a seller's promise becomes an express warranty if it is a part "of the basis of the bargain" made between the parties. How would you compare the capability problems provoked by § 2-313 and § 2-715?

2. A strong case can be made that the practice of deference to precedent is in part a response to the "pressure of work." Precedent may be compared to habit; it is, among other things, a device whereby we may quickly deal with recurring situations without elaborate rethinking of those situations on each recurrence. This may explain, in some measure, why "when 'a rule is well established by decisions, it is not necessary to give any reasons in its support, or to say anything to show it to be a good and useful one.'"

But deference to precedent, like action by habit, raises problems of its own. As this essay points out, if circumstances have changed, habitual conduct may make more work than it eliminates. A capability problem of cruel dimensions therefore emerges. We rationally deal with one capability problem (limited time and energy) by rarely rethinking rules, while another capability

---

*Quoted in William Twining, Karl Llewellyn and the Realist Movement 116 (1973).

problem (changing circumstances) makes it imperative to repeatedly rethink at least some rules. Does the legal historian help at all
to resolve these problems?

3. "This article notes that Judge Richard Posner endorses
the rule of *Hadley v. Baxendale* because he thinks it contributes
to allocative efficiency. Judge Posner has been a leading actor in
effecting an intimate union between law and economics, particularly 'Chicago school' economics. This marriage of disciplines has
much to be said for it. But the weaknesses of the kind of economic
analysis propounded by Judge Posner and the Chicago school are
so like the weaknesses of appellate legal analysis that one fears
that the marriage is incestuous — its offspring may be crippled by
the compounded weaknesses of the parents.

Principal among these weaknesses is the lack of attention in
both disciplines to distributional considerations. Beyond this, and
of more central concern here, is the fact that an economist, like an
appellate judge, typically ignores capability questions. Both traffic
in hypotheticals or in cases where the facts are assumed. Both ignore what the economist calls 'transaction costs': information, negotiation, and litigation are assumed to be flawless and cost-free
for businessmen, consumers and judges. The capability problem
undermines Professor Posner's work fully as much as it does that
of the judge."

Do you agree? If not, why not? If so, does that mean that Judge
Posner's analysis is irrelevant?

4. Economic analysis has also been deployed to criticize the
rule in *Hadley* as inefficient. Consider this passage:

> I argue that an extensive (although admittedly incom-
> plete and methodologically informal) survey of hundreds
> of cases on consequential damages over the last 120 years
> … finds few cases where the promisee claimed to have
> done what the information-forcing theory says she should
> have done: nobody seems to have claimed that they told
> the promisor that they would suffer unusually large con-
> sequential damages. At the same time, there are scores of
> recent cases in which the parties apparently accepted the
> more expansive "foreseeability" version of *Hadley*. I do not
> contend that any of this constitutes conclusive empirical

proof that most people like the "foreseeability" limitation and that those who do not are able to bargain around it. Rather, I contend merely that there is no conclusive evidence one way or the other. . . . Just as people sometimes fail to bargain around a default rule not because the default is efficient for them but because there are strategic impediments to bargaining around it, the observation that lots of people bargain around a default rule does not imply that the rule they bargain to is the optimal default rule. It may be that the bargained-to rule would, for strategic reasons, not be bargained around were it the default rule. . . .

Jason Johnston, Strategic Bargaining and the Economic Theory of Contract Default Rules, 100 Yale L.J. 615, 619 (1990). What kind of "strategic impediments" might impede people from bargaining around the rule in *Hadley*? Do such impediments imply that the rule in *Hadley* has replaced one set of capability problems (e.g., those arising when juries decide damages without much guidance from judges) with another?

5. Another commentator argues:

[T]he principle of *Hadley v. Baxendale* should be dropped from contract law in favor of a regime of proximate cause — or more accurately, a regime of proximate cause, contractual allocations of loss, and fair disclosure. The precise standard of foreseeability under this regime should depend not on whether the action is labeled contract or tort, but on the nature of the interest invaded and the wrong involved — on whether, for example, the injury involves harm to the person, physical injury to property, lost profits, out-of-pocket costs, or opportunity costs, and on whether the breach was inadvertent or opportunistic.

Melvin Eisenberg, The Principle of *Hadley v. Baxendale*, 80 Cal. L. Rev. 563, 567-68 (1992). Would such a rule diminish or exacerbate capability problems?

6. Make an argument for the rule in *Hadley v. Baxendale* on the theory that it limits damages and that a perception of capability problems underscores the desirability of limiting the run of damages.

7. Make an argument against the rule in *Hadley v. Baxendale* by contending that the rule demands a judicial capability thought conceivable by Victorian judges, but, which is, in fact, unachievable by a twentieth century court.

8. How would you phrase the rule in *Hadley v. Baxendale* if you had to decide that case today?

III. JACOB AND YOUNGS v. KENT

FIRST QUESTIONS

In May of 1913, George Edward Kent, on the advice of his architect, entered a contract with the New York firm of Jacob and Youngs. The contract provided that the firm would construct a mansion for Kent on Jericho Long Island. Amidst several hundred "specifications," the contract provided that "Reading Pipe" must be exclusively used in the plumbing. (Reading was a prominent pipe manufacturing company at the time.)

After moving into the house and making all but the final payment due under the contract, Mr. Kent discovered that pipe manufactured by a company or companies other than Reading was inadvertently used, and now was embedded in the foundations of the building. All parties recognized that (1) this was not the pipe called for; (2) it was the contractor's responsibility to meet the specifications; (3) the pipe actually used was the equivalent in every tangible respect to that specified; (4) it would be prohibitively expensive to change the pipe now; to do so would require the demolition of large parts of the house.

Given this state of affairs, Mr. Kent refused to make the payment of $3,483.46 due the Jacob and Youngs firm on their completion of the house; Jacob and Youngs sued for this amount.

How do you think this case should be decided? Excerpts from the contract which controlled this transaction are printed below to aid your thinking. Note in this regard, that Kent proceeded by invoking Articles IV and V of the contract and having his architect give proper notice, etc., to Jacob and Youngs that "the plumbing work installed by you and your sub-contractors is not in full accordance with the specifications of the contract. . . ."

After you have read the contract and thought through your own recommended resolution of the dispute, read Justice Cardozo's and Justice McLaughlin's opinions on the matter. (These are reproduced after the contract.) Justice Cardozo is often acclaimed as the greatest state court justice of this century. (He also, late in his career, wrote several important opinions as a Justice of the Supreme Court of the United States.) You, as you no doubt know, are a beginning law student. How do your layman's intuitions about result in this case differ, if at all, from Justice Cardozo's? How do your modes of reasoning or justification differ? Given only this opinion (a famous one) as your datum, is there any basis for thinking Cardozo a great judge?

* * *

Excerpts from the Contract and "Specifications" agreed to by Jacob and Youngs ("Contractor") and George Edward Kent ("Owner"):

Art. II. It is understood and agreed by and between the parties hereto that the work included in this contract is to be done under the direction of the said Architect, and that his decision as to the true construction and meaning of the drawings and specifications shall be final. It is also understood and agreed by and between the parties hereto that such additional drawings and explanations as may be necessary to detail and illustrate the work to be done are to be furnished by said Architect, and they agree to conform to and abide by the same so far as they may be consistent with the purpose and intent of the original drawings and specifications referred to in Art. I.

* * *

Art. III. No alterations shall be made in the work except upon written order of the Architect; the amount to be paid by owner or allowed by the Contractors by virtue of such alterations to be stated in said order. Should the Owner and Contractors not agree as to amount to be paid or allowed, the work shall go on under the order required above, and in case of failure to agree, the determination of said amount shall be referred to arbitration, as provided for in Art. XII of this contract.

Art. IV. The Contractors shall provide sufficient, safe and proper facilities at all times for the inspection of the work by the

Architect or his authorized representatives; shall, within twenty-four hours after receiving written notice from the Architect to that effect, proceed to remove from the grounds or buildings all materials condemned by him, whether worked or unworked, and to take down all portion of the work which the Architect shall by like written notice condemn as unsound or improper, or as in any way failing to conform to the drawings and specifications, and shall make good all work damaged or destroyed thereby.

Art. V. Should the Contractors at any time refuse or neglect to supply a sufficiency of properly skilled workmen, or of materials of the proper quality, or fail in any respect to prosecute the work with promptness and diligence, or fail in the performance of any of the agreements herein contained, such refusal, neglect or failure being certified by the Architect, the Owner shall be at liberty, after three days written notice to the Contractors, to provide any such labor or materials, and to deduct the cost thereof from any money then due or thereafter to become due to the Contractors under this contract; and if the Architect shall certify that such refusal, neglect or failure is sufficient ground for such action, the Owner shall also be at liberty to terminate the employment of the Contractors for the said work and to enter upon the premises and take possession, for the purpose of completing the work included under this contract, of all materials, tools and appliances thereon, and to employ any other person or persons to finish the work, and to provide the materials therefor; and in case of such discontinuance of the employment of the Contractors they shall not be entitled to receive any further payment under this contract until the said work shall be wholly finished, at which time, if the unpaid balance of the amount to be paid under this contract shall exceed the expense incurred by the Owner in finishing the work, such excess shall be paid by the Owner to the Contractors; but if such expense shall exceed such unpaid balance, the Contractors shall pay the difference to the Owner. The expense incurred by the Owner as herein provided, either for furnishing materials or for finishing the work, and any damage incurred through such default, shall be audited and certified by the Architect, whose certificate thereof shall be conclusive upon the parties.

Art. VI. The Contractors shall complete the several portions and the whole of the work comprehended in this Agreement by and at the time or times hereinafter stated, to wit: December 15th 1913.

Art. VII. Should the Contractors be delayed in the prosecution or completion of the work by the act, neglect or default of the Owner, of the Architect, or of any other contractor employed by the Owner upon the work, or by any damage caused by fire or other casualty for which the Contractors are not responsible, or by combined action of workmen in no wise caused by or resulting from default or collusion on the part of the Contractors, then the time herein fixed for the completion of the work shall be extended for a period equivalent to the time lost by reason of any or all the causes aforesaid, which extended period shall be determinated and fixed by the Architect; but no such allowance shall be made unless a claim therefor is presented in writing to the Architect within forty-eight hours of the occurrence of such delay.

*　*　*

Art. IX. It is hereby mutually agreed between the parties hereto that the sum to be paid by the Owner to the Contractors for said work and materials shall be Seventy thousand five hundred ($70,500) dollars, subject to additions and deductions as hereinbefore provided, and that such sum shall be paid by the Owner to the Contractors, in current funds, and only upon certificates of the Architect, as follows:

On or about the first day of each month a certificate will be given by the architect to the contractors for a payment on account of value of the work finished and erected at the site, which represents in his judgment a fair proportion to the whole of the contract price less a fifteen per cent (15%) margin which shall be withheld until after the completion and acceptance of the entire work. The final payment shall be made within thirty (30) days after the completion of the work included in this contract and all payments shall be due when certificate for the same are issued.

The final payment, or 15% of the total amount of this contract, shall be made within thirty days after the completion of the work included in this contract, and all payments shall be due when certificates for the same are issued.

*　*　*

Art. XII. In case the Owner and Contractors fail to agree in relation to matters of payment, allowance or loss referred to in Arts. III or VIII of this contract, or should either of them dissent from the decision of the Architect referred to in Art. VII of this contract, which dissent shall have been filed in writing with the Architect within ten days of the announcement of such decision, then the matter shall be referred to a Board of Arbitration to consist of one person selected by the Owner, and one person selected by the Contractors, these two to select a third. The decision of any two of this Board shall be final and binding on both parties hereto. Each party hereto shall pay one-half of the expense of such reference.

* * *

(Extracts from Specifications.)

GENERAL CONDITIONS

* * *

(19) The Contractor is responsible for, and must make good any defects arising or discovered in his work within two years after completion of work and acceptance, or faults in labor or material, unless hereinafter changed.

* * *

(22) Where any particular brand of manufactured article is specified, it is to be considered as a standard. Contractors desiring to use another shall first make application in writing to the Architect, stating the difference in cost, and obtain their written approval of the change.

* * *

Character of Work and Labor:
(24) The decision of the Architect as to the character of any material or labor furnished by the Contractor is to be final and conclusive on both Contractor and Owner.

Access to Works:

(25) The Architect or his authorized agents are to have free access at all times to the works or to any place where any of the material for the same is in preparation.

* * *

Certificates:

(28) For each and every payment the Architect will issue his regular form of certificate, and the term "Entitled to" which appears on the certificate is hereby understood by each and all of the parties signing the contract to mean that in the Architect's judgment the work called for under said payment has been satisfactorily executed, entitling the Contractor to the money.

* * *

The payment by the Owner of such certificates, including the final certificate, will not constitute an acceptance of the work thus paid for as far as the Contractor is concerned, and the Owner shall hold the Contractor solely responsible for any and all defects that may appear in said work, at any time, before or after said payments, excepting such as may result from imperfections in the plans and specifications. Each certificate of payment to be issued by the Architect within not less than ten (10) days after the receipt of a written request from the Contractor for such payment, provided the Architect considers such payment due.

* * *

Approved material:

(225) The approval of the quality of any material will not be considered as acceptance of the work when installed should such material or work prove defective.

* * *

Wrought iron pipe:

(227) All wrought iron pipe must be well galvanized lap welded pipe of the grade known as "Standard Pipe" of Reading manufacture. Burrs formed in cutting must be reamed out. Fittings shall be extra heavy, galvanized, malleable iron fittings.

THE OPINION

JACOB & YOUNGS, INC. v. KENT
Court of Appeals of New York, 1921.
230 N.Y. 239, 129 N.E. 889, 23 A.L.R. 1429.
Reargument denied 230 N.Y. 656, 130 N.E. 933.

CARDOZO, J. The plaintiff built a country residence for the defendant at a cost of upwards of $77,000, and now sues to recover a balance of $3,483.46, remaining unpaid. The work of construction ceased in June, 1914, and the defendant then began to occupy the dwelling. There was no complaint of defective performance until March, 1915. One of the specifications for the plumbing work provides that —

"All wrought-iron pipe must be well galvanized, lap welded pipe of the grade known as 'standard pipe' of Reading manufacture."

The defendant learned in March, 1915, that some of the pipe, instead of being made in Reading, was the product of other factories. The plaintiff was accordingly directed by the architect to do the work anew. The plumbing was then encased within the walls except in a few places where it had to be exposed. Obedience to the order meant more than the substitution of other pipe. It meant the demolition at great expense of substantial parts of the completed structure. The plaintiff left the work untouched, and asked for a certificate that the final payment was due. Refusal of the certificate was followed by this suit.

The evidence sustains a finding that the omission of the prescribed brand of pipe was neither fraudulent nor willful. It was the result of the oversight and inattention of the plaintiff's subcontractor. Reading pipe is distinguished from Cohoes pipe and other brands only by the name of the manufacturer stamped upon it at intervals of between six and seven feet. Even the defendant's architect, though he inspected the pipe upon arrival, failed to notice the discrepancy. The plaintiff tried to show that the brands installed, though made by other manufacturers, were the same in quality, in appearance, in market value, and in cost as the brand stated in the contract — that they were, indeed, the same thing, though manufactured in another place. The evidence was excluded, and a verdict directed for the defendant. The Appellate Division reversed, and granted a new trial.

We think the evidence, if admitted, would have supplied some basis for the inference that the defect was insignificant in its relation to the project. The courts never say that one who makes a contract fills the measure of his duty by less than full performance. They do say, however, that an omission, both trivial and innocent, will sometimes be atoned for by allowance of the resulting damage, and will not always be the breach of a condition to be followed by a forfeiture. Spence v. Ham, 163 N.Y. 220, 57 N.E. 412, 51 L.R.A. 238; Woodward v. Fuller, 80 N.Y. 312; Glacius v. Black, 67 N.Y. 563, 566; Bowen v. Kimbell, 203 Mass. 364, 370, 89 N.E. 542, 133 Am.St.Rep. 302. The distinction is akin to that between dependent and independent promises, or between promises and conditions. Anson on Contracts (Corbin's Ed.) § 367; 2 Williston on Contracts, § 842. Some promises are so plainly independent that they can never by fair construction be conditions of one another. Rosenthal Paper Co. v. Nat. Folding Box & Paper Co., 226 N.Y. 313, 123 N.E. 766; Bogardus v. N. Y. Life Ins. Co., 101 N.Y. 328, 4 N.E. 522. Others are so plainly dependent that they must always be conditions. Others, though dependent and thus conditions when there is departure in point of substance, will be viewed as independent and collateral when the departure is insignificant. 2 Williston on Contracts, §§ 841, 842; Eastern Forge Co. v. Corbin, 182 Mass. 590, 592, 66 N.E. 419; Robinson v. Mollett, L. R., 7 Eng. & Ir.App. 802, 814; Miller v. Benjamin, 142 N.Y. 613, 37 N.E. 631. Considerations partly of justice and partly of presumable intention are to tell us whether this or that promise shall be placed in one class or in another. The simple and the uniform will call for different remedies from the multifarious and the intricate. The margin of departure within the range of normal expectation upon a sale of common chattels will vary from the margin to be expected upon a contract for the construction of a mansion or a "skyscraper." There will be harshness sometimes and oppression in the implication of a condition when the thing upon which labor has been expended is incapable of surrender because united to the land, and equity and reason in the implication of a like condition when the subject-matter, if defective, is in shape to be returned. From the conclusion that promises may not be treated as dependent to the extent of their uttermost minutiae without a sacrifice of justice, the progress is a short one to the conclusion that they may not be so treated without a perversion of intention. Intention not otherwise revealed may be presumed to hold in contemplation the reasonable and probable. If something else is in view, it must not be left to implication. There will be no assumption of a purpose to visit venial faults with oppressive retribution.

Those who think more of symmetry and logic in the development of legal rules than of practical adaptation to the attainment of a just result will be troubled by a classification where the lines of division are so wavering and blurred. Something, doubtless, may be said on the score of consistency and certainty in favor of a stricter standard. The courts have balanced such considerations against those of equity and fairness, and found the latter to be the weightier. The decisions in this state commit us to the liberal view, which is making its way, nowadays, in jurisdictions slow to welcome it. Dakin & Co. v. Lee, 1916, 1 K.B. 566, 579. Where the line is to be drawn between the important and the trivial cannot be settled by a formula. "In the nature of the case precise boundaries are impossible." 2 Williston on Contracts, § 841. The same omission may take on one aspect or another according to its setting. Substitution of equivalents may not have the same significance in fields of art on the one side and in those of mere utility on the other. Nowhere will change be tolerated, however, if it is so dominant or pervasive as in any real or substantial measure to frustrate the purpose of the contract. Crouch v. Gutmann, 134 N.Y. 45, 51, 31 N.E. 271, 30 Am.St.Rep. 608. There is no general license to install whatever, in the builder's judgment, may be regarded as "just as good." Easthampton L. & C. Co., Ltd., v. Worthington, 186 N.Y. 407, 412, 79 N.E. 323. The question is one of degree, to be answered, if there is doubt, by the triers of the facts (Crouch v. Gutmann; Woodward v. Fuller, supra), and, if the inferences are certain, by the judges of the law (Easthampton L. & C. Co., Ltd., v. Worthington, supra). We must weigh the purpose to be served, the desire to be gratified, the excuse for deviation from the letter, the cruelty of enforced adherence. Then only can we tell whether literal fulfillment is to be implied by law as a condition. This is not to say that the parties are not free by apt and certain words to effectuate a purpose that performance of every term shall be a condition of recovery. That question is not here. This is merely to say that the law will be slow to impute the purpose, in the silence of the parties, where the significance of the default is grievously out of proportion to the oppression of the forfeiture. The willful transgressor must accept the penalty of his transgression. Schultze v. Goodstein, 180 N.Y. 248, 251, 73 N.E. 21; Desmond-Dunne Co. v. Friedman-Doscher Co., 162 N.Y. 486, 490, 56 N.E. 995. For him there is no occasion to mitigate the rigor of implied conditions. The transgressor whose default is unintentional and trivial may hope for mercy if he will offer atonement for his wrong. Spence v. Ham, supra.

In the circumstances of this case, we think the measure of the allowance is not the cost of replacement, which would be great, but the difference in value, which would be either nominal or nothing. Some of the exposed sections might perhaps have been replaced at moderate expense. The defendant did not limit his demand to them, but treated the plumbing as a unit to be corrected from cellar to roof. In point of fact, the plaintiff never reached the stage at which evidence of the extent of the allowance became necessary. The trial court had excluded evidence that the defect was unsubstantial, and in view of that ruling there was no occasion for the plaintiff to go farther with an offer of proof. We think, however, that the offer, if it had been made, would not of necessity have been defective because directed to difference in value. It is true that in most cases the cost of replacement is the measure. Spence v. Ham, supra. The owner is entitled to the money which will permit him to complete, unless the cost of completion is grossly and unfairly out of proportion to the good to be attained. When that is true, the measure is the difference in value. Specifications call, let us say, for a foundation built of granite quarried in Vermont. On the completion of the building, the owner learns that through the blunder of a subcontractor part of the foundation has been built of granite of the same quality quarried in New Hampshire. The measure of allowance is not the cost of reconstruction. "There may be omissions of that which could not afterwards be supplied exactly as called for by the contract without taking down the building to its foundations, and at the same time the omission may not affect the value of the building for use or otherwise, except so slightly as to be hardly appreciable." Handy v. Bliss, 204 Mass. 513, 519, 90 N.E. 864, 134 Am.St.Rep. 673. Cf. Foeller v. Heintz, 137 Wis. 169, 178, 113 N.W. 543, 24 L.R.A.(N.S.) 321; Oberlies v. Bullinger, 132 N.Y. 598, 601, 30 N.E. 999; 2 Williston on Contracts, § 805, p. 1541. The rule that gives a remedy in cases of substantial performance with compensation for defects of trivial or inappreciable importance has been developed by the courts as an instrument of justice. The measure of the allowance must be shaped to the same end.

The order should be affirmed, and judgment absolute directed in favor of the plaintiff upon the stipulation, with costs in all courts.

McLAUGHLIN, J. I dissent. The plaintiff did not perform its contract. Its failure to do so was either intentional or due to gross neglect which, under the uncontradicted facts, amounted to the same thing, nor did it make any proof of the cost of compliance, where compliance was possible.

Under its contract it obligated itself to use in the plumbing only pipe (between 2,000 and 2,500 feet) made by the Reading Manufacturing Company. The first pipe delivered was about 1,000 feet and the plaintiff's superintendent then called the attention of the foreman of the subcontractor, who was doing the plumbing, to the fact that the specifications annexed to the contract required all pipe used in the plumbing to be of the Reading Manufacturing Company. They then examined it for the purpose of ascertaining whether this delivery was of that manufacture and found it was. Thereafter, as pipe was required in the progress of the work, the foreman of the subcontractor would leave word at its shop that he wanted a specified number of feet of pipe, without in any way indicating of what manufacture. Pipe would thereafter be delivered and installed in the building, without any examination whatever. Indeed, no examination, so far as appears, was made by the plaintiff, the subcontractor, defendant's architect, or any one else, of any of the pipe except the first delivery, until after the building had been completed. Plaintiff's architect then refused to give the certificate of completion, upon which the final payment depended, because all of the pipe used in the plumbing was not of the kind called for by the contract. After such refusal, the subcontractor removed the covering or insulation from about 900 feet of pipe which was exposed in the basement, cellar, and attic, and all but 70 feet was found to have been manufactured, not by the Reading Company, but by other manufacturers, some by the Cohoes Rolling Mill Company, some by the National Steel Works, some by the South Chester Tubing Company, and some which bore no manufacturer's mark at all. The balance of the pipe had been so installed in the building that an inspection of it could not be had without demolishing, in part at least, the building itself.

I am of the opinion the trial court was right in directing a verdict for the defendant. The plaintiff agreed that all the pipe used should be of the Reading Manufacturing Company. Only about two-fifths of it, so far as appears, was of that kind. If more were used, then the burden of proving that fact was upon the plaintiff, which it could easily have done, since it knew where the pipe was obtained. The question of substantial performance of a contract of the character of the one under consideration depends in no small degree upon the good faith of the contractor. If the plaintiff had intended to, and had, complied with the terms of the contract except as to minor omissions, due to inadvertence, then he might be allowed to recover the contract price, less the amount necessary to fully compensate the defendant for damages caused by such omissions. Woodward v. Fuller, 80 N.Y. 312; Nolan v. Whitney, 88 N.Y. 648. But that is not this case. It installed between 2,000 and 2,500 feet of pipe, of which only 1,000 feet at most complied with the contract. No explanation was given why pipe called for by the contract was not used, nor that any effort made to show what it would cost to remove the pipe of other manufacturers and install that of the Reading Manufacturing Company. The defendant had a right to contract for what he wanted. He had a right before making payment to get what the contract called for. It is no answer to this suggestion to say that the pipe put in was just as good as that made by the Reading Manufacturing Company, or that the difference in value between such pipe and the pipe made by the Reading Manufacturing Company would be either "nominal or nothing." Defendant contracted for pipe made by the Reading Manufacturing Company. What his reason was for requiring this kind of pipe is of no importance. He wanted that and was entitled to it. It may have been a mere whim on his part, but even so, he had a right to this kind of pipe, regardless of whether some other kind, according to the opinion of the contractor or experts, would have been "just as good, better, or done just as well." He agreed to pay only upon condition that the pipe installed were made by that company and he ought not to be compelled to pay unless that condition be performed. Schultze v. Goodstein, 180 N.Y. 248, 73 N.E. 21; Spence v. Ham, supra; Steel S. & E. C. Co. v. Stock, 225 N.Y. 173, 121 N.E. 786; Van Clief v. Van Vechten, 130 N.Y. 571, 29 N.E. 1017; Glacius v. Black, 50 N.Y. 145, 10 Am.Rep. 449; Smith v. Brady, 17 N.Y. 173, and authorities cited on page 185, 72 Am.Dec. 442. The rule, therefore, of substantial performance, with damages for unsubstantial omissions, has no application. Crouch v. Gutmann, 134 N.Y. 45, 31 N.E. 271, 30 Am.St.Rep. 608; Spence v. Ham, 163 N.Y. 220, 57 N.E. 412, 51 L.R.A. 238.

What was said by this court in Smith v. Brady, supra, is quite applicable here:

"I suppose it will be conceded that every one has a right to build his house, his cottage or his store after such a model and in such style as shall best accord with his notions of utility or be most agreeable to his fancy. The specifications of the contract become the law between the parties until voluntarily changed. If the owner prefers a plain and simple Doric column, and has so provided in the agreement, the contractor has no right to put in its place the more costly and elegant Corinthian. If the owner, having regard to strength and durability, has contracted for walls of specified materials to be laid in a particular manner, or for a given number of joists and beams, the builder has no right to substitute his own judgment or that of others. Having departed from the agreement, if performance has not been waived by the other party, the law will not allow him to allege that he has made as good a building as the one he engaged to erect. He can demand payment only upon and according to the terms of his contract, and if the conditions on which payment is due have not been performed, then the right to demand it does not exist. To hold a different doctrine would be simply to make another contract, and would be giving to parties an encouragement to violate their engagments, which the just policy of the law does not permit." (17 N.Y. 186, 72 Am.Dec. 442).

I am of the opinion the trial court did not err in ruling on the admission of evidence or in directing a verdict for the defendant.

For the foregoing reasons I think the judgment of the Appellate Division should be reversed and the judgment of the Trial Term affirmed.

HISCOCK, C. J., and HOGAN and CRANE, JJ., concur with CARDOZO, J.

POUND and ANDREWS, JJ., concur with McLAUGHLIN, J.

Order affirmed, etc.

———————————

On motion for reargument:

PER CURIAM. The court did not overlook the specification which provides that defective work shall be replaced. The promise to replace, like the promise to install, is to be viewed, not as a condition, but as independent and collateral, when the defect is trivial and innocent. The law does not nullify the covenant, but restricts the remedy to damages.

The motion for a reargument should be denied.

HISCOCK, C. J., and CARDOZO, POUND, McLAUGHLIN, CRANE, and ANDREWS, JJ., concur.

Motion denied.

SUPPLEMENTARY COMMENTS[*]

A basic question worth asking yourself both in pondering an individual case and in assessing the performance of a judicial system, is: why do people engage in litigation? Interviews with surviving contemporaries, a study of the records in the case, and research in collateral contemporary materials (newspapers, *Who's Who*, phone books, land records, etc.) permit the following description of the events leading up to the litigation in *Jacob and Youngs v. Kent.*

George Edward Kent, the defendant in this case, was a successful New York lawyer who maintained two offices and two apartments in Manhattan as well as the mansion in Jericho (Long Island) whose construction provoked this litigation. In addition, George Kent acquired substantial wealth and political connections by his marriage (at age 38) to a daughter of W. R. Grace, then the owner of a large shipping line, and later Mayor of New York.

In 1913 when the Kents decided to build on land Mrs. Kent had acquired in Jericho during an earlier period, they hired an architect, William Welles Bosworth of New York City, who drew plans and specifications for a mansion on the property. In response to these plans Jacob and Youngs, a substantial, though not eminent, New York construction firm, tendered a "proposal" (an estimate of cost) for construction which was accepted. The contract and specifications for construction reprinted above were drawn and dated May 5 and May 7, 1913.

Why was pipe manufactured by the Philadelphia and Reading Iron and Coal Company specified? If Mr. Kent had a professional or financial connection with the Reading Company it remains buried. His surviving daughters, one born in 1898, another in 1911, are unaware of any such connection, as is his personal secretary of 20 years. While the latter entered Kent's employ in 1927, he saw most of Kent's papers and was consequently aware of his stockholdings and major clients for some years before that. In addition veteran employees at the remnants of what were the Reading Companies

[*]We are grateful to Jim Liebman for the exceptional talent and energy he brought to bear as a research assistant working on this essay. Mr. Liebman is now the Simon H. Rifkind Professor of Law at Columbia University.

have never heard of a Kent or Grace connection and no member of either family shows up in the companies' annual reports as a director or officer from 1915-1945.

The contract specified a standard of pipe which cost 30% more than steel pipe — then the most widely used (and now the almost universally used) pipe. The makers of wrought iron pipe, however, claimed that the savings due to durability and low maintenance more than made up for the added expense.[1] The years from 1905-1920 saw a peak in the popularity of wrought iron pipe. For example Byers Co. reported a rise in the use of wrought iron pipe from 40-50% of the total market in New York City in the "few years" previous to 1916.[2] This rise occurred, according to Byers, not in "cheap buildings sold to the public at large," but rather "in sky-scraper construction as well as in other large buildings planned and constructed with expertness and care."[3] As an example of such a building a Byers publication printed a picture of a house built in Southampton, Long Island, another area like Jericho into which wealthy New Yorkers were moving after 1910. The house is very like that constructed for the Kents.

The Reading Company was by its account the largest manufacturer of wrought iron pipe in the country, having provided it for such famous New York buildings as the Metropolitan Life Insurance Building and the Chrysler Building.[4] Indeed, its 1911 brochure asserted that "the majority of the modern and most prominent buildings in New York City are equipped with READING wrought iron pipe" and that "many leading architects and engineers have drawn their specifications in favor of wrought iron pipe, in instances prohibiting steel pipe entirely."[5]

Interestingly, as this last comment suggests, these trade publications made their comparative claims not so much with reference to their competitors who made wrought iron pipe, as to those who made steel pipe. According to a pipe wholesaler interviewed in New York City in 1975, genuine wrought iron pipe was manufac-

---

1. A. M. Byers Co., The Selection of Pipe for Modern Buildings 7 (1916).
2. Id. at 12.
3. Id.
4. Reading Iron Co., Court of Actual Experience: Wrought Iron Pipe vs. Steel Pipe 37 (9th ed., 1911).
5. Id., p. 2.

tured in the pre-war period by four largely noncompeting companies: Reading, Cohoes, Byers and Southchester. According to this informant, all of these brands "were of the same quality and price. The manufacturer's name would make absolutely no difference in pipe or in price."

The testimony prepared for the Kent trial was to the same effect. If one reads between and around objections and exclusions of evidence it is apparent that Jacob and Youngs were prepared to show equality of price, weight, size, appearance, composition, and durability for all four major brands of wrought iron pipe. Indeed, in addition to other witnesses, an employee of the Reading Company was prepared to testify to this effect. Probably because of this evidence, Kent's briefs on appeal conceded that "experts could have testified that the substitute pipe was the same in quality in all respects . . . ."[6] It appears that this concession crystallized into a "stipulation" before argument in the Court of Appeals, and that Cardozo's reference was to this when he directed a judgment for Jacob and Youngs.

Why then was Reading Pipe specified? Apparently because it was the normal trade practice to assure wrought iron pipe quality by naming a manufacturer. In contemporary trade bulletins put out by Byers and Reading, prospective buyers were cautioned that some steel pipe manufacturers used iron pipe and often sold under misleading names like "wrought pipe." To avoid such inferior products, Byers warned: "When wrought iron pipe is desired, the specifications often read 'genuine wrought iron pipe' but as this does not always exclude wrought iron containing steel scrap, it is safer to mention the name of a manufacturer known not to use scrap." Reading's brochure said: "If you want the best pipe, specify 'Genuine wrought iron pipe made from Puddled Pig Iron' and have the Pipe-Fitter furnish you with the name of the manufacturer."[7]

The contract makes it especially clear that the use of Reading was primarily as a standard. Specification twenty-two says: "Where

6. Appellant's Brief, New York Court of Appeals, p. 13.

7. This area of plumbing metallurgy had apparently been productive of conflict between builders and owners. The Reading pamphlet cited above, at p. 2, notes: "In some cases, where wrought iron was specified and steel pipe was substituted, it resulted after discovery in heavy fines to the contractor, and in some instances the steel pipe was ordered torn out and replaced with wrought iron pipe at a

any particular brand of manufactured article is specified, it is to be considered as a standard. Contractors desiring to use another shall first make application in writing to the Architect stating the difference in cost and obtain their written approval of change." (Jacob and Youngs stressed the implications of this first sentence in their court of appeals brief.[8])

Why, given a realistic indifference to the maker of the pipe, did Kent refuse to pay for anything but Reading Pipe through three levels of litigation? Mr. Kent, according to some who knew him, carried cost consciousness "to an extreme point." As one put it: "The old man would go all over town to save a buck." Perhaps having paid the extra cost of wrought iron pipe, he felt cheated when not indisputably assured of the highest quality and purity with which Reading's name was associated. However, a Reading representative's willingness to testify for the plaintiff, and the apparent ability of Jacob and Youngs to show the equality of Byers, Cohoes, Southchester and Reading pipes (an equality probably realized by Kent's architect) suggest that Kent may have seized upon the pipe substitution as an expression of other dissatisfactions in his relationship with Jacob and Youngs. A summary of the construction process as revealed during the suit suggests anything but a harmonious relationship between builder and owner.

The first shipment of pipe arrive in June 1913, soon after the contract was signed. It was examined by Youngs, his foreman, Wal-

---

large expense." The Appellants' Brief in Jacob and Youngs, p. 13-14, quoted from Shultze v. Goodstein, 180 N.Y. 248, 73 N.E. 21, a case in which some type of pipe, probably steel, was substituted for the specified iron pipe. In that case, complete performance as to iron pipe was deemed a condition to the buyer's duty to pay. (The case is cited by McLaughlin in dissent, but Cardozo passed it off as a case relevant only to wilful breaches.)

8. The imprecision of the specifications is underscored by the fact that apparently it was not possible to make *lap welded* wrought iron in all of the sizes (¾"-2" in diameter) necessary for such a house. (Trial testimony of Parke H. Holton, a pipe marketing expert from Nason Mfg. Co. And see *Byers Pipe*, a magazine put out by Byers Co. in July 1921, bulletin no. 34 which shows that lap welding is only done on pipes of 1¼, 1½ and 2". A different kind of welding is used on smaller pipe.) Thus it is apparent that the specifications could NOT have been met. See also testimony by Henry S. Carland, a sales representative for Reading, showing that the specifications called for a non-existent pipe. This evidence was ruled inadmissible on the ground both sides had accepted the specifications in the contract.

lace Heidtman, and the subcontractor's worker, Louis Simpson. At this point, Heidtman reminded Simpson that the "specification calls for Reading." (Testimony of Simpson, Heidtman, Youngs.) This batch, probably 1000 feet (or two fifths of the total used in the house) was found to be Reading. Note that it was built into the foundation and was the least discoverable later. Thus while only 70 of the 700-800 feet of pipe exposed in cellar and attic were of Reading Pipe (testimony of William H. Healy, architect's assistant) it is not surprising that more Reading wasn't found. After that point, none of the three, nor Healy, whose duties included "in a general way" making sure the specifications were met, examined any later shipments of pipe. (Testimony of Healy, Simpson, Youngs.) Simpson was to blame for not ordering Reading Pipe. (This, by his own testimony). His error was probably negligent. Healy, the architect's watchdog, may share some of the blame as Jacob and Youngs argued in their brief and as Cardozo hinted in his opinion. Kent later hired Healy on a full time basis to prepare for trial.

As the work progressed, additional work became necessary in the amount of $7,244.44. (Complaint, paragraph 4). While work was originally to be completed on the fifteenth of December, 1913, a modification was written and signed on the twenty-third of that month, extending the contract for an unspecified time and adding $580.00 to Kent's bill. (Complaint, paragraphs 6, 12, 13). The reason given for the delay is that "the defendant failed to perform what he was to do under the said contract in time so the plaintiff's work could be completed by the said time," and because of "the defaults and delays of defendant." This language parallels one excuse for delay allowed in Art. III of the contract. The only duty which Kent seems to have owed Jacob and Youngs was to make payment, although the missing specifications may have detailed some preparatory work which Kent or his agents were to have done. Thus the delay and need for modification may have hinged on other troubles causing Kent to withhold payment at certain points. Paragraph 8 of the complaint notes "certain alterations and omissions entitled the defendant to a deduction of $4,031.41." Here again, there is evidence of unhappiness on Kent's part with work done by Jacob and Youngs. The whole price paid under the subcontract for the plumbing was only $6,000, so the earlier disputes were over equally large aspects of the contract.

The Kents moved into the house in June 1914, after twice as much time had passed for completion as the contract specified. Yet, even Jacob and Youngs averred no more in their complaint than that "substantial completion" occurred by November 13, 1914. At that time a new modification entitled Jacob and Youngs to $240, and specified several "minor details of work" yet to be completed. The $3483.46 outstanding on the contract would not be paid until these defaults were cured. (Complaint, paragraphs 14, 15.)

Moreover, though Kent occupied the house in June 1914 and work stopped except for "minor details" by November, Jacob and Youngs had not received the final payment or certificate by March 1915, 2 years after the contract was signed, and 1½ years after it was to have been completed. (World War I began in Europe in the summer of 1914, probably complicating supply conditions). Yet until then, Reading pipe was never mentioned as a subject of dispute. In fact, on October 10, 1914 Healy had written the subcontracting plumber on behalf of his principal, as follows:

> New York
> October 10, 1914
>
> Re: Kent Residence
>
> McKenna Bros.,
> Westbury,
> L.I.
>
> Gentlemen:
>
> In response to the request in your letter to us under date of October 6th, we write to inform you that your work at the above residence is satisfactory. It is understood that this statement in no way releases you from obligations as per your contract and guarantee.
>
> Yours very truly,
> W. W. Bosworth
> per H
>
> WH/K

On March 19, 1915, Jacob and Youngs received a letter from Bosworth noting that some non-Reading pipe had been discovered. Healy, Bosworth's assistant, probably discovered the error. According to his testimony he was employed by Kent full time at some point. Kent's lawyer went out of his way to be sure that Healy not explain the nature of that employment, but it is plausible to suppose that Healy's satisfaction with the plumbing, expressed in the letter of the previous October, changed to dissatisfaction at Kent's prompting. Perhaps Healy then set to looking for specification errors by Jacob and Youngs. Jacob and Youngs hinted in their brief that were Youngs allowed to testify what he was told by the architect as to why the certificate was withheld, it would show that it was solely at Kent's insistence.[9]

Later in March, Youngs, Healy, McKenna (the plumbing subcontractor) and representatives from Reading and Cohoes examined about 150' of pipe and found some to be Cohoes, some Reading, and most unmarked. (Testimony of John A. McKenna). A March 19 letter demanded that Jacob and Youngs replace the offending pipe. It was from the architect and followed the procedure in article IV of the contract, for dealing with unsatisfactory work or materials. By Nov. 23, 1915, the pipe had not been replaced and a letter from Bosworth to Jacob and Youngs referred to still other details of work yet undone, as well as reiterating the replacement demand.

On January 16, 1916, Bosworth sent a letter to Jacob and Youngs giving the latter three days notice of termination unless the builders replaced the pipe, as specified in article V of the contract. After this nothing seems to have happened until November 10, 1916 when Jacob and Youngs formally demanded and was refused the architect's certificate. These delays are intriguing, but unexplained. One wonders if Kent believed himself absolved of the duty to pay as of January 1916, only to receive a new demand for the architect's certificate in November and a legal complaint in December. Perhaps, also, it was Jacob and Youngs' initial intention to forget the $3,400 still owing, but some new pressure led the firm to change its mind.

The complaint was filed on December 11, 1916. Paragraph three alleged "That . . . the plaintiff proceeded to perform the conditions of said contract on its part to be performed, and furnished and de-

---

9. Appellee's Brief, New York Court of Appeals, pp. 6-7.

livered substantially all the materials and performed substantially all the work required by the said contract on the part of the plaintiff to be furnished and performed." On December 29, 1916, Kent responded by denying the claim of substantial performance.

FURTHER QUESTIONS

1. Judge Cardozo says "[t]here was no complaint of defective performance until March, 1915." The supplementary essay suggests that this observation is misleading. What do you think Judge Cardozo meant by his statement? What capability problem is suggested by the divergence between the supplementary comments and Judge Cardozo's statement? What function does the quoted statement perform in Judge Cardozo's opinion? Is it important to the question of whether there was "substantial performance" in this case?

2. A doctrinaire enforcement of the law of conditions would hold that if a seller breached a condition of a contract then a buyer had no obligation to pay the contract price.* Judge Cardozo refuses to be subservient to lines of "symmetry and logic" and seeks instead to attain "a just result."† He says that to achieve this, "[w]e must weigh the purpose to be served, the desire to be gratified, the excuse for deviation from the letter, the cruelty of enforced adherence." Argue against judging by a standard of "symmetry" and judging by a standard of the "just result" on the basis of the capability problems that they raise. Which position, if either, seems preferable to you on this count?

3. Judge Cardozo says that "the willful transgressor must accept the penalty of his transgression . . . . The transgressor whose default is unintentional and trivial may hope for mercy . . . ." Are distinctions commonly drawn in contract law between willful and unintentional transgressions? When the mill shaft in *Hadley v. Baxendale* was shipped by canal because it was cheaper than transportation by rail, was that "transgression" intentional or unintentional? Should it make a difference? What faith do you have in the court's capacity to determine whether a transgression is

---

*Note that a buyer might still be forced to make payment to the extent that he had benefited from services or goods received. Such a payment would be "off the contract," that is it would be measured by the actual value to the buyer of the goods or services received rather than by the contract price. Payment is directed in such a circumstance not on a theory of breach of promise but rather on a theory that the defendant ought not to be "unjustly enriched" at the expense of the plaintiff.

†For more on Cardozo's desire for a "fair result" in this and other cases, see Andrew L. Kaufman, Cardozo 350-56 (1998).

willful? Do the majority and dissent agree here on whether the breach was willful?

4. If Kent attempted to introduce evidence that he specified Reading Pipe because all other pipe companies discriminated against women, should that evidence have been admissible? If it were admissible, could Jacob and Youngs respond by attempting to show that the pipe installed was manufactured by a company which treated women no less favorably than Reading? How, if at all, would the courts have determined what Kent's motive was and to what extent that motive was satisfied? If you distrust the court's capacity to make such judgments, how does that affect your position in this case?

5. Professor Alan Schwartz of Yale has criticized the "court centeredness" of the opinion in *Kent*. "The contract . . . gave defendant the power to choose between the cost of completion and diminution in value damage measures, but the court reserved this power for itself." Alan Schwartz, The Myth that Promisees Prefer Supracompensatory Remedies: An Analysis of Contracting for Damage Measures, 100 Yale L. J. 369, 406 (1990). In Professor Schwartz's view, parties are in the best position to draft contracts with efficient liquidated remedies clauses. Professor Schwartz concludes that "courts should enforce all liquidated damage and specific performance clauses," except in cases involving unconscionability or other invalidating cause. Id. at 405.

By contrast, Professor George Cohen of the University of Virginia has characterized the dilemma in *Kent* as a "classic case of the negligence-opportunism tradeoff." George M. Cohen, The Negligence-Opportunism Tradeoff In Contract Law, 20 Hofstra L. Rev. 941, 996 (1992). In his view, "The court had to choose between deterring the contractor's negligence in allowing nonconforming pipe to be used, and the homeowner's potential opportunism in insisting on strict performance when he had no real interest in it." Id. Professor Cohen contends that Cardozo's opinion justifiably gives priority to deterring opportunism. Cohen argues further that Schwartz neglects the transaction costs that will prevent parties from drafting the most efficient liquidated-damage clauses, and Cohen sees an important role for courts in policing such bargains. Id. at 996-1000. With which professor do you agree?

IV. DANIEL MILLS v. SETH WYMAN

MILLS v. WYMAN
Supreme Court Of Massachusetts, Worcester, 1825.
20 Mass. 207, 3 Pick. 207.

PARKER, C. J. General rules of law established for the protection and security of honest and fair-minded men, who may inconsiderately make promises without any equivalent, will sometimes screen men of a different character from engagements which they are bound in foro conscientioe to perform. This is a defect inherent in all human systems of legislation. The rule that a mere verbal promise, without any consideration, cannot be enforced by action, is universal in its application, and cannot be departed from to suit particular cases in which a refusal to perform such a promise may be disgraceful.

The promise declared on in this case appears to have been made without any legal consideration. The kindness and services towards the sick son of the defendant were not bestowed at his request. The son was in no respect under the care of the defendant. He was twenty-five years old, and had long left his father's family. On his return from a foreign country, he fell sick among strangers, and the plaintiff acted the part of the good Samaritan, giving him shelter and comfort until he died. The defendant, his father, on being informed of this event, influenced by a transient feeling of gratitude, promises in writing to pay the plaintiff for the expenses he had incurred. But he has determined to break this promise, and is willing to have his case appear on record as a strong example of particular injustice sometimes necessarily resulting from the operation of general rules.

It is said a moral obligation is a sufficient consideration to support an express promise; and some authorities lay down the rule

119

thus broadly; but upon examination of the cases we are satisfied
that the universality of the rule cannot be supported, and that
there must have been some preexisting obligation, which has become inoperative by positive law, to form a basis for an effective
promise. The cases of debts barred by the statute of limitations,
of debts incurred by infants, of debts of bankrupts, are generally
put for illustration of the rule. Express promises founded on such
preexisting equitable obligations may be enforced; there is a good
consideration for them; they merely remove an impediment created by law to the recovery of debts honestly due, but which public policy protects the debtors from being compelled to pay. In all
these cases there was originally a quid pro quo; and according to
the principles of natural justice the party receiving ought to pay;
but the legislature has said he shall not be coerced; then comes the
promise to pay the debt that is barred, the promise of the man to
pay the debt of the infant, of the discharged bankrupt to restore to
his creditor what by the law he had lost. In all these cases there is
a moral obligation founded upon an antecedent valuable consideration. These promises therefore have a sound legal basis. They
are not promises to pay something for nothing; not naked pacts;
but the voluntary revival or creation of obligation which before
existed in natural law, but which had been dispensed with, not
for the benefit of the party obliged solely, but principally for the
public convenience. If moral obligation, in its fullest sense, is a
good substratum for an express promise, it is not easy to perceive
why it is not equally good to support an implied promise. What
a man ought to do, generally he ought to be made to do, whether
he promise or refuse. But the law of society has left most of such
obligations to the interior forum, as the tribunal of conscience has
been aptly called. Is there not a moral obligation upon every son
who has become affluent by means of the education and advantages bestowed upon him by his father, to relieve that father from
pecuniary embarrassment, to promote his comfort and happiness,
and even to share with him his riches, if thereby he will be made
happy? And yet such a son may, with impunity, leave such a father
in any degree of penury above that which will expose the community in which he dwells, to the danger of being obliged to preserve
him from absolute want. Is not a wealthy father under strong moral obligation to advance the interest of an obedient, well disposed

son, to furnish him with the means of acquiring and maintaining a becoming rank in life, to rescue him from the horrors of debt incurred by misfortune? Yet the law will uphold him in any degree of parsimony, short of that which would reduce his son to the necessity of seeking public charity.

Without doubt there are great interests of society which justify withholding the coercive arm of the law from these duties of imperfect obligation, as they are called; imperfect, not because they are less binding upon the conscience than those which are called perfect, but because the wisdom of the social law does not impose sanctions upon them.

A deliberate promise, in writing, made freely and without any mistake, one which may lead the party to whom it is made into contracts and expenses, cannot be broken without a violation of moral duty. But if there was nothing paid or promised for it, the law, perhaps wisely, leaves the execution of it to the conscience of him who makes it. It is only when the party making the promise gains something, or he to whom it is made loses something, that the law gives the promise validity. And in the case of the promise of the adult to pay the debt of the infant, of the debtor discharged by the statute of limitations or bankruptcy, the principle is preserved by looking back to the origin of the transaction, where an equivalent is to be found. An exact equivalent is not required by the law; for there being a consideration, the parties are left to estimate its value: though here the courts of equity will step in to relieve from gross inadequacy between the consideration and the promise.

These principles are deduced from the general current of decided cases upon the subject, as well as from the known maxims of the common law. The general position, that moral obligation is a sufficient consideration for an express promise, is to be limited in its application, to cases where at some time or other a good or valuable consideration has existed.[1]

1. Cook v. Bradley, 7 Conn. 57; Littlefield v. Shee, 2 Barnw. & Adol. 811; Yelv. (Metcalf's ed.) 4 a, note 1; Parker v. Carter, 4 Munf. 273; M'Pherson v. Rees, 2 Penrose & Watts, 521; Pennington v. Gittings, 2 Gill & Johns. 208; Smith v. Ware, 13 Johns. R. 259; Edwards v. Davis, 16 Johns. R. 281, 283, note; Greeves v. M'Allister, 2 Binn. 591; Chandler v. Hill, 2 Hen. & Munf. 124; Fonbl. on Eq. by Laussat, 273, note; 2 Kent's Comm. (2nd ed.) 465. Contra, Glass v. Beach, 5 Vt. 172; Barlow v. Smith, 4 Vt. 139; Commissioners of the Canal Fund v. Perry,

A legal obligation is always a sufficient consideration to support either an express or an implied promise; such as an infant's debt for necessaries, or a father's promise to pay for the support and education of his minor children. But when the child shall have attained to manhood, and shall have become his own agent in the world's business, the debts he incurs, whatever may be their nature, create no obligation upon the father; and it seems to follow, that his promise founded upon such a debt has no legally binding force.

The cases of instruments under seal and certain mercantile contracts, in which considerations need not be proved, do not contradict the principles above suggested. The first import a consideration in themselves, and the second belong to a branch of the mercantile law, which has found it necessary to disregard the point of consideration in respect to instruments negotiable in their nature and essential to the interests of commerce.

Instead of citing a multiplicity of cases to support the positions I have taken, I will only refer to a very able review of all the cases in the note in 3 Bos. & Pul. 249. The opinions of the judges had been variant for a long course of years upon this subject, but there seems to be no case in which it was nakedly decided, that a promise to pay the debt of a son of full age, not living with his father, though the debt were incurred by sickness which ended in the death of the son, without a previous request by the father proved or presumed, could be enforced by action.

It has been attempted to show a legal obligation on the part of the defendant by virtue of our statute, which compels lineal kindred in the ascending or descending line to support such of their poor relations as are likely to become chargeable to the town where they have their settlement. But it is a sufficient answer to this position, that such legal obligation does not exist except in the very cases provided for in the statute, and never until the party charged has been adjudged to be of sufficient ability thereto. We do not know from the report any of the facts which are necessary to create such an obligation. Whether the deceased had a legal settlement in this commonwealth at the time of his death, whether he was

5 Ohio 56. See also Seago v. Deane, 4 Bingh. 459; Welles v. Horton, 2 Carr. & Payne, 383; Davis v. Morgan, 6 Dowl. & Ryl. 42.

likely to become chargeable had he lived, whether the defendant was of sufficient ability, are essential facts to be adjudicated by the court to which is given jurisdiction on this subject. The legal liability does not arise until these facts have all been ascertained by judgment, after hearing the party intended to be charged.[2]

For the foregoing reasons we are all of opinion that the nonsuit directed by the Court of Common Pleas was right, and that judgment be entered thereon for costs for the defendant.

2. Cook v. Bradley, 7 Conn. 57; Wethersfield v. Montague, 3 Conn. 507; Dover v. McMurphy, 4 N.H. 158.

FIRST QUESTIONS

1. Imagine three different reasons why Seth Wyman, having once promised to pay Daniel Mills, now refuses to pay him. Would the differing reasons affect your view of whether the courts should force him to keep his promise? To what extent do you think a court would be good at discerning his true reason? Does your view of this capability affect your conclusion as to the appropriate rule of law?

2. Chief Justice Parker distinguishes sharply between law and morality — between promises supported by consideration that will be enforced by courts and "moral" obligations that are left to the "internal forum" or the "tribunal of conscience." Almost a century later, Holmes echoed this sentiment, arguing that the tendency to confuse the two was "no more pronounced than in the law of contract." Do you agree? Is there any place for a doctrine of "moral obligation" in contract law at all?

3. In considering *Hadley v. Baxendale* we discussed the social utility of the rule the court formulated. Does Chief Justice Parker consider issues of this kind?

Suppose it were argued: "Parents generally love their children and would want them cared for by Good Samaritans. If the common law creates an obligation for parents to pay for that care, it will increase the frequency with which that care will be provided. Accordingly, the common law should make that presumption — and especially when there is a promise to pay, that promise will be enforced." How do you think Chief Justice Parker would respond to this argument? How would you respond if you were a judge ruling on this case today?

4. When did Wyman promise to pay Mills? Does the timing matter?

5. Was young Wyman dead or alive at the time of this promise? Does it matter?

6. Suppose Seth Wyman died before he could fulfill his promise and Daniel Mills brought suit against the Wyman estate. Suppose further that the estate had assets of just $100 and there was a claim outstanding for $100 for food that had been sold to Seth Wyman in return for his promise to pay. How do you think a court should allocate the estate between Daniel Mills' claim and that of

the grocer who provided the food? Does your answer to this question affect your view of *Mills v. Wyman*?

7. The Chief Justice acknowledges that it was sometimes necessary to "disregard" the traditional requirement of consideration in cases involving certain mercantile commercial instruments. Enforcement of these instruments, he says, is "essential to the interests of commerce." Are you persuaded that there is a stronger ground for overlooking consideration in that case than in Daniel Mills' case?

8. Likewise, Chief Justice Parker acknowledges that some gratuitous promises to pay otherwise unenforceable past debts are enforceable, despite the lack of any bargaining for new consideration. For example, if a debtor who has been "discharged by the statute of limitations or bankruptcy" nonetheless promises to make good on his original debt, that new promise will be binding. In that case, the law will bind the promisor even absent any return promise "by looking back to the origin of the transaction, where an equivalent is to be found." Is there any meaningful difference between the debtor's case and that of Daniel Mills?

9. Did Daniel Mills have a *restitution* claim against Seth Wyman? Mills conferred a benefit on Wyman, presumably, by expending time and money in an effort to save the life of Wyman's son. Two traditional defenses against restitution are "gratuitousness" and "officiousness." It seems unlikely that Mills was an "officious intermeddler." Did he act gratuitously — that is, as if he were making a gift, or otherwise behaving simply as a Good Samaritan? Or is it fair to infer that Mills, an innkeeper, would normally expect compensation from people for emergency medical services rendered while they stay in his inn?

10. Is the law's treatment of Good Samaritans appropriate? On the one hand, tort law seems to discourage Good Samaritans from helping those in distress: if the Bad Samaritan walks by a drowning baby, she usually incurs no liability. But if the Good Samaritan attempts to save the baby and, in so doing, worsens the situation or otherwise causes harm, she will be liable in tort. Likewise, the criminal law will rarely punish the bystander who watches a rape in a pool hall and does nothing. And contract law apparently holds that Daniel Mills can expect nothing for his good deeds. Are these rules justifiable? Consistent?

SUPPLEMENTARY COMMENTS*

Levi Wyman was born on November 25, 1795, in Shrewsbury, Massachusetts, a suburb of Worcester.[15] He was the seventh and last child of Seth and Mary Wyman.[16] This Levi Wyman was almost certainly the same sick young man whose medical expenses became the center of the controversy in *Mills v. Wyman*. Levi's birth date would have made him twenty-five-years-old at the time of his illness in 1821, and the report of the case indicates that Levi was "about twenty-five years of age" at that time.

Not much is known of Levi's childhood. He grew up in a relatively prosperous household, on a homestead of more than a hundred acres.[18] . . .

Sometime between 1815 and 1821, Levi left home. By 1821, according to the trial court in *Mills v. Wyman*, Levi "had long ceased to be a member of his father's family."[22] Where he went, and why, is a mystery.[23] The next we hear of him, Levi was in Hartford,

*Excerpted from Geoffrey R. Watson, In the Tribunal of Conscience: *Mills v. Wyman* Reconsidered, originally published in 71 Tulane L. Rev. 1749-1806 (1997). Reprinted with the permission of the Tulane Law Review Association, which holds the copyright. We have made a few minor revisions in the text and omitted some footnotes. We have retained the original footnote numbers.

15. See Andrew H. Ward, Family Register of the Inhabitants of the Town of Shrewsbury, Mass. from its Settlement in 1717 to 1829, and of Some of them to a Later Period 276 (Boston, Samuel G. Drake 1847) [hereinafter Ward, Family Register]; Vital Records of Shrewsbury, Massachusetts, to the End of the Year 1849, at 114 (Franklin P. Rice 1904) (LC Call F74.S63 S6) [hereinafter Vital Records of Shrewsbury]; see also Massachusetts Vital Records (manuscript on file at the Library of Congress Microform Reading Room) (recording the birth of Levi Wyman to Seth and Mary Wyman on Nov. 25, 1795).

16. See Ward, Family Register, supra note 15, at 276 (listing children as Sarah, Ross, Seth, Oliver, Mary, Clarissa, and Levi); Vital Records of Shrewsbury, supra note 15, at 114 (listing children as Sally, Ross, Seth, Oliver, Polly, Clarisa, and Levi). . . .

18. See Vincent D. Wyman, Wyman Historic Genealogy Ancestors and Descendants (1595-1941) of Asa Wetherby Wyman 17-20 (1941) (describing Seth Wyman's land holdings).

22. Record, Mills v. Wyman (Ct. Comm. Pleas, Dec. Term 1824) (Howe, J.) (unpublished manuscript on file with the Massachusetts State Archives, Boston, Mass., Box 203, 33.B.5, 826-28) [hereinafter Record, Mills].

23. A Levi Wyman does appear in the 1820 federal census for Connecticut. This Wyman lived in Union, Connecticut, in Tolland County. See Connecticut 1820 Census Index 123 (Ronald Vern Jackson et al. eds., 1977). But it is unlikely that this was our Levi Wyman, for a similar entry appears in the 1810 Connecticut

Connecticut in February 1821, "on his return from a voyage at sea" — indeed, on his return from a "foreign country"[25] — when he became very ill.

Precisely when Levi became sick is unclear. By some accounts, Levi fell ill on February fifth at the house of Daniel Mills, the Good Samaritan of *Mills v. Wyman*: "one Levi Wyman at Hartford . . . on the fifth day of February [1821] was at the house of [Mills] and then and there fell dangerously sick . . . ."[26] Other accounts agree that Levi became sick at Mills's house, but not until February twentieth.[27] None of the accounts says he became ill while abroad or at sea, though this is surely a possibility.

The nature of Levi's illness is also a mystery. Court papers provide some tantalizing details. The illness . . . lasted at least two weeks. Daniel Mills, the Good Samaritan who housed and cared for Levi Wyman, arranged for two men to guard Levi for four days and nights while Levi "was in this derang'd state."[29] Levi was so sick that "he leaped out of a chamber window to the imminent hazard of his life, and to the very great alarm of the family and the boarders."[30] Mills provided Wyman with "1 gallon Spirits" and with "pills" provided by a Doctor Linde. Mills also hired John Lee Comstock, a prominent Hartford physician, to care for Wyman. Comstock found Levi "in a state of indisposition" and, for some time, "in a state of delirium" that required two or three persons "to prevent him from injuring himself."[35] Although Dr. Comstock published dozens of books on subjects ranging from mineralogy to Greek history to philosophy,[36] he left little further record of his diagnosis and treatment of Levi Wyman.

census, when our Levi — then age 15 — probably still lived with his parents. See Connecticut 1810 Census Index 109 (Roland Vern Jackson et al. eds., 1977). . . .

25. *Mills*, 20 Mass. (3 Pick.) at 209.

26. Record, *Mills*, supra note 22 (Report of Abijah Bigelow, Clerk of the Worcester County Courts). . . .

27. See id. (Deposition of Nathaniel Wales and Norman Pease, Nov. 29, 1824). . . .

29. Id. (itemized expenses of Daniel Mills, in Letter of Daniel Mills to Seth Wyman, Mar. 3, 1821); see also id. (Depositions of Wales and Pease) (noting that Mills "procured a Mr. Morton and a Mr. Powers to attend upon Mr. Wyman").

30. Id. (Depositions of Wales and Pease).

35. Id. (Deposition of John Lee Comstock).

36. See, e.g., John Lee Comstock, History of the Precious Metals (1849); John Lee Comstock, Introduction to Mineralogy (1832); John Lee Comstock,

Perhaps the most interesting aspect of Levi's illness was the end of it. The Supreme Judicial Court pronounced Levi dead. It said that Mills "acted the part of the Good Samaritan, giving [Levi] shelter and comfort until he died." This finding might influence one's view of the case, since Mills is a less sympathetic plaintiff if his ministrations were ineffective.[38] But the court's report of Levi's death was somewhat exaggerated.[39] All available evidence suggests that Levi in fact recovered and eventually settled in Springfield, Massachusetts. On March 3, 1821, Mills wrote to Levi's father, Seth Wyman, stating that "it is with satisfaction that I can announce to you - that he has recovered his health in a measure so far that he has left this place a day or two since."[40] In a postscript, Mills added: "Levi Started from here and contemplated on going home by the way of Springfield should his health admit — was tolerable smart when he left here." Two of Mills's acquaintances, Nathaniel Wales and Norman Pease, also spoke of Levi's "recovery."[44]

Moreover, there is evidence that Levi survived for years or even decades after the illness. In 1829 one Levi Wyman executed a quitclaim deed in favor of Seth Wyman, Jr., administrator of the estate of Colonel Seth Wyman.[45] In exchange for five hundred dollars, this Levi Wyman quitclaimed all his rights in the "Real Estate whereof *my Hon. Father Seth Wyman* ... died seized."[46] Colonel Seth Wyman had only one son named Levi, the Levi Wyman of

System of Natural Philosophy (1831); John Lee Comstock, History of the Greek Revolution (variously dated at 1828 or 1829), cited in Appletons' Cyclopaedia of American Biography, supra note 33, at 702. His *System of Natural Philosophy* went through 94 editions, was translated into many languages, and sold nearly 900,000 copies. . . .

38. But cf. Cotnam v. Wisdom, 104 S.W. 164, 167 (Ark. 1907) (permitting restitutionary recovery by doctor even when patient died).

39. Cf. John Bartlett, Familiar Quotations 625 (Emily Morison Beck ed., 14th ed. 1968) ("The reports of my death are greatly exaggerated.") (quoting Mark Twain, Cable from London to the Associated Press (1897)).

40. Record, *Mills*, supra note 22 (Letter of Daniel Mills to Seth Wyman, Mar. 3, 1821).

44. Record, *Mills*, supra note 22 (Depositions of Wales and Pease); see also Curtis Nyquist, Contract Theory, Single Case Research and the Massachusetts Archives, 3 Mass. L. Hist. 53, 79-81 (1997).

45. See 264 Probate Recs. of Worcester County 392 (Quitclaim Deed from Levi Wyman to Seth Wyman, Jr., dated Jan. 9, 1829) [hereinafter Quitclaim Deed].

46. Id. (emphasis added).

Mills v. Wyman. What's more, the deed mentions that this Levi Wyman lived in Springfield, Massachusetts, the town to which he headed after leaving the home of Daniel Mills. Incidentally, the deed also mentions that Levi now had a wife named Lucinda. One history of Springfield families indicates that he married her on September 19, 1824, just seven months after he left Hartford.[49]

Other evidence also suggests that, while Levi outlived the Supreme Judicial Court's pronouncement of his death, he did not outgrow his habit of getting into trouble. Worcester County probate records from the 1820s and 1830s indicate that a Levi Wyman, a spendthrift and drunkard, had been assigned a legal guardian.[50] In 1829, the Worcester County Probate Court appointed Henry Snow of Shrewsbury as guardian of "Levi Wyman of said Shrewsbury, who spends and wastes his estate by excessive drinking and idleness."[51] The guardian's accounting of Levi's assets suggests that this is indeed our Levi Wyman, for the accounting mentions "One Bond for one hundred and fifty Dollars, signed by Seth Wyman" — presumably Seth Wyman, Jr. — and dated January 8, 1829.[52] This was the day before Levi executed the quitclaim deed releasing his claims to any of the estate of his father. The only other property in Levi's name was "an old riding Saddle worth about one Dollar." This Levi, like the Levi Wyman in the 1829 deed, was married. He also had one or more daughters. Again, it seems likely that this was the Levi Wyman of *Mills v. Wyman*.

It is not clear why the Supreme Judicial Court thought Levi was dead. No surviving court records suggest that he had died. Perhaps a stray suggestion of counsel at oral argument influenced the court; only the plaintiff's attorneys appeared in person.[57] But it

49. See 3 Thomas B. Warren, Springfield Families 782 (1934-1935) ("Levi Wyman m 19 Sept 1824 Lucinda Edwards").

50. See 142 Probate Recs. of Worcester County 103 (Mar. 3, 1829) (Docket No. 67894); 194 Probate Recs. of Worcester County 196 (Mar. 3, 1829); 67 Probate Recs. of Worcester County 557 (May 28, 1829) (inventory of Levi Wyman's possessions).

51. 194 Probate Recs. of Worcester County 196 (Mar. 3, 1829) (Docket No. 67894)

52. 73 Probate Recs. of Worcester County 468-69 (Apr. 1, 1834) (Docket No. 67894) (Levi Wyman's Guardians Acct.).

57. See Mills v. Wyman, 20 Mass. (3 Pick.) 207, 208 (1825) (noting in a headnote that defense counsel furnished a written argument "in vacation").

would hardly have been in Mills's interest to suggest that Levi had died while under his care.

Whatever his physical health in 1821 — sick or well, dead or alive — Levi's financial health was indisputably wretched. He was a "stranger" in Hartford, "totally unable to pay" for his room, board, and medical expenses.[58] Those expenses amounted to about twenty-two dollars — a considerable sum in those days — and included six dollars for fourteen days' board and lodging, three dollars for "Room pine & Candles," one dollar for a gallon of "Spirits," six dollars in expenses for the two men hired to restrain Levi, and six dollars for Dr. Comstock's fee.[59] Levi apparently did, however, volunteer that his father Seth Wyman would reimburse Mills. He was "confident that his father, Col. Seth Wyman, would readily pay" the bill.[60] This confidence was either misplaced or feigned.

Levi Wyman left Hartford without paying Daniel Mills a penny. As Mills's acquaintances put it: "We never have known of any property of Levi Wyman since his sickness nor have we ever seen him since."[61] The date of Levi's departure is uncertain. That date is of interest because it roughly corresponds with the date on which Seth Wyman supposedly promised to pay for Levi's expenses. Mills billed Seth for fourteen days lodging, but Mills didn't clearly indicate which fourteen days were involved. One bill carries the date February 20; another carries the date February 27. But on March 3, Mills reported to Seth Wyman that Levi Wyman had "left this place a day or two since,"[63] suggesting that Levi had left Mills's house at the very end of February or even early March.

Daniel Mills was not willing to let this bill go unpaid. He does not appear to have been wealthy. . . . Unlike Seth Wyman, Mills is

58. Record, *Mills*, supra note 22 (Report of Abijah Bigelow, Clerk of the Worcester County Courts).

59. See id. (Letter of Daniel Mills to Seth Wyman, Mar. 3, 1821 and bill of Dr. Comstock). These figures changed slightly as the dispute progressed. In April, 1824, Mills calculated the total expenses at $22.93, plus $4.50 interest. Levi's 14 days' room and board was now assessed at $6.15. The bill reflected only two quarts of "Spirits," at a cost of 50 [cents]. It also reflected 13 [cents] "cash paid for Laudanum" and 15 [cents] for "pills." See id.

60. Id. (Depositions of Wales and Pease).

61. Id.

63. Id. (Letter of Daniel Mills, to Seth Wyman, Mar. 3, 1821).

never referred to as a "gentleman" in the papers.[65] Little else about Mills is certain. A "master mariner" named Daniel or D.A. Mills lived with a Hetta Mills at a boarding-house at 118 Front Street in Hartford, near the Connecticut River, in the 1830s and 1840s, but it is not clear that this was our Mills.[66] . . .

Anxious to be paid, Mills did not wait to contact Levi's father until Levi had departed. In early or middle February, Mills contacted Seth Wyman and advised him of Levi's condition. We don't have the text of Mills's first communication to Wyman, but Mills apparently suggested that Seth Wyman come see his son.[71] On February 24, while Levi was probably still at Mills's house, Seth Wyman responded. This was the ostensible promise to pay Mills for services already rendered and the writing on which the litigation in *Mills v. Wyman* turned. It is worth quoting in full:

> Dear Sir
> I received a line from you relating to my Son Levi's sickness and requesting me to come up and see him, but as the going is very bad I cannot come up at the present, but I wish you to take all possible care of him and if you cannot have him at your house I wish you to remove him to some convenient place and if he cannot satisfy you for it I will.
> I want that you should write me again immediately how he does and greatly oblige your most obedient servant
>
> Seth Wyman   Feb 24th 1821

By this letter, Seth Wyman supposedly promised to pay Mills for services already rendered, for so-called "past consideration." But the letter does not clearly promise to pay for the services already rendered. It seems more directed at procuring future services from Daniel Mills — i.e., that he either "have him at your house" or "remove him to some convenient place." Wyman can be

---

65. See id.

66. See Gardner's Hartford City Directory for 1838, at 32 (1838). . . .

71. See Record, *Mills*, supra note 22 (Letter of Col. Seth Wyman to Daniel Mills, Feb. 24, 1821).

more fairly said to have been bargaining for future conduct and for real consideration than to have been making a sterile promise to pay for past services. The letter is understandably preoccupied with ensuring his son's safety hereafter, not in settling his debts heretofore. Not surprisingly, when the case came to trial, Wyman's first defense was that he never promised to pay Mills for past expenses.[74]

Mills, however, interpreted Wyman's letter as a promise to pay Levi's existing debt, not just an offer to pay for future services. Mills was not concerned with arranging future accommodations for Levi. Mills wanted Levi's bill paid. By the time Mills received Seth Wyman's letter, i.e., in late February or even early March, Levi Wyman was leaving or perhaps already gone. Anxious to collect on his debt, Mills interpreted Wyman's letter as a guarantee of Levi's existing obligations. After advising Seth of Levi's departure, Mills wrote:

> [Levi] did not nor was not in any situation for to compensate me or the Phisitian in the Least For my trouble and expense I shall therefore agreeable to your Letter of guarantee make out any bill against you which you will find annexed to this — amounting to — $16.00 — Which I can assure you is more reasonable than it otherwise would have been — had it not been so unfortunate on your part — you will have the goodness to enclose said amount and forward it to me by mail as soon as convenient and oblige yours etc.
>
> Daniel Mills   City of Hartford   3d March 1821[76]

The letter included Mills' itemized expenses and Dr. Comstock's bill for six dollars. There is no record of any response from Seth Wyman. Mills repeated his demand, to no avail, one month later.[77]

---

74. See id. (Report of Abijah Bigelow, Clerk of Worcester County Courts).

76. Id. (Letter of Daniel Mills to Col. Seth Wyman, Mar. 3, 1821). [The authors are grateful to Professor Chuck Knapp for helping us decipher the word "Least" in this letter.]

77. See id. (Bill of Apr. 5, 1824).

Why did Seth Wyman decline to visit his son? Was he just an uncaring father? His age may offer an explanation. Seth was born on April 5, 1758[78] in Shrewsbury. Thus, when Mills invited him to Hartford in 1821, Seth Wyman was almost sixty-three years old — not a young man for his day. Perhaps when Seth wrote "the going is very bad," he meant he was too frail to travel to Hartford .... Indeed, Seth died on December 29, 1827, less than seven years after the events in question, and just three months before his seventieth birthday.[81] There is no evidence that he traveled much at all in his last years ...

Even when they were healthy, Seth and Mary were hardly world travelers.... Apart from [a] possible stint in the militia, there is little evidence that [Seth] traveled much at all. After Seth and Mary were married at Shrewsbury in August of 1782, the newlyweds settled in Buckland, Massachusetts and stayed for six years. In 1788, they returned to Shrewsbury, where they lived the remaining forty years of their lives.[90]

It is also possible that Seth and Mary may have refused to visit Levi because he had become estranged from his family. This possibility cannot be discounted, especially given the evidence that Levi was later adjudicated a spendthrift who needed a guardian to manage his affairs. Nonetheless, Seth's letter suggests that the father still cared for the son. "I wish you to take all possible care

78. See Vital Records of Shrewsbury, supra note 15, at 114; Massachusetts Vital Records, supra note 15 (listing Seth's birth date as April 5, 1758).

Seth Wyman's parents were Ross and Dinah Wyman, also of Shrewsbury. See id. at 114, 282.... According to one account, Ross . . .was a blacksmith, a "stout, athletic man" who supported the Revolution and refused to work for Tories. He once defended himself from impressment onto a British man-of-war by "snatching up a cod fish with both hands in the gills, [and] beating them off by slapping them in the face with its slimy tail!" Id. at 274 n*.

81. See Ward, Family Register, supra note 15, at 484. Another source suggests he was "aged 70" when he died. See American Antiquarian Society, Worcester, Mass., Index of Dates in Massachusetts Centinel and Columbian Centinel 1784-1840 (available in the Genealogy Section of the Library of Congress).

90. Deeds and probate records from Worcester County support this conclusion. Seth Wyman was involved in at least 30 real estate transactions in Worcester County between 1780 and 1827. See Grantee Index 1731-1839 Wh. – Wy.-Y.Z. of Worcester County; Grantor Index 1731-1839 Wh. – Wy.-Y.Z. of Worcester County. In every deed after 1800, he lists his home as Shrewsbury. . . .

of him," Seth wrote. "If you cannot have him at your house I wish you to remove him to some convenient place . . . . I want that you should write me again immediately how he does . . . ." If Seth had disowned his son, he might not have bothered to write back at all, and he certainly would not have offered to pay for any further expenses. Even the Supreme Judicial Court, no friend of Seth Wyman, thought he liked his son enough to experience a "transient feeling of gratitude."

Whatever his reason for not visiting Levi, why did Seth refuse to pay the man who nursed Levi back to health? When Seth spoke of the "going being bad," did he mean his financial rather than physical health? At first blush, poverty seems an unlikely explanation for Seth's refusal to pay Mills. Seth Wyman was a man of means who became a moderately prominent citizen of his small home town. One source offers this laconic description of his life: "He had a farm and built the grist mill and saw mill. He was colonel of the militia, and selectman of the town. He was a large lumber dealer."[95] Wyman's political career was short-lived; he served as a selectman for only one term, from 1814 to 1815.[96] But he owned a considerable amount of property right up to the end of his life. Property records from Worcester County, for example, indicate that he bought and sold substantial amounts of real estate throughout his life.[97] After his death in 1827, his real estate holdings were appraised at $ 7,924 and his personal property was valued at $ 2,033.76, for a grand total of almost $10,000.[98] That was a large sum of money in those days, far more than most people earned in a year or even a decade. The probate court's inventory of

95. IV Historic Homes and Institutions and Genealogical and Personal Memoirs of Worcester County Massachusetts with a History of Worcester Society of Antiquity 136 (Ellery Bicknell Crane ed. 1907).

96. See Ward, Family Register, supra note 15, at 81. Wyman was one of five selectmen. See id. Seth Wyman did not leave office because of any term limit; other selectmen held office for more than a single one-year term. See id.

97. . . . Some of the deeds involved significant amounts of land and money. See, e.g., 205 Worcester County Deeds 202-03 (Deed from Seth Wyman to John Davis, June 1, 1815; recorded Feb. 19, 1817) (recording sale of 60 acres of land for $1,200); 198 Worcester County Deeds 476 (Deed from Seth Wyman to Elijah Brigham, Nov. 1, 1815; recorded Nov. 23, 1815) (recording sale of 38 acres for $1,000).

98. See 63 Probate Recs. of Worcester County, 614 (Jan. 29, 1828) (Seth Wyman's Inventory).

the couple's possessions suggests they led a very comfortable life in the country.[99]

Still, Seth's financial situation was not perfect. He had sizable debts. The administrator of his estate was ordered to sell $3,400 worth of property to satisfy Seth's creditors.[100] In fact, the administrator ended up selling almost $5,000 worth of real and personal property to meet Seth's debts.[101] Nor was Mary Wyman wealthy. She died with assets appraised at $246.78.[102] Moreover, although Seth bought and sold property actively up until 1817, from 1817 until his death in 1827 he continued to sell real estate, but stopped buying it. Perhaps he sold land to keep cash flowing in as he grew too old to manage the family farm and the mills he had erected on it. What's more, he died intestate, even though he was survived by his wife, several children, and a number of other living relatives.[104] The absence of a will again suggests uncertainty about his financial situation. While Seth could doubtless afford to pay Mills his $25, perhaps Seth's financial circumstances had deteriorated sufficiently that he was willing to fight a debt he did not think he

---

99. In addition to Seth's substantial real estate holdings, his inventory lists hundreds of personal items, including the following: three yokes of oxen; one bull; nine cows; two calves; one horse; one mare; 27 sheep; 24 lambs; 27 tons of hay; all sorts of farming tools, including rakes, wheelbarrows, screwdrivers, sickles, and a gun; one buffalo robe; two barrels of feathers; three barrels of vinegar; 11 bushels of wheat; 75 bushels of potatoes; four wine glasses; a loom; four pewter platters; several sets of clothes; and a healthy array of furniture. See id. at 612-14.

Mary Wyman's inventory includes "One black Silk Gown"; a collection of other clothing; "Seven Silver Tea Spoons" a cherry table; various kitchen items including a coffee mill, kettle, and wine glasses; and a variety of linens and the like. See 67 Probate Recs. of Worcester County 457-59 (Mar. 27, 1829) (Mary Wyman's Inventory).

100. See 263 Probate Recs. of Worcester County 431 (May 1828) (Seth Wyman Esq. Estate, Petition for Sale).

101. See The Account of Seth Wyman Administrator on the Estate of Col. Seth Wyman Late of Shrewsbury Deceased 3 (undated unpublished manuscript on file at Massachusetts State Archives, Boston, Mass.). Much of it was sold at a public auction on June 7, 1828. . . .

102. See 67 Probate Recs. of Worcester County 457, 459 (Mar. 27, 1829) (Mary Wyman's Inventory).

104. Seth's wife, Mary, inherited a third of his property as her dower interest. See 65 Probate Recs. of Worcester County 371 (Sept. 22, 1828) (Seth Wyman's Widow's Dower).

owed. He took that determination with him to his grave: Seth's estate did not pay Daniel Mills anything.

One question of motive remains. Why did these two men take a twenty-five dollar dispute all the way to the Supreme Judicial Court of Massachusetts? Granted, twenty-five dollars was a significant sum of money, the equivalent of a month's pay or more, but it was not that large a sum when compared to court costs and attorney's fees. Moreover, not only did the Massachusetts court award costs to the victor, as is the practice today;[105] it also still followed the English rule on attorney's fees,[106] thereby magnifying the risks of litigation for both parties. At the trial level, for example, Daniel Mills was ordered to pay Wyman's costs and fees, which totaled $10.74, $1.50 of which represented the attorney's fee. When Mills lost again on appeal, he was saddled with Wyman's costs in the Supreme Judicial Court as well; these totaled an additional $9.94, $2.50 of which represented defense counsel's fee on appeal, for a total of $20.68. In addition to all this, Mills presumably had to pay his own attorneys; he was represented by respected counsel at trial and by fairly prominent attorneys on appeal, and they presumably charged similarly for fees and costs.[109] Thus he paid out more than he expected to win. In retrospect, it seems remarkable that either Mills or Wyman took the risk of being saddled with costs and fees that exceeded the actual amount in controversy. But they did.

The Legal Proceedings

Daniel Mills brought his suit in the Worcester County Court of Common Pleas in Worcester, Massachusetts in 1824.[110] ... [T]he

---

105. See, e.g., Fed. R. Civ. P. 54(d)(1) (stating that "costs other than attorneys' fees shall be allowed as of course to the prevailing party unless the court otherwise directs").

106. Precisely why American courts moved away from the English rule is unclear. See, e.g., Richard A. Field et al., Civil Procedure 165 (6th ed. 1990) ....

109. A fee schedule adopted by the Worcester County Bar shortly after *Mills v. Wyman* gives a sense of the prevailing rates. A "writ on demand" between $20 and $100 cost $2.50; a continuance cost between $2.00 and $5.00, depending on the court and matter; a demurrer in the court of common pleas cost $4.00; arguing fees in that court cost not less than $5.00; and arguing fees in the supreme judicial court cost not less than $10.00. See generally Rule 10, Bar Rules, Worcester County, Mass., Sept. 2, 1828. ...

110. Although Mills was from Connecticut and Wyman from Massachusetts, federal diversity jurisdiction was unavailable because the amount in controversy

case was set for trial in June. It was continued until December, 1824, when it finally went to trial before a jury.

The presiding Judge was Samuel Howe, who had been appointed to the newly established court of common pleas three years earlier. Before his appointment, he was regarded as a leading member of the bar of western Massachusetts.[113] He was a solid but not flamboyant attorney. Howe was a more effective advocate before a judge than a jury; he relied on "sound reasoning," not "display."[114] Howe's mind was more noteworthy for its "discipline" than its "original intuition."[115] Descriptions suggest that he possessed the steady temperament of a good judge, if not the brilliant imagination of a great one.[116] Even so, he did not find his work on this "court of despatch" to be "enough to satisfy his love of judicial investigation."[117] The job "rarely offered occasion for the deeper researches" because the docket was full and his was not a court of last resort.[118]

Judge Howe's "court of despatch" heard *Mills v. Wyman* in December, 1824. . . . [N]o briefs or records of testimony or oral argument appear to have survived. The existing record consists of nine documents, all of them handwritten copies of important

---

did not exceed $500, then the required minimum. See Act of Sept. 24, 1789, 11, 1 Stat. 73, 78. . . .

113. See, e.g., Charles Warren, A History of the American Bar 318 (1912) (citing Howe as an example of leading lawyers in Massachusetts outside of Boston).

114. Address of Chief Justice Parker 8 (Boston, Nathan Hale 1828) (speech at a memorial service for Judge Howe). The author of these words was the same Chief Justice Parker who wrote the opinion affirming Howe's decision in *Mills v. Wyman*.

115. Rufus Ellis, Memoir of the Hon. Samuel Howe 51-58 (Boston, Wm. Crosby and H.P. Nichols 1850) (letter from Samuel Willard to Rufus Ellis).

116. Nonetheless, Howe's appointment to the reorganized bench apparently provoked some resentment. It was "a trying situation, because the order of things was new, and the friends of the old judges were dissatisfied." Id. at 25. Judge Howe eventually did earn the respect of the bench and bar, however. See Address of Chief Justice Parker, supra note 114, at 9 (noting that Judge Howe was a "popular judge" and that the bar was "full of his praises").

117. Address of Chief Justice Parker, supra note 114, at 9.

118. Id. at 10. Judge Howe was so eager for "deeper researches" that he decided to teach law. In 1823, he and Elijah Mills, a U.S. Senator, established a law school in Northampton. The school was modeled after the lecture style of Howe's alma mater, the Litchfield Law School. Howe was an "excellent teacher" who "attracted many students." Foster W. Russell, Mount Auburn Biographies 90 (1953). . . .

documents: the correspondence between the parties, the depositions of various witnesses, the expenses of each party, a summary
of the proceedings, a copy of the jury's verdict, and a copy of the
court's opinion. . . .

Daniel Mills's lawyer at trial was John Williams Hubbard.
Hubbard was born in Brookfield, Vermont, on November 22,
1793. He graduated from Dartmouth in 1814. After studying law
in Vermont and in Worcester, he was admitted to the bar in 1817
and practiced in Worcester until his death in 1825 — while the appeal in *Mills v. Wyman* was pending.[124] . . .

David Brigham was counsel for the defendant, Seth Wyman,
both at trial and on appeal. . . . Brigham apparently practiced in
Shrewsbury for a number of years before and after the case. . . .

The plaintiff's case focused on Wyman's letter of February 24.
On that day, Seth Wyman "undertook and faithfully promised"
to reimburse Mills if Levi could not pay.[130] Consideration for this
promise was the father's "natural affection" for his son; the "great
expense, and trouble in providing for and assisting" Levi; and the
plaintiff's undertaking to "take all proper care of the sd. Levi and
procure medicine and medical and other attendance." Brigham's
main line of defense was that Wyman never promised to reimburse Mills for expenses already incurred. Brigham said "he never
promised the plaintiff in manner and form as he in the declaration
of his writ has alledged against him, and of this he puts himself
on the Country." The record contains no evidence that Brigham
argued lack of consideration during the trial itself.

After a "full hearing," the case was submitted to the jury, and
the jury returned a verdict for the plaintiff. The record contains
two versions of the jury verdict. One, on a separate sheet copied
by clerk Bigelow, reads: "The Jury agree that the Plaintiff has
supported his action and have assessed damages to the amount
of $26.95. Bernard Fowler foreman."[134] The other is more inter-

124. See Inscriptions from the Old Burial Grounds in Worcester, Massachusetts,
from 1727 to 1859: With Biographical and Historical Notes 97-98 (1878) [herein-
after Inscriptions] (providing a biographical sketch). . . .

130. Record, *Mills*, supra note 22 (Writ of Attachment).

134. Id. (Verdict). Not much is known about Bernard Fowler, the foreman. A
Bernard Fowler of "a very respectable family" lived in Northbridge, Massachusetts,
in Worcester County, in the late eighteenth century. William A. Mowry, The

esting. The record of the case reports that the jury "find that the defendant did promise in manner and form as the plaintiff in the declaration of his writ has alledged, and assess damages for the plaintiff in the sum of twenty six dollars and ninety five cents."[135] In other words, this version of the verdict contains a finding that Seth Wyman made the promise alleged. This verdict cites no evidence to support this finding.

Wyman moved that the verdict be set aside. From Judge Howe's opinion, it appears that Brigham argued that Wyman's supposed promise lacked consideration. The record does not disclose whether Brigham also argued that the jury's factual finding, that Wyman made the promise, was supported by sufficient evidence. After a hearing, Judge Howe granted the motion and directed a nonsuit. Judge Howe explained that he "suffered the Jury . . . to assess" plaintiff's damages to save the expense of a new trial in the event the judgment was reversed on appeal.[138] . . . Judge Howe provided a brief, one-page opinion that cited no authority for its conclusion.

His opinion began by asserting that Seth Wyman had in fact made the promise alleged: "After all the expenses had been incurred the defendant wrote a letter to the plaintiff promising to pay him said expenses." As noted, the letter is more plausibly read as a promise to pay for expenses incurred after the date of the letter. It is not clear why Judge Howe let the jury's finding on this point stand. There is no surviving evidence that Seth made the promise alleged. True, early American judges generally paid more deference to juries than is the case today.[141] In the colonial era, for example, juries had the power to find the law as well as the facts.[142] But the jury's law-finding role had largely disappeared by

Descendants of Nathaniel Mowry of Rhode Island 127-28 (Providence, Sidney S. Rider 1878). We don't know whether this man was the same Bernard Fowler who sat on the jury in *Mills*. . . .

135. Record, *Mills*, supra note 22 (Report of Abijah Bigelow, Clerk of the Worcester County Courts).

138. Id. (Judgment).

141. See generally William E. Nelson, Americanization of the Common Law 3-4, 20-30 (1975) (describing the power of colonial juries).

142. See id. at 21 (stating that pre-Revolutionary juries had "vast power to find both the law and the facts").

the 1820s.[143] Even if the jury's finding was purely a conclusion of fact, it could have been overturned if it was "manifestly against the weight of the evidence."[144] Indeed, Howe's own treatise on civil procedure supported the use of a sufficiency standard in reviewing verdicts.[145] Moreover, since the Revolution, Massachusetts courts had become increasingly vigilant in enforcing the express terms of a contract over any implied terms. The law would "not imply a promise, where there was an express promise."[146] It is thus surprising that Judge Howe found sufficient evidence to support the jury's finding that Wyman had promised to pay Mills for past services when Wyman's letter is more plausibly read as bargaining only for future services.

Having found that Wyman made the promise, Judge Howe declared: "There was no evidence of any consideration for this promise except what grew out of the relation which existed between Levi Wyman & the defendant & thinking this not to be sufficient to support the action I directed a non suit."[147] Thus in one sentence Judge Howe found the promise lacked consideration. The brevity of this reasoning brings to mind the famous analysis from *Kirksey v. Kirksey*, decided only twenty-two years after Judge Howe's opinion in *Mills*: "My brothers . . . think that the promise on the

---

143. The Massachusetts judiciary greatly curtailed the jury's law-finding power in the first decade of the nineteenth century. See id. at 168-69; Gerald W. Gawalt, The Promise of Power: The Emergence of the Legal Profession in Massachusetts 1760-1840, at 105 & n.62 (1978).

144. Hammond v. Wadhams, 5 Mass. 353, 355 (1809). This rule again reflected a recent diminution in the power of juries. In the colonial era, courts set aside verdicts only if they had "no support" in the evidence. See Nelson, supra note 141, at 170. But just as the jury's law-finding powers had waned by 1810, the jury's fact-finding powers had come under closer supervision by judges. See id. at 169-70. Why this happened is a complex question that invites further research. Cf. A.W.B. Simpson, The Horwitz Thesis and the History of Contracts, 46 U. Chi. L. Rev. 533 (1979) ("What needs to be explained is this progressive dethronement of the jury. . . .").

145. See Samuel G. Howe, Lectures on the Practice of Courts 351 (1825) (available at the Harvard Law School Library, Cambridge, Mass.).

146. Nelson, supra note 141, at 140 (quoting Whiting v. Sullivan, 7 Mass. 107, 109 (1810) ("One set of cases articulated more precisely than had been necessary in the colonial period the dominance of express over implied contract")).

147. Record, *Mills*, supra note 22 (Judgment).

part of the defendant was a mere gratuity, and that an action will not lie for its breach."[148]

Daniel Mills appealed. After the death of his first attorney, John W. Hubbard, Daniel Mills hired new counsel for appeal: the prominent partnership of John Davis and Charles Allen of Worcester. Whether Davis or Allen or both argued the appeal in *Mills v. Wyman* is unknown. The Supreme Judicial Court did not keep regular records of oral or written pleadings at that time. . . .

Davis and Allen were not successful with the three New England justices who heard their appeal. Chief Justice Isaac Parker,[163] writing for a unanimous panel, held that Seth Wyman was not liable to Daniel Mills. Like Judge Howe, Justice Parker assumed that Seth Wyman made the promise at issue. Nowhere in the opinion does he quote the actual text of Seth's February 24 letter, the only document that even arguably evidences a promise to pay for Levi's expenses. Justice Parker even attributed motives to Seth Wyman that may not fairly explain Wyman's behavior. Wyman, he wrote, was "influenced by a transient feeling of gratitude." He made a promise and then was "determined to break this promise, and is willing to have his case appear on record as a strong example of particular injustice sometimes necessary resulting from the operation of general rules." As noted, the facts suggest less despicable motives. Wyman did not make the promise and thus never "determined" to break any promise. Wyman's "transient feeling of gratitude" might have been a sincere expression of willingness to pay for Levi's future expenses, but not his past ones. Wyman's "willing-

148. 8 Ala. 131 (1845).

163. Justice Parker was born in Boston on June 17, 1768. He graduated from Harvard in 1786, entered the practice of law, and in 1796 was elected a member of Congress. He declined re-election in 1798 and was instead appointed Marshal of the District of Maine. In 1806 he was appointed to the supreme judicial court, and in 1814 he was appointed Chief Justice of Massachusetts. He was the first Royall Professor of Law at Harvard University, and his plan for the establishment of a Harvard Law School was adopted in 1817. Parker served as Chief Justice until the end of his life, in 1830. . . .

This Isaac Parker is not to be confused with the "hanging judge" Isaac Parker of the American West. See, e.g., Henry Sinclair Drago, Outlaws on Horseback 114 (1964) (noting that the western Judge Parker sentenced 88 men to death by hanging).

ness" to stand as an example of an "injustice" was more likely a determination to fight for his rights. . . .

If Seth Wyman did not make the promise in question, he certainly would not have been liable for breach of contract and probably would not have been liable in restitution either. Daniel Mills would have had to overcome both the traditional requirement that Seth Wyman himself benefited by Mills's acts and the presumption that Mills acted gratuitously. Because Seth was no longer legally responsible for the necessaries of his adult son, it seems unlikely that a court would have held him liable in restitution. Indeed the courts in Mills did not even appear to consider this a possibility. That Levi actually survived adds some weight to Mills's restitution claim, but probably not enough to overcome these doctrinal hurdles.

If Wyman did make the promise in question, however, the court let him off too easily, and in so doing missed an opportunity to reform the doctrine of consideration. The law on moral obligation was not as settled at the time as the court implied. English authorities were still struggling with the scope of moral-obligation doctrine and indeed with the consideration doctrine itself. In a 1765 case, the influential Lord Mansfield announced a drastic reform of the doctrine of consideration. When an agreement was reduced to writing, he said, "there was no objection to the want of consideration . . . In commercial cases amongst merchants, the want of consideration is not an objection."[176] In 1778 this new rule was rejected by English authorities,[177] but Mansfield's view retained lingering importance in America, both because news of the rejection did not reach America until after the turn of the century and because of the "congeniality of Mansfield's . . . views to American judges."[178]

---

176. Pillans & Rose v. Van Mierop & Hopkins, 3 Burr. 1663, 1669 (K.B. 1765). Oddly, the report of *Mills v. Wyman* indicates that Mills's attorney did not cite Van Mierop but that Wyman's attorney did - just the opposite of what one might expect. See *Mills*, 20 Mass. (3 Pick.) at 208. Brigham, counsel for Wyman, apparently sought to distinguish the case on the grounds that a promissory note is a "privileged contract" and not subject to the normal consideration rules. See id.

177. Rann v. Huges, 101 Eng. Rep. 1014 (1778) ("If [contracts] be . . . written and not specialties, they are parol, and a consideration must be proved.")).

178. See Morton J. Horwitz, The Historical Foundations of Modern Contract Law, 87 Harv. L. Rev. 917, 943 (1974).

Moreover, Lord Mansfield kept up his assault on the consideration doctrine and, in particular, on moral-obligation doctrine. In a 1782 case he declared: "Where a man is under a moral obligation, which no Court of Law or Equity can inforce, and promises, the honesty and rectitude of the thing is a consideration."[180] Lord Mansfield gave as examples promises to revive antecedent debts, but his statement of the "rule" was not explicitly limited to these cases. Lord Mansfield's broad statement of the rule met with resistance. In the early nineteenth century, writers went to great trouble to show that Lord Mansfield really intended to limit his dictum to cases of antecedent debt. In 1802, for example, the reporter of the English case *Wennall v. Adney* wrote, "Lord Mansfield appears to have used the term moral obligation not as expressive of any vague and undefined claim arising from the nearness of relationship, but of those imperative duties which would be enforceable by law, were it not for some positive rule."[181]

. . . . Chief Justice Parker chose to side with the reporter in *Wennall*, adopting his theory that moral-obligation doctrine extended only to promises based on pre-existing debt. . . . In so doing, Chief Justice Parker explicitly rejected his own 1813 opinion in *Bowers v. Hurd*,[189] in which the Supreme Judicial Court enforced a promise based solely on past good deeds. In *Bowers*, one Sarah Thompson gave promissory notes to three of her friends, including the plaintiff. Thompson wished to leave something for the plaintiff because the plaintiff had been a good friend and had "frequently attended" Thompson when she was ill. Indeed, Thompson felt an "obligation" to leave something for the plaintiff even though no antecedent debt was involved. Thompson gave promissory notes in order to avoid the expense of drafting a will. After she passed away, her executor refused to honor the notes, and one of the promisees sued. At trial, the defense pleaded lack of consideration, but the judge "directed the jury to lay that evidence out of the case, and

180. Hawkes v. Saunders, 98 Eng.Rep. 1091 (1782).
181. Wennall v. Adney, 3 Bos. & Pul. 247, 249 n. (1802). He added this: "However general the expressions used by Lord Mansfield may at first sight appear, yet the instances adduced by him as illustrative of the rule of law, do not carry that rule beyond . . . its proper limits" of antecedent debt. Id.
189. 10 Mass. 427 (1813).

that a verdict might notwithstanding be found for the plaintiff."[195] It was.

On appeal, the Supreme Judicial Court affirmed.[196] Justice Parker, writing for the court, rejected the executor's contention that the promise lacked consideration. He acknowledged that consideration was a defense to enforcement of a note between the original two parties.[198] But he offered a radical theory of consideration:

> Now, we do not admit that, when one voluntarily makes a written promise to another to pay a sum of money, the promise can be avoided merely by proving there was no legal and valuable consideration subsisting at the time; any more than, if he actually paid over the amount of such note, he can recover it back again because he repents of his generosity.

In other words, Justice Parker analogized a promise to delivery of a gift. This is precisely the analogy that consideration doctrine supposedly rejects. A gratuitous promise is revocable absent reliance; a gratuitous gift is irrevocable. Justice Parker went on to justify enforcement of this gratuitous promise by stressing the sham recital of consideration in the note. By this recital, the promisor has "precluded himself and his representatives from denying a consideration, when he has under his hand acknowledged one." The court's refusal to weigh parol evidence showing lack of consideration was later overruled, though the Massachusetts courts insisted the *Bowers* case itself was correctly decided on "other principles."[201] ... *Bowers* doesn't fit neatly into the universe of moral obligation described by the same Chief Justice Parker in *Mills v. Wyman*. *Bowers* suggests that moral obligation could bind a gratuitous promise that did not revive an antecedent debt.

Not surprisingly, Davis & Allen, counsel for Mills, cited *Bowers* prominently in support of Mills' position. "If there was no moral obligation on the part of the defendant, it is sufficient that his promise was in writing, and was made deliberately, with a knowl-

195. Id. at 428.
196. See id. at 430.
198. See id. at 429.
201. See Hill v. Buckminster, 5 Pick. 393 (1828).

edge of all the circumstances."[202] Mills' lawyer added: "A man has a right to give away his property," to which Chief Justice Parker replied, "There is a distinction between giving and promising." Mills' counsel responded by pointing out that *Bowers* "does not take that distinction." To which Justice Parker replied ominously: "That case has been doubted." David Brigham, counsel for Seth Wyman, distinguished *Bowers* in his written pleadings by contending that a promissory note that recites consideration is a "privileged contract." It is not clear whether Chief Justice Parker accepted this distinction or simply thought his own earlier opinion was wrong. His opinion in *Mills* did not discuss his opinion in *Bowers*. Thus Chief Justice Parker passed up an opportunity to build on his holding in *Bowers* and to establish that a promise founded on moral obligation should always be binding if there is sufficient evidence of intent to be bound.

One unanswered question is whether Chief Justice Parker's narrow doctrine of moral obligation comported with the view taken by early American juries, who until around 1810 had enjoyed broad powers to find the law as well as the facts. The anecdotal evidence from *Mills v. Wyman* itself might suggest not. Despite doubts that Seth Wyman made the promise at all, Bernard Fowler and the other citizens on the jury in *Mills v. Wyman* had no trouble finding him liable. Without a thorough study of the behavior of juries in the eighteenth and early nineteenth centuries, no definitive conclusion can be reached. However, the demise of the jury's law-finding power suggests that there was a vacuum in American common law and that Justice Parker and his contemporaries had a unique opportunity to fill that void. As Professor Simpson puts it, the "dethronement of the jury" was "accompanied by the generation or reception of law in order not so much to replace or transform older doctrine as to provide law where before there was little or none."[208]

Insofar as there was doubt about the "reception" of Mansfield's broad rule into American law, *Mills* helped seal its fate. Certainly that is how *Mills* would later be remembered by Massachusetts courts and, even later, by national commentators — as the case

202. *Mills*, 20 Mass. at 207.
208. Simpson, supra note 144, at 600.

that settled doubts about the scope of the moral-obligation rule.[209] In the 180 years since the decision in *Mills*, there is no mistaking its influence. It is one of the two or three leading American cases on moral obligation as consideration, along with cases like *Webb v. McGowin* (Chapter 5) and *Harrington v. Taylor* (Chapter 6). *Mills* is a staple of the first-year contracts curriculum and is reprinted in virtually every American casebook on the subject. Its facts are the basis of the first illustration to section 86 of the most recent Restatement of Contracts.[213] . . .

The most important factor in *Mills'* rise to prominence was its inclusion in Langdell's first casebook on contracts.[227] Langdell devoted sixty-seven pages of his casebook to the subject of "Moral Consideration" and included a full report of *Mills*.[228] Although *Mills* was just one of more than a dozen cases in this section of the book, it was the first American moral-obligation case encountered by the student, and its facts were among the most accessible.

Mills has not left the contracts curriculum since. . . . Surely *Mills*, like *Webb*, deserves its place in the casebooks. The facts of *Mills*, even if inaccurately rendered, are compelling, and the opinion, even if misguided, is provocative.

But does the rule in *Mills* still deserve its place as a "fixed star in the jurisprudential firmament"?[230] What, if any, theory of moral obligation justifies the *Mills* doctrine? . . . . [The article goes on to criticize not only the doctrine in *Mills*, but also the doctrine of consideration as a whole. It notes that civil-law systems and public international law generally do not require consideration, and it concludes by arguing that a writing requirement or some other formality would be a better test for enforcing promises.]

209. See Dearborn v. Bowman, 36 Mass. 155, 158 (1841) ("The rule of law seems to be now well settled — though it may have formerly been left in doubt. . . .") (citing *Mills* and other cases).

213. See Restatement (Second) of Contracts 86, cmt. a, illus. 1 (1981).

227. See Christopher Columbus Langdell, A Selection of Cases on the Law of Contracts 367 (Boston: Little, Brown & Co., 1871).

228. See id. at 339-406.

230. Grant Gilmore, The Death of Contract 83 (1974) (referring to *Hadley v. Baxendale*).

FURTHER QUESTIONS

1. Recall that Alice Sullivan, the plaintiff in *Sullivan v. O'Connor* (in Chapter 1), felt betrayed by the legal system even though she won her case. Do you suppose Seth Wyman, the winner in *Mills v. Wyman*, had reason to feel the same way? Consider the opening sentence of the opinion in *Mills*: "General rules of law established for the protection and security of honest and fair-minded men, who may inconsiderately make promises without any equivalent, will sometimes screen men of a different character from engagements which they are bound in foro conscientioe to perform." The court adds that Seth "has determined to break this promise, and is willing to have his case appear on record as a strong example of particular injustice sometimes necessarily resulting from the operation of general rules." Was Seth Wyman a man of a "different character" from "honest and fair-minded men"?

2. Seth Wyman's initial defense was not lack of consideration, but rather that he hadn't made any promise to pay for services already rendered. Seth's lawyer argued that Seth's letter was bargaining for future services by Daniel Mills, and Seth should be bound only to the extent that Mills rendered any such services. Why did the trial court and the Supreme Judicial Court reject Seth's reading of the letter?

3. Chief Justice Parker is obliged to explain his judgment, and he offers a carefully reasoned opinion benefiting from his study of the law and his research of relevant precedents. The jury is in a quite different position. A group of laymen, they are required to explain nothing. Note that the jury's view of *Mills v. Wyman* differed from that of both the trial and appellate judges.

Why have juries in civil cases? Do they add any capabilities or compensate for any limitations in judges? Why not simply have Judge Howe (the trial judge) decide this case? Note that the United Kingdom, from which the United States inherited the jury, has done away with the jury in most civil cases.

4. "In the colonial era . . . juries had the power to find the law as well as the facts. But the jury's law-finding role . . . disappeared . . . ." Why do you think this happened? (Recall the discussion of *Hadley v. Baxendale*.) Does it matter? (Recall *Sullivan v. O'Connor*.) If it

does matter, is the demise of the jury's law-finding role good or bad (especially considering your answer to #1, above)?

5. Who is the best decision-maker here: Chief Justice Parker, Judge Howe, or the jury? By what standard do you answer this question? Who amongst these three "made the decision" in *Mills v. Wyman*? If you think more than one did, can you identify the parts each contributed?

6. As noted, Massachusetts in 1825 compelled losing litigants to pay costs, including the prevailing party's attorney's fees. This is still the prevailing rule in Britain. The modern American rule does not generally require payment of attorney's fees. Can you identify the different biases that will result in the two systems? Which do you prefer?

7. How did the Supreme Judicial Court come to the conclusion that Levi Wyman had died in Mills' care? Or, as the SJC put it, that Mills had given Levi "shelter and comfort until he died"? Written depositions in the record clearly state that Levi left town after the litigation, and the foregoing essay presents additional evidence that Levi lived for many more years. What kind of capability problems could possibly account for this confusion over the facts?

8. Why should consideration be the test of enforceability of promises at all? In much of the rest of the world, particularly civil-law countries, the test is not whether a promise is supported by consideration, but whether the promisor made his or her promise in good faith and with sufficient formality to suggest intent to be legally bound. Does your perception of capability problems affect your view of whether the common law or the civil law position is preferable?

9. Note the discussion of *Bowers v. Hurd* in this essay. Can you identify some differences in the rules of procedure and of substance that apply in determining whether to enforce wills and contracts? Why are there such differences?

V. JOE WEBB v. N. FLOYD McGOWIN & JOSEPH F. McGOWIN, AS EXECUTORS OF ESTATE OF J. GREELEY McGOWIN

WEBB v. McGOWIN
Court of Appeals of Alabama, 1935.
27 Ala. App. 82, 168 So. 196.

Action by Joe Webb against N. Floyd McGowin and Joseph F. McGowin, as executors of the estate of J. Greeley McGowin, deceased. From a judgment of nonsuit, plaintiff appeals.

Reversed and remanded.

BRICKEN, Presiding Judge.

This action is in assumpsit. The complaint as originally filed was amended. The demurrers to the complaint as amended were sustained, and because of this adverse ruling by the court the plaintiff took a nonsuit, and the assignment of errors on this appeal are predicated upon said action or ruling of the court.

A fair statement of the case presenting the questions for decision is set out in appellant's brief, which we adopt.

"On the 3d day of August, 1925, appellant while in the employ of the W. T. Smith Lumber Company, a corporation, and acting within the scope of his employment, was engaged in clearing the upper floor of mill No. 2 of the company. While so engaged he was in the act of dropping a pine block from the upper floor of the mill to the ground below; this being the usual and ordinary way of clearing the floor, and it being the duty of the plaintiff in the course of his employment to so drop it. The block weighed about 75 pounds.

"As appellant was in the act of dropping the block to the ground below, he was on the edge of the upper floor of the mill.

149

As he started to turn the block loose so that it would drop to the ground, he saw J. Greeley McGowin, testator of the defendants, on the ground below and directly under where the block would have fallen had appellant turned it loose. Had he turned it loose it would have struck McGowin with such force as to have caused him serious bodily harm or death. Appellant could have remained safely on the upper floor of the mill by turning the block loose and allowing it to drop, but had he done this the block would have fallen on McGowin and caused him serious injuries or death. The only safe and reasonable way to prevent this was for appellant to hold to the block and divert its direction in falling from the place where McGowin was standing and the only safe way to divert it so as to prevent its coming into contact with McGowin was for appellant to fall with it to the ground below. Appellant did this, and by holding to the block and falling with it to the ground below, he diverted the course of its fall in such way that McGowin was not injured. In thus preventing the injuries to McGowin appellant himself received serious bodily injuries, resulting in his right leg being broken, the heel of his right foot torn off and his right arm broken. He was badly crippled for life and rendered unable to do physical or mental labor.

"On September 1, 1925, in consideration of appellant having prevented him from sustaining death or serious bodily harm and in consideration of the injuries appellant had received, McGowin agreed with him to care for and maintain him for the remainder of appellant's life at the rate of $15 every two weeks from the time he sustained his injuries to and during the remainder of appellant's life; it being agreed that McGowin would pay this sum to appellant for his maintenance. Under the agreement McGowin paid or caused to be paid to appellant the sum so agreed on up until McGowin's death on January 1, 1934. After his death the payments were continued to and including January 27, 1934, at which time they were discontinued. Thereupon plaintiff brought suit to recover the unpaid installments accruing up to the time of the bringing of the suit.

"The material averments of the different counts of the original complaint and the amended complaint are predicated upon the foregoing statement of facts."

In other words, the complaint as amended averred in substance: (1) That on August 3, 1925, appellant saved J. Greeley McGowin, appellee's testator, from death or grievous bodily harm; (2) that in doing so appellant sustained bodily injury crippling him for life; (3) that in consideration of the services rendered and the injuries received by appellant, McGowin agreed to care for him the remainder of appellant's life, the amount to be paid being $ 15 every two weeks; (4) that McGowin complied with this agreement until he died on January 1, 1934, and the payments were kept up to January 27, 1934, after which they were discontinued.

The action was for the unpaid installments accruing after January 27, 1934, to the time of the suit.

The principal grounds of demurrer to the original and amended complaint are: (1) It states no cause of action; (2) its averments show the contract was without consideration; (3) it fails to allege that McGowin had, at or before the services were rendered, agreed to pay appellant for them; (4) the contract declared on is void under the statute of frauds.

1. The averments of the complaint show that appellant saved McGowin from death or grievous bodily harm. This was a material benefit to him of infinitely more value than any financial aid he could have received. Receiving this benefit, McGowin became morally bound to compensate appellant for the services rendered. Recognizing his moral obligation, he expressly agreed to pay appellant as alleged in the complaint and complied with this agreement up to the time of his death; a period of more than 8 years.

Had McGowin been accidentally poisoned and a physician, without his knowledge or request, had administered an antidote, thus saving his life, a subsequent promise by McGowin to pay the physician would have been valid. Likewise, McGowin's agreement as disclosed by the complaint to compensate appellant for saving him from death or grievous bodily injury is valid and enforceable.

Where the promisee cares for, improves, and preserves the property of the promisor, though done without his request, it is sufficient consideration for the promisor's subsequent agreement to pay for the service, because of the material benefit received. Pittsburg Vitrified Paving & Building Brick Co. v. Cerebus Oil Co., 79 Kan. 603, 100 P. 631; Edson v. Poppe, 24 S.D. 466, 124 N.W.

441, 26 L.R.A.(N.S.) 534; Drake v. Bell, 26 Misc. 237, 55 N.Y.S. 945.

In Boothe v. Fitzpatrick, 36 Vt. 681, the court held that a promise by defendant to pay for the past keeping of a bull which had escaped from defendant's premises and been cared for by plaintiff was valid, although there was no previous request, because the subsequent promise obviated that objection; it being equivalent to a previous request. On the same principle, had the promisee saved the promisor's life or his body from grievous harm, his subsequent promise to pay for the services rendered would have been valid. Such service would have been far more material than caring for his bull. Any holding that saving a man from death or grievous bodily harm is not a material benefit sufficient to uphold a subsequent promise to pay for the service, necessarily rests on the assumption that saving life and preservation of the body from harm have only a sentimental value. The converse of this is true. Life and preservation of the body have material, pecuniary values, measurable in dollars and cents. Because of this, physicians practice their profession charging for services rendered in saving life and curing the body of its ills, and surgeons perform operations. The same is true as to the law of negligence, authorizing the assessment of damages in personal injury cases based upon the extent of the injuries, earnings, and life expectancies of those injured.

In the business of life insurance, the value of a man's life is measured in dollars and cents according to his expectancy, the soundness of his body, and his ability to pay premiums. The same is true as to health and accident insurance.

It follows that if, as alleged in the complaint, appellant saved J. Greeley McGowin from death or grievous bodily harm, and McGowin subsequently agreed to pay him for the service rendered, it became a valid and enforceable contract.

2. It is well settled that a moral obligation is a sufficient consideration to support a subsequent promise to pay where the promisor has received a material benefit, although there was no original duty or liability resting on the promisor. . . . State ex rel. Bayer v. Funk, 105 Ore. 134, 199 P. 592, 209 P. 113, 25 A.L.R. 625, 634; Hawkes v. Saunders, 1 Cowper 290; Park Falls State Bank v. Fordyce, 206 Wis. 628, 238 N.W. 516, 79 A.L. R. 1339 [citations omitted]. In the case of State ex rel. Bayer v. Funk, supra, the court

held that a moral obligation is a sufficient consideration to support an executory promise where the promisor has received an actual pecuniary or material benefit for which he subsequently expressly promised to pay.

The case at bar is clearly distinguishable from that class of cases where the consideration is a mere moral obligation or con-scientious duty unconnected with receipt by promisor of benefits of a material or pecuniary nature. Park Falls State Bank v. Fordyce, supra. Here the promisor received a material benefit constituting a valid consideration for his promise.

3. Some authorities hold that, for a moral obligation to support a subsequent promise to pay, there must have existed a prior legal or equitable obligation, which for some reason had become unen-forceable, but for which the promisor was still morally bound. This rule, however, is subject to qualification in those cases where the promisor, having received a material benefit from the promisee, is morally bound to compensate him for the services rendered and in consideration of this obligation promises to pay. In such cases the subsequent promise to pay is an affirmance or ratification of the services rendered carrying with it the presumption that a previous request for the service was made. [Citations omitted.]

Under the decisions above cited, McGowin's express promise to pay appellant for the services rendered was an affirmance or ratification of what appellant had done raising the presumption that the services had been rendered at McGowin's request.

[handwritten margin notes: "Promised to pay", "McGowin requested this… + promised"]

4. The averments of the complaint show that in saving McGowin from death or grievous bodily harm, appellant was crip-pled for life. This was part of the consideration of the contract de-clared on. McGowin was benefited. Appellant was injured. Benefit to the promisor or injury to the promisee is a sufficient legal con-sideration for the promisor's agreement to pay. Fisher v. Bartlett, 8 Greenl. 122, 22 Am. Dec. 225; State ex rel. Bayer v. Funk, supra.

5. Under the averments of the complaint the services rendered by appellant were not gratuitous. The agreement of McGowin to pay and the acceptance of payment by appellant conclusively shows the contrary.

6. The contract declared on was not void under the statute of frauds (Code 1923, § 8034). The demurrer on this ground was not well taken, 25 R.C.L. 456, 457 and 470, § 49.

The cases of Shaw v. Boyd, 1 Stew. & P. 83, and Duncan v. Hall, 9 Ala. 128, are not in conflict with the principles here announced. In those cases the lands were owned by the United States at the time the alleged improvements were made, for which subsequent purchasers from the government agreed to pay. These subsequent purchasers were not the owners of the lands at the time the improvements were made. Consequently, they could not have been made for their benefit.

From what has been said, we are of the opinion that the court below erred in the ruling complained of; that is to say, in sustaining the demurrer, and for this error the case is reversed and remanded.

Reversed and remanded.

SAMFORD, Judge (concurring).

The questions involved in this case are not free from doubt, and perhaps the strict letter of the rule, as stated by judges, though not always in accord, would bar a recovery by plaintiff, but following the principle announced by Chief Justice Marshall in Hoffman v. Porter, Fed. Cas. No. 6,577, 2 Brock. 156, 159, where he says, "I do not think that law ought to be separated from justice, where it is at most doubtful," I concur in the conclusions reached by the court.

FIRST QUESTIONS

1. Do you believe that the outcomes in *Webb v. McGowin* and *Mills v. Wyman* can be reconciled?

2. The method of the majority opinion in *Webb* reflects a belief in traditional legal positivism. Through research, the majority apparently discovers what the legal rule is, and then it applies that rule to the facts before it. Compare Justice Kaplan's opinion a generation later in *Sullivan v. O'Connor* (Chapter 1), in which he frankly weighs the competing merits of the reliance and expectancy measures of damages.

Judge Samford, in his concurrence, says that "the strict letter of the rule" might favor McGowin, but "justice" leads him to vote for Webb. Is his reasoning more like that of the majority opinion, or more like that of Justice Kaplan in *Sullivan*? Which is the role of a judge — to follow the "strict letter" of the law, or to do "justice"? To which view, or to what third view, do you think Justice Kaplan would say he subscribed?

3. "It is well settled," the court says in section 2 of its opinion, "that a moral obligation is a sufficient consideration to support a subsequent promise to pay where the promisor has received a material benefit, although there was no original duty or liability resting on the promisor." Do you think that rule was "well settled" then? Or now?

4. From reading the opinion, how much do you know about McGowin's promise? Was it written or oral? If it was oral, were there witnesses other than Webb and McGowin themselves? What was the precise language McGowin used? Did he make the promise directly to Joe Webb, or through an intermediary?

5. What if McGowin had made no promise at all? Would Webb have had a claim against him in restitution?

SUPPLEMENTARY COMMENTS*

Joe Webb

Joe Webb was not a man of means, and he did not leave behind an extensive paper trail. He was born in the southern United States shortly after the Civil War. One of his granddaughters remembers a "handed-down" story that Joe was adopted when he was very young. According to this story, Joe had been traveling with his family across Texas when he became very sick — too sick to make the rest of the trip across the state. The family was unable to care for Joe, and accordingly they gave him away to another family more capable of dealing with the illness and rearing a child. Joe's new stepfather eventually may have taken him to Tennessee.[1]

The 1920 U.S. Census shows a 53-year-old white man named Joe Webb living in the area of Chapman, Alabama — site of the mill in *Webb v. McGowin*.[2] That would mean he was about 58 years old at the time of the mill accident. It seems likely that this Census record identifies the Joe Webb of *Webb v. McGowin*.[3]

Charles Howard Webb has a "very clear" recollection of his grandfather Joe.[4] Charles was born in 1938, and thus he was about five or six years old when Joe died in 1943 or 1944. During that

*Geoff Watson compiled this account from documentary evidence and telephone interviews with descendants of the parties and others involved in the case. The authors are grateful to Lewis ("Pete") Hamilton, Esq., N. Floyd McGowin, Jr., Calvin Poole III, Esq., Elisha Poole, Esq., Charles Howard Webb, Jani Webb Daron, and Janice Hammond Webb for participating in telephone interviews about the case. We are especially grateful to Calvin Poole III for supplying us with a raft of helpful documents.

1. Telephone Interview with Janice Webb Hammond, Feb. 10, 2004.

2. Fourteenth Census of the U.S., Butler County, Ala., Precinct 3, vol. 8, E.D. 19, Sheet 5, Line 39 (Jan. 14-15, 1920).

3. The Census record lists Joe's wife as "Emmie Webb." Joe Webb's granddaughter, Janice Webb Hammond, says her grandmother's maiden name was Emma Lessie Graves, though she was always known as Lessie. Likewise, the Census record lists a James Webb age "0/12," which presumably meant a newborn, and Janice's father's name was James Eugene Webb. The only disconnect is that James Eugene Webb's children are sure their father was born several years earlier than 1920. E.g., Telephone Interview with Janice Webb Hammond, Feb. 10, 2004; Telephone interview, Charles Howard Webb, Feb. 11, 2004; e-mail of Jani Suzanne Webb, May 17, 2004 (putting James Eugene Webb's date of birth at Nov. 27, 1913).

4. Telephone interview, Charles Howard Webb, Feb. 11, 2004.

period, Joe Webb lived in a house about a mile and a half outside Georgiana, a small town not far from Chapman, the company town run by W.T. Smith Lumber Company. (Hank Williams, the country singer, was born near Georgiana; the Hank Williams Museum is located in Georgiana today. Williams also lived in Chapman for a time, and one of his songs mentions Chapman by name.[5]) Charles lived in Georgiana itself, and he made frequent visits to his grandparents' home.

To five- or six-year-old Charles, grandpa Joe seemed "very imposing," but today Charles guesses that Joe was about six feet tall. Charles recalls that Joe was thin but not "emaciated or undernourished." He had a full head of brown hair, but no facial hair or glasses. Charles says he thinks Joe could read and write, but Charles can't recall ever seeing him reading. Joe enjoyed listening to the news on his battery-powered radio, though it produced "more static than news." Charles remembers that his grandfather was fun to talk with — that he constantly injected humor into conversation.

Charles remembers that Joe didn't get around much. He was hobbled by his injuries from the accident at the W.T. Smith Lumber Company. He had a limp, and "he was always in pain." He didn't own a car or wagon. He was a Protestant, but he didn't go to church much, nor was he active in politics.

According to Charles, Joe and his wife were "very, very poor." Neither Joe nor his wife Lessie were healthy enough to work outside the home. The house itself was their main asset: it stood on several acres of farmland. As we'll see, both Charles and his sister Janice are convinced that this property was provided by J. Greeley McGowin after the accident reported in *Webb v. McGowin*.

Charles recalls that Joe and his wife grew their own food, maintained their own canning house, and had a "traditional Southern diet." A typical meal would include cornbread, peas, and tomatoes, but Sunday dinner would feature chicken as well. Charles recalls going there every Sunday after church for dinner. Everyone wore their Sunday best, Charles recalls, but he never saw Grandpa Joe in a coat and tie. "I don't even now if he owned one," Charles says.

---

5. See Hank Williams, "The Log Train," The Complete Hank Williams (Mercury Records 2000).

Charles enjoyed visiting his grandfather because of his great sense of humor and the fun "tricks he used to play on me." Joe gave young Charles chewing tobacco on at least two occasions, and Joe enjoyed watching Charles squirm as he chomped on the wad. Joe and Charles had spitting contests, aiming for one of the fireplaces in the house. Joe used to make his own blackberry wine, and he enjoyed giving young Charles wine — "more than a sip" — because "he used to like to hear me talk when I'd had a few drinks."

Joe teased young Charles in one other way. In those years, Joe Webb's house had no electricity or indoor plumbing, and Joe enjoyed scaring Charles just before Charles made his nightly trip outside to the outhouse. Charles recalls:

> I was afraid of the outhouse after it got dark. You could see the spider webs during the day time. [Joe] used to tell me about gooses and goblins before. I'd always have to go at night. Like clockwork. He would tell me, as I was getting my coat on, about the gooses and the goblins. I didn't know what a goose or goblin was, but I knew it was bad. He'd convince me it was best to take a lantern and go out in the pasture. He'd start telling me stories that would scare the hell out of me.[6]

J. Greeley McGowin

James Greeley McGowin was the patriarch of what was (and still is) one of south Alabama's most prominent families. Mr. Greeley, as he was often known, was born on June 24, 1871, on a farm in southern Alabama.[7] While he was growing up, Greeley worked for his father, who was in the timber business. Greeley was raised as a Universalist, and he developed very strong ties to his

6. Telephone Interview with Charles Howard Webb, Feb. 11, 2004.

7. His employees also referred to him as "Mr. Greel." John Applegate, The W. T. Smith Lumber Co. 34 (2000). For more on Mr. Greeley's childhood, see Elwood R. Maunder, Oral History with Earl M. McGowin, Mar. 17, 1976 (Forest History Society, 1976), [hereafter Earl McGowin Oral History], at 3; Elwood R. Maunder, Oral History with N. Floyd McGowin, Mar. 16, 1976 (Forest History Society, 1976) [hereafter Floyd McGowin Oral History], at 2. These and other oral histories are available at the website of the Duke University library. See http://www.lib.duke.edu.

church.[8] He did not receive much formal education, although one of his sons recalled that he did spend "a few weeks in a business school" in Lexington, Kentucky.[9]

Nonetheless, Mr. Greeley proved to be a quick study in the ways of business. In 1892, when he was just 21, he and his brother-in-law opened a mercantile business that did very well. He made enough money to acquire a nice home in Brewton, and in 1898 he married Essie Theresa Stallworth, a member of another prominent south Alabama family. A portrait of McGowin made around that time depicts a thin young man with neatly parted dark hair and a trim moustache.[10] Eventually the McGowins had six children. In 1903 Greeley sold his interest in the mercantile company. In 1905 he and his brothers acquired a controlling interest in the W. T. Smith Lumber Company in Chapman, Alabama. According to one disputed account, the seller, Mr. Smith, said he was happy to have "unloaded that lemon in Chapman."[11]

Some lemon. The company thrived, at least initially. It did face stiff competition, and it had to adjust its business strategy to accommodate a rapidly changing economy. In the early days it sold timber to markets in New England, but the opening of the Panama Canal brought competition from West Coast lumber companies, and the company's sales shifted to the interior of the country.[12]

Mr. Greeley served as the company's secretary and treasurer, and he became its President in 1925 — the year in which Joe Webb deflected a pine block that was falling toward Greeley's head. Greeley remained President until his death in 1934. Even during the Depression he was able to keep the lumber mills going.[13] When asked how and why he managed to stay in business, he wrote: "[I]f we shut down there is nowhere for our men to make a living."[14]

8. See, e.g., McGowin is Named as Church Official, Greenville Advocate, Dec. 1, 1926, at 6, col. 2.

9. Earl McGowin Oral History, at 3, 4.

10. Appleyard, The W.T. Smith Lumber Co., supra note 7, at 33.

11. Id. at 6. Smith's sons later told *Life* magazine that Smith had never said that. Id.

12. Earl McGowin Oral History, at 10; Floyd McGowin Oral History, at 6.

13. Floyd McGowin Oral History, at 21-22.

14. Id. at 22 (quoting letter of J. Greeley McGowin to S. E. Moreton, May 10, 1932). In fact, the McGowins kept the company in business until 1966, when they sold it to Union Camp. See generally id. at 261-69.

The McGowins, like their predecessor Mr. Smith, ran Chapman as a company town. They provided housing, schools, and churches for the entire workforce — although white people and black people lived in separate neighborhoods and attended separate schools and churches.[15] Only a "handful" of people in Chapman ever voted in local elections, and most of these were whites. "Very few blacks voted."[16] But McGowin "was strongly opposed to the periodic activities of the Ku Klux Klan in neighboring communities. He kept them out of Chapman."[17] While some area mills employed all-white or all-black labor forces, the McGowins employed about an even mix. Mr. Greeley's son, Earl, had "no recollection" of any "racial unrest" during his childhood.[18] Likewise, labor relations seem to have been peaceful during McGowin's tenure. The mills at W.T. Smith Lumber Company weren't unionized until after World War II.[19]

Mr. Greeley was regarded as an honest, hard-working man who had high expectations of others. One of his sons recalls him as a pretty strict father. "He made us work. He was a keen disciplinarian. We didn't dare contradict our father. We didn't dare argue with him about a thing."[20] He is said to have loved his family and his home, and while he took his family to the Mississippi coast on vacation many summers, he generally didn't like to travel. He enjoyed relaxing at a farm he bought near Chapman. He fished; he raised peacock, horses, deer, guineas, and turkeys; he hunted quail; and he grew tangerines, pecans, pears, and peaches.[21]

McGowin was conservative in bearing and in his politics, "one of the few in Butler County who may have voted Republican in na-

15. Floyd McGowin Oral History, at 6-10. See also Appleyard, The W.T. Smith Lumber Co., at 209-10 (depicting the "white neighborhood," "colored neighborhood," "White School," "Colored School," etc.); id. at 206 (quoting "one old timer") ("The attendance of the colored church was generally better than at the white church").

16. Appleyard, The W.T. Smith Lumber Co., at 206.

17. Id. at 37.

18. Earl McGowin Oral History, at 15.

19. Appleyard, The W.T. Smith Lumber Co., at 253.

20. Earl McGowin Oral History, at 16.

21. Appleyard, The W.T. Smith Lumber Co., at 35-36; N. Floyd McGowin Oral History, 15-16.

tional elections."[22] He "kept a picture of President Calvin Coolidge in his office."[23] While Mr. Greeley didn't always like the laws emanating from the federal government, he taught his children always to respect the law, even laws they disliked.[24] Less than six months before he died, he opined at length on needed reforms in Alabama government, but he was reluctant to comment on the judiciary: "Fortunately," he wrote, "my contact with the courts has been relatively small. . . ."[25]

McGowin's death was, not surprisingly, front-page news in Greenville.[26] Newspapers eulogized him as one of Alabama's "really great men," a man who loved his employees and whose employees loved him.[27] The death of the lumberman was "like the fall of the mightiest pine in all the forests of Alabama."[28]

The accident

There are a variety of accounts of the accident in the lumber mill at the W. T. Smith Lumber Company on the morning of August 3, 1925. These accounts differ significantly, at least in emphasis. The Court of Appeals opinion simply relied on the statement of facts in Webb's appellate brief, which in turn reiterated the facts alleged in the complaint. This was appropriate given that the case went up on demurrer, in which the court must assume the facts in the complaint are true. According to this statement of facts, Webb diverted the falling pine block in order to save McGowin from serious injury or death, and in so doing Webb was "badly crippled for life" and "unable to do physical or mental labor."

22. Appleyard, The W.T. Smith Lumber Co., at 37. See also Division of Voters is Unnatural — McGowin, Greenville Advocate, Dec. 22, 1926, at 4, col. 2 (arguing that conservative Southern Democrats might find a more comfortable home in the Republican Party).

23. Appleyard, The W.T. Smith Lumber Co., at 37.

24. Earl McGowin Oral History, at 11.

25. M'Gowin Tells Editors of Necessary Reforms, Greenville Advocate, July 26, 1933, at 2, col. 1, 6.

26. Butler County Loses Outstanding Citizen, Greenville Advocate, Jan. 5, 1934, at 1, col. 5.

27. See Appleyard, The W.T. Smith Lumber Co., at 294 (reprinting various newspaper obituaries).

28. John Temple Graves II, This Morning, Birmingham Age-Herald, reprinted in id. at 295 & 296.

Charles Howard Webb, Webb's grandson, visited the mill and has this understanding of the facts:

> [T]hey would take big logs and turn it into lumber. Now, part of a log, when they turn it into lumber, turns into waste. You have slabs that are cut off, which is the bark and stuff, and all that becomes . . . some of it is salvageable . . . . All of that waste was put on a conveyor that went several hundred feet away from the plant, and several feet high, to a burn pile. They had a chain, and pieces of metal attached to that chain, pick up scrap, take all way to end, drop into burn pile. To support the structure that the chain was on, you had a post . . . . and sometimes lumber not properly placed on that chain would turn sideways, get caught on the post [and] actually stop the chain from moving. It would be a logjam.
>
> My grandfather had to go up and free up a logjam. Well, the piece of lumber that was causing it was big enough that he could just barely pick it up. He got it to the point where he could throw it off the chain and dispose of it. As he was getting ready to throw it, Mr. McGowin was on the spot where it would have landed. So he diverted it to go away from McGowin, and in the process he fell . . . . He followed the piece of lumber down. It resulted in a serious injury to [his] hip and leg. It was probably something [that would be] correctable today. [But it] was not [then].[29]

But a much shorter, more "pro-defense" version of the facts appears in a Workmen's Compensation Report, apparently filed by W. T. Smith Lumber Co. on September 26, 1925 — less than two months after the accident, and three and a half weeks after McGowin allegedly made his promise. The Report states simply: "In building saw mill when sawing a piece of timber off he was holding it up and he became over balanced and fell to the ground."[30] The Report makes no mention of any altruistic motive on Webb's

---

29. Telephone interview, Charles Howard Webb, Feb. 11, 2004.

30. Employer's First Report of Injury for which Compensation is Claimed or Paid Under the Workmen's Comp. Law of Alabama, Sept. 25, 1925, § C, ¶ 3.

part. It does not indicate that Webb was trying to save McGowin's life. It simply says Webb lost his balance. Then again, the Report form doesn't leave much space for a more elaborate description.

What's more, one of the estate's initial grounds for demurrer was that the complaint failed to allege that Mr. Greeley "was, at or before the plaintiff received his injuries, in danger of suffering death or serious bodily harm."[31] Indeed, the original complaint alleged only that Webb suffered his injuries "in attempting to save ... J. Greeley McGowin from death or serious bodily harm. Later an amended complaint deleted the word "attempting" and alleged flatly that Webb "saved" McGowin from death or serious harm.[32]

Privately, too, the estate's lawyer seemed reluctant to concede that Webb had saved McGowin's life. In a letter to a colleague seeking advice about the Statute of Frauds issue in the case, Calvin Poole acknowledged the plaintiff's allegation that Webb had saved McGowin's life, but then described the "real facts" slightly differently. "[T]he timber was about to fall just as Mr. McGowin was passing under it, and the plaintiff intercepted the timber to keep it from falling and fell himself and was rather badly hurt."[33] In other words, Poole's version of the real facts didn't necessarily admit that Webb saved McGowin from death or serious injury.

In its later pleadings, however, the McGowin estate seemed to acknowledge at least that Webb acted to protect McGowin from "danger." In its answer, the estate generally denied the allegations of the complaint but also alleged

> that J. Greeley McGowin was inspecting the works and machinery of the plant of ... W. T. Smith Lumber Company; that the plaintiff was working on the upper floor of one of the mills of said lumber company removing some pieces of sawed-off timbers throwing the same to the ground floor; that as said J. Greeley McGowin approached the point

31. Demurrer to amended complaint, April 8, 1935, ¶ 11, in Record, Webb v. McGowin, Appeal to Ct. of App. Ala., Cir. Ct. No. 7565, at 3, filed May 8, 1935. Some later pleadings are also reprinted in Appleyard, The W.T. Smith Lumber Co., at 207-303.

32. Compare Complaint, Webb v. McGowin, Aug. 11, 1934, ¶ 1 ("attempting") with Amended Complaint, April 8, 1935, ¶ 4 ("saved").

33. Letter of Calvin Poole to T. M. Stevens, Jan. 11, 1935.

where plaintiff was working, the plaintiff was about to throw down a piece of timber; that plaintiff seeing the danger of [*sic*] said J. Greeley McGowin, undertook to catch or intercept the falling timber and lost his balance and fell, thereby sustaining the injuries complained of.[34]

There is general agreement that Webb's injuries were serious, and that as a result he was unable to work for the rest of his life. But the initial medical report, filed with the Workmen's Compensation report, described the injuries in somewhat less permanent terms. The attending physician, one Dr. James C. Watson[35] of the clinic in nearby Georgiana, Alabama, described a "Colle's fracture of right forearm; fracture of tibia and fibula 2" below knee (right); fracture of *Os calcis*."[36] (A Colle's fracture is a broken wrist; the *os calcis* is the heel bone.) Dr. Watson reported that Webb was confined to bed for four weeks, and that he was "yet incapacitated from earining [*sic*] wages because he is not fully recovered." But he predicted that the disability would exist only "about 6 to 8 weeks longer."[37] In fact, Webb never worked again, and the estate did not dispute the extent of his disability in the course of the litigation.

Incidentally, the medical professionals who treated Joe Webb most certainly did not work for free. According to the executor of Mr. Greeley's estate, W. T. Smith Co. paid Dr. Watson's bill of about $600 as well as a hospital fee of $62.90, and the company paid $7.50 to a Dr. Boswell and $50.00 to a Dr. Blue.[38]

A review of local newspapers from 1925 reveals no press reports of the accident. That's not to say that the W. T. Smith Lumber Company never made news. Four months before Joe Webb's accident, the *Greenville Advocate* published two short front-page

34. Answer, Webb v. McGowin, Cir. Ct. of Butler Co., Ala., 1936, ¶ 2.

35. No relation to either author. Dr. Watson was the great-great uncle of the present mayor of Georgiana, Alabama, Lynn Watson. Telephone interview with Mayor Lynn Watson, Mar. 5, 2004.

36. James C. Watson, M.D., Surgeon's First Report, W.T. Smith Lumber Co., Sept. 26, 1925, ¶ 4.

37. Id. ¶¶ 14 & 15.

38. Letter of N. Floyd McGowin to Calvin Poole, May 23, 1934.

stories about fires at the lumber company.[39] The McGowins themselves frequently made the papers, sometimes for business doings,
sometimes in the society pages.[40] Calvin Poole, attorney for the defendant in *Webb v. McGowin*, had his name in the paper on occasion, as did his family.[41] The trial judge's golf matches, as we'll see,
were reported in meticulous detail. But the accident that crippled
Joe Webb stayed out of the papers.[42]

The disputed promise

Whatever discrepancies there are about the circumstances of
the accident and injury, they pale in comparison to the disagreement over what, if any, promise McGowin made to Webb on
September 1, 1925. Again, the Court of Appeals opinion simply
adopted the plaintiff's allegations, as is to be expected on demurrer. The court reported that "in consideration of appellant having
prevented him from sustaining death or serious bodily harm and
in consideration of the injuries appellant had received, McGowin
agreed with him to care for and maintain him for the remainder of
appellant's life at the rate of $15 every two weeks . . . ."[43]

39. Smith Lumber Co. Has Two Fire Losses, Greenville Advocate, April 1, 1925,
at 1, col. 3; Smith Lumber Co. Has Fire Damage, Greenville Advocate, April 18,
1925, at 1, col. 4.

40. See, e.g., Mrs. McGowin Entertains, Greenville Advocate, May 13, 1925,
at 5, col. 2 (reporting on a wedding reception); Officers are Elected by Chapman Masons, Greenville Advocate, June 25, 1925, at 1, col. 4 (election of N.F.
McGowin); McGowin is Butler's Foremost Sportsman, Greenville Advocate, Mar.
17, 1926, at 1, col. 6.

41. See, e.g., Commercial Club Elects Officers, Greenville Advocate, April 8,
1925, at 1, col. 5 (listing C. Poole as one of the new members of the Chamber of
Commerce); Mrs. Poole Entertains at Bridge, Greenville Advocate, Aug. 8, 1925,
at 3, col. 2.

42. At this time, the *Greenville Advocate* was published twice a week. Here
are all the front-page headlines from the August 5 issue, the first to appear after
Webb's accident: "Cave-Ins Do Damage to Birmingham Homes"; "Road Con-
tractor is Seriously Injured"; "Dr. Bell to Preach Here Sunday Night"; "'Miss
Greenville' Writes of Gotham"; "Greenville to Have Another City School"; "Bibb
Graves Enters Governor's Race"; "State Veterans Will Meet at Tuscaloosa"; "S.S.
Conference to Meet in Selma"; "Negro Boy Drowned Near Halso's Mill"; "Rain-
bow Café is New Name Adopted"; and a report on driving hand-signals.

43. Webb v. McGowin, 168 So. at 197.

The parties, however, had sharply different positions on whether any promise was made at all, what its content was, and whether it was made by Mr. Greeley or one of his employees. In an answer to interrogatories, the plaintiff asserted that "the wife and daughter of the plaintiff . . . witnessed a statement made by Mr. McGowin to the Plaintiff" to pay Webb, in accordance with the court's reported version of the facts.[44] But the estate's position was that McGowin made no such promise at all; that at most he merely instructed his bookkeeper to pay Webb; and that the term of such payments was to be limited by the statutory period for Workmen's Compensation.

For some living descendants of Webb and McGowin, it is this aspect of the case — whether McGowin made a promise, and if so precisely what the promise contained — that seems most important. The technical issue decided — the presence or absence of consideration — is at best secondary to the non-lawyers in each family who look back on the decision now. When family members do ponder the legal issue, they might focus on the oral nature of the promise, or on questions of proof; they tend not to focus on the actual legal issue decided, consideration. To the families, the case isn't about consideration. To at least some of these family members, the case is about integrity.

In a telephone interview, for example, Joe Webb's grandson Charles Howard Webb went out of his way to emphasize that his grandfather was a man of honor. Toward the end of the interview, he interjected that there was one question the interviewer hadn't asked:

> Was Joe Webb an honest man? From my own experience
> . . . I remember comments from older gentlemen later on
> speaking very highly of [my] grandfather's integrity. It was
> always very important to me that they said good things.
> 'Yeah, I knew Joe Webb; a man of his word.'[45]

Even lawyers with a family connection to the case don't speak of it primarily in terms of consideration. The Greenville firm of Powell & Hamilton represented Joe Webb. Dempsey Powell prob-

44. Letter of Calvin Poole to T.M. Stevens, Jan. 11, 1935, at 2.
45. Telephone interview, Charles Howard Webb, Feb. 11, 2004.

ably did most of the legal work on the case, but C.E. Hamilton and his son were both active members of the firm at the time.[46] Pete Hamilton, grandson of C.E. Hamilton, recalls Pete's father describing the case to him this way:

> Greeley McGowin had started paying the guy, basically for saving his life. And then when [McGowin] died, his children quit paying [Webb]. My feeling all along was that just was the wrong thing to do. The court was going to make sure the old boy got paid. Because it was . . . he wasn't getting much money as I remember.[47]

The McGowin family is especially sensitive to any implication that the case is a stain on the family's honor. That's not to say that they impugn the integrity of Joe Webb. Mr. Greeley's grandson, N. Floyd McGowin, Jr., says he'd always heard Joe Webb was a man of integrity. As Floyd recalls, Webb was regarded as "honest," "upstanding," and "well thought of."[48] Indeed, Floyd employed Webb's granddaughter, Janice Webb Hammond, for many years as a trusted executive secretary and administrative assistant.[49]

But Floyd also emphasizes that his grandfather, Mr. Greeley, had a reputation as "a person who was fair and ethical in his dealings with people, regardless of the circumstances."[50] He says he and other family members have long worried that the case has cast their family in an unfair light, by suggesting that Mr. McGowin made a solemn promise and that his estate later reneged on it, despite a moral and legal obligation to pay. At one point in an interview, Floyd said he understood *Webb v. McGowin* as involving a "verbal remark that was somehow interpreted as a contract."[51]

46. Powell's signature appears on some documents connected with the case. See, e.g., Letter of Powell & Hamilton to N. Floyd McGowin, May 19, 1934 (enclosing the complaint and requesting payment in full). Hamilton's grandson Pete Hamilton also thinks Powell was primarily responsible for it. Telephone interview with Lewis S. ("Pete") Hamilton, May 4, 2004.

47. Telephone interview with Lewis S. ("Pete") Hamilton, May 4, 2004.

48. Telephone interview with N. Floyd McGowin, Jr., Jan. 23, 2004.

49. In his memoirs, Floyd describes Janice as a "star performer," and says he "trusted her implicitly." N. Floyd McGowin, Jr., Rocky Creek: A Southern Memoir 359, 360 (unpublished manuscript). She worked diligently and showed "great loyalty," earning a "steady stream of promotions." Id. at 360.

50. N. Floyd McGowin, Jr., Rocky Creek, supra (p. 1 of the Foreword).

51. Telephone interview with N. Floyd McGowin, Jr., Jan. 23, 2004.

In a memoir, though, Floyd gives credence to Webb's insistence that Mr. Greeley had made the promise. In fact, Floyd disagrees with the initial decision of his family and the company's lawyer, Calvin Poole, to litigate:

> My view of the case is different from that of Mr. Poole, my father [one of the executors of the estate] and his family and based on what seems to be the moral high ground as opposed to the legal niceties. There is no disputing the fact that Mr. Webb was grievously injured in trying to prevent harm to Mr. Greeley, which permanently disabled him. I don't know if Mr. Webb's claim that my grandfather promised to pay him for the rest of his life was provable, but it seems just and likely. It is also likely that to Mr. Webb, Mr. Greeley and The Company were one and the same, and that as the head man he had the authority to make such a commitment on behalf of the business, over and above its obligations under the Workman's Compensation Law. Mr. Poole's feelings were that if the family had not been under pressure to settle the Estate, he could have successfully litigated the case and proved that Mr. Webb was not entitled to any further compensation. This may have been true, but I feel that it would have been far better for all concerned if the family, The Company or both acting together had volunteered a fair and acceptable settlement to Mr. Webb and resolved the matter in the beginning.[52]

As Floyd says, though, other McGowin family members took a harder line. In a letter to Poole, Mr. Greeley's son N. Floyd McGowin — one of the two executors of the estate — asserted that the matter "was handled by the company and not by my father and payments were made on the basis of the compensation law ...." The implication is that Mr. Greeley did not make a direct promise to Webb. The executor continued: "[W]hen full compensation had been paid, Papa continued payments to [Webb] out of sympathy, but each year when it came up questioned the advisability of doing so." And the executor's instructions to his lawyer were clear: "I suggest that you tell Mr. Powell to go ahead and sue if he wants

---

52. N. Floyd McGowin, Jr., *Rocky Creek: A Southern Memoir*, at 361.

to. We are not going to pay anything as we have already done much more than the law required."[53]

Accordingly, the McGowin estate initially did litigate, and it took the position that McGowin never made the promise alleged — or at least not the precise promise alleged. According to Calvin Poole III, grandson of the Calvin Poole who handled the case for the McGowin estate, McGowin never made a promise directly to Webb.[54] Instead, Poole says, McGowin instructed the company bookkeeper to send Webb $15 every two weeks in accordance with the Workmen's Compensation statute. Indeed, Poole's grandfather planned to present the jury with evidence that it was W. T. Smith Lumber Co., not Mr. McGowin, who made the payments to Joe Webb.[55]

It's not clear whether this version of the facts, if eventually found to be accurate by a court, would have precluded Webb's claim. But it certainly would have complicated it. One common basis for distinguishing *Webb v. McGowin* from *Mills v. Wyman* is the "directness" of the promise in *Webb*. That is, in *Webb*, the "benefited party" (McGowin) supposedly made the promise directly to the Good Samaritan (Webb). By contrast, the "benefited party" in *Mills* (Levi Wyman) made no promise at all; his father promised on his behalf. If, as Poole suggests, McGowin never spoke directly to Webb, and instead the bookkeeper made an express or implied promise to Webb, the facts look somewhat more like *Mills v. Wyman*. To Joe Webb, though, it surely didn't matter whether the promise came from McGowin or his company. As Floyd McGowin says, Joe Webb no doubt regarded Mr. Greeley and his company as "one and the same."[56]

The estate also took the position, in the alternative, that even if McGowin did make some sort of oral promise to Webb, it was

53. Letter of N. Floyd McGowin to Calvin Poole, May 23, 1934.

54. Telephone interview with Calvin Poole III, Mar. 5, 2004.

55. Letter of Calvin Poole to N. F. McGowin, April 2, 1935 ("We will, of course, show in the course of the trial that no payments were ever made to the plaintiff by your father [Mr. Greeley], individually, but that all payments were made by the W.T. Smith Lumber Company as compensation for an injured employee..."). Company records do show that the $15 payments were made by the company. W.T. Smith Lumber Co., Ledger book, Joe Webb Cas. Ins., 1925-1934 (on file with authors).

56. N. Floyd McGowin, Jr., *Rocky Creek: A Southern Memoir*, at 361.

nothing more than a promise to make Workmen's Compensation payments — which, under Alabama law, would indeed have amounted to $15 every two weeks, but only for 300 weeks, not for life. "When the statutory requirements for the payment of workmen's compensation benefits ran out," the estate's attorneys argued, "Mr. McGowin, purely out of the kindness of his heart and prompted by appreciation for what Mr. Webb had done for him, caused W.T. Smith Lumber Company to continue the payments paid to Mr. Webb."[57]

The legal proceedings

Powell & Hamilton[58] filed its complaint on behalf of Joe Webb on August 11, 1934, about seven months after Mr. Greeley passed away. The complaint sounded in contract only; it contained no count demanding relief in restitution. On September 13, defendant's counsel Calvin Poole[59] filed a demurrer asserting that the alleged contract lacked consideration and that enforcement of the contract was barred by the Statute of Frauds.

The demurrer made no mention of the Alabama Workmen's (now "Workers'") Compensation statute. Alabama adopted its first such statute in 1919, making it one of the last states in the union

---

57. Memorandum of Calvin Poole, undated, at 1-2, reprinted in John Appleyard, The W.T Smith Lumber Co. 245 (2000). As to the statutory period of 300 weeks, see id. at 244 (reprinting letter of Nov. 11, 1936 from Floyd McGowin to Nick S. McGowin, a family member then studying at Harvard Law School).

58. This firm, like Poole & Poole, is still operating in Greenville today. At the time of the litigation in *Webb*, the two partners were Dempsey M. Powell and Claude Edward (C.E.) Hamilton. Powell practiced law, including civil and criminal litigation, from as early as 1886 into the 1940s. Powell was a "leader in the fight" against repeal of Prohibition. D. M. Powell Issues Interesting Statement, Greenville Advocate, July 12, 1933, at 1, col. 3. Powell seems to have handled most of the plaintiff's case in *Webb v. McGowin*.

59. Calvin Poole received his A.B. and L.L.B. degrees from the University of Alabama, and he was admitted to the bar in 1917. He served with distinction as a lieutenant in World War I and then returned home, taking up the practice of law in 1920. He practiced law from 1920 to 1987, primarily in private practice, though he also served as Butler County Solicitor and Circuit Solicitor. "His fame spread far and wide as a trial lawyer whose services were much sought after." C.H. "Buster" McGuire, Chamber Music and Camellia Bouquets 22 (1995). Mr. Poole was regarded as a "learned man" with "astounding recall" and a "gruff" manner that "soon dissolved into a most pleasant interlude as a conversation lengthened." Editorial, It Ends, Greenville Advocate, Sept. 27, 1990.

to embrace workers' compensation. Like most such statutes, the Alabama law established a presumption that employers and employees would resolve on-the-job injuries through the process of Workmen's Compensation, in which the employee got the benefit of no-fault liability and the employer got the benefit of limited damage remedies. The statutory remedy was exclusive: once the worker received Workmen's Compensation payments, the worker was precluded recovery for the same injury on a common-law theory of tort or contract.[60] In many respects Alabama's system was typical, though it had one unusual feature: disputes were resolved primarily by the judiciary, not an administrative body.[61]

Given that W. T. Smith Lumber Company apparently did file a Workmen's Compensation Report immediately after the accident, it seems surprising that the estate didn't set up the Workmen's Compensation Act as a defense in *Webb v. McGowin*. It may be that Poole felt his consideration argument was so strong that he didn't need to raise the Workmen's Compensation Act, or it may be that the Act was more appropriate to raise during a trial on the merits.

It's not that Poole was unaware of the issue. In fact, he drafted but did not file an answer that asserted that the company was "subject to the provisions of the Workmens' [*sic*] Compensation Law of Alabama, said injuries being received in the course of [Webb's] employment," and that after the statutorily-required period of payments expired, the company continued the payments out of kindness. The draft answer further asserted that any contract was with the company, not McGowin.[62]

60. See generally 1919 Acts Ala. 245; Ala. Code 1923 §§ 7545-47, § 7596; Robert W. Lee & Steven W. Ford, Alabama Workers' Compensation Law and Handbook §1-2 & § 2-1 through § 3-1. For the modern version of the exclusivity rule, see Ala. Code. § 25-5-52.

61. See Woodward Iron Co. v. Bradford, 206 Ala. 447, 449-50 (Ala. Supr. Ct. 1921) (describing the development of the original system); Lee & Ford, supra, §18-1 ("Unlike many other states, workers' compensation disputes in Alabama are resolved by courts of general jurisdiction, rather than through a specialized administrative system. However, the Alabama Department of Industrial Relations (DIR) does play a significant role in administering Alabama's workers' compensation system.").

62. This undated draft answer, provided to us by Calvin Poole III, bears the handwritten words "not filed." The allegations about Workmen's Compensation are in paragraph 3; the assertion about the proper party is in the final clause.

Had the estate raised Workmen's Compensation, the plaintiff might have countered that the parties agreed to opt out of the compensation scheme and replace it with McGowin's more generous stream of payments. The alleged oral agreement took place weeks before the Workmen's Compensation report was filed, which might suggest that the parties agreed to enlarge upon what was required by the Compensation law. And Webb did in fact receive payments for longer than the limited time then set by the law.

Poole did spend some time researching the Statute of Frauds question. Then, as now, the Alabama Statute prevented enforcement of an oral agreement "which, by its terms, is not to be performed within one year from the making thereof."[63] Poole reluctantly came to the conclusion that the contract was not within the Statute, but he wrote to a colleague seeking confirmation of his view.[64] His colleague agreed that the Statute did not apply to contracts that "may or may not" be performed within one year, but he added that he thought Poole had a good consideration defense.[65]

The trial judge in the case was A. E. Gamble, who presided over the Butler County Circuit Court for decades.[66] His son remembers Judge Gamble as a "great man" whose court was one of general jurisdiction. "He tried everything there was to try. He was the only circuit judge in the circuit. He tried all the cases, domestic relations, family law, civil cases." When asked whether his father ever wanted to join an appellate court, Judge Gamble's son replies that his father was happy as a trial judge.[67]

Judge Gamble probably had social contact with lawyers on both sides of the case and with Mr. Greeley. The judge was a charter member of the Greenville Country Club, and he was an avid

---

63. Ala. Code 1923, § 8034, now codified at Ala. Code § 8-9-2(1).

64. See Letter of Calvin Poole to T.M. Stevens, Jan. 11, 1935.

65. Letter of T.M. Stevens to Calvin Poole, Jan. 14, 1935.

66. Judge Arthur E. Gamble was repeatedly elected to serve as presiding judge of what was in 1934 the second judicial circuit, which embraced several counties. See, e.g., He's Elected, Greenville Advocate, May 4, 1934, at 8, col. 3. His name can be found on reported appeals from the Butler County Circuit Court as early as 1917 and as late as 1949. See, e.g., Smith v. State, 16 Ala. App. 153 (1917); Goggans v. Goggans, 252 Ala. 19 (1949). His name appears in cases from other counties as late as 1950 and as early as 1911. See Bailey v. McQueen, 253 Ala. 471 (1950); Millsapp v. Woolf, 1 Ala. App. 599 (1911).

67. Telephone Interview with Arthur E. Gamble, Jr., Mar. 4, 2004.

golfer.[68] In 1925 Judge Gamble played in a club tournament in the same field as "D. M. Powell" — probably Dempsey M. Powell, attorney for the plaintiff in *Webb v. McGowin* nine years later.[69] Judge Gamble and J. Greeley McGowin belonged to the same Sportsmen Club; in November 1925, McGowin was elected President of the club at a "meeting held in the court house," and Judge Gamble was selected to serve on the Executive Committee.[70] Of course, fraternization among bench, bar and litigants still takes place today and was even more widely accepted in Judge Gamble's day.[71]

Judge Gamble also had frequent professional contact with the lawyers on both sides, as one would expect in a small town. For a time, Judge Gamble worked closely with Calvin Poole, counsel for the defense in *Webb*, who served as Circuit Solicitor.[72] Dempsey Powell appeared before Judge Gamble many times, winning some and losing some, again as one would expect.[73] And *Webb* was not the only case in which Poole and Powell battled against each other in Judge Gamble's courtroom.[74]

68. See, e.g., Committees Named by Country Club Board, Greenville Advocate, April 18, 1925, at 1, col. 3; Barnes is Medalist in Club Tournament, Greenville Advocate, June 6, 1925, at 1, col. 4 (reporting Judge Gamble's score of 103).

69. Id. Mr. Powell lost in his first match. Interesting Matches in Golf Tournament, Greenville Advocate, June 10, 1925, at 1, col. 4. Judge Gamble trounced his first opponent, easily beat his second, id., only to lose his final round. Barnes Wins Golf Tourney Second Time, Greenville Advocate, June 13, 1925, at 1, col. 2.

The June 13 issue of the *Advocate* carried two other interesting stories, also on the front page: "Klan Ceremonial is Unqualified Success," id., col. 4; and "Hugo L. Black to Enter Senate Race," id., col. 3.

70. McGowin is President of Sportsmen Club, Greenville Advocate, Nov. 18, 1925, at 1, col. 6. It does not appear, however, that McGowin played golf with Judge Gamble. According to his grandson, Mr. Greeley was not particularly fond of golf. Telephone interview with N. Floyd McGowin, Jr., Jan. 23, 2004.

71. Cf. Cheney v. United States District Court, 124 S. Ct. 1391 (2004) (Memorandum of Scalia, J.).

72. See, e.g., Greenville Advocate, Nov. 18, 1925, at 1, col. 3 ("Hon. Calvin Poole and Judge Gamble are at Luverne for the next three weeks it looks like. All last week they were there during the civil week of the Fall Term of Circuit Court and the indications are that it will take three weeks to try the criminal cases . . .").

73. See, e.g., Stallings v. State, 249 Ala. 580 (1947) (affirming murder conviction, before Judge Gamble, of one of Powell's clients); Finlay v. Kennedy, 250 Ala. 33 (1947) (reversing Judge Gamble's ruling in favor of Powell's client in an equity proceeding); Coker v. Hughes, 205 Ala. 344 (1920) (sustaining Judge Gamble's ruling in favor of Powell's client in an action for ejectment).

74. See, e.g., Woodmen of the World Life Ins. Soc. v. Braden, 242 Ala. 606 (1942); Sovereign Camp, W. O. W. v. Waller, 232 Ala. 170 (1936).

Poole and Powell also worked together occasionally. In 1933 they jointly represented W. M. McGowin in a real-estate dispute.[75] In 1932 they teamed up to challenge a conviction in Judge Gamble's court of a black defendant accused of murdering a white man. The Supreme Court of Alabama unanimously overturned the conviction in *Ballard v. State* on the grounds, among other things, that Judge Gamble had erred by failing to remove a juror for cause after the juror had "winked" at the prosecutor.[76]

Three years after *Ballard*, Poole and Powell squared off against each other in the same courtroom, before the same judge, in *Webb v. McGowin*. On April 8, 1935, Judge Gamble sustained Poole's demurrer. The record contains no opinion apart from the Judgment in the case, which sustained the demurrer "separately and severally as to each count of the amended complaint."[77]

The plaintiff immediately appealed. The lawyers' briefs focused on the consideration issue. The appellant's brief distinguished

---

75. Reznik v. McGowin, 227 Ala. 125 (1933).

76. Ballard v. State, 225 Ala. 202 (1932). For other examples of cases in which Powell & Hamilton joined forces with Calvin Poole, see Crum v. Crum, 253 Ala. 163 (1949); Piper v. Halford, 247 Ala. 530 (1946).

For another case in which Dempsey Powell successfully sought reversal of a conviction of an African-American defendant accused of killing a white person, see Goldsmith v. State, 232 Ala. 436 (1936). Again Judge Gamble was the trial judge. The Alabama Supreme Court said the evidence justified at most a finding of manslaughter, and it wrote:

> Had all these parties been of the same race, or if conditions had been reversed, we feel sure that there would have been a different verdict and that the present one was actuated by passion or race prejudice; not perhaps from corrupt motives, but from an inborn and uncontrollable antagonism between the two races, when a negro kills a white man or when a white man kills a negro.

Id. at 437.

Calvin Poole also took on cases raising racial issues throughout his career. In Donald v. Matheny, 276 Ala. 52 (1963), a civil tort suit, Poole argued unsuccessfully that a verdict against his black client be overturned because of opposing counsel's statement that a black witness would "change her testimony" because of "the breed of the race." Poole also defended city officials of Greenville against a class action suit brought by Jack Greenberg and other lawyers on behalf of black plaintiffs seeking to march in Greenville. See Cottonwood v. Johnson, 252 F. Supp. 492 (M.D. Ala. 1966) (entering injunctions against both the plaintiffs and the defendants).

77. Judgment, Webb v. McGowin (Cir. Ct., Butler Co., Ala.), April 8, 1935, in Record, Webb v. McGowin, at 7.

between a "mere moral obligation," which alone was not consideration, and "a moral obligation arising from a material benefit conferred upon the person making the express promise to pay," which was enforceable.[78] In response, Calvin Poole stressed the traditional rule that past consideration is no consideration.[79] As one would expect, each advocate's methodology was traditional legal positivism: the lawyers mostly argued about what the law was, not which rule made the most sense, and certainly not which rule was most efficient.

Neither party relied on the Workmen's Compensation statute. The appellant's brief did rebut the Statute of Frauds defense raised in the estate's demurrer, noting that it was not impossible for the contract to be performed within one year of the making thereof.[80] Judging by his brief, Poole does not seem to have pressed the Statute of Frauds issue.

In November 1935 the Alabama Court of Appeals reversed Judge Gamble in the opinion reprinted at the beginning of this chapter. The court found for Webb on the consideration issue, made no mention at all of Workmen's Compensation, and dispensed with the estate's Statute of Frauds argument in a few short sentences at the end of the opinion.

Calvin Poole considered what to do next. He wrote to counsel for the estate for advice on whether to press forward or settle.[81] Poole also wrote to his client Floyd McGowin and explained the procedural posture of the case. If the case were tried, Poole wrote, "we might have a chance to win it on the facts."[82] And Poole apparently asked Mr. Greeley's son Nick McGowin, a student at Harvard, not only whether Nick might help researching the legal issues but also whether the *Harvard Law Review* might print a note on the case. Nick replied that the *Review* wouldn't be likely to publish anything on the case until it was published in the

---

78. Appellant's Brief, Webb v. McGowin, Ct. App. Ala., May 8, 1935, at 6. The appellant's reply brief also quoted Lord Mansfield's broad endorsement of liability for moral obligation in Hawkes v. Saunders, 1 Cowper 289 (1782) ("Where a man is under a moral obligation . . . and promises, the honesty and rectitude of the thing is a consideration. Reply Brief, Webb v. McGowin, July 3, 1935, at 4.

79. Appellee's Brief, id., May 1935, at 11.

80. Id. at 8-9.

81. Letter of Calvin Poole to T.M. Stevens, Nov. 14, 1935.

82. Letter of Calvin Poole to Floyd McGowin, Nov. 14, 1935.

official case reports, which in those days took months.[83] Nick also spent "2 afternoons looking around the library for something on the Webb case" and provided Poole with some citations.[84] Poole eventually included some of these suggestions in briefs before the Alabama Supreme Court.[85]

Ultimately Poole did press his appeal further. He first sought, unsuccessfully, a rehearing from the Court of Appeals. Then he filed a petition for review by the Alabama Supreme Court. On May 14, 1936, it issued this opinion:

WEBB v. McGOWIN
Supreme Court of Alabama, 1936.
232 Ala. 374, 168 So. 199.

Petition of N. Floyd McGowin and Joseph F. McGowin, as executors of the estate of J. Greeley McGowin, deceased, for certiorari to the Court of Appeals to review and revise the judgment and decision of that court in Joe Webb v. McGowin, et al. Ex'rs, 168 So. 196.

Writ denied.

FOSTER, Justice.

We do not in all cases in which we deny a petition for certiorari to the Court of Appeals approve the reasoning and principles declared in the opinion, even though no opinion is rendered by us. It does not always seem to be important that they be discussed, and we exercise a discretion in that respect. But when the opinion of the Court of Appeals asserts important principles or their application to new situations, and it may be uncertain whether this court agrees with it in all respects, we think it advisable to be specific in that respect when the certiorari is denied. We think such a situation here exists.

---

83. Letter of Nick McGowin to Calvin Poole, Jan. 5, 1936.

84. Letter of Nick McGowin to Calvin Poole, Jan. 8, 1936. Among other things, Nick noted that "due to Lord Mansfield the English rule was against us for a while, but it is definitely settled our way there now, and in all but a few jurisdictions here.").

85. Letter of Calvin Poole to Nick McGowin, Feb. 15, 1936 ("You will note that I have adopted largely the suggestions which you made . . . .").

Neither this court nor the Court of Appeals has had before it questions similar to those here presented, though we have held that the state may recognize a moral obligation, and pay it or cause it to be paid by a county, or city. State v. Clements, 220 Ala. 515, 126 So. 162; Board of Revenue of Mobile v. Puckett, 227 Ala. 374, 149 So. 850; Board of Revenue of Jefferson County v. Hewitt, 206 Ala. 405 (6), 90 So. 781; Moses v. Tigner, 168 So. 194.

Those cases do not mean to affirm that the state may recompense for nice ethical obligations, or do the courteous or generous act, without a material and substantial claim to payment, though it is not enforceable by law; nor that an executory obligation may be so incurred.

The opinion of the Court of Appeals here under consideration recognizes and applies the distinction between a supposed moral obligation of the promisor, based upon some refined sense of ethical duty, without material benefit to him, and one in which such a benefit did in fact occur. We agree with that court that if the benefit be material and substantial, and was to the person of the promisor rather than to his estate, it is within the class of material benefits which he has the privilege of recognizing and compensating either by an executed payment or an executory promise to pay. The cases are cited in that opinion. The reason is emphasized when the compensation is not only for the benefits which the promisor received, but also for the injuries either to the property or person of the promisee by reason of the service rendered.

Writ denied.

ANDERSON, C. J., and GARDNER and BOULDIN, JJ., concur.

The settlement

After the Alabama Supreme Court decision came down, Poole wrote to Floyd McGowin that the decision "places us in a rather difficult position." He noted that the case would be set for trial in the fall of 1936, and he added: "I suggest that you be thinking about the matter in the mean time to determine whether we should undertake to make some amicable adjustment of it in preference to going to trial."[86] The summer of 1936 passed, however, without any settlement.

---

86. Letter of Calvin Poole to N. Floyd McGowin, May 16, 1956.

In September 1936 the *Yale Law Journal* wrote to Poole and asked to borrow his briefs from *Webb v. McGowin*. The *Journal* was considering publishing a note on the case because it "presents an interesting development in the idea of moral obligation."[87] Poole promptly complied with the request, but it does not appear that the *Journal* ever published a note.[88] *Webb* was noted in the *Missouri Law Review* that year, and in a few other law journals later.[89] But the decision in *Webb v. McGowin* was not "marketed" in the same way as *Hadley v. Baxendale* (described in Chapter 2).

Webb filed a new complaint in Judge Gamble's court in October 1936.[90] It's not clear why the plaintiff filed a new complaint, but Calvin Poole III (grandson of Poole) speculates that it "was filed . . . as a procedural matter to correctly posture the case for trial in Circuit Court."[91] In any case, the estate filed a new demurrer that reiterated, in identical language, the original demurrer's contention that the alleged contract was "without consideration."[92] The new demurrer made no reference to the Statute of Frauds. But it did fault the complaint for failing to allege that Mr. Greeley (as opposed to his company) had made any payments to Webb. The estate also filed its first answer in the case, which acknowledged that Webb acted after "seeing the danger of" McGowin, but otherwise denied the allegations of the complaint.

The case never got to trial. In November 1936 the estate agreed to pay Webb a lump sum of $900 in exchange for dismissal of the suit.[93] This sum represented less than three years' worth of payments, much less than Webb would have received had he collected

87. Letter of Roy Parker to Calvin Poole, Sept. 17, 1936.

88. See Letter of Calvin Poole to Yale Law Journal, Sept. 21, 1936; Letter of Roy Parker to Calvin Poole, Oct. 22, 1936 ("We have not yet definitely decided whether to publish the note on the case or not.").

89. See Recent Cases, 1 Missouri L. Rev. 350 (1936); see also Merton L. Ferson, Consideration and Contracts, 28 Rocky Mt. L. Rev. 31, 43 (1955); W. Jack Grosse, Moral Obligation as Consideration in Contracts, 17 Villanova L. Rev. 1 (1971).

90. This new complaint is reprinted in Appleyard, The W.T. Smith Lumber Company 297 (2000).

91. Letter of Calvin Poole III to Prof. David Epstein, Aug. 18, 2000, at 2.

92. Compare, e.g., Demurrer, Webb v. McGowin, Nov. 1936, ¶ 3, with Demurrer, id., Sept. 1934, ¶ 3.

93. See Agreement of Nov. 16, 1936 (unsigned) (on file with author); Letter of N. Floyd McGowin to Calvin Poole, Nov. 14, 1936 (enclosing a check for $900 as "settlement in full of the Joe Webb case").

$15 every two weeks until he died in 1943 or 1944. (If a court had awarded Webb the $15 payments retroactive to January 1934, Webb would have received a total of at least $3,500, although most of it would have come in $15 installments.) And Webb doubtless had to use some of the $900 settlement to pay his attorney, who did not normally work for free.[94]

At least two of Joe Webb's grandchildren think that the McGowin family — most likely Mr. Greeley himself — also gave Webb use of a home and several acres of land outside Georgiana. These grandchildren have detailed memories of visiting that property while one or both grandparents lived there.[95] This arrangement does not seem to have been part of the formal settlement in the case. Charles Howard Webb speculates that before Mr. Greeley died, he made an "oral agreement" with Joe Webb in which he gave Webb and his wife use of the house and land until they both passed away.[96] When asked about such an arrangement, both Calvin Poole III and Pete Hamilton — grandsons of lawyers on each side — say they know nothing about it.[97]

Calvin Poole came to regret the decision to settle, and some of the McGowins may have as well. Long after Poole settled the case, he remembered it this way:

> There was no basis for a claim against the McGowin estate, and such a claim could not have been proven. The case was settled on the basis of expediency alone. It was desired to settle the administration of the estate, and the executors decided to settle the lawsuit for a more or less nominal sum rather than incur the expense and inconvenience of delaying the settlement of the estate.
>
> In the light of afterthought and for the vindication of the McGowin family in the court records, it would proba-bly have been better to have had the record clarified by fol-

94. Neither Pete Hamilton nor Calvin Poole III has records of what fees were paid in the case. Letter of Calvin Poole III to Geoffrey R. Watson, May 14, 2004; Telephone Interview with Lewis S. ("Pete") Hamilton, May 4, 2004.

95. Telephone Interview with Janice Webb Hammond, Feb. 10, 2004; Telephone Interview with Charles Howard Webb, Feb. 11, 2004.

96. Telephone Interview with Charles Howard Webb, Feb. 11, 2004.

97. Telephone Interview with Calvin Poole III, Mar. 5, 2005; Telephone Interview with Lewis S. ("Pete") Hamilton, May 4, 2004.

lowing up the case after reversal and requiring the plaintiff to prove the averments of his complaint.[98]

Or, as Poole's grandson puts it today:

> Papa (my grandfather) always said that if had known of the widespread publicity which the case would receive, he would have taken the case to trial so as to clear the McGowin family name. I always wondered if he weren't just as concerned about the Poole family name, since our name goes down in the law books as having lost the case in the Alabama Supreme Court.[99]

Powell & Hamilton, for its part, doesn't seem to have regarded *Webb v. McGowin* as its most important case. C.E. Hamilton's grandson recalls that when Dempsey Powell was called on to eulogize Hamilton, Powell didn't list *Webb v. McGowin* among Hamilton's great successes. To be sure, Powell himself, rather than Hamilton, did most of the work on *Webb*. But there's no evidence that Powell thought of the case as his most important victory. The lawyer who now runs the office, Pete Hamilton, says he doesn't keep any mementos to the case on his office walls.[100] To an experienced litigator like Dempsey Powell, a case that settled for $900 probably didn't rank among his most storied successes.

Epilogue

No one involved in *Webb v. McGowin* seems to have anticipated that it would become a nationally-known case, reprinted in every Contracts casebook — almost invariably to draw a contrast with *Mills v. Wyman* (discussed in Chapter 4) or *Harrington v. Taylor* (Chapter 6). Calvin Poole would later say that the case was "magnified out of all proportion by the commentators because of the novelty of the legal question involved."[101]

---

98. Memorandum of Calvin Poole, undated, at 1-2, reprinted in Appleyard, The W.T. Smith Lumber Co., at 247. This passage is also excerpted in E. Allan Farnsworth, et al., Contracts 45 n. c (6th ed. 2001).

99. Letter of Calvin Poole III to Norman F. McGowin, July 26, 2000.

100. Telephone Interview with Lewis S. ("Pete") Hamilton, May 4, 2004.

101. Appleyard, The W.T. Smith Lumber Co., at 243-44.

But while *Webb's* moral-obligation rule is still rejected in many jurisdictions,[102] it has occasionally found favor in others,[103] it is still good law in Alabama,[104] and it has found approval in the influential Restatement (2d) of Contracts. Section 86 of the Restatement provides: "A promise made in recognition of a benefit previously received by the promisor from the promisee is binding to the extent necessary to prevent injustice." Illustration 7 for this provision is based on *Webb v. McGowin.*

Moreover, Alabama courts have occasionally approved of the broader proposition — articulated in Judge Samford's concurrence in *Webb* — that courts should "refrain from a strict construction to prevent grave injustice and technical miscarriage."[105] Indeed, Justice Foster, author of the Alabama Supreme Court's opinion in *Webb*, later cited *Webb* approvingly when upholding against constitutional challenge a state statute appropriating money to compensate a woman who was "injured when the automobile in which she was riding ran into a washed out bridge on a certain county road."[106] Justice Foster suggested that the moral-obligation principle of *Webb* might extend to public promisors as well.[107]

But whatever influence *Webb* has had on courts, the case also illustrates a persistent problem with the doctrine of consideration:

102. See, e.g., Estate of Graham v. Morrison, 576 S.E.2d 355, 359 (N.C. App. 2003) ("Past consideration or moral obligation is not adequate consideration to support a contract").

103. See, e.g., Old American Life Ins. Co. v. Biggers, 172 F.2d 495 (10th Cir. 1949) (citing *Webb*); Park Falls State Bank v. Fordyce, 206 Wis. 628 (1932); Holland v. Martinson, 119 Kan. 43 (1925); See also Alliance Mut. Casualty Co. v. Scheufler, 203 Kan. 171 (1969) (Fromme, J., dissenting); cf. also N.Y. Gen. Oblig. L. § 5-1105 (providing for enforcement of some written promises supported only by "past consideration").

104. See Slayton v. Slayton, 55 Ala. App. 351, 354, 315 So. 2d 588, 590 (1975) ("it is well settled that a moral obligation is a sufficient consideration to support a subsequent promise to pay where the promisor has received a material benefit, although there was no original duty or liability resting on the promisor") (citing *Webb*).

105. In re Rice, 18 B.R. 562, 565 (Bankr. N.D. Ala. 1982).

106. Stone v. State, 252 Ala. 240, 242 (1948).

107. Id. at 244. Cf. also First Nat'l Bank v. Walker County Board of Education, 243 Ala. 576, 578 (1943) (Foster, J.) (citing *Webb* for a similar proposition); Downs v. Birmingham, 240 Ala. 177, 185 (1940) (Foster, J.) (similar).

most Americans don't know it exists. Certainly the non-lawyers in
Webb don't talk about the case in terms of consideration or bar-
gained-for exchange. To the non-lawyers connected to the case,
the main issue is whether there was a promise, and if so what the
terms were. In no area of law is the gulf between popular perception and legal doctrine wider than consideration. *Webb* might have
narrowed that gulf a few millimeters, but it still exists. Of course,
the fact that a rule of law is misunderstood by the public doesn't
necessarily mean that the rule is hopelessly flawed. But it ought to
give pause.

FURTHER QUESTIONS

1. "In no area of law is the gulf between popular perception and legal doctrine wider than consideration." If such a basic requirement of contract formation is not understood, is it a wise rule?

2. We've already seen that Alice Sullivan and Seth Wyman, the "winners" in their lawsuits, had reason to be disappointed with their supposed victories. Is that true of Joe Webb, too? Why do you suppose he settled for less than three years' worth of payments?

3. The absence of a trial means that the major factual issues in *Webb* remain unresolved. Is that a good thing? Is there something to be said for leaving some questions unresolved — that it allows each side to maintain its own narrative over succeeding generations? Or does "constructive ambiguity" make for festering wounds?

4. Would a trial have conclusively "resolved" the crucial factual issues — e.g., the precise nature and circumstances of the promise made to Webb? What kind of evidence (including testimony) would have been used to prove the promise? What kind of evidence (including testimony) would have been used to disprove it?

5. Greenville, Alabama, is a small town; even today, it has only around 8,000 inhabitants. The essay notes that Judge Gamble had frequent social and professional contacts with lawyers on both sides of the cases and with the McGowins. As the essay suggests, such contacts were commonplace in Judge Gamble's day. Do they bother you? To what extent does a formal system that emphasizes legal positivism protect against distortion from such contacts? To what extent is a system that emphasizes "justice" vulnerable to misjudgment or abuse in settings like the one described here?

6. The estate was obviously much wealthier than the plaintiff, Joe Webb. Even so, Webb was well-represented by respected counsel, and he won a significant victory in the state Supreme Court. Did the parties' comparative wealth play any role in the court decisions? What if Webb had been the wealthier one, and McGowin the poorer one? Same result then? Conversely, what if Webb had been unable to secure the services of a lawyer. Would he have had a chance *pro se*?

7. After the litigation was over, Calvin Poole and the McGowins frequently asserted that Webb was put on a schedule of Workmen's Compensation payments, and that the W.T. Smith Lumber Company paid him more than he was entitled to. And it's true that the company, not McGowin himself, made the payments. Why didn't Poole rely more heavily on the Workmen's Compensation statute in his pleadings and briefs? Is it possible that such a tactic might have undermined his case?

8. Is the rule in *Webb v. McGowin* efficient? Will it exacerbate capability problems by creating uncertainty about what moral obligations do and do not qualify for judicial enforcement? Or will it ameliorate capability problems by harmonizing notions of the law and of justice?

VI. LENA HARRINGTON v. LEE WALTER TAYLOR

HARRINGTON v. TAYLOR
Supreme Court of North Carolina, Dec. 12, 1945.
225 N.C. 690, 36 S.E.2d 227.

Appeal of plaintiff from Olive, Special J., May 1945 Civil Term of Richmond Superior Court.

GEORGE S. STEELE, Jr. — For Plaintiff, Appellant.

No Counsel *Contra*.

PER CURIAM:

The plaintiff in this case sought to recover of the defendant upon a promise made by him under the following peculiar circumstances:

The defendant had assaulted his wife, who took refuge in plaintiff's house. The next day the defendant gained access to the house and began another assault on his wife. The defendant's wife knocked him down with an axe, and was on the point of cutting his head open or decapitating him while he was laying on the floor, and the plaintiff intervened, caught the axe as it was descending, and the blow intended for defendant fell upon her hand, mutilating it badly, but saving defendant's life.

Subsequently, defendant orally promised to pay the plaintiff her damages; but, after paying a small sum, failed to pay anything more. So, substantially, states the complaint.

The defendant demurred to the complaint as not stating a cause of action, and the demurrer was sustained. Plaintiff appealed.

The question presented is whether there was a consideration recognized by our law as sufficient to support the promise. The Court is of the opinion that however much the defendant should be impelled by common gratitude to alleviate the plaintiff's misfortune, a humanitarian act of this kind, voluntarily performed, is not such consideration as would entitle her to recover at law.

The judgment sustaining the demurrer is

Affirmed.

FIRST QUESTIONS

1. Four actors figure in the events described in this opinion: (a) the husband — Lee Taylor; (b) the wife — Arnisea Taylor; (c) the intervenor who was injured — Lena Harrington; and, as we shall see, (d) the police. If among them they must total 100% of the responsibility for Ms. Harrington's injury, what percent of that responsibility would you attribute to each? How confident are you of your rankings? Are they relevant to how you would decide the contracts case? Compare your views to those of your classmates. Are the disparities relevant?

2. The trial court disposed of the court on demurrer; i.e., it found that the complaint stated no claim upon which relief could be granted. We also saw use of a demurrer in *Webb v. McGowin*. See also Fed. R. Civ. P. 12(b)(6). The rationale for such a rule is that the courts should not waste time on a trial if the facts in the complaint, even if proved, would not amount to a legally cogniza-ble claim. Are there any reasons in addition to those stated by the court that might explain why the North Carolina trial court chose not to "waste time" on this matter?

3. If the North Carolina courts allowed this complaint to stand and then determined that Mr. Taylor was obliged to pay Ms. Harrington for breach of contract, what do you think would hap-pen next? Does your view of this affect your view of whether a suit should be allowed for the alleged breach?

4. Do the facts in the opinion support a claim in tort against Lee Walter Taylor? Do they support a claim against the ax-wield-ing Arnisea Taylor? (Tort law requires that the defendant should have "reasonably foreseen" that his or her conduct would lead to the injury.) Should the state be more generous in allocating and enforcing remedies for tort than for contract?

5. In cases like *Harrington v. Taylor*, *Sullivan v. O'Connor*, and *Mills v. Wyman*, are we seeing injustices merely because law-yers, trial judges, or juries are invoking the wrong doctrines? (Or because lawyers and their clients choose, for whatever reason, not to sue the most appropriate defendant?) If you are a trial judge and a plaintiff advances an apparently meritorious case under the wrong heading (or against the wrong party), what should you do? If you are an appellate judge, what can you do?

SUPPLEMENTARY MATERIAL*

First consider the following documents from Lena Harrington's contract claim against Lee Walter Taylor.

*   *   *

COMPLAINT
[Caption omitted]

The plaintiff, complaining of the defendant, says and alleges:

1. That the plaintiff and the defendant are residents of the Town of Hamlet, Richmond County, North Carolina.

2. That on or about the 7th day of January, 1945, as plaintiff is informed and believes, the defendant assaulted and beat up his wife, Arnisea Taylor, and that the said Arnisea Taylor left defendant's home and went to the police to report the assault; that about 12:45 A.M., the police of the Town of Hamlet brought the said Arnisea Taylor to the plaintiff's house to spend the night for the protection of the said Arnisea Taylor; that the said Arnisea Taylor spent the night with the plaintiff.

3. That about 3 o'clock in the afternoon of January 8, the defendant came to plaintiff's house and talked to his wife, and that shortly thereafter he left without having been admitted to plaintiff's house.

4. That about 4:30 in the same afternoon, the defendant returned to plaintiff's house and his wife, Arnisea Taylor, locked all the doors to the house to keep him from coming in, because of her fear of him, he having threatened to kill her; that, at that time, the plaintiff was in the yard picking up wood to take into the fire, and that when the plaintiff went into the house, the defendant followed her in, and, as plaintiff is informed and believes, assaulted his wife; that thereupon his wife hit defendant with an axe, knocking him down; that the said Arnisea Taylor started to cut the defendant's head open with the axe, and that the plaintiff intervened by grabbing the axe, which, as it was descending, cut plaintiff's hand se-

*Geoff Watson assembled these materials with the energetic assistance of Sabrina Hilliard, to whom we offer thanks.

verely, the plaintiff receiving the blow intended for the defendant; that thereby the plaintiff saved the defendant's life.

5. That the plaintiff's fingers were cut to the bone by the aforesaid blow, and that the plaintiff suffered great pain and suffering thereby; that the plaintiff's hand is permanently injured and is practically useless to her.

6. That the plaintiff has spent considerable sums of money for treatment of her hand, and will have to continue to spend money for treatment thereof.

7. That the plaintiff is a washwoman, making her living by washing clothes, and that the injury to her hand has made it impossible for a number of weeks for her to carry on her occupation; that she will never be able to wash with the skill and efficiency that she has had heretofore, and the number of washes which she will be able to do has been substantially reduced.

8. That the defendant promised the plaintiff that he would pay her damages but, after paying twenty dollars ($20), he has failed to pay any more, though his wife has paid plaintiff the sum of twenty three dollars ($23).

9. That the plaintiff has been damaged by reason of the matter set forth above in the sum of twelve thousand, five hundred dollars ($12,500).

Wherefore, the plaintiff prays the court that she have and recover of the defendant the sum of twelve thousand, four hundred, sixty seven dollars ($12,467), and the costs of this action, and that she have such other and further relief as to the court may seem just and proper.

G. S. Steele
Attorney for Plaintiff

* * *

DEMURRER
[Caption omitted]

The Defendant, Lee Walter Taylor, files the following Demurrer to the Complaint of the Plaintiff for that the complaint fails to state a cause of action against the defendant and for the reasons:

1. That it appears from the complaint of the plaintiff that the defendant was not a trespasser on the property of the plaintiff and

whatever the plaintiff did for the protection of the defendant was gratuitous.

2. That "in saving the defendant's life" as alleged in the complaint the plaintiff was under no legal obligation to defend the defendant and assumed whatever risks were incident to her conduct in seeking to protect the defendant.

3. That while the defendant may have been placed under moral obligations to the plaintiff for her conduct as alleged in her complaint, he has not been placed under any legal obligations for which he is liable in damages to the plaintiff.

4. That whatever injury or harm the plaintiff may have sustained under the allegations of the complaint, the same are damnum abseque injuria.

5. That it appears from the complaint that whatever promise the defendant made to the plaintiff as to payment was for a past consideration, is not enforcible in law and is nudum pactum.

6. That it appears from the complaint that no definite amount was agreed upon to be paid plaintiff by defendant for any damages she sustained and was based on no present consideration.

Wherefore, Defendant prays the Court that the action of the plaintiff be dismissed.

Fred W. Bynum
Attorney for Defendant

*   *   *

ORDER GRANTING LEAVE TO SUE AS A PAUPER
[Caption omitted]

. . . [I]t is ordered:

1. That the above named Lena Harrington be allowed to prosecute her said suit as a pauper.

2. That G.S. Steele be assigned to her as counsel to prosecute said action.

This the 26th day of March, 1945.

Thomas L. Corrington
Clerk Superior Court

*   *   *

JUDGMENT
[Caption omitted]

This cause coming on to be heard before Judge Hubert E. Olive, presiding over the May Term, 1945 of Richmond County Superior on the demurrer of the defendant, and the Court being of the opinion the complaint does not state a cause of action against the defendant;

It is now, on motion of Fred W. Bynum, counsel for defendant, ordered and adjudged that the demurrer of the defendant be, and the same hereby is, sustained and the action of the plaintiff is dismissed.

Hubert E. Olive
Judge Presiding

*   *   *

APPEAL ENTRIES
[Caption omitted]

To the foregoing judgment, the plaintiff excepts and gives notice of appeal to the Supreme Court. Further notice waived. The record and case on appeal shall consist of the summons, complaint, demurrer and judgment and the appeal entries.

Hubert E. Olive
Judge Presiding

*   *   *

June 28, 1945

Honorable Adrian J. Newton, Clerk
Supreme Court of North Carolina
Department of Justice Building
Raleigh, North Carolina

In Re: Harrington v. Taylor, #594

Dear Adrian:

I enclose herein the original certified copy of the record and case on appeal in the above entitled case together with 9 typewritten copies thereof. I also enclose the application for leave to sue as a pauper, the certificate of attorney and the order granting leave to sue as a pauper, and the affidavit to be allowed to appeal as a pauper, the certificate of counsel and the order allowing the appeal in forma pauperis.

I also enclose a check for $2 in payment of the docketing fee in this case.

I enjoyed seeing you and the members of your staff on Tuesday, and I hope I will be able to get up there again before November.

With best regards,

G. S. Steele

* * *

BRIEF OF PLAINTIFF-APPELLANT
[Caption and Statement of Facts omitted]

ARGUMENT

I. LIABILITY IN CONTRACT — Past Consideration.

A. Legal Obligation.

It is the general rule of the common law that a legal duty to the promisee on the part of the promisor, though the legal duty is already existent at the time of the promise, is a sufficient consideration for the promise. Jones v. Winstead, 186 N.C. 536, 120 S.E. 89; 12 Am. Jur. 587-588, Contracts, Sec. 94; 17 C. J. S. 472, Contracts, Sec. 122. Hence, if the defendant be liable in tort or on a quasi-contract for the damage to the plaintiff, then without doubt, he is liable on his promise to pay. The defendant's liability in tort for the damage to the plaintiff is discussed in the second part of this brief.

B. Moral Obligation.

However, even though the Court should find that the defendant was not liable in tort for the damage to the plaintiff, if the Court follows the trend of modern authority, it will hold that he is liable on his promise to pay supported by his moral obligation to pay. There is considerable authority to the effect that past benefit of a material or pecuniary nature to the promisor — and there can be no doubt that the past benefit to defendant was of a material nature, since the benefit to defendant was the saving of his life —, which created on his part a moral obligation to pay, is a sufficient consideration for his subsequent promise. 12 Am. Jur. 601 and 603, Contracts, Secs. 107 and 110; 17 C. J. S. 471, Contracts, Sec. 118; See Jacobs Kull & Sons v. Farmer, 78 N.C. 339.

The law certainly should hold that a moral obligation is sufficient consideration to support a promise to pay. If I should fall in the Pee Dee River in the winter time, and Mr. Bynum should jump in and pull me out, and I should then promise to pay him whatever his damage should be, and he should take pneumonia and have a large hospital bill and be unable to work for several months, and I should then be ungrateful enough to refuse to pay him, the law should certainly require me to do it.

* * *

D. Quasi Contract — Promise Implied in Law.

It is well settled that were a physician treats a patient who is unconscious when brought to the physician — and hence he and the physician are unable to make either an express contract or one implied in fact —, the physician may recover from the patient because of the promise of the patient which the law implies. 41 Am. Jur. 256, Physicians and Surgeons, Sec. 166. "In an emergency case, requiring immediate attention to save life, the physician when called, or when he volunteers his services, should not stop to inquire by whom he will be paid, or to make it known that he expects to be paid." Schoenberg v. Ross, 145 N.Y.S. 831, 834.

The law implies this promise when the patient is incapable of promising because he is unconscious. It implies a promise which he would make — or rather that he should make — were he conscious.

The law implies the contract because it is his duty to make the promise or make the payment, and natural justice requires that he should do so. ". . . As has been well said, in the case of actual contracts the agreement defines the duty, while in the case of quasi contracts the duty defines the contract . . . In quasi contracts the obligation arises, not from the consent of the parties, as in the case of contracts, express or implied in fact, but from the law of natural immutable justice and equity." 12 Am. Jur. 502-503, Contracts, Sec. 6. The law implies this promise in some cases where there would be no promise implied in fact were the patient conscious.

In this case, the plaintiff and defendant were unable to make an express contract or a contract implied in fact, not because defendant was unconscious, but because there was not enough time. Certainly defendant has a duty to pay plaintiff and the "law of natural immutable justice and equity" requires that he do so. Essentially, this case is no different from the case of the physician and his patient: Therefore, it would certainly seem that the law would imply a promise to pay.

II. LIABILITY IN TORT

In the first place, the plaintiff was not a mere volunteer as stated in the demurrer. (R., p. 7.) She not only had a moral duty to prevent defendant's wife from killing him, but she had a legal duty to prevent the homicide. It is a common law crime to observe that a crime is about to be committed and do nothing to prevent it. This crime is known as misprision of felony. "It is described as a criminal neglect either to prevent a felony from being committed or to bring the offender to justice after its commission." 15 C. J. S. 703, Compounding Offenses, Sec. 2 (especially pocket part). Since the plaintiff was thus discharging her duty in a situation which had been brought about by defendant's wrongdoing — by his violation of a duty he owed both his wife and the plaintiff —, he certainly should be liable to the plaintiff for the damages she suffered.

An intentional tort differs from a negligent tort in that in the case of a negligent tort, the defendant is liable to the plaintiff for plaintiff's damage only if the injury to the plaintiff was reasonably foreseeable, while in the case of an intentional tort, the defendant is liable regardless of whether or not the injury is foreseeable, provided his actions are the proximate cause of the injury. 52 Am. Jur. 382, Torts, Sec. 32; See Steffan v. Meiselman, 223 N.C. 154, 157. In this case, the defendant having been the aggressor and his wife having picked up the axe only after he commenced the assault on her, certainly his actions in assaulting his wife are the proximate cause of plaintiff's injury.

In an affray, each participant is liable for any injury to a third person. 2 C. J. S. 1006, Affray, Sec. 29. This case differs from an affray only in that an affray is an altercation in a public place, whereas the altercation here occurred in plaintiff's home. The reason that all of the participants in an affray are liable for any injury to a third person is because they are all deemed to have caused the injury since they are all engaged in an unlawful fight out of which the injury arose. The elements of, and reasons for, liability in this case and in the case of an affray are the same. The distinction between them makes no difference as to the liability.

It is well recognized that if a person assaults one person, and in so doing strikes a third person, then he is liable to the third person for an assault. 4 Am. Jur. 144, Assault and Battery, Sec. 30; 6 C. J. S. 804, Assault and Battery, Sec. 10(2). And there would seem to be no reason for a different rule where the defendant by his assault caused the person assaulted to strike a third person, and indeed this seems to be the law. 4 Am. Jur. 144, Assault and Battery, Sec. 30.

However, regardless of whether or not defendant is liable to plaintiff on direct tort grounds, it would seem that he is liable because of the doctrine of rescue. "It is generally held that when a person is exposed to imminent peril of life or limb, through the negligent act of another, the latter will be liable in damages for the injuries sustained by a third party in a reasonable effort to rescue the one so imperiled, the rescuer not being precluded from recovery because of his apparent immunity from danger or his voluntary incurrence of risk, provided his acts do not constitute contributory negligence, as being rash and reckless in the eyes of men of ordinary prudence acting in emergency." 23 N. C. L. Rev. 251-252 (April, 1945). To like effect is the holding in Norris v. RR., 152 N.C. 505, 67 S.E. 1017, 27 L. R. A. (N. S.) 1069. Of course, that statement differs in two respects from this case:

1. It contemplates that the peril shall have been the result of negligence; and

2. It contemplates that the person imperiled shall have been someone other than the person at fault. However, I don't think either of those distinctions make any material difference. As to the first, the liability for an intentional tort is greater than the liability for a negligent tort, as was pointed out above. Hence, if a person who negligently caused a peril would be liable for the injuries received by a rescuer, a person who by his intentional acts created a situation wherein there was peril would certainly be liable for the injury to the rescuer. As to the second, there seems to be no reason why a person who creates a peril should be liable for injury to the

rescuer of a third person and yet should not be liable for injury to the rescuer of himself. If there were any distinction, it would seem that there is more cause for liability for injury to his own rescuer. The language of this court in Norris v. RR., supra, p. 514, is appropriate on this question, though directed to the question of contributory negligence: ". . . and when one sees his fellowman in such peril he is not required to pause and calculate as to court decisions, nor recall the last statute as to the burden of proof, but he is allowed to follow the promptings of a generous nature and extend the help which the occasion requires; . . ."

Thus it seems that whatever view is taken of the tort question in this case, it is apparent that defendant is liable to plaintiff for her damages. It follows that there was error in the ruling of the court below sustaining the demurrer, and it is respectfully suggested that the ruling be reversed.

Respectfully submitted,

George S. Steele, Jr.
Attorney for Plaintiff-Appellant

*   *   *

The record contains no reply brief from the defendant. Taylor was represented by counsel at trial but was apparently unrepresented on appeal. Even so, Taylor won on appeal when the North Carolina Supreme Court issued the opinion set forth at the outset of this chapter.

But that holding did not end the litigation in *Harrington v. Taylor*. After her unsuccessful contract action against Lee Taylor, Lena Harrington brought a separate tort suit against him. Here are some documents from the tort case, including oral testimony of witnesses and the final opinion of the Supreme Court of North Carolina. As you read these materials, consider how they bear on the contract issue decided in the first *Harrington v. Taylor*, and ask yourself what capability problems they raise.

*   *   *

PLAINTIFF'S EVIDENCE*

Dorothy Strickland
Dorothy Strickland, having been duly sworn, testified as follows:

DIRECT EXAMINATION
My name is Dorothy Strickland. Lena Harrington is my mother. I remember the occasion when she got her hand cut. I remember about Arnisea Taylor spending the night with us. She come between eleven thirty and a quarter 'til twelve on Sunday night, the 7th of January. The polices brought her. She spend the night there. I know the defendant, Lee Walter Taylor, and he came there the next day. The first time he came was around twelve o'clock. He axed to speak to his wife, Arnisea, and she went on the porch and talked with him, and he left, and she came back. He come back about three thirty or something like that and axed her to go home with him. She told him she would be there when his brother came. His brother gets off at four o'clock. So he told her, "All right." Between four and four thirty, he came back. And when he come back she saw him coming, and she locked all the doors. My mother was out in the backyard picking up some wood, and when she came in he came in too. Mother called and axed Arnisea to open the door, and she opened the door. Then Mother came in. Mother came on in the living room to put the wood on the fire, and Lee followed her. Arnisea was in the living room then and when he went in Mother went on to the fireplace, and he went in and Arnisea got up then. She was holding my baby. She layed the baby on the couch, and he grabbed for her, for Arnisea. He was trying to pull her through the bedroom, and she would get loose from him, and she was standing there side of the dresser, and she grabbed up the ax and hit him with the back of the ax the first lick, and she said, "Let me kill him! He is going to kill me if I don't."

He fell when she hit him with the ax, and that is when she said, "Let me kill him! He is going to kill me if I don't."

---

*All testimony is reprinted in the form in which it appears in the official record in the case. Punctuation and spelling are as they appear in the original, except that headings are boldfaced instead of underlined.

Then she hit him again. This time with the blade. That time she struck him on the neck, and he went to get up, and he fell over on his face.

And she was fixing to come down again, and by that time, Mother looked up and said, "Don't kill him! Don't kill him!" And Mother looked around, and just then, she was coming down, and she run out of the living room. That was right in between the bedroom door and the living room, and she run up and said, "Oh, God, don't kill him!" Just as Mother run up, Arnisea brung the ax down, and as Mother went to grab the ax by the handle, she reached too far and caught the blade and it knocked her hand up against the door, and that is how she got her hand cut. Then Mother stepped across him, and he was still lying down there, and she and I took the ax from her.

After we got the ax from her, she looked at her hand, and her hand was bleeding so, and we seed her fingers were off, and we carried her next door and poured kerosene on it to try to stop the bleeding until we could get to the doctor, and we got somebody down below to carry her to the doctor.

CROSS EXAMINATION

I live with my Mother all the time, and am still living with her. I didn't help her was and look after the house as I was married, and my baby was young then. That is the child there. My husband does not live there. We are not living together. I am not helping my mother because I am not able to. I do the best I can, but there is not very much I can do. I can help pretty well though. I don't help much to make some of the stuff Mother gives me to eat. I don't do any washing or anything like that.

On this occasion, Lee Walter Taylor's wife and I were in the house together in what we call the living room. As far as I know, she seemed to be all right. We had windows in the house, and I could see Mother and Lee Walter out in the yard, and Arnisea could look out as well as I could. Arnisea locked the doors after he had already been there twice and talked to her. He came there at twelve o'clock, and there wasn't any trouble between them at all, and he came back at three o'clock, and she went out on the porch and talked to him. The house was not locked or anything then.

She hadn't any occasion to lock the house on the second occasion either.

On the third trip, the house was locked after he got there. When she saw him out there in the yard, heard him talking, she locked the doors. She did this although she had gone out there on the porch to talk to him just an hour before, and yet on this occasion she locked the doors.

Arnisea is larger than I am. Mother was out in the yard getting wood. I heard Lee Walter talking to my mother. When he walked up, he just asked where Arnisea was. He said, "I called her, and she didn't come. Where is she?" And Mother says, "She is in the house." He talked like he was mad then. He was not talking in a gentle voice. It sounded like he was very mad and impatient because she hadn't come to him. Mother said she would be glad for him to come in to see his wife if he wanted to speak to her, and somebody unlocked the door. Mother and Lee Walter got in the kitchen, but I didn't hear them say anything. Then he went on with Mother into the room where Arnisea was. Arnisea didn't say anything to him, but he said, "I thought I told you to come on home." And she said, "I was coming when Rob come." And he made a grab for her, and she had put the baby down on the couch.

I saw him take hold of her. He was pulling her as rough as a man could pull a woman. He had her by the arm. He said, "Come on." He said, "I thought I told you to come on home." And she said, "I was coming when Rob come." Rob is his brother. He was pulling her into the bedroom then. The ax was standing in the bedroom, standing by the dresser. He was carrying her through the room where the ax was up side of the dresser. She pulled loose from him and stepped back and grabbed the ax. When he stepped back, she took the back of the ax and hit him. She hit him and he fell. Then she turned the blade over, right there in the middle of the room. I don't know whether he is a pretty strong colored man or not. She picked up the ax and hit him side of the head. It made one scar up there and one on his neck, and she cut him in the back somewhere. She was treating him pretty badly. Then Mother came in there, and when she started to use the ax again, Mother grabbed it to keep her from slicing his face. He turned over. He went to get up and fell over on his face, and then she was fixing . . . She said, "Let me kill him! If I don't, he is going to kill me." Then Mother went to catch the handle, and she reached too far and caught the blade, and it knocked her hand against the wall.

Arnisea was trying to protect herself. I don't know what he had. When Mother went back, she stepped in to stop Arnisea, and Arnisea hit her with the ax.

REDIRECT EXAMINATION

My husband and I separated the last time in March of this year. When Lee Walter spoke to her and said, "I thought I told you to come on home," he spoke in a loud, angry voice.

EXAMINATION BY THE COURT

The defendant was lying down on the floor at the time his wife had drawn back to hit him with the ax in the face.

Lena Harrington

Lena Harrington, the plaintiff, having been first duly sworn, testified as follows:

DIRECT EXAMINATION

I am the plaintiff in this action, and I live on East Main Street in Hamlet. That is South of the railroad tracks. I have been living in Hamlet fourteen years the fifth of next month. My husband does not live with me. Me and him been separated right here in this courthouse twelve years ago the ninth of July.

I wash and iron for a living. I have been doing that ever since 1934. My husband does not contribute anything to my support. I don't know where he is. The last time I heard of him, he was in South Carolina. I don't know where Arnisea Taylor lives. The last time I heard of her, she was at her home. Her home is at Leesville, South Carolina.

I recall the occasion, January a year ago, when Arnisea Taylor came to my house to spend the night. Two of the polices brought her there. She spent the night there. Her husband came there the next day. I was out in the yard picking up some wood to start a fire in the fireplace, and he came down on his bicycle. He stopped at the kitchen door. He said, "I want to see Arnisea, Mrs. Harrington," after he told me, "Howdy." I looked around at him, and I seed he was mad. I said, "Well, I can't stop you." I said, "You can speak to her." Just like dat. So I said, "You go on in," and I kept picking wood. So he said, "The door is locked." I said, "Go around to the front door." And he went around there, and then he said, "Mrs. Harrington, the front door is locked." And he came on back, and he started back walking like he were going back towards home, right fast, and I seed he was good and mad. Then I said, "Come on, I am going in the house, and you can go in." And so he come on then, and I hollered and called for some of them to open that door. I said, "What the devil are you doing with the door fastened?" Just like that. And so the door opened, and I turned and went on in, so he came on in, and when he got in there, I told him Arnisea was in the living room with the baby. So I had the wood, and so he walked on, and when he got there to the living room door there, Arnisea layed the baby on the little studio couch I have got in there. I had a trunk and a chair behind the door, and Arnisea had started hiding there to go out. She tried to get out, but he seen her. When I looked around, they was tied up and a scuffling. I was down there at the fireplace putting the wood there and scratching in the hot ashes, trying to get a fire. She is as good a woman as he is a man. He is good, but his being good ain't nothing to her, and she got loose from him. I have my ax there. You see I has a lot of oak wood, and I have to get different boys to cut wood for me, and they say they don't want to cut no wood with no old dull ax, so I got me another ax. And this ax was beside the old wardrobe — washstand, setting there so when they gets to scuffling, she got loose, and she grabbed that ax, and when she grabbed that ax, she give him a blow with it. So the blood excited me, and I had this wood. I just stood there and I couldn't even move, just standing there with the wood in my hands, so when he got up and aimed to grab her, she hit him again, and he got on back down then. She hit him again, and he fell. And the next time she was going to hit him in his face, and I said, "Lord, don't kill him!" Then she started to hit him again, and I grabbed for the handle of the ax. Instead of getting the handle, I won't close enough, being excited, and I grabbed the ax. It hit my hand and knocked it up against the door. Then I jumped over top of him and taken the ax from her with this hand, after she had done knocked him down and I had got cut.

When I looked around — you see, I was down there by the fireplace — I am going to tell you the truth. You asked me to, and

I am going to tell you. I was down there at the fire with my back turned to them people, and when I looked around they got tied up to what they were doing, but when I seed them, he had done pulled her — I reckon he pulled her. I didn't see it at first, and when I looked around, she had done hit him then. She had done run back, and she said, "If I don't kill him, he will kill me!"

My right hand was cut. It is hurting yet. I am left-handed and right-handed when I am washing, but left-handed to write anything. They took me and carried me to Dr. Robinson. He tried to do something about it, but he couldn't do anything. He done the best he could, but he didn't fix it so I could use it. That was done the eighth of January, and he took the stitches out of it in March. I never got to unwrap that hand until the warm weather. He said for fear it would catch cold. It stayed so raw. I believe the weather got warm along in April sometime.

I paid Dr. Robinson twenty-two dollars, but the whole thing was fifty-nine or forty-nine dollars. I disremember now. I still owe him for it.

I didn't know how much I spent for medicine, for I bought so much.

Before this happened, I had eighteen washings regular, and I made $26.75 a week. Now, I have six washings. I make anywhere from twelve to thirteen dollars. I couldn't cook with my hand wrapped up like that. Ruby done the cooking. My daughter did the washing. I ain't done no washing since. I tried to hang up some clothes and rinse some out yesterday; that was the first day. I tried to wash some, but that corner of my hand swells up across there, and I can't wash. When I say I make thirteen a week on washings, I mean Ruby makes it. I don't make nothing. And she is done married now, and I ain't going to make even that.

(At the request of counsel, the witness here exhibited her right hand and her left hand to the jury.)

I ain't been able to use them two fingers whatever since the eighth day of January, a year ago, I tried to do a washing yesterday, but my shoulder has been hurting ever since. It hurts me right through here (indicating the right shoulder).

I heard Lee Walter and Arnisea talking in the living room. Both was talking. He told her that he told her to come on home and "I mean for you to come," and she said, "Well, he come to kill me.

Turn me loose! Turn me loose!" I didn't pay any attention to their talking because they always be talking, you know. They talk loud all the time. But I could tell he was mad by looking at his face.

I am fifty years old if I live to see the fourteenth day of next March.

CROSS-EXAMINATION

I rents my home in Hamlet. I don't own it. On this occasion, Lee Walter's wife had spent the night at my house, the part what she got there. I don't know whether he came to see her the next day about twelve o'clock or not; I don't know what the time was, but I know he came. I guess he came back about three o'clock. Everything was pleasant as far as I know, because me and a white lady what brought clothes there was in the house when he came and he said he wanted to see her, and I said, "There she is." And she went out there. He said he wanted to talk to his wife. I reckon it was about four o'clock when he came back. No, it won't no four. It was about two because Rob gets off at four, and she hadn't gone home. I don't remember whether he had been to my house that day three times or two times. He come there the first time. I don't remember Lee coming there but twice because he come there the first time, and me and a white girl I washed for was standing there talking.

I said I reckon about three-thirty in the afternoon when I let him in the house. I tells you as close as I can get to it; I know the Briarhoppers was on, I know that. They was on the radio. And they come on around about three-thirty. They done changed the time, and it comes on at four, but at that time, it was three-thirty.

I was out in the yard when Lee came up, and he spoke to me pleasantly. No, I didn't go to the door and find it locked. He went and found both of them locked. I certainly did say I wanted to know who in the devil locked the door. He started somewhere. I guess he started home, and I reckon if I hadn't called him back, he would have gone. He left his bicycle. I reckon he would have come back later and got that. I said, "Lee, come on." I said, "I am going in the house now," and I said, "You can go with me." He looked pretty mad. You see, I never seen Lee mad, but he didn't talk mad, because I didn't reckon a man would talk mad when he was going to kill you. I don't reckon so. But he talked pleasantly to me. I talked the same as he did.

Arnisea wasn't behind the door. She couldn't have gotten behind the door with her size, but she was somewhere around that door. She could not have gotten behind the door because I had a trunk behind there, a big trunk that takes up the door behind. I saw her, and her and Lee was together, and she was on him or he was on her, I don't know what because I was scared. We went in the kitchen door off the back porch right on to the kitchen to another door in the bedroom. He was in front of me until me and him got to the living room. He said to me — he said, "Mrs. Harrington, she ain't in there." I said, "Yes, she is. I left her in there," and I passed right on by him with my wood, and I went to the fireplace den. When I heard this calamity, I got up from the fire, and looked back and they had it on then. My relations with Lee Walter are perfectly pleasant, just as pleasant now as was then. I just want him to help me some.

Lee ain't done nothing yet. You see, I hold Lee responsible, for when that gal come down there, Lee didn't have no business coming down to my house. He knowed that he was mad; they knowed they was not on good terms. Now Lee ought to have stayed there. He done told her to come and he done called her. How come Lee to come out to my house when he knowed both of them had the devil in them? He ought to have stayed there. Then I wouldn't have my hand cut. Lee didn't do anything to harm me but come to my house. I hold him responsible for that.

My hand don't give me no little trouble about washing; it gives me all the trouble. I tried to wash yesterday, and them fingers give me trouble and hurts all through here. I didn't rest a bit last night, and I come over here, and now I can't get a long breath because that hand just hurts me. My other hand does not hurt me a bit, no sir. I can raise up my hand all right, and I can use this one very good (indicating left hand).

Q. And you can use the thumb and fingers on this one? (Indicating the right hand.)

A. Well, how can I wash white folks' clothes with two fingers?

Q. Well, it is a slight inconvenience.

A. How can I make a living with both of my children grown and married?

Q. Well, I don't know. You still take care of six or eight washings a day?

A. I said I had them six, but since my baby is married, I ain't got them now.

Q. Isn't Dorothy with you?

A. Dorothy's husband does, is supporting her and her baby, such as 'tis.

Q. Well, I say —

A. What good is Dorothy shaped like she is? What can she do? Nothing but sit there on my hands.

Well, Arnisea wouldn't never had hit me if Lee had not come there. You see, Arnisea was trying to take care of herself, and I was trying to take care of him. I don't know who picked the ax up. She is the one that had it. I can't say how Arnisea got the ax first, or who got it first. I couldn't swear to it. I don't know whether there were any marks on Arnisea or not. I didn't look.

THE PLAINTIFF RESTED.

MOTION FOR NONSUIT

The defendant, through counsel, moved that the Court grant a judgment as in case of nonsuit. The motion was allowed, and plaintiff excepted.

*   *   *

The trial judge, the Hon. Henry L. Stevens, Jr., entered judgment for Lee Taylor. The judgment stated that the Court was "of the opinion that the plaintiff was not entitled to recover anything of the defendant. . . ." Lena Harrington appealed to the North Carolina Supreme Court. Here are documents from the appeal.

*   *   *

BRIEF OF PLAINTIFF-APPELLANT

QUESTION INVOLVED

Where defendant commenced an assault on his wife, and his wife, defending herself, seized an ax and knocked defendant down and raised the ax and started to hit him again with it, and plaintiff intervened to save defendant's life and received the blow intended for defendant was thereby badly damaged, may plaintiff recover from defendant her damages?

FACTS

At the Fall Term, 1945, this Court affirmed the action of the Superior Court in sustaining a demurrer to the plaintiff's complaint for failure to state a cause of action, holding that there was no sufficient consideration for defendant's promise to pay. Harrington v. Taylor, 225 N. C. 690, 36 S. E. 2d 227. In that case, plaintiff sued on defendant's promise to pay; in this case plaintiff sues in tort. In that case, defendant filed a demurer to the complaint; in this case, defendant moved for judgment as in case of nonsuit.

Defendant went to plaintiff's house and tried to force his wife to leave with him and go to his house. (R., pp. 5 and 8.) While he was attempting to drag her from the house, she seized an ax and knocked him down with it and was on the point of hitting him with it again when the plaintiff intervened and grabbed the ax. (R., pp. 6, 8, 10-11.) His wife was frightened, for she said, as she started to hit him the second or third time, "If I don't kill him, he will kill me!" (R., p. 11.)

Plaintiff received the blow of the ax on her hand, and that was the blow intended for defendant. (R., pp. 8 and 11.) Her hand was badly cut, so that at the time of the trial — over one year after it was cut — plaintiff was unable to wash with it. (R., p. 12.) Plaintiff is a wash woman, and used to make her living washing clothes. (R., p. 12.)

ARGUMENT

The defendant set in motion the series of acts which resulted in the injury to the plaintiff. Without his original wrongful act, the injury to the plaintiff would not have occurred, and she would still be washing clothes and supporting herself. Consequently, he is liable to plaintiff, both because his original fault was the cause of plaintiff's injury, and because he engaged in mutual combat with his wife.

Care must be taken to distinguish between proximate cause and negligence. An act may be the proximate cause of an injury even though the injury is not reasonably foreseeable. However, if the result is not reasonably foreseeable and is not otherwise wrongful, then there is no liability because there is no negligence. The negligence is in the failure to foresee the result or in the failure to heed if the actor does foresee; that is what makes an act, which is otherwise harmless, wrongful. This distinction is clearly made by Justice Walker in Drum v. Miller, 135 N. C. 204 at 212, 47 S. E. 421. . . .

Since defendant's act in assaulting his wife was wrongful, it is not material whether or not he could reasonably foresee the injury to the plaintiff. The only question is, was the defendant's act the proximate cause of the injury? The defendant's act does not have to be the sole proximate cause of the injury [citations omitted], for "where the independent tortuous acts of two or more persons supplement one another and concur in contributing to and producing a single indivisible injury, such persons have in legal contemplation been regarded as joint tort-feasors, notwithstanding the absence of concerted action. This rule has been regarded as applicable where the acts are concurrent as to place and time and unite in setting in operation a single destructive and dangerous force which produces the injury . . . ." [Citations omitted.]

Both the act of the defendant and the act of his wife were proximate causes of plaintiff's injury, for the injury would not have occurred without the occurrence of both acts.

Of course, if the defendant and his wife are joint tort-feasors, the plaintiff may sue either or both of them, and she is not required to sue both. 52 Am. Jur. 456, Torts, § 119; [two case citations omitted].

On the other hand, if defendant's wife was so crazed with fear of defendant that she did not know what she was doing or felt that there was no time for her to consider the consequences of her act, then there was no wrongful act on her part and defendant is solely liable for plaintiff's injury. . . . [Citations omitted.] There is evidence tending to show that defendant's wife was so crazed with fear that she was irresponsible for, otherwise, she would not have shouted: "Let me kill him! He is going to kill me if I don't." (R., p. 6.)

There is a scarcity of authority on the particular circumstances of this case, though the general principles point to the liability of the defendant, as pointed out above. Certain other authorities lead to the same conclusion.

In an affray, each participant is liable for any injury to a third person. 2 C. J. S. 1006, Affray, § 29. This case differs from an affray only in that an affray is an altercation in a public place, whereas the altercation here occurred in the plaintiff's home. The reason that all of the participants in an affray are liable for any injury to a third person is because they are all deemed to have caused it since they are all engaged in an unlawful fight out of which the injury arises. The elements of, and reason for, liability in this case and in the case of an affray are the same. The distinction between them makes no difference as to the liability.

It is well recognized that if a person assaults one person and in so doing strikes a third person, he is liable to the third person for the assault. 4 Am. Jur. 144, Assault and Battery, § 30; 6 C. J. S. 804, Assault and Battery, § 10(2). And there would seem to be no reason for a different rule where the defendant by an assault on one person caused that person to strike a third person. It is said: "Of course, liability exists if the plaintiff is struck by the defendant while the latter is assaulting a third person, or if such third person, during the assault, is caused to strike, or is thrown against, the plaintiff." 4 Am. Jur. 144, Assault and Battery, § 30 (last sentence).

The doctrine of rescue, i.e., the doctrine that when a person is placed in a position of peril by the negligent act of the defendant, the defendant is liable to a third person who is injured in an attempt to rescue the person placed in peril, is settled law. [Citations omitted.] Though all of the rescue cases examined have been negligence cases, it would seem that that would make no difference, as negligence is just one division of wrongful acts for which recovery may be had, and a person who commits a willful wrongful act is liable in many cases where he would not have been liable if the wrongful act had been merely negligent. Drum v. Miller, 135 N. C. 204, 47 S. E. 421, 65 L. R. A. 890, 102 Am. St. Rep. 528; 52 Am. Jur. 382, Torts, § 32.

However, practically all of the rescue cases deal with defendant's who have placed innocent persons in peril, though occasionally there is one in which the defendant and the person in peril were both negligent, and in those cases it is generally held that the defendant is not relieved of liability merely because the person in peril was also negligent.

In Brugh v. Bigelow, 310 Mich. 74, 16 N.W.2d 668, 158 A. L. R. 184, the Supreme Court of Michigan held that where the defendant, himself, was placed in peril by his own wrongful act, and the plaintiff was injured while rescuing him, the plaintiff could recover her damages from him.

There can be no doubt that in this case the defendant's wrongful act placed him in peril, and therefore, it would seem that the plaintiff in this case should be allowed to recover from the defendant on authority of Brugh v. Bigelow, supra.

Respectfully submitted,

George S. Steele, Jr.
Attorney for Plaintiff-Appellant.
[Filed Nov. 11, 1946.]

* * *

BRIEF FOR DEFENDANT, APPELLEE

Since the record comprises only the evidence of two people the Court can get a picture of this action quickly. To state the evidence succinctly, it seems that Arnisea Taylor, wife of the defendant, had gone to a neighbor's house, the plaintiff, and I will assume it was because of some domestic troubles at home. The record says on page 5, "The polices brought her," referring to the wife of the defendant and from the agility with which this record shows she wields an axe it could be that the "polices" were taking away from home to protect the defendant.

However, the facts seem to be that defendant's wife had left home and there still flowed in his breast a love for her and a yearning for her to return to his home where she rightfully should have been. The defendant seems to be a courteous negro as Dorothy Strickland testified that the defendant came to plaintiff's home and "He came there at 12 o'clock and there wasn't any trouble at all, and he came back at 3 o'clock and she went on the porch and talked to him. The house wasn't locked or anything then." (Page 7 of typed record, cross-examination.) The owner of the house, the plaintiff in the action, was out in the yard washing clothes when the defendant came up. There was nothing hostile in his conversation and the plaintiff insisted on defendant going in the house. When he found the door locked he started on back home and plaintiff called him back and when he told her the door was locked the plaintiff showed more anger than the defendant had shown by going to her door and asking: "What the devil are you doing with the door fastened?" (Page 10 of typed record.)

The evidence comes from the injured plaintiff and her daughter and it discloses nowhere that the defendant actually assaulted his wife in the house as contended by plaintiff in her brief. He merely insisted on his wife coming on home and caught her by the hand to lead her out of the house and before he knew what happened this great big woman located an axe and with probably no notice knocked the defendant down and was on the verge of killing him, lying prostrate and helpless on the floor, when the plaintiff intervened. Except for the fact that counsel for plaintiff is so insistent in his views about this case I would not be disposed to take the time of this Court to file any brief for the defendant. The case was here before and when it came up again before Judge Stevens I think his mind was made up when he examined the witness about the defendant's position in the house of the plaintiff and was informed: "The defendant was lying down on the floor at the time his wife had drawn back to hit him with the axe in the face." (Page 9 of the typed record.)

There is quite a difference in the law of rescue and the rights of the proper parties to recover from the facts in this case. Our court has held that if a man sees a child in danger before an approaching train and he dives forward to rescue the child and is killed, the railroad is liable because of its primary negligence. In the present case, the plaintiff says if the defendant had not been in her house, to which she invited him, she would not have gotten hurt. She can just as logically argue that if she had not been at home she wouldn't have gotten injured and the same argument apply to defendant's wife. As a matter of fact, if the plaintiff had allowed the defendant to go on home when he found the doors locked, the injury would not have occurred and this Court knows the plaintiff would not have invited the defendant in her home if he had had the demeanor of one desiring to raise a fuss. The defendant went in plaintiff's house at her invitation and, legally speaking, having been invited he was entitled to her defense of him against an assault.

Before this Court could hold the defendant liable to the plaintiff in this case I submit it would have to hold that he was a trespasser and had forced his entrance in plaintiff's home. Except for the inference that defendant and his wife may have had some family bickering, all the evidence shows he came to plaintiff's house in good humor, had evidently pleaded peacefully with his wife at 12 o'clock to come home and had repeated his desire for her to come on home where she should have been at the 3 o'clock period as the first witness said his wife went out and told him she would come on home when her brother came. When she did not come, defendant naturally felt the brother may have been delayed and he made another trip. Old "Aunt Lena," a good natured old soul, was out at the wash pot and said defendant was all right. I merely repeat these portions of the evidence to impress on the Court the righteousness of Judge Henry L. Stevens' judgment in dismissing the action of the plaintiff.

Like myself, the Court and my client have a great deal of sympathy for the plaintiff and I am quite confident the defendant hopes to help the plaintiff voluntarily but when he had been knocked violently to the floor by an axe that would have killed some people and while in an evidently dazed condition and helpless on the floor and hardly cognizant of what was taking place over his helpless body, to the defendant it is passing strange that learned counsel can be found who will charge him with what was occurring over his almost dead body as something for which he should be held liable in damages. There is no effort to charge the wife with any liability. It is all against the poor defendant.

I respectfully submit this poor negro is entitled to freedom from further civil litigation and that the judgment in this case should meet the approval of this Court.

Respectfully submitted,

Fred W. Bynum
Attorney for Defendant, Appellee.
[Filed Nov. 14, 1946.]

*   *   *

Less than two weeks after Bynum submitted his brief for the appellee, the North Carolina Supreme Court issued the following opinion:

HARRINGTON v. TAYLOR
North Carolina Supreme Court, Nov. 27, 1946.
226 N.C. 769, 40 S.E.2d 367.

Appeal by plaintiff from Stevens, J., at May Term, 1946, of Richmond.

Civil action to recover damages for personal injuries alleged to have been caused by the negligence of the defendant.

On January 8, 1945, defendant went to the home of the plaintiff to get his wife who had gone there for protection. The defendant and his wife fell to fighting in the plaintiff's house. The defendant's wife had floored him with an axe and had it raised to strike him again when the plaintiff intervened and saved his life, but received a severe cut on the hand when she "got the lick which was intended for him."

From judgment of nonsuit, entered at the close of plaintiff's evidence, she appeals, assigning errors.

George S. Steele, Jr., for plaintiff, appellant.
Fred. W. Bynum for defendant, appellee.

PER CURIAM: The action is against the defendant and not his wife who inflicted the injury. The plaintiff first sued on contract — defendant's promise to pay damages — reported in 225 N.C. 690, 36 S.E.(2d) 227. She now sues in tort.

The evidence is wanting in sufficiency to carry the case to the jury. The injury is not one which the defendant could have reasonably foreseen or anticipated. Butner v. Spease, 217 N.C. 82, 6 S.E. (2d) 808. The judgment of nonsuit will be upheld.

Affirmed.

FURTHER QUESTIONS

1. This case demonstrates that clients don't walk in the door with "tort" or "contract" stamped on their foreheads — that is, that the same transaction can give rise to starkly different legal theories. Which of Lena Harrington's claims was stronger — the tort claim or the contract claim? Presumably you are now familiar with the applicable contract doctrine: generally "past consideration is no consideration," but there may be some exception for promises motivated by strong pre-existing "moral obligations," and promises to compensate another for a benefit conferred may also be enforceable on a "promissory restitution" theory. By contrast, Lena Harrington's tort claim required her to prove that it was reasonably foreseeable to Lee Taylor that his conduct might injure her. Which theory seems stronger to you?

2. The case also raises questions of civil procedure. In the first ("contract") suit, plaintiff's brief made arguments in both tort and contract. But the North Carolina Supreme Court didn't discuss any tort issues in its brief *per curiam* opinion upholding dismissal of the suit. Why didn't the courts in the first suit reach the tort claim?

In plaintiff's brief in the second suit — the tort suit — plaintiff's counsel asserted that the first suit had been in contract, not in tort, even though plaintiff's brief in the first suit argued both. Should the plaintiff have been precluded from litigating the tort claim in the second suit?

3. Are the facts reported by the courts consistent with those set forth in the trial testimony? Does Lee Taylor sound more or less sympathetic now that you've read the transcripts? Lena Harrington? Anisea Taylor? Does the presence of the baby affect your view of the case one way or another? Was the court's statement of the facts complete enough to assess whether this might be a plausible claim for "moral obligation," along the lines of *Webb v. McGowin*?

4. In the contract suit, counsel for the plaintiff did raise the "moral obligation" theory of consideration espoused by the Alabama courts in *Webb*, but the plaintiff didn't cite *Webb* itself. Instead, the plaintiff cited *Jacob Kull & Sons v. W.D. Farmer*, 78 N.C. 339 (1878), in which the North Carolina Supreme Court enforced

a seemingly gratuitous promise to pay a past debt, collection of which was otherwise barred by discharge in bankruptcy. That court reasoned that "the promise itself becomes or may become the cause of action and the unpaid prior legal obligation, notwithstanding the discharge, is a sufficient consideration to support it." Was *Jacob Kull & Sons* distinguishable?

5. The plaintiff's brief also argued that Lee Taylor could be liable in "quasi-contract," or restitution. "It is well settled," plaintiff's counsel wrote, "that were a physician treats a patient who is unconscious when brought to the physician ... the physician may recover from the patient because of the promise of the patient which the law implies." And indeed there is now, and was then, substantial authority to support that assertion. See, e.g., *Cotnam v. Wisdom*, 83 Ark. 601 (1907) (permitting recovery in quasi-contract by a physician). Restatement (2d) of Contracts §86 now also endorses the theory of "promissory restitution." Do you find that theory applicable in *Harrington v. Taylor*?

Suppose it is suggested that physicians are in a special category and should be given a right of recovery that others lack. Argue for this proposition. Argue against it. What do you conclude?

6. What do you make of the defense counsel's brief in the second suit (the tort suit)? How much precedent did it cite? Note that this argument proves to be the winning one. Did the "best brief" win the legal contest?

7. Do you think the race, class or gender of the participants affected the court's judgment? Should these factors be discussed in the court's opinion? In contracts casebooks and treatises?

VII. FULLERTON LUMBER CO. v. TORBORG

FULLERTON LUMBER CO. v. TORBORG
Supreme Court of Wisconsin, 1955.
270 Wis. 133, 70 N.W.2d 585.

[Appeal from a judgment of the circuit court for Waupaca county: Herbert A. Bunde, Circuit Judge. Reversed.]

Action by plaintiff Fullerton Lumber Company, a foreign corporation, against defendant Albert C. Torborg, for an injunction restraining defendant from breach of contract. Upon findings of fact and conclusions of law filed by the trial court, judgment was entered dismissing plaintiff's complaint. From that judgment plaintiff appeals.

Plaintiff is a Minnesota corporation with its principal office in Minneapolis. It operates a number of retail lumber yards in Wisconsin and other states. Defendant began working for the plaintiff in a managerial capacity in 1938. In December 1942 he entered the military service and when he returned to civilian life in November 1945 he was rehired by the company and placed in charge of a yard at Gaylord, Minnesota. At the time of his rehiring he was advised that the pension plan provided for the company's employees had been made applicable to managers who had been employed five years; that the time spent in military service could be counted in the five-year period required to qualify; and that it was the company's policy to require employment agreements with employees who were eligible to participate in such plan. In March 1946 defendant was transferred to Clintonville, Wisconsin, as manager of the company's yard there. On April 15, 1946 he entered into an employment contract with the company which provided, in part:

"If, I cease to be employed by the company for any reason;*
I will not, for a period of ten years thereafter, work directly
or indirectly for any establishment or on my own account
handling lumber, building material or fuel at retail in any
city, village or town, or within a radius of fifteen miles
thereof, where I have served as manager for the company
within a period of five years preceding the date of termination of my employment, unless first obtaining permission,
in writing, from the company."

... In November 1953 [Torborg] voluntarily quit, advising
plaintiff that he intended to open his own lumber yard in that city.
He thereafter incorporated the Clintonville Lumber and Supply,
Inc. and on December 1, 1953 commenced business in Clintonville, taking with him three other of the plaintiff's Clintonville yard
employees.

Plaintiff thereafter brought this action to enjoin defendant
from working for the Clintonville Lumber and Supply, Inc., for
himself or for any other lumber and fuel business within a radius
of fifteen miles of Clintonville during a period of ten years following the termination of his employment by the plaintiff, as provided
in that portion of the contract set out above. The trial court found
that the restraint as to time was unreasonably long and not reasonably necessary for the fair protection of plaintiff's business, and
granted judgment dismissing the complaint.

MARTIN, Justice....

There is no question that restrictive covenants of the type involved in this contract are lawful and enforceable if they meet the
tests of necessity and reasonableness.

As stated in Restatement of the Law, Contracts, sec. 516, p.
995:

"The following bargains do not impose unreasonable restraint of trade unless effecting, or forming part of a plan
to effect, a monopoly: ...

*Punctuation as in original. –RD/GW.

"(f) A bargain by an assistant, servant, or agent not to compete with his employer, or principal, during the term of the employment or agency, or thereafter, within such territory and during such time as may be reasonably necessary for the protection of the employer or principal, without imposing undue hardship on the employee or agent."

At sec. 515, p. 988, of the same text it is stated:

"A restraint of trade is unreasonable, in the absence of statutory authorization or dominant social or economic justification, if it

"(a) is greater than is required for the protection of the person for whose benefit the restraint is imposed . . . ."

It is established that:

"The burden rests upon the employer to establish both the necessity for, and the reasonableness of, the restrictive covenant he seeks to enforce by enjoining the employee from violating its terms." Annotation, 52 A.L.R. 1364.

Cases such as Midland Lumber & Coal Co. v. Roessler, 1930, 203 Wis. 129, 233 N.W. 614; Kradwell v. Thiesen, 1907, 131 Wis. 97, 111 N.W. 233; My Laundry Co. v. Schmeling, 1906, 129 Wis. 597, 109 N.W. 540, and Cottington v. Swan, 1906, 128 Wis. 321, 107 N.W. 336, where this court has upheld restrictive covenants, are not very helpful in this instance because they grow out of the sale of a business rather than employment. As pointed out in the Restatement of the Law, Contracts, sec. 515, Comment (b):

"No identical test of reasonableness applies to bargains for the transfer of land or goods or of a business, on the one hand, and to bargains for employment on the other. The elements that must be considered in order to determine reasonableness differ in the two cases, especially where the employment is of a specialized character, and familiarity and skill in it are assets of the employee. Limitations of his use of these assets are less readily supported than limitations of the use of property or in carrying on a business."

See, also, Annotation 9 A.L.R. 1456, et seq.

Our court has consistently recognized this difference with respect to applying the test of reasonableness, Milwaukee Linen Supply Co. v. Ring, 1933, 210 Wis. 467, 246 N.W. 567, and has allowed a much greater scope of restraint in contracts between vendor and vendee than between employer and employee. As there stated, 210 Wis. at page 473, 246 N.W. at page 569, "There is 'small scope for the restraint of the right to labor and trade and a correspondingly small freedom of contract.' "In all these cases the facts must be carefully scrutinized to determine whether the employee is restrained beyond the point where he could be reasonably anticipated to injure his employer's business. Where the facts warrant such a conclusion this court has held that the entire covenant must fall.

> ". . . if full performance of a promise indivisible in terms, would involve unreasonable restraint, the promise is illegal and is not enforceable even for so much of the performance as would be a reasonable restraint." Restatement, Contracts, sec. 518, p. 1004.

We agree with the trial court that the ten-year period of restraint imposed by the instant contract is unreasonably long. There is no case cited where this court has upheld a covenant in an employment contract restricting the employee from engaging in competitive activity for so long a time, and the evidence in this case does not establish that a ten-year restraint is necessary for the protection of plaintiff's business.

It cannot be seriously disputed, however, that defendant was plaintiff's key employee in the Clintonville yard. Being a foreign corporation with all its officers and supervisory employees outside of the state, the plaintiff necessarily depended for the growth and maintenance of good will in the Clintonville area upon the efforts and personal assets of the defendant. In the first three years of his employment as manager there he tripled the business of the yard and thereafter (with the exception of 1952 when the entire country experienced a building "boom") he maintained the sales at a level averaging well over $200,000 per year. He terminated his employment at the end of 1953 and immediately commenced operations in Clintonville in competition with the plaintiff. The sales of plaintiff's yard for 1954, based upon its business for the first five months of that year, were estimated at approximately $60,000, a decline of more than two-thirds of the average annual sales of the previous years (excluding the peak year 1952).

These facts conclusively show not only that the business of plaintiff's Clintonville yard depended largely on the efforts, and customer contacts of the defendant, but that it suffered an irreparable loss when defendant took those efforts and customer contacts, as well as three other employees of plaintiff's yard, into a competitive business immediately after he left its employ.

Defendant states in his brief:

> "We concede at this point that plaintiff does have a legitimate interest in its business and good will which it is entitled to preserve by exacting a reasonable restrictive covenant from its manager. The testimony in this case clearly shows that defendant has been able to establish a business at Clintonville which has substantially cut into the business of plaintiff. This, of course, was possible because defendant started his business immediately after he quit plaintiff, while all of his connections with the customers of the plaintiff were still strong. It is obvious that if defendant were removed from the scene for any extended period, and his place were taken by another Fullerton manager, the good will and trade of the plaintiff would be safe in the hands of the new manager."

There has been no case in this court where the facts presented such a clear need for the kind of protection plaintiff thought it was bargaining for when this contract was made. The facts show that it had every reason to anticipate its business would suffer if defendant, after developing and establishing personal relations with its customers in Clintonville, chose to leave its employ and enter into competition with it in that vicinity.

It is, of course, necessary to consider whether the legality of the covenant is open to objection on the ground of coercion or interference with individual liberty.

"... injunctive relief will not be awarded against breach of a covenant the real purpose of which was to prevent the employee from quitting the employers' service." Annotation 52 A.L.R. 1363.

There is no evidence that such a purpose existed when this contract was drawn and the fact that defendant did in fact terminate the employment to carry on competitive operations shows that the restrictive covenant had no such deterring effect upon him. There is no showing that it had had that effect at any time while he was working for the plaintiff.

The evidence of irreparable damage to the plaintiff is so strong in this case that we have undertaken a thorough reconsideration of the rule that has obtained in Wisconsin — that a covenant imposing an unreasonable restraint is unenforceable in its entirety. ...

In 5 Williston on Contracts (Rev.Ed.) secs. 1659 and 1660, the author discusses the divisibility of promises and states that the traditional test of severability is the "blue-penciling" test (which this court [has] applied) .... But he points out that in England, which is the source of this rule (as evident from the Massachusetts cases following it), it has been held that:

"... where a negative restrictive covenant, indivisible in terms, extended beyond a time that the court in its discretion thought appropriate for an injunction, it granted an injunction for the period during which it deemed that remedy reasonable." Sec. 1659, p. 4683.

In Oregon Steam Nav. Co. v. Winsor, 1874, 20 Wall. 64, 22 L.Ed. 315, 319, the plaintiff purchased a steamer from the California Steam Navigation Company subject to a stipulation that it should not be run upon any of the water routes of the state of California for ten years from May 1, 1864. In February 1867 plaintiff sold the steamer to the defendants subject to the stipulation that it should not be employed on such routes for ten years from May 1, 1867. In a suit based on breach of the latter agreement it was held that the restrictive covenant was necessary in order that the plaintiff might keep its covenant with the California Company, but since it extended three years beyond the period for which plaintiff was bound to the California Company, the extra period of three years was not necessary to the protection of the plaintiff. The court said:

> "But the suit is brought and the breach is alleged for a portion of time during which the Oregon Company is bound to protect the California Company from the interference of said steamer. And the question arises whether the contract is so divisible in relation to the California portion that it can stand for the seven years for which the Oregon Company is bound, though it be void as to the remaining three years. We think it is so divisible. It is laid down by Chitty as the result of the cases, and his authorities support the statement, 'that agreements in restraint of trade, whether under seal or not, are divisible; and, accordingly, it has been held that when such an agreement contains a stipulation which is capable of being construed divisibly, and one part thereof is void as being in restraint of trade, whilst the other is not, the court will give effect to the latter, and will not hold the agreement to be void altogether.' . . . We see no reason why this principle should not be followed in the present case. The line of division between the period which is properly covered by the restriction and that which is not so, is clearly defined and easily drawn. It is subject to no confusion or uncertainty, and the court can have no difficulty in applying it."

. . . As stated in 6 Corbin on Contracts, sec. 1394, p. 524:

> "As in the case of contracts restraining the seller of a business with its good will, the fact that the restriction on an employee goes too far to be valid as a whole does not prevent a court from enforcing it in part insofar as it is reasonable and not oppressive. The injunction may be made operative only as to reasonable space and time . . ."

It is our considered opinion that this view should be adopted in Wisconsin. While we recognize that the rule of partial enforcement of indivisible promises is a departure from that which this court has adhered to in the past, there is no departure from the general principle that contracts in restraint of trade are void as against public policy if they deprive the public of the restricted party's industry or injure the party himself by precluding him from pursuing his occupation and thus prevent him from supporting himself and his family. Where the terms of a restrictive covenant, not otherwise invalid, restrain an employee beyond either the area or the time within which an employer needs protection from competition by him, it is that excess of territory or time that is contrary to public policy and void.

As set out above, this court has been willing to apply the "blue-pencil" test to area restrictions, . . . but we do not see why the basic reason for such willingness to enforce a contract after removing terms which are literally divisible should not also exist in the case of indivisible promises where the evidence is ample to support a finding as to the extent the restriction would be necessary and valid. Territory limits are by their nature more susceptible to separate specification than time and are often so expressed, but we see no difficulty in making a finding as to time upon evidence which is available to show the necessity for restraint in that respect.

In considering this rule many authorities point to the danger that its application might tend to encourage employers and purchasers possessing superior bargaining power to insist upon oppressive restrictions. However, these contracts are always subject to the test of whether their purpose is contrary to public policy, and if there is any credible evidence to sustain a finding that they are deliberately unreasonable and oppressive, such covenants must be held invalid whether severable or not.

The judgment is reversed and the cause remanded for a determination by the trial court of the extent of time as to which the restrictive covenant with respect to defendant's operations in Clintonville is reasonable and necessary for plaintiff's protection, and for judgment enjoining defendant from a breach thereof. It appears to us that a minimum period of three years would be supported by the evidence. It was established that after defendant took over the managership of plaintiff's yard in 1945 he built the business to a fairly constant level in that period of time, and it must be assumed that any manager taking his place could accomplish the same thing if the restrictions of the contract were enforced against the defendant during that time. In view of the fact that defendant has engaged in continuous competitive activities since December

1, 1953, employing the advantage gained while he was in the service of the plaintiff, the injunction should run from the date of the judgment rather than the date the employment terminated.

We are not passing upon the reasonableness of the restrictive covenant with respect to competition by defendant in Arcadia and Gaylord, Minnesota. The record contains no evidence that restrictions are necessary for the plaintiff's protection in those areas, and a showing of necessity must be made before the covenant will be upheld as to those locations.

Judgment reversed and cause remanded for further proceedings in accordance with this opinion.

GEHL, Justice (dissenting).

The majority agree that the ten-year restraint imposed by the contract is unreasonably long. This court has consistently held that an unreasonably long restraint is unenforceable, void and illegal [five citations omitted] and that a void contract, one against public policy, cannot be made the foundation of any action, whether in law or equity. Brill v. Salzwedel, 235 Wis. 551, 292 N.W. 908.

It is true, as the majority say, that there has been a tendency on the part of some courts to ascertain whether a contract in restraint of trade is divisible and, if found to be, to hold it unreasonable only to the extent necessary for the protection of the covenantee. Unless that position is limited, however, as it has been by this court, it gives effect to the court's notion as to what should be included in the contract, rather than to the intent of the parties as expressed in the contract, the parties who, had they desired a narrower or a broader provision, should and could have expressed it in the writing. If the provision is to be treated as being divisible, such purpose must be found in the contract itself; that quality should not be supplied by the court simply because it might be considered that the parties should have made broader or narrower provision against possible competition than they did. That is the rule of this state. . . .

The question in Wisconsin Ice & Coal Co. v. Lueth, 213 Wis. 42, 250 N.W. 819, 821, was whether the territory covered by a restrictive covenant was unreasonably large in view of the circumstances. We said in that case:

"If the contract is unreasonable in its territorial scope, and if the contract itself furnishes no basis for dividing the territory to which the restriction applies, the restrictive covenant is void, and is not aided by the plaintiff's willingness to accept in the injunctional order a restriction that is proper in scope." (Emphasis supplied.)

I have found no Wisconsin case which suggests that the court, rather than the parties who made the contract, should be permitted to substitute arbitrarily for the parties a provision making an indivisible covenant divisible. The citation of text authorities and of cases from other jurisdictions "is but misplaced industry." They are of no help to this court which has so clearly stated the rule that if a covenant is to be treated as being divisible and therefore enforceable to the extent that it is a reasonable restriction, the fact of divisibility must appear from the contract itself. If it can be said that a single provision as to time, ten years as is this case, is divisible and it is possible to read that quality out of the terms of the contract, then it is only reasonable to ask, how could a provision indivisible as to time be effectively expressed?

It is apparent that the majority have construed the contract and applied a rule in the light of what has taken place since its execution. It occurs to me to inquire: as of what time are we to determine that the terms of a contract are or are not unreasonable? Is it to be determined as of the time of its execution, or as of a later time? May we say that a contract is void and then, not because of its terms, but because of the manner in which one of the parties to it has subsequently construed its terms, or because he has violated its provisions to the loss of the other party, still hold it enforceable in whole or in part? I doubt it.

In Sheffield-King Milling Co. v. Jacobs, 170 Wis. 389, 175 N.W. 796, 801, we said:

"The validity of a contract is to be determined as of the date of its execution, and a contract valid when made cannot be rendered invalid even by legislative action. [City of] Superior v. Douglas County Tel. Co., 141 Wis. 363, 122 N.W. 1023. It is the situation of the parties at the time of the inception of the contract that governs. Davis v. La Crosse Hospital Ass'n, 121 Wis. 579, 99 N.W. 351."

It would seem that if a provision of a contract valid when made cannot be rendered invalid even by legislative action, one invalid when made cannot be validated, in whole or in part, by action of the parties.

The mere fact that developments subsequent to the execution of the contract show that the parties, or one of them, should have made a better bargain for himself does not affect the situation. Miller Saw-Trimmer Co. v. Cheshire, 172 Wis. 278, 178 N.W. 855.

I would affirm.

FIRST QUESTIONS

1. Do the facts cited by the Court "conclusively show . . . that the business of plaintiff's Clintonville Yard depended largely on the efforts and customer contacts of the defendant . . ."? Conceive alternative explanations for the decline of Fullerton Lumber's Clintonville sales. How much confidence do you have in the Court's judgment on this point?

2. Assume that the Court is correct that the loss to Fullerton is attributable to Torborg's defection. What supports the court's judgment that the loss is "irreparable"? What evidence could possibly justify such a judgment?

3. Criticize the rule of law articulated by the Supreme Court in terms of the capability problems it will encounter. Taking account of these capability problems would you vote with the majority in this case? (Consider, among other things, the capability problems encountered by alternatives to the majority's rule.)

4. As the dissent notes, the Supreme Court here changes the law of Wisconsin. Quite apart from the merits of the new rule, what capability problems are posed by changing the law in the way it was changed here?

5. On remand the trial court held that Torborg was restrained from competing with Fullerton Lumber for three years. What do you think subsequently happened to Fullerton Lumber and to Torborg? (Imagine all the capability problems that you think might impede Fullerton Lumber's securing the protection that the appellate court thought desirable.)

SUPPLEMENTARY COMMENTS[*]

Usually, a law school casebook reprints only an appellate opinion. On one level, this can be misleading because it is easy to draw the wrong inference about what actually happened to the parties in the case or to similarly situated people after the decision was issued. It is one thing to win a judgment; it is another to enforce it. It is fine to get a trial court judgment against you reversed on appeal; it may be less than fine if it leads to an expensive second trial which you lose for other reasons. On another level, a single appellate opinion can be misleading because it is but one step in a process of statement and correction over time. One can understand the law sometimes only by reading a series of opinions by the same court dealing with the same or related problems. Sometimes one must read a series of opinions, statutes, administrative regulations and law review commentaries to understand the process which is taking place. Sometimes one must turn to unofficial sources as well.

What can we learn about *Fullerton Lumber Co. v. Torborg* beyond the edited opinion? Law professors and practicing lawyers share the problem of resources. Ideally, one would interview officials of Fullerton, Mr. Torborg, their lawyers and people in Clintonville as well as read all of the documents available. However, this would be extremely costly, involving at least a week in Clintonville and several days in Minneapolis, the home of Fullerton Lumber. Moreover, the events are generally over fifty years in the past, and those involved may have reasons to bury that past. What follows then is what can be found in records available in Madison and Milwaukee. Reliance is placed on the briefs and records on the two appeals before the Supreme Court, the bill file in the Wisconsin Legislative Reference Library, the files of the United States District Court for the Eastern District of Wisconsin, the annual corporate reports in the office of the Secretary of State, the micro-film copies of the weekly *Clintonville Tribune-Gazette*, and the

---

[*]These comments were written by Professor Stewart Macaulay of the University of Wisconsin Law School. They are reprinted with his permission. We have made a few minor updates, mostly at the end of the essay.

Clintonville telephone directory. Also, there was correspondence with some of the participants.

First, let us turn to the arguments made on the appeal which yielded the opinion reprinted above. The trial judge had found unreasonable the ten year restriction on competition in the employment contract, and thus Fullerton Lumber had to convince the Supreme Court to overturn this judgment. Fullerton's brief assembled the facts to support two major arguments. The first was that Fullerton had been seriously injured when Al Torborg quit as its yard manager, hired away other Fullerton employees and opened his competing yard, Clintonville Lumber and Supply, Inc. Fullerton Lumber Co. introduced in evidence exhibits showing the impact on its business during the first five months of 1954 (the trial was in June). The sales at Fullerton's Clintonville yard had decreased from $68,821 during January to May in 1953, to $17,012, during the same period in 1954. The $51,809 decrease in business was a 75.2% loss. At the same time, Mr. Torborg's Clintonville Lumber and Supply had sales of $46,745 for these five months in 1954. The sales at several other Fullerton yards in nearby Wisconsin cities indicated that the loss was not due to factors peculiar to Fullerton Lumber or general economic conditions.

Fullerton sought to show that its customers had followed Al Torborg to his Clintonville Lumber and Supply, Inc. He was well known in Clintonville, and, as part of his job with Fullerton, he had been active in civic affairs. It was front page news in the *Clintonville Tribune-Gazette* of November 26, 1953, that "Torborg to Start Lumber Company . . . Clintonville will have a third lumber outlet Dec. 1 when Al Torborg opens a retail building materials center and construction contracting service . . .". The article mentioned that "the manager of sales and construction will be I. C. (Ike) Hokenstein, another former Fullerton employee." In fact, the only Fullerton employees left at its Clintonville yard were two truck drivers who had had little contact with the public. On December 17, 1953, Clintonville Lumber and Supply ran an advertisement announcing that "we are now open for business." The ad featured Mr. Torborg's name prominently. Undoubtedly, in a small town such as Clintonville, people talked about Torborg's new business.

The second major point in the Fullerton brief was that Torborg had been a well treated employee. In 1946, when he took over the

Clintonville yard, he was paid $200 a month. When he quit in 1953, he was making $600 a month. In addition, he received yearly bonuses based on sales. In 1953, his bonus was $2,039; in 1952, $1,536; in 1951, $1,000. Finally, Fullerton made contributions to a pension plan. While Torborg's 1953 compensation of $9,239 may not seem too impressive today, one must recall that this was 1953, and it was paid to a man working in a small town. In 1953, for example, beginning lawyers received about $5,000 a year, and sirloin steak cost 79¢ a pound in Clintonville. Al Torborg's own letter of resignation stated, "I enjoyed working for you and your Company, and leaving your organization is the only regret I have in the move."

Why did Fullerton Lumber Co., Inc. lay stress on these two points? In what way are they relevant to show that the trial judge was wrong and that a ten year restriction from competition in Clintonville was reasonable? To the extent that they do not seem particularly relevant to that point, why did Fullerton make them? To what extent, if at all, is it relevant that Fullerton is a Minnesota corporation, doing business in nine states and a Canadian province with total sales of $27,888,531 in 1953?

Torborg was in a strong tactical position on appeal. The trial judge had found in his favor because the judge had determined that a ten year restriction was unreasonable. Since the existing Wisconsin case law clearly followed the all or nothing rule — that is, if the employer obtained an unreasonable restraint on competition, he would be denied any protection — it seemed that all Torborg had to do was defend the finding that ten years was too much. Thus, his lawyer stated in his brief:

> Even the time limit of ten years as applied to the Clintonville area is unreasonable.
>
> We concede at this point that plaintiff does have a legitimate interest in its business and good will which it is entitled to preserve by exacting a reasonable restrictive covenant from its manager. The testimony in this case clearly shows that defendant has been able to establish a business at Clintonville which has substantially cut into the business of plaintiff. This, of course, was possible because defendant started his business immediately after he quit

plaintiff, while all of his connections with the customers of the plaintiff were still strong. It is obvious that if defendant were removed from the scene for any extended period, and his place were taken by another Fullerton manager, the good will and trade of the plaintiff would be safe in the hands of the new manager.

There is no evidence that defendant was the only capable manager that plaintiff had in its system of over one hundred stores. The testimony shows that the year before defendant went to Clintonville the gross sales of that yard were about $88,000.00 (R. 299, A-Ap. 178). At the end of about three years the gross sales had about tripled (R. 299, A-Ap. 178), and defendant had reached a peak in building up the business (R. 299, A-Ap. 179). Thereafter the fluctuations were not significant. While it is true that defendant may have increased his acquaintance in the community and in business circles after three years, it may be safely assumed that if the manager who preceded defendant had returned after three years, he would not have been able materially to affect plaintiff's business because of any hold that he might have acquired during his tenure as manager.

Likewise the trial court in viewing all of the evidence presented is entitled to find that if defendant were barred from Clintonville for some period substantially shorter than ten years, it would have been sufficient for plaintiff's protection.

From the evidence of the increase in gross sales during defendant's first three years, it may be inferred that a three year period would be long enough. Certainly five years would have been ample. Plaintiff could have sent to Clintonville another manager of skill, experience and ability equal to that of defendant. In a period of from three to five years the new manager would have acquired the same hold on the business and good will of plaintiff's yard that defendant had when he quit.

On the basis of these facts it is submitted that the findings of the trial court that the restraint is unreasonable must be sustained. Not only are the findings not against the great weight and clear preponderance of the evidence; they are sustained by the preponderance of the credible evidence and the reasonable inferences therefrom.

Here, and not in the Fullerton Lumber Co. brief, the idea was introduced into the case that a three year restriction would be reasonable. The paragraph beginning "We concede at this point that plaintiff does have a legitimate interest in its business . . ." is marked in pencil in the set of briefs in the University of Wisconsin Law School Library; very possibly one of the Justices of the Supreme Court made these marks. Torborg's three-or-five-but-not-ten argument was a perfectly good one as long as it was assumed that the Wisconsin court would follow its past cases and insist that restrictions as drafted be entirely valid or entirely without legal effect. Once that assumption fell, then such a concession was very damaging to Torborg's position.

It appears that Torborg's attorney had placed great reliance on what prior Wisconsin cases had held concerning the validity of restrictions on competition by former employees. After the Supreme Court had unpleasantly surprised him by its opinion, he sought a rehearing and made the following arguments:

> It is obvious from this testimony that Mr. Torborg had been advised that the contract was void because the time limit was too long and he was willing to act upon this advice and invest his funds in his own venture. Under the law of the state of Wisconsin prior to the decision in the present case, it must be admitted that Mr. Torborg received sound advice. The Circuit Court found that the restrictive covenant for ten years was unreasonable and void. The Supreme Court affirmed the findings of the Circuit Court that the ten year restriction is unreasonable, but because of sympathy for the corporation, it determined to overrule its former decisions and apply a new rule under which no restrictive covenants will ever be void no matter how long a time or how great an area is involved.
>
> Relying upon the decisions of this court which stood for over twenty years, Mr. Torborg invested all his funds and the funds of his family in a new venture to the extent of in excess of $60,000.00. Because of his rather unusual suc-

cess in establishing his business the court concluded that it must not apply the rules which have been established for many years and upon which Mr. Torborg relied when he invested his money, but that it must overrule the existing decisions so that it may protect the Fullerton Lumber Company from Mr. Torborg.

Since the attorney who wrote this brief also prepared the articles of incorporation for Mr. Torborg's Clintonville Lumber and Supply which were filed on November 16, 1953, it is likely that the attorney is reporting the advice which he gave to Mr. Torborg. Doesn't Mr. Torborg's attorney have a point? Wasn't Torborg entitled to rely on the law as settled, the promise as void, and his consequent freedom to enter business with, for him, a large investment? What does this incident suggest to you about your future role as an attorney giving legal advice to clients? What does the concession in the brief suggest about the tactics of legal argument?

When the case was remanded to the trial court, it held a hearing on December 15, 1955. The judge stated: "The injunction will be issued for a period of three years from 3 October, 1955 . . . . The provisions of the injunctional order are those as suggested by Mr. Moss [the attorney for Fullerton Lumber]. I will expect Mr. Moss will submit the proposed injunctional order to the attorneys for the defendant before submitting the same to the Court for signature." Notice who gets to write the first draft of an official governmental order. Does the practice trouble you? Is it fair to Mr. Torborg? What burdens does it place on Mr. Torborg's attorneys?

The court signed the following order on February 28, 1956:

> IT IS HEREBY ORDERED, ADJUDGED AND DECREED that the defendant, Albert C. Torborg, should be and he hereby is enjoined and restrained for a period of three (3) years commencing at twelve o'clock Noon on October 3, 1955, from working directly or indirectly for the Clintonville Lumber & Supply, Inc., a corporation, located at Clintonville, Wisconsin, engaged in the sale of lumber, building material and fuel at retail in said City of Clintonville and within a radius of fifteen (15) miles of said City and he is hereby enjoined and restrained from working directly or indirectly for any firm, corporation, business or

person or for himself, handling lumber, building material or fuel at retail in the City of Clintonville or within a radius of fifteen (15) miles thereof.

IT IS FURTHER ORDERED, ADJUDGED AND DE-CREED that the defendant, Albert C. Torborg, should be and he hereby is enjoined and restrained for a period of three (3) years, commencing at twelve o'clock Noon on October 3, 1955, from:

1. Continuing, remaining or becoming an officer, director, or stockholder of the Clintonville Lumber & Supply, Inc., a corporation, located at Clintonville, Wisconsin, or any other firm, corporation, or business, handling lumber, building material or fuel at retail in the City of Clintonville or within a radius of fifteen (15) miles of said City of Clintonville.

2. Attending any corporate meetings, directors' meetings or stockholders' meetings of the Clintonville Lumber & Supply, Inc., a corporation, located at Clintonville, Wisconsin, or any other firm, corporation or business, handling lumber, building material or fuel at retail in the City of Clintonville or within a radius of fifteen (15) miles of said City of Clintonville.

3. Furnishing advice or counsel to the Clintonville Lumber & Supply, Inc., a corporation, located at Clintonville, or to its officers, directors or employees, or to any other firm, corporation or business or its employees, handling lumber, building material or fuel at retail in the City of Clintonville or within a radius of fifteen (15) miles of said City of Clintonville.

4. Authorizing or permitting the use of his name by the Clintonville Lumber & Supply, Inc., a corporation, located at Clintonville, Wisconsin, on its stationery, accounts, statements or advertising; or in connection with any phase of the business or operation of the Clintonville Lumber & Supply, Inc., or any other firm, corporation or business, handling lumber, building material or fuel at retail in the City of Clintonville or within a radius of fifteen miles of said City of Clintonville.

5. Inducing or soliciting, or attempting to induce or solicit, any person, firm, corporation or business to purchase lumber, building material or fuel from the Clintonville Lumber & Supply, Inc., a corporation, located at Clintonville, Wisconsin, or any other firm.

6. Inducing or soliciting, or attempting to induce or solicit, any person, firm, corporation or business not to purchase lumber, building material or fuel from the Fullerton Lumber Company, located at Clintonville, Wisconsin.

Before you read on, consider the injunction and predict its consequences. Has Mr. Moss neglected to cover any important point? Will this injunction destroy Clintonville Lumber and Supply, Inc.? Whether or not it does this, will it send the customers back to Fullerton Lumber or will they go to O & N Lumber Co., the third lumber yard doing business in Clintonville? In light of the Supreme Court's opinion is the injunction fair to Mr. Torborg? Can you suggest improvements in the terms of the injunction?

While the trial court granted the three year injunction, it refused to hold a hearing on the issue of Fullerton Lumber's damages caused by Mr. Torborg's breach of contract and competition from December of 1953 to April 3, 1954, when a temporary injunction was issued. Again the case was taken to the Supreme Court of Wisconsin, and it reversed and remanded the case for a hearing on the issue of damages. On December 24, 1959, the Circuit Court of Waupaca County entered judgment against Mr. Torborg, for $9,500.00; indeed, an unpleasant Christmas gift to him. How do you suppose that sum was arrived at? What would Fullerton have to show to establish its claim?

The Supreme Court's second opinion in *Fullerton Lumber Co. v. Torborg* was issued on January 7, 1957. On February 26, 1957, Assemblyman Richard E. Peterson, a Republican who represented Waupaca County and who had law offices in Clintonville, wrote a letter to the head of the Wisconsin Legislative Drafting Service. He requested that a bill be drafted for him to introduce. He said, "I respectfully request that you draw a bill which will have the effect of preventing the recovery of damages under any of these restrictive covenants, which are held unreasonable by the Court in any respect, but divisible to the extent that the Court will hold them enforceable as to area or time determined by the Court to be reasonable." The letter, then, requested a bill to overturn the second opinion in *Fullerton Lumber Co. v. Torborg*.

The original draft of the bill is in longhand written by pencil. It is almost the same as the statute ultimately passed by the legislature (reproduced below). The last lines of the longhand draft have been erased and the present last lines of the statute were written over the erasure. Insofar as one can read what was erased, it appears to be language dealing with the employee's liability for damages. Perhaps the change was only for ease of drafting as the erased draft appears to have been rather complex while the revised version is fairly simple and straightforward. Assemblyman Peterson's letter did attack the first Supreme Court opinion concerning revising overbroad clauses. He said, "at the time the contract was entered into, the bargaining position of the two contractors appears to me to be relatively unequal in that the party seeking enforcement must, if he desires employment with the contracting party, consent to almost any restrictive covenant imposed." The bill was approved on July 24, 1957. It now appears on the statute books as Wisconsin Statute §103.465 and reads as follows:

Restrictive covenants in employment contracts

A covenant by an assistant, servant or agent not to compete with his employer or principal during the term of the employment or agency, or thereafter, within a specified territory and during a specified time is lawful and enforceable only if the restrictions imposed are reasonably necessary for the protection of the employer or principal. Any such restrictive covenant imposing an unreasonable restraint is illegal, void and unenforceable even as to so much of the covenant or performance as would be a reasonable restraint.

One of Mr. Torborg's former attorneys has written, "The case has created an unusual amount of interest by other attorneys representing clients in the same or similar positions, and it was . . . the uncertainty in the case law that prompted Assemblyman Peterson, who at the time was a practicing attorney in the City of Clintonville, to introduce a bill which reversed the rule of this case." What does this suggest about the source and nature of legislative oversight of decisions of the State Supreme Court which change the law? About the need for certainty of legal rules in business affairs? What is it which must be predictable, if not certain? How would you define the opposing interests: who would be in favor of the Supreme Court's position and who in favor of the legislative solution? Does the lawyer-assemblyman source of the statute suggest how the interests of one group are fed into the law making process? What group?

The draft bill, as originally introduced by Assemblyman Peterson, had the phrase, "without imposing undue hardship on the employee or agent" after the phrase "reasonably necessary for the protection of the employer or principal" which is in the statute as passed. What does this deleted phrase indicate about the uncertainty explanation for Assemblyman Peterson's action? About the interests involved in the passage of the bill? Interestingly, the Supreme Court of Wisconsin, in Lakeside Oil v. Slutsky, 8 Wis.2d 157, 98 N.W.2d 415 (1958), in interpreting the statute, read in a requirement that the restriction from competition not be unreasonable to the employee or to the general public. To what extent, did the court overturn the amendment which deleted the employee hardship language? Under a separation of powers theory, was the court warranted in doing this?

So much for the statute. What about the parties in the case? Fullerton Lumber Company's presence in Clintonville seems to have gradually faded away. By the early 1970s, its sales in Wisconsin were less than half of those reported in 1953, when the Torborg case began. Today, Fullerton Lumber Co. is still in business in Wisconsin and several other states, but its website lists no office in Clintonville. By contrast, Clintonville Lumber and Supply, Inc. maintained a business in Clintonville for decades after the decision, and a web search still shows a Clintonville Lumber Co. in Clintonville. Interestingly, however, the first listing under "Lumber" in a search of internet yellow pages for Clintonville yields this entry: Torborg's Lumber. Fullerton Lumber may have won its lawsuit against Torborg, but not the fight for market share in Clintonville.

That's not to say that Torborg didn't honor the injunction. While the temporary injunction pending the original trial was in effect, Clintonville Lumber and Supply, Inc., advertised, "Business as Usual. The only completely locally owned firm of its kind in Clintonville, will continue to give you the best products, materials and service available." *Clintonville Tribune-Gazette*, April 22, 1954, § 3, p. 16. The original Supreme Court opinion was handed down on June 1, 1955, and the motion for rehearing was denied on September 13, 1955. On December 1, 1955, a letter was sent to the Secretary of State indicating that Albert C. Torborg had withdrawn as Secretary-Treasurer of Clintonville Lumber and Supply. In the *Clintonville Tribune-Gazette*, March 1, 1956, p. 2, col. 5, it was stated that "Al Torborg, who operates Steel Building Sales, Inc., 227 Monroe Street, Green Bay, will leave Sunday for Detroit, Michigan, where he will attend the annual national dealer meeting of Stran-Steel Corp., Mar. 6 & 7." In the annual report for 1956, filed with the Secretary of State on January 8, 1957, Clintonville Lumber and Supply, Inc. indicated that Betty Torborg had become its Vice-President sometime in 1956. Betty Torborg's address was the same as listed for Albert C. Torborg on the firm's 1955 report. She was again listed as Vice-President in the report for 1957. The injunction against Albert C. Torborg's association with Clintonville Lumber and Supply, Inc., expired in October of 1958. In the report for 1958, filed in January of 1959, A. C. Torborg was listed as Secretary-Treasurer. In the reports filed for 1970 and 1971, A. C. Torborg is listed as President and Betty Torborg as Secretary-Treasurer. Mr. Torborg filed for bankruptcy on January 27, 1959, and received a discharge on December 26, 1961. The major debt wiped out by the discharge was Fullerton Lumber Company's judgment for $9,500.00.

Apparently, Fullerton Lumber Co. won most of the legal battles before the courts but lost the war in Clintonville. How would you explain the reasons for this seemingly paradoxical outcome?

And what were the costs of all this legal warfare? One cost of extended litigation is delay and uncertainty while awaiting results. You will recall matters started with Mr. Torborg's resignation on November 4, 1953. The action for an injunction was commenced on January 6, 1954. The first trial was on June 28th and 29th. The original judgment was filed on October 7th. The first Supreme Court opinion was filed on June 1, 1955, and became final on September 13th. The trial court held a hearing on the injunction on December 15, 1955, and filed its order on February 28th. The second appeal on the damages issue gave rise to a Supreme Court opinion remanding the case for additional proceedings, which was filed on January 7, 1957. There was a judgment against Mr. Torborg for $9,500 on December 24, 1959, finally discharged in bankruptcy in 1961. Not quite up to a Dickens novel, but still very slow.

The major cost probably was lawyers' fees. We do not know what each side paid its lawyers. However, we can get a very rough sense of the amounts likely involved by consulting the State Bar Association of Wisconsin suggested minimum fee schedules and making some estimates. The schedules for 1955-56, would apply to the entire injunction proceeding; those for 1957 likely would cover the damages issue involved in the second Supreme Court case. The 1972 rates are given to indicate what might be involved if the case had been tried then. In 1975, the U.S. Supreme Court held that suggested minimum fee schedules violate the antitrust laws,[1] but it's still possible to estimate recent rates by consulting reports on the practice of law in Wisconsin.[2]

Before Circuit Court	1955	1957	1972	2001
Appearance in court, per day	$75	$150	$300	$1000
Preparation of law or facts, per day	75	100	30/hr	120/hr
Before Supreme Court				
Appearance and argument	150	200	300	500
Preparation of appendix and brief, per day	75	100	30/hr	120/hr
Motion for rehearing		100		
Preparation brief for motions, per day	75	100	30/hr	120/hr
Hourly rate	10	15	30	120

In the injunction proceeding, there were two days of trial, and so both the lawyer for Fullerton and the lawyer for Torborg each should bill at least $150 for this. Each should bill at least another

1. Goldfarb v. Virginia State Bar, 421 U.S. 773 (1975).

2. Billing data for 2001 show a mean hourly rate of $125 and a median of $146 for East/Central Wisconsin, and a mean hourly rate of $117 and a median of $120 for towns with fewer than 5,000 people. See The Economics of Practicing Law:

$150 for the appearance before the Supreme Court. Now comes the hard part: How many hours or days should the client be billed for to represent the legal research and writing done by both attorneys? Fullerton Lumber's attorney wrote a 56 page appellant's brief, citing 23 cases. He edited a 103 page appendix containing what he thought to be the relevant parts of the record of the trial, including the transcript of testimony and the exhibits. He wrote a 15 page reply brief, and he wrote a 17 page brief opposing Torborg's petition for rehearing. Torborg's attorney produced a 30 page respondent's brief and a 29 page brief on his motion for rehearing. Both sides were aided by A.L.R. annotations which made the research somewhat easier. Each attorney, it would seem, could bill for no less than four full days of research and writing to produce these documents. (Ask yourself how long it would take you to write the number of pages produced by the attorneys; four days is likely a very conservative estimate.) Four days at $75 per day would come to $300 for each. So far we've run up $600 for each side, but undoubtedly there was also research and writing to prepare for circuit court too. Add another $100 for a minimum estimated fee of $700. Of course, lawyers do not have to charge the suggested minimum: the fees could have been much more since one or both lawyers could have put in for more time than these estimates or one or both could bill at substantially higher rates. Fullerton Lumber's lawyer, particularly, is very unlikely to have billed at the suggested minimum fees.

The damages litigation through the Supreme Court should have been billed at the higher 1957 rates. There was somewhat less involved in this proceeding. (We do not know what was involved in trying the case when it was remanded.) One also can suggest $700 more as a minimum estimate in this part of the case. You can make your own guesses about the case if it were tried today.

A Snapshot, 74 Wisconsin Lawyer (Dec. 2001), Table 6, reprinted at the website of the Wisconsin State Bar Association, www.wisbar.org. Clintonville is in East-Central Wisconsin, and it has a population of just under 5,000 people, so $120/hour seems like a fair estimate.

FURTHER QUESTIONS

1. If Fullerton Lumber could have foreseen all that followed Torborg's resignation, what course of action should it have adopted when he served notice that he was leaving the yard?

2. If Fullerton Lumber could have foreseen all that this essay describes, what, if anything, could it have done to better protect itself when it hired Torborg?

3. "When the Wisconsin Supreme Court said that Fullerton Lumber would suffer 'irreparable damage' from Torborg's immediate competition, what it really meant was not that the damage was irreparable, but rather that it was incalculable. In an effort, however, to finesse this capability problem it unwisely opted for a course of action (specific performance) which encountered a yet greater capability problem." Do you agree? What should a court do in cases like this?

4. Which better takes account of capability problems, the statute passed by the Wisconsin Legislature or the majority opinion reprinted here?

5. Try to envision the conclusions you would draw if you simply read the appellate opinion in this case and not Professor Macaulay's essay. How would those conclusions differ from the point of view you now have about the workings of the law? Against this backdrop, try to inventory other ideas that you have acquired thus far in your legal education. Can you determine any about which you now feel uneasy?

6. The presence of the third lumberyard in Clintonville raises a consideration not normally directly confronted by appellate courts. (Note that this third yard is not mentioned in the Supreme Court opinion.) Almost any transaction regulated by the law of contracts will have effects on others besides those who directly participate in the transaction. Economists call effects like these "externalities."

> An externality arises when an economic activity performed by one person generates an effect, beneficial or otherwise, on some other person who is not a party to the activity. Beneficial externalities are often termed external economies and harmful ones external diseconomies. Such effects can arise either from production or consumption. External

diseconomies of production would include all forms of pollution emanating from industrial sources, while detergent pollution from the home would be a diseconomy of consumption. A classic case of reciprocal external economies in production is that of neighboring orchards and apiaries; the blossom provides the bees with pollen to make honey, while the bees fertilize the trees. Amateur gardeners generate externalities of consumption of both kinds; the beauty and scent of their flowers is a gift to their neighbors while the noise of the power lawnmower is a nuisance.*

What were the external effects of Torborg's leaving the employ of Fullerton Lumber? What were the external effects of the majority's decision in this case? To what extent does the Court appear to have considered these effects? To what extent do courts generally consider such effects in contracts litigation? How well equipped are they to consider these effects? (In answering these questions you may want to consider the following: "The fundamental principle underlying legal procedure is that parties to a controversy shall have the right to litigate the same, free from interference of strangers." Consolidated Liquor Co. v. Scotello & Nizzi, 155 Pac. 1089, 21 New Mexico 485, 494-95 (1916).)

7. Two commentators have described the rule against unreasonably restrictive covenants as an example of an "immutable" rule, one that parties cannot alter by contract. They distinguish these from "default rules," such as the rule in *Hadley v. Baxendale*, that can be altered by contract but otherwise serve as gap-fillers.

> An important difference between default and immutable rules is that if parties attempt to contract around a default rule and fail, they will simply be bound by the default, whereas if parties attempt to contract around an immutable rule and fail, the law may choose to penalize the attempt by imposing a penalty different from (and, from the parties' ex ante perspectives, worse than) the immutable standard. . . .
>
> [In *Fullerton*, the court] struggled in deciding whether it should reformulate the contract to impose a duty not to

---

*Winch, D. M., Analytical Welfare Economics 123 (1971).

compete for a reasonable period or penalize the employer for transgressing the immutable limitation by allowing the former employee to compete immediately.

If the goal of an immutable rule is to discourage people from even attempting to contract around a provision, then it would seem that the penalty reconstruction would be the favored result.

Ian Ayres & Robert Gertnert, Filling Gaps in Incomplete Contracts: An Economic Theory of Default Rules: 99 Yale L.J. 87, 125-26 (1989). Do you agree? Does a rule of "penalty reconstruction" minimize capability problems by establishing a clear and easily enforceable rule? Or does it magnify capability problems by encouraging courts to use covert tools to avoid operation of an overly punitive rule? Cf. Karl Llewellyn, Book Review, 52 Harv. L.Rev. 700, 702 (1939) ("Covert tools are never reliable tools.").

VIII. FRANCIS B. ORTELERE v.
TEACHERS' RETIREMENT BOARD OF
THE CITY OF NEW YORK

ORTELERE v. TEACHERS' RETIREMENT BD.
Court of Appeals of New York, 1969.
25 N.Y.2d 196, 303 N.Y.S.2d 362, 250 N.E.2d 460.

BREITEL, Judge.

This appeal involves the revocability of an election of benefits under a public employees' retirement system and suggests the need for a renewed examination of the kinds of mental incompetency which may render voidable the exercise of contractual rights. The particular issue arises on the evidently unwise and foolhardy selection of benefits by a 60-year-old teacher, on leave for mental illness and suffering from cerebral arteriosclerosis, after service as a public schoolteacher and participation in a public retirement system for over 40 years. The teacher died a little less than two months after making her election of maximum benefits, payable to her during her life, thus causing the entire reserve to fall in. She left surviving her husband of 38 years of marriage and two grown children.

There is no doubt that any retirement system depends for its soundness on an actuarial experience based on the purely prospective selections of benefits and mortality rates among the covered group, and that retrospective or adverse selection after the fact would be destructive of a sound system. It is also true that members of retirement systems are free to make choices which to others may seem unwise or foolhardy. The issue here is narrower than any suggested by these basic principles. It is whether an otherwise irrevocable election may be avoided for incapacity because

242

of known mental illness which resulted in the election when, except in the barest actuarial sense, the system would sustain no unfavorable consequences.

The husband and executor of Grace W. Ortelere, the deceased New York City schoolteacher, sues to set aside her application for retirement without option, in the event of her death. It is alleged that Mrs. Ortelere, on February 11, 1965, two months before her death from natural causes, was not mentally competent to execute a retirement application. By this application, effective the next day, she elected the maximum retirement allowance (Administrative Code of City of New York, § B20-46.0). She thus revoked her earlier election of benefits under which she named her husband a beneficiary of the unexhausted reserve upon her death. Selection of the maximum allowance extinguished all interests upon her death.

Following a nonjury trial in Supreme Court, it was held that Grace Ortelere had been mentally incompetent at the time of her February 11 application, thus rendering it "null and void and of no legal effect." The Appellate Division, by a divided court, reversed the judgment of the Supreme Court and held that, as a matter of law, there was insufficient proof of mental incompetency as to this transaction (31 A.D.2d 139, 295 N.Y.S.2d 506).

Mrs. Ortelere's mental illness, indeed, psychosis, is undisputed. It is not seriously disputable, however, that she had complete cognitive judgment or awareness when she made her selection. A modern understanding of mental illness, however, suggests that incapacity to contract or exercise contractual rights may exist, because of volitional and effective impediments or disruptions in the personality, despite the intellectual or cognitive ability to understand. It will be recognized as the civil law parallel to the question of criminal responsibility which has been the recent concern of so many and has resulted in statutory and decisional changes in the criminal law (e.g., A.L.I. Model Penal Code, § 4.01; Penal Law, § 30.05; Durham v. United States, 214 F.2d 862).

Mrs. Ortelere, an elementary schoolteacher since 1924, suffered a "nervous breakdown" in March, 1964 and went on a leave of absence expiring February 5, 1965. She was then 60 years old and had been happily married for 38 years. On July 1, 1964 she came under the care of Dr. D'Angelo, a psychiatrist, who diagnosed her breakdown as involutional psychosis, melancholia type. Dr. D'Angelo prescribed, and for about six weeks decedent underwent, tranquilizer and shock therapy. Although moderately successful, the therapy was not continued since it was suspected that she also suffered from cerebral arteriosclerosis, an ailment later confirmed. However, the psychiatrist continued to see her at monthly intervals until March, 1965. On March 28, 1965 she was hospitalized after collapsing at home from an aneurysm. She died 10 days later; the cause of death was "Cerebral thrombosis due to H[ypertensive] H[eart] D[isease]."

As a teacher she had been a member of the Teachers' Retirement System of the City of New York (Administrative Code, § B20-3.0). This entitled her to certain annuity and pension rights, pre-retirement death benefits, and empowered her to exercise various options concerning the payment of her retirement allowance.

Some years before, on June 28, 1958, she had executed a "Selection of Benefits under Option One" naming her husband as beneficiary of the unexhausted reserve. Under this option upon retirement her allowance would be less by way of periodic retirement allowances, but if she died before receipt of her full reserve the balance of the reserve would be payable to her husband. On June 16, 1960, two years later, she had designated her husband as beneficiary of her service death benefits in the event of her death prior to retirement.

Then on February 11, 1965, when her leave of absence had just expired and she was still under treatment, she executed a retirement application, the one here involved, selecting the maximum retirement allowance payable during her lifetime with nothing payable on or after death. She also, at this time, borrowed from the system the maximum cash withdrawal permitted, namely, $8,760. Three days earlier she had written the board, stating that she intended to retire on February 12 or 15 or as soon as she received "the information I need in order to decide whether to take an option or maximum allowance." She then listed eight specific questions, reflecting great understanding of the retirement system, concerning the various alternatives available. An extremely detailed reply was sent, by letter of February 15, 1965, although by that date it was technically impossible for her to change her selection. However, the board's chief clerk, before whom Mrs. Ortelere executed the application, testified that the questions were "answered verbally by me on February 11th." Her retirement reserve totalled $62,165 (after deducting the $8,760 withdrawal), and the difference between electing the maximum retirement allowance (no option) and the allowance under "option one" was $901 per year or $75 per month. That is, had the teacher selected "option one" she would have received an annual allowance of $4,494 or $375 per month, while if no option had been selected she would have received an annual allowance of $5,395 or $450 per month. Had she not withdrawn the cash the annual figures would be $5,247 and $6,148 respectively.

Following her taking a leave of absence for her condition, Mrs. Ortelere had become very depressed and was unable to care for herself. As a result her husband gave up his electrician's job, in which he earned $222 per week, to stay home and take care of her on a full-time basis. She left their home only when he accompanied her. Although he took her to the Retirement Board on February 11, 1965, he did not know why she went, and did not question her for fear "she'd start crying hysterically that I was scolding her. That's the way she was. And I wouldn't upset her."

The Orteleres were in quite modest circumstances. They owned their own home, valued at $20,000, and had $8,000 in a savings account. They also owned some farm land worth about $5,000. Under these circumstances, as revealed in this record, retirement for both of the Orteleres or the survivor of them had to be provided, as a practical matter, largely out of Mrs. Ortelere's retirement benefits.

According to Dr. D'Angelo, the psychiatrist who treated her, Mrs. Ortelere never improved enough to "warrant my sending her back [to teaching]." A physician for the Board of Education examined her on February 2, 1965 to determine her fitness to return to teaching. Although not a psychiatrist but rather a specialist in internal medicine, this physician "judged that she had apparently recovered from the depression" and that she appeared rational. However, before allowing her to return to teaching, a report was requested from Dr. D'Angelo concerning her condition. It is notable that the Medical Division of the Board of Education on February 24, 1965 requested that Mrs. Ortelere report to the board's "panel psychiatrist" on March 11, 1965.

Dr. D'Angelo stated "[a]t no time since she was under my care was she ever mentally competent"; that "[m]entally she couldn't make a decision of any kind, actually, of any kind, small or large." He also described how involutional melancholia affects the judgment process: "They can't think rationally, no matter what the situation is. They will even tell you, 'I used to be able to think of anything and make any decision. Now,' they say, 'even getting up, I don't know whether I should get up or whether I should stay in bed.' Or, 'I don't even know how to make a slice of toast any more.' Everything is impossible to decide, and everything is too great an effort to even think of doing. They just don't have the effort, actually, because their nervous breakdown drains them of all their physical energies."

While the psychiatrist used terms referring to "rationality," it is quite evident that Mrs. Ortelere's psychopathology did not lend itself to a classification under the legal test of irrationality. It is undoubtedly, for this reason, that the Appellate Division was unable to accept his testimony and the trial court's finding of irrationality in the light of the prevailing rules as they have been formulated.

The well-established rule is that contracts of a mentally incompetent person who has not been adjudicated insane are voidable. Even where the contract has been partly or fully performed it will still be avoided upon restoration of the *status quo*. (Verstandig v. Schlaffer, 296 N.Y. 62, 64, 70 N.E.2d 15, 16; Blinn v. Schwarz, 177 N.Y. 252, 262, 69 N.E. 542, 545; see, also, Ann., Contracts with Incompetent, 95 A.L.R. 1442; Ann., Incompetent — Contract Before Adjudication, 46 A.L.R. 416.)

Traditionally, in this State and elsewhere, contractual mental capacity has been measured by what is largely a cognitive test (Aldrich v. Bailey, 132 N.Y. 85, 30 N.E. 264; 2 Williston, Contracts [3d ed.], § 256; see 17 C.J.S. Contracts § 133[1], subd. e, pp. 860-862). Under this standard the "inquiry" is whether the mind was "so affected as to render him wholly and absolutely incompetent to comprehend and understand the nature of the transaction" (Aldrich v. Bailey, supra, at p. 89, 30 N.E. at p. 265). A requirement that the party also be able to make a rational judgment concerning the particular transaction qualified the cognitive test (Paine v. Aldrich, 133 N.Y. 544, 546, 30 N.E. 725, 726, Note, "Civil Insanity": The New York Treatment of the Issue of Mental Incompetency in Non-Criminal Cases, 44 Cornell L.Q. 76). Conversely, it is also well recognized that contractual ability would be affected by insane delusions intimately related to the particular transaction (Moritz v. Moritz, 153 App. Div. 147, 138 N.Y.S. 124, affd. 211 N.Y. 580, 105 N.E. 1090, see Green, Judicial Tests of Mental Incompetency, 6 Mo.L.Rev. 141, 151).

These traditional standards governing competency to contract were formulated when psychiatric knowledge was quite primitive. They fail to account for one who by reason of mental illness is unable to control his conduct even though his cognitive ability seems unimpaired. When these standards were evolving it was thought that all the mental faculties were simultaneously affected by mental illness. (Green, Mental Incompetency, 38 Mich.L.Rev. 1189, 1197-1202.) This is no longer the prevailing view (Note, Mental Illness and the Law of Contracts, 57 Mich.L. Rev. 1020, 1033-1036).

Of course, the greatest movement in revamping legal notions of mental responsibility has occurred in the criminal law. The nineteenth century cognitive test embraced in the *M'Naghten* rules has long been criticized and changed by statute and decision in many jurisdictions (see *M'Naghten's Case*, 10 Clark & Fin. 200; 8 Eng. Rep. 718 [House of Lords, 1843]; Weihofen, Mental Disorder as a Criminal Defense [1954], pp. 65-68; British Royal Comm. on Capital Punishment [1953], ch. 4; A.L. I. Model Penal Code, § 4.01, supra; cf. Penal Law, § 30.05).

While the policy considerations for the criminal law and the civil law are different, both share in common the premise that policy considerations must be based on a sound understanding of the human mind and, therefore, its illnesses. Hence, because the cognitive rules are, for the most part, too restrictive and rest on a false factual basis they must be re-examined. Once it is understood that, accepting plaintiff's proof, Mrs. Ortelere was psychotic and because of that psychosis could have been incapable of making a voluntary selection of her retirement system benefits, there is an issue that a modern jurisprudence should not exclude, merely because her mind could pass a "cognition" test based on nineteenth century psychology.

There has also been some movement on the civil law side to achieve a modern posture. For the most part, the movement has been glacial and has been disguised under traditional formulations. Various devices have been used to avoid unacceptable results under the old rules by finding unfairness or overreaching in order to avoid transactions (see, e. g., Green, Proof of Mental Incompetency and the Unexpressed Major Premise, 53 Yale L.J. 271, 298-305).

In this State there has been at least one candid approach. In Faber v. Sweet Style Mfg. Corp., 40 Misc.2d 212, at p. 216, 242 N.Y.S.2d 763, at p. 768, Mr. Justice Meyer wrote: "[i]ncompetence to contract also exists when a contract is entered into under the compulsion of a mental disease or disorder but for which the contract would not have been made" (noted in 39 N.Y.U.L. Rev. 356). This is the first known time a court has recognized that the traditional standards of incompetency for contractual capacity are inadequate in light of contemporary psychiatric learning and applied modern standards. Prior to this, courts applied the cognitive standard giving great weight to objective evidence of rationality (e. g., Beisman v. New York City Employees' Retirement System, Sup., 81 N.Y.S.2d 373, revd. 275 App.Div. 836, 88 N.Y.S.2d 411, affd. 300 N.Y. 580, 89 N.E.2d 876; Schwartzberg v. Teachers' Retirement Bd., 273 App.Div. 240, 76 N.Y.S.2d 488, affd. 298 N.Y. 741, 83 N.E.2d 146; Martin v. Teachers' Retirement Bd., Sup., 70 N.Y.S.2d 593).

It is quite significant that Restatement, 2d, Contracts, states the modern rule on competency to contract. This is in evident recognition, and the Reporter's Notes support this inference, that, regardless of how the cases formulated their reasoning, the old cognitive test no longer explains the results. Thus, the new Restatement section reads: "(1) A person incurs only voidable contractual duties by entering into a transaction if by reason of mental illness or defect . . . (b) he is unable to act in a reasonable manner in relation to the transaction and the other party has reason to know of his condition." (Restatement, 2d, Contracts [T.D. No. 1, April 13, 1964], § 18C.) (See, also, Allen, Ferster, Weihofen, Mental Impairment and Legal Incompetency, p. 253 [Recommendation b] and pp. 260-282; and Note, 57 Mich.L.Rev. 1020, supra, where it is recommended "that a complete test for contractual incapacity should provide protection to those persons whose contracts are merely uncontrolled reactions to their mental illness, as well as for those who could not understand the nature and consequences of their actions" [at p. 1036]).

The avoidance of duties under an agreement entered into by those who have done so by reason of mental illness, but who have understanding, depends on balancing competing policy considerations. There must be stability in contractual relations and protection of the expectations of parties who bargain in good faith. On the other hand, it is also desirable to protect persons who may understand the nature of the transaction but who, due to mental illness, cannot control their conduct. Hence, there should be relief only if the other party knew or was put on notice as to the contractor's mental illness. Thus, the Restatement provision for avoidance contemplates that "the other party has reason to know" of the mental illness (id.).

When, however, the other party is without knowledge of the contractor's mental illness and the agreement is made on fair terms, the proposed Restatement rule is: "The power of avoidance under subsection (1) terminates to the extent that the contract has been so performed in whole or in part or the circumstances have so changed that avoidance would be inequitable. In such a case a court may grant relief on such equitable terms as the situation requires." (Restatement, 2d, Contracts, supra, § 18C, subd. [2].)

The system was, or should have been, fully aware of Mrs. Ortelere's condition. They, or the Board of Education, knew of her leave of absence for medical reasons and the resort to staff psychiatrists by the Board of Education. Hence, the other of the conditions for avoidance is satisfied.

Lastly, there are no significant changes of position by the system other than those that flow from the barest actuarial consequences of benefit selection.

Nor should one ignore that in the relationship between retirement system and member, and especially in a public system, there is not involved a commercial, let alone an ordinary commercial, transaction. Instead the nature of the system and its announced goal is the protection of its members and those in whom its members have an interest. It is not a sound scheme which would permit 40 years of contribution and participation in the system to be nullified by a one-instant act committed by one known to be mentally ill. This is especially true if there would be no substantial harm to the system if the act were avoided. On the record none may gainsay that her selection of a "no option" retirement while under psychiatric care, ill with cerebral arteriosclerosis, aged 60, and with a family in which she had always manifested concern, was so unwise and foolhardy that a factfinder might conclude that it was explainable only as a product of psychosis.

On this analysis it is not difficult to see that plaintiff's evidence was sufficient to sustain a finding that, when she acted as she did on February 11, 1965, she did so solely as a result of serious mental illness, namely, psychosis. Of course, nothing less serious than medically classified psychosis should suffice or else few contracts would be invulnerable to some kind of psychological attack. Mrs. Ortelere's psychiatrist testified quite flatly that as an involutional melancholiac in depression she was incapable of making a voluntary "rational" decision. Of course, as noted earlier, the trial court's finding and perhaps some of the testimony attempted to fit into the rubrics of the traditional rules. For that reason rather than reinstatement of the judgment at Trial Term there should be a new trial under the proper standards frankly considered and applied.

Accordingly, the order of the Appellate Division should be reversed, without costs, and the action remanded to Special Term for a new trial.

JASEN, Judge (dissenting).

Where there has been no previous adjudication of incompetency, the burden of proving mental incompetence is upon the party alleging it. I agree with the majority at the Appellate Division that the plaintiff, the husband of the decedent, failed to sustain the burden incumbent upon him of proving deceased's incompetence.

The evidence conclusively establishes that the decedent, at the time she made her application to retire, understood not only that she was retiring, but also that she had selected the maximum payment during her lifetime.

Indeed, the letter written by the deceased to the Teachers' Retirement System prior to her retirement demonstrates her full mental capacity to understand and to decide whether to take an option or the maximum allowance. The full text of the letter reads as follows:

February 8, 1965

*   *   *

Gentlemen:

I would like to retire on Feb. 12 or Feb. 15. In other words, just as soon as possible after I receive the information I need in order to decide whether to take an option or maximum allowance. Following are the questions I would like to have answered:

1. What is my 'average' five-year salary?

2. What is my maximum allowance?

3. I am 60 years old. If I select option four-a with a beneficiary (female) 27 years younger, what is my allowance?

4. If I select four-a on the pension part only, and take the maximum annuity, what is my allowance?

5. If I take a loan of 89% of my year's salary before retirement, what would my maximum allowance be?

6. If I take a loan of $5,000 before retiring, and select option four-a on both the pension and annuity, what would my allowance be?

7. What is my total service credit? I have been on a leave without pay since Oct. 26, 1964.

8. What is the 'factor' used for calculating option four-a with the above beneficiary?

Thank you for your promptness in making the necessary calculations. I will come to your office on Thursday afternoon of this week.

It seems clear that this detailed, explicit and extremely pertinent list of queries reveals a mind fully in command of the salient features of the Teachers' Retirement System. Certainly, it cannot be said that the decedent could possess sufficient capacity to compose a letter indicating such a comprehensive understanding of the retirement system, and yet lack the capacity to understand the answers.

As I read the record, the evidence establishes that the decedent's election to receive maximum payments was predicated on the need for a higher income to support two retired persons — her husband and herself. Since the only source of income available to decedent and her husband was decedent's retirement pay, the additional payment of $75 per month which she would receive by electing the maximal payment was a necessity. Indeed, the additional payments represented an increase of 20% over the benefits payable under option 1. Under these circumstances, an election of maximal income during decedent's lifetime was not only a rational, but a necessary decision.

Further indication of decedent's knowledge of the financial needs of her family is evidenced by the fact that she took a loan for the maximum amount ($8,760) permitted by the retirement system at the time she made application for retirement.

Moreover, there is nothing in the record to indicate that the decedent had any warning, premonition, knowledge or indication at the time of retirement that her life expectancy was, in any way, reduced by her condition.

Decedent's election of the maximum retirement benefits, therefore, was not so contrary to her best interests so as to create an inference of her mental incompetence.

Indeed, concerning election of options under a retirement system, it has been held: "Even where no previous election has been made, the court must make the election for an incompetent which would be in accordance with what would have been his manifest and reasonable choice if he were sane, and, in the absence of convincing evidence that the incompetent would have made a different selection, it is *presumed that he would have chosen the option yielding the largest returns in his lifetime.*" (Schwartzberg v. Teachers' Retirement Bd., 273 App.Div. 240, 242-243, 76 N.Y.S.2d 488, affd. 298 N.Y. 741, 83 N.E.2d 146; emphasis supplied.)

Nor can I agree with the majority's view that the traditional rules governing competency to contract "are, for the most part, too restrictive and rest on a false factual basis."

The issue confronting the courts concerning mental capacity to contract is under what circumstances and conditions should a party be relieved of contractual obligations freely entered. This is peculiarly a legal decision, although, of course, available medical knowledge forms a datum which influences the legal choice. It is common knowledge that the present state of psychiatric knowledge is inadequate to provide a fixed rule for each and every type of mental disorder. Thus, the generally accepted rules which have evolved to determine mental responsibility are general enough in application to encompass all types of mental disorders, and phrased in a manner which can be understood and practically applied by juries composed of laymen.

The generally accepted test of mental competency to contract which has thus evolved is whether the party attempting to avoid the contract was capable of understanding and appreciating the nature and consequences of the particular act or transaction which he challenges. (Schwartzberg v. Teachers' Retirement Bd., supra; Paine v. Aldrich, 133 N.Y. 544, 30 N.E. 725; Beisman v. New York City Employees' Retirement System, 275 App.Div. 836, 88 N.Y.S.2d 411, affd. 300 N.Y. 580, 89 N.E.2d 876.) This rule represents a balance struck between policies to protect the security of transactions between individuals and freedom of contract on the one hand, and protection of those mentally handicapped on the other hand. In my opinion, this rule has proven workable in practice and fair in result. A broad range of evidence including psychiatric testimony is admissible under the existing rules to establish a party's mental condition. (See 2 Wigmore, Evidence [3d ed.], §§ 227-233.) In the final analysis, the lay jury will infer the state of the party's mind from his observed behavior as indicated by the evidence presented at trial. Each juror instinctively judges what is normal and what is abnormal conduct from his own experience, and the generally accepted test harmonizes the competing policy considerations with human experience to achieve the fairest result in the greatest number of cases.

As in every situation where the law must draw a line between liability and nonliability, between responsibility and nonresponsibility, there will be borderline cases, and injustices may occur by deciding erroneously that an individual belongs on one side of the line or the other. To minimize the chances of such injustices occurring, the line should be drawn as clearly as possible.

The Appellate Division correctly found that the deceased was capable of understanding the nature and effect of her retirement benefits, and exercised rational judgment in electing to receive the maximum allowance during her lifetime. I fear that the majority's refinement of the generally accepted rules will prove unworkable in practice, and make many contracts vulnerable to psychological attack. Any benefit to those who understand what they are doing, but are unable to exercise self-discipline, will be outweighed by frivolous claims which will burden our courts and undermine the security of contracts. The reasonable expectations of those who innocently deal with persons who appear rational and who understand what they are doing should be protected.

Accordingly, I would affirm the order appealed from.

FULD, C. J., and BURKE and BERGAN, JJ., concur with BREITEL, J.

JASEN, J., dissents and votes to affirm in separate opinion in which SCILEPPI, J., concurs.

Order reversed, without costs, and a new trial granted.

FIRST QUESTIONS

Decisions about competence rest on intuitions about the facts underlying a particular transaction rather than on commonly applied, "objective" inferences drawn from the wording of a contract. It should not be surprising, therefore, that *Ortelere* raises difficult capability problems. Judge Breitel seems rather sure about a number of things he has occasion to comment on in the course of his opinion. Considering the following factual questions, first decide (a) what your intuition is as to the "realities" underlying this case; (b) how much confidence you have in that intuition; (c) how much confidence you have in Judge Breitel's intuition about these "realities"; and (d) whether the courts' capabilities are too limited to make the doctrine of *Ortelere* workable. Then read the excerpts from the record in *Ortelere* which follow these questions, and consider the questions again.

1. Note the impersonal and assertive language used by Judge Breitel. Though the document is called an "opinion," it uses language of fact. Examine, for instance, the beginning of each sentence of the second paragraph of the opinion. These sentences begin with the following: "There is no doubt . . ."; "It is also true . . ."; "The issue here is . . . "; "It is . . .". In the crucial fifth paragraph he says: "Mrs. Ortelere's mental illness . . . is undisputed. It is not seriously disputable . . . . A modern understanding . . . suggests . . . It will be recognized . . . ." Argue that this impersonal deductive logical language helps our legal system function appropriately. Argue that it is inappropriate. (Note Judge Breitel's praise of "the candid approach" in Faber v. Sweet Style Mfg. Corp.)

2. Judge Breitel says that "the criminal law and the civil law . . . both share in common the premise that policy considerations must be based on a sound understanding of the human mind and, therefore, its illnesses." He goes on to conclude that previously there was no such understanding, but now there is. Do you agree that we have reached that position? If it seems that we haven't, do we have any choice but to take the best knowledge we have and use it accordingly? Or should modesty about our insights lead us to be more modest in our legal doctrines? Does Judge Breitel manifest such modesty when he writes "of course, nothing less serious than medically classified psychosis should suffice or else few contracts

would be invulnerable to some kind of psychological attack." Is this proviso appropriate? If you were skeptical about your insight into "the human mind," how would that affect your decision in *Ortelere*? Is Judge Breitel in that position?

3. Was Mrs. Ortelere happily married? (What is the significance of question 3 in her letter of inquiry about retirement benefits?)

Consider the following excerpt from T. Szasz, Law, Liberty, and Psychiatry 150-151 (1968):

> [T]here are powerful forces in society which seek to demote the mental patient from the position of a contracting individual to that of occupant of the status of insanity. This sort of social degradation is one of the ways the group punishes those of its members that fail to fulfill some of their contractual obligations .... [F]ailure to fulfill certain contractual obligations does not necessarily mean 'inability' to honor 'all' of them. There are other possibilities .... It could ... be that breaking the contract was a means of communicating to his partner the wish to redefine the relationship.... I submit that, except in cases of gross disability, adults should always be treated as if they were capable of fulfilling the contractual obligations they have assumed. If people are to remain responsible, contracting individuals, it is important to respond to their failure to fulfill obligations by punishing them, not by redefining them as inferior beings, unfit to enter into contracts.*

4. What were Mrs. Ortelere's and her husband's immediate needs at the time of her retirement as compared with her husband's needs after her death?

5. Did Mrs. Ortelere know that she had cerebral arteriosclerosis at the time she selected her retirement option?

6. What was Mrs. Ortelere's life expectancy at the time she retired?

7. Why was the Board of Education specialist in internal medicine inclined to let Mrs. Ortelere return to teaching?

---

*Quoted in J. Zusman and W. Carnahan, 1 Mental Health: New York Law and Practice 14-2—14-3.

8. What did "the system" know about Mrs. Ortelere's mental health at the time of her retirement?

9. Who wrote the letter that asked such detailed questions about the retirement benefits?

10. When did Mr. Ortelere learn which benefit scheme Mrs. Ortelere had selected?

11. Who do you believe offered a more truthful and more accurate insight into Mrs. Ortelere's state of mind at the time of her retirement, Dr. D'Angelo or the School Board's internist?

12. Do defenses like capacity, duress, and undue influence tend to reinforce stereotypes about the people they are intended to protect? At common law, married women lacked the capacity to enter into many contracts. This rule gradually disappeared from American law as states enacted reforms beginning in the nineteenth century. See, e.g., Reva B. Siegel, The Modernization of Marital Status Law: Adjudicating Wives' Rights to Earnings, 1860-1930, 82 Georgetown L.J. 2127, 2150-54 (1994) (describing the process of reform in nineteenth-century New York).

Do you see evidence of stereotyping in *Oretelere*? Stereotyping of mental illness? Of gender? Would the case have gone the same way had it been Frank Ortelere who was ill and Grace Ortelere was seeking to prove Frank's incapacity?

13. In *Ortelere*, Judge Breitel endorses both a "cognitive" and "volitional" theory of mental infirmity, and he suggests that the civil law and criminal law are moving toward acceptance of both. (The "cognitive" theory applies to an actor who doesn't understand what she's doing; the "volitional" theory applies to an actor who can't control her impulses.)

In 1982, thirteen years after *Ortelere*, John Hinckley was acquitted of attempting to assassinate President Reagan on grounds of insanity after the jury was instructed that Hinckley should be acquitted if he could not conform his conduct to law. This instruction was a variant of the volitional theory adopted in *Ortelere*. In the wake of *Hinckley*, a majority of states revised their laws to restrict the insanity defense, and Congress and a number of states enacted laws that essentially abolished the volitional prong of the insanity defense. As a result, many jurisdictions now confine the insanity defense to the cognitive theory embodied in the *M'Naghten* rule

– a rule Judge Breitel says has "long been criticized and changed by statute and decision in many jurisdictions."

Does this history suggest that *Ortelere* is no longer good law? Are legislatures better-equipped than courts to define mental infirmity? Should the legal rule be crafted by psychiatrists rather than lawyers?

SUPPLEMENTARY MATERIAL

Transcript of Proceeding.
SUPREME COURT,
NEW YORK COUNTY,
Trial Term, Part XXII.
60 Centre Street,
New York, New York,
November 8-9, 1967.

Before: Honorable JOHN M. MURTAGH, Justice
   Appearances:
A. Mark Levien, Esq., Attorney for plaintiff.
Hon. J. Lee Rankin, Corporation Counsel of the City of New York, attorney for defendant; by Isidore Heyman, Esq., Assistant Corporation Counsel, of Counsel.

*   *   *

MR. HEYMAN: [Opening Statement]

*   *   *

I also want to go one step further, your Honor: The claim is that the decedent was incompetent on February 11, 1965 at the time she filed her application for retirement, and counsel for plaintiff has stated that she had been sick and under psychiatric care. We will show your Honor that as recent as less than two weeks before she filed the application, January 29, 1965, she submitted to the Board of Education, her employer, a medical certificate stating that she has fully recovered and is able to resume her duties, which clearly should be entitled to great weight on this question of whether or not she —

THE COURT: I think it would be hearsay, counselor. I think you would have to bring a medical expert who would state that she was. The mere fact that she — and the plaintiff now contends that she was incompetent at the time — attempted to give you evidence as the employer that she was competent, I don't think would be competent.

MR. HEYMAN: Well, your Honor, this is a medical statement that she —

THE COURT: It's hearsay though.

MR. HEYMAN: Pardon me?

THE COURT: It's hearsay.

MR. HEYMAN: Yes, but it's something that she submitted. If I was getting something —

THE COURT: But you start trying to bind the plaintiff who urges that she was not competent at the time.

MR. HEYMAN: But he has to establish that. I mean the burden — the burden is on the plaintiff, your Honor.

THE COURT: Of course it is.

MR. HEYMAN: To establish the incompetency of this particular teacher. There is no doubt about that.

THE COURT: Yes, but should the Court receive evidence of a doctor made outside of the Court simply because it was submitted by the deceased? I am inclined to think not. I would certainly think it would be appropriate for you to bring into Court the medical authority who made that statement. Otherwise, if I receive it at all, it wouldn't be entitled to much credence.

MR. HEYMAN: Your Honor, I intend to introduce that as part of the public records kept by the Board of Education in the regular course of —

THE COURT: Frankly, if it is received, and I am not sure that I will, as the trier of the fact I wouldn't be inclined to give it much weight. I know I have enough background in matters psychiatric to know how reliable a mere statement as to a person's competency is without having a witness in court to assert it.

MR. HEYMAN: We will try to get this witness. I have tried previously. He is out of town, and I don't know whether he is still alive, but I will try; but I merely try to indicate that as part of our proof we have records that were submitted by this decedent herself, and I think it might even be considered as part of the res gestae, the entire situation, with reference to her mental condition.

THE COURT: Res Gestae is a handy term that expresses the fact that alleged hearsay is in fact not hearsay; in other words, that you are not interested in the truth of the statement being given to the Court. In this instance, we would clearly be interested in the statement for the truth of the matter contained in the statement, and so res gestae is not at all applicable.

MR. HEYMAN: Well, the probity of the evidence of course is for your Honor, and for whatever value your Honor wishes to place upon it. This is for the Court, and I have —

THE COURT: I am not sure that it is competent, aside from its very limited probative force.

MR. HEYMAN: Well, be that as it may, then I merely thought I would indicate to the Court the position of the Teachers' Retirement Board who, as your Honor understands, doesn't examine applicants who file applications for retirement, and as I will show under the law, they have to accept these —

THE COURT: I don't think anyone is criticizing the Board.

MR. HEYMAN: Well, I just wanted to make that clear.

THE COURT: Even counsel for the plaintiff.

MR. HEYMAN: All right, thank you, your Honor. With that statement I will close.

*   *   *

Francis B. Ortelere, 137-46 229th Street, Laurelton, New York 11413, the plaintiff, called as a witness in his own behalf, having been first duly sworn, testified as follows:

Direct Examination by MR. LEVIEN:

Q. Mr. Ortelere, you are the plaintiff in this case?   **A.** Yes.

Q. Grace W. Ortelere was your wife?   **A.** Yes.

Q. When did you marry?   **A.** August 6, 1927.

Q. At that time was your wife a school teacher?   **A.** Yes.

Q. What is your occupation?   **A.** Electrician.

Q. In March of 1963 what was the condition, so far as you could observe it, of your wife?   **A.** Well, all right, In '64 I had to give up my job because my wife had a nervous breakdown, so I was home taking care of her, because she was taking tranquilizers at the time; and I was afraid to leave her alone.

So in the meantime, while I was home, she become very depressed and irritable and as time went on, she lost her appetite, she wouldn't eat. At night she'd wake up hysterically crying and shaking, and I'd have to hold her. Then she got so she wouldn't go out of the house; she'd just sit by herself.

And then in the mornings at times she'd wake up; she was forever taking her pulse. She claimed she had an awful fast heartbeat, but I never took her pulse because I didn't know how. And —

Q. Did you take her to a psychiatrist? **A.** Yes, took her — well, she was going to the psychiatrist.

Q. When? **A.** Oh, I don't remember—

THE COURT: Just relax now and —

A. I am not good on dates. Well, it was some time in '64 that I took her to the psychiatrist. Just when I don't know.

So she was going to the psychiatrist. It's getting away from what I want to tell. I get confused. Just let me think.

Q. What was his name?

THE COURT: Let the witness speak.

A. The psychiatrist's name was Dr. D'Angelo; and she went in for these shock treatments. I used to take her there and bring her back.

THE COURT: When did she go in for shock treatments? Was that back in '64?

THE WITNESS: In '64, yes, and some time in '64. Just when I couldn't say.

THE COURT: What is the doctor's full name?

THE WITNESS: His full name —

MR. LEVIEN: Ernani.

THE WITNESS: I think it's Angelo. I think it's Angelo.

MR. LEVIEN: E-r-n-a-n-i D-apostrophe-A-n-g-e-l-o.

THE COURT: Where is his office?

THE WITNESS: In Jamaica.

THE COURT: Where in Jamaica?

THE WITNESS: It's right by the park. I'd say about a hundred fifty some-odd street. You will have to give me a minute. I lost my train of thought now.

Well, as time went on, as I said, she wouldn't sleep.

MR. HEYMAN: I don't think there is a question before the witness.

THE WITNESS: Let me finish my story.

MR. LEVIEN: 88-92 150th Street, Jamaica.

THE WITNESS: Something like that.

MY. HEYMAN: Your Honor, may I for clarification inquire whether or not the witness is asked to tell a story, or he is asking, "Did you take her for — "

THE COURT: He asked him when she started going to a psychiatrist, and he is telling us that as best he can.

THE WITNESS: I wish nobody would ask. Let me just tell the story as I lived it for fifteen months with my wife.

THE COURT: We are sympathetic to you.

THE WITNESS: If they ask me, they confuse me.

THE COURT: Relax. We are asking you to relax. Let your lawyer ask questions, and we will get further.

Q. Did you take her to the psychiatrist's office each time? **A.** I always did.

Q. And do you know how long she was receiving shock treatments? **A.** I don't know how long, but I know in all she had taken twelve treatments, and then we used to have to go back every once in a while for consultation. He'd sit with her and talk to her. Then it got so he was telling her what he thought she'd have to take more treatments, and she didn't want it. She had a dreaded fear of them —

Q. All right.   **A.** — and she never did take more.

Q. Do you remember the date — **A.**   May I continue now?

THE COURT: No, please; you will have to relax.

Q. Describe what her condition was between the time you first took her to the psychiatrist and until February 10, 1965?   **A.** Well, that was the time there in between where we thought she was improving a little, but it only lasted a short time, and then she started to get worse all the time. It got so that she — I had to get her a black mask for her eyes, and she wanted to stay in bed all the time crying she couldn't sleep, she couldn't sleep. But at night at times she'd fall asleep and during the night she'd wake up hysterically crying tears and trembling. I started to get in her bed and hold her like you would a baby. Then it got so at times she'd even say, "Frank, if it wasn't for my religion, I'd take my own life" she was so depressed.

MR. HEYMAN: Your Honor, may I object at this point and have the witness fix a date, because this is quite important. It begins in '64.

THE WITNESS: I am coming —

THE COURT: Roughly what time are you referring to now?

THE WITNESS: This was towards the end, getting nearer to '65, the end of it. As time went on she was getting worse, started to threaten to take her life. Then February the 10th, that night she put in a terrible night. She didn't sleep at all. So the morning of the 11th she said, "I want to go down to the pension board," which I put her in the car, I drove her down. It was after lunch we got there. She went in there, and I walked in, and there was a long counter. She went to the counter, and whatever she done I don't know. And then from there we went to another place where there was a gentleman sitting that she spoke to. Would that have been you?

Q. Don't ask.   **A.** No. And then we come out, and I took her home. She never mentioned a word to me. Now, two and a half weeks later she said to me, "Frank, I want to go see D'Angelo."

MR. HEYMAN: Your Honor, I object to any conversations between the decedent and her husband after February 10 or 11. I think it's —

THE COURT: I will allow them. All right. After the date of filing I will sustain the objection.

THE WITNESS: I can't say anything?

THE COURT: Nothing after that date.

THE WITNESS: Well, it's very important. That's when I found out what she had done.

MR. HEYMAN: Your Honor, I move to strike that out.

THE COURT: All right, strike it out. I will admit evidence after February 10th only to the degree that it reflects on her mental condition on February 10th.

THE WITNESS: Now, one more thing I forgot to mention.

MR. HEYMAN: I object to —

THE COURT: We haven't got a jury here.

MR. HEYMAN: But, your Honor, I don't mind — I am going to allow the witness free opportunity, but I don't think he should go all over the field. I have a client to protect in this case, and I want to give the witness every fair opportunity.

THE COURT: All right. He is not greatly abusing this situation. He is a troubled man. I will allow him to add what he has in mind.

THE WITNESS: I lost my train of thought. These things — it's pretty near three years since these things happened, and these things come back slowly. There was something I wanted to mention that was very important. You stopped me. Oh, about — she had terrible loss of memory. Towards the end there I'd make supper, serve her her supper, she wouldn't eat. She lost a lot of weight. She'd come to me a half hour later, an hour later, and say, "Frank, when are we going to eat?" I'd say, "Grace, we had supper. You didn't eat it." And also she'd ask the same question many times about certain things over and over again, and never have any — never knew that she'd asked the same thing before. Well, that's about all I can say.

Q. On the way down to the Teachers' Retirement System, did she discuss with you anything about options?   A. No, no, and if she had, I wouldn't know. I don't know anything about them yet. In fact, she never did speak much while she was sick towards the end.

Q. When you left the Teachers' Retirement System, did she tell you anything about what she had done?   A. No.

Q. After February 11th, did there come a time when you had to take her to the psychiatrist again?   A. That's what I wanted to mention before. Two and a half weeks later she said to me, "Frank, I want to go down and see the psychiatrist."

* * *

Q. Did you have occasion to take Mrs. Ortelere to the psychiatrist, Dr. D'Angelo, after February 11th?   A. Yes, I did. Two and half weeks — two to two and a half weeks later, she says, "Frank, I want to see Dr. D'Angelo." I took her down there, and he brought us both into his office, and she says, "Doctor, I think I have made a terrible mistake," and that's when I had heard what she had done. And he says, "Well, you are in no condition to make any changes like that," he said to her; and he immediately wrote a letter and mailed it to the board.

MR. HEYMAN: I am going to object to what the doctor told him.

THE COURT: I heard your objection.

THE WITNESS: He didn't tell me. He told her.

THE COURT: Your objection is sustained. It will be stricken out. It is hearsay.

A. And then, after we come out of there — that was two and a half weeks later — then on the 28th, in the morning, I heard an unmerciful scream. I went into the bathroom, and she is laying on the floor, because all the time she had been ill, she always complained — I just thought of it — of the pains in the back of her head. And this morning, I found her on the floor. So I said, "What happened?" She says, "I had such a pain I thought I was going to fall, and I slid off the john onto the floor." I picked her up, put her in bed. I went to the bathroom myself. I must have flushed the water when she screamed, because when I come in she was in the bed unconscious. And that's when I run to the phone, called the doctor, called the ambulance. That was March 28th, and to the hospital she went. She was there ten days and that was it. That's about everything I can recall.

* * *

MR. LEVIEN: I have no further questions of this witness at this time. I couldn't be sure when this trial would start, so I didn't have anybody but the plaintiff present. There is a witness, an elderly lady, who lives all the way out in Stony Brook, Long Island. We didn't want to drag her down here in case the case didn't start. We expect to have her here tomorrow morning; and his daughter we expect, lives in Philadelphia —

THE WITNESS: Norristown.

THE COURT: But we are trying the case today. When is your next witness going to be here?

MR. LEVIEN: We can't have any other witnesses except this gentleman at this time.

MR. HEYMAN: Mr. Levien indicated to the Court he was ready with his witnesses. I have no objection, your Honor —

THE COURT: We will declare a recess until 2 P.M., but I want witnesses here then.

MR. LEVIEN: Doesn't he want to cross examine him?

THE COURT: I don't know if he does.

MR. HEYMAN: I will cross examine, your Honor. Shall I proceed now?

THE COURT: And I want the other witnesses in at 2 P.M.

MR. LEVIEN: It takes more than two hours.

THE WITNESS: I can't get my daughter from Pennsylvania in that time. She has five children. I can always have her the following morning by calling the afternoon before.

THE COURT: This is a matter that is the responsibility of your lawyer.

MR. LEVIEN: We were here five days in succession and each time this gentleman asked for an adjournment, put it off this day and put it off that day; and this lady out in Stony Brook is physically not too well, and we didn't want to drag her down.

THE COURT: She can be here by 2 P.M.

MR. LEVIEN: He has to go out there to bring her here.

THE WITNESS: I couldn't get her in here. She is a teacher roommate of my wife's. She did live right around the corner from me, and we tried to have the case come up last Friday, but since then she's moved out to Stony Brook. That was the date she moved, so I can't very well get her.

THE COURT: All right, proceed with your cross examining.

Cross Examination by MR. HEYMAN:

Q. Mr. Ortelere, you stated that your occupation was that of electrician? **A.** Correct.

Q. And were you employed or in your own business? **A.** No, I worked for a contractor.

Q. Until when did you last work for a contractor approximately? **A.** That was it, when I packed in. If I — when I quit my job, that was in — I can't tell you that.

Q. You have no — **A.** I can look it up at home.

THE COURT: When roughly?

THE WITNESS: I was off the whole year of '64 with her, so what could I say, January 1st? I don't know when to say.

Q. Well, roughly, as the judge pointed out. Would you say about January 1, 1964?   **A.** All right, say January 1st.

Q. It isn't what I say.   **A.** I will say — okay, I'll say —

Q. January 1, 1964?   **A.** All right, so if you find it's a few months difference, it doesn't mean anything.

Q. Mr. Ortelere, please believe me, I don't want to argue with you. I just want to get the facts, so don't argue. Just tell me what your best recollection is; that's all.   **A.** Yes.

Q. What was your income just prior to the time that you said you gave up the job, approximately January?   **A.** What has that got to do with that, what I earned?

MR. LEVIEN: I object as immaterial and incompetent.

THE COURT: The witness asks him a very good question. What are we going into this for? Is there a question of the man's veracity?

THE WITNESS: I am retired now.

THE COURT: Please, you are making a mistake all through.

THE WITNESS: I am sorry, your Honor. I am awfully sorry.

THE COURT: Why are we going into this?

MR. HEYMAN: Your Honor, the reason for the questions with reference to income and assets bear importantly on the question of the kind of selection the decedent might have made; and in all these cases, I am allowed, either on the question of veracity or —

THE COURT: All right, I will allow it. Go ahead.

A. My weekly gross pay is about $222.

Q. $222 per week?   **A.** That's right.

Q. And after you quit your job, as you say, around January 1964, did you have any income from employment at all?   **A.** None whatsoever.

Q. Did you have income of any kind after January 1964?   **A.** You mean as earnings? By labor?

Q. No, no. You said no income from employment.   **A.** Nothing.

Q. Did you have income from any other assets?   **A.** Yes, I had a little money of my own.

Q. Approximately what would you say your assets totalled at the time you quit your job?   **A.** I don't know whether I am right or wrong, but what is that to your business what my possessions are?

> THE COURT: Now please, Mr. Witness.
> THE WITNESS: Do I have to tell him?
> THE COURT: Yes, you do, so just relax. Tell him to the best of your knowledge.

A. I own my own home. It's free and clear.

Q. Pardon me? You owned your own home?   **A.** Yes, we did, my wife and I; and — well, I have a little property in Connecticut, just farmland. It's worth about $5,000. I had about eight thousand in the bank at the time. And that's, I guess, about it.

* * *

Re-cross Examination by MR. HEYMAN:

Q. Mr. Ortelere, did there come a time in 1964 after Mrs. Ortelere's illness began that she was on sick leave from her position without pay?   **A.** That I wouldn't know because I never knew what she earned or what she was doing as far as whether she got her pay or not.

Q. You wouldn't know anything about that?   **A.** She handled the money; I didn't.

* * *

THE COURT: Do you have any other evidence today?

MR. LEVIEN: No, I just will have some evidence from the Board of Education which they are supposed to bring over.

THE COURT: That will only take two minutes.

MR. LEVIEN: That's right.

THE COURT: All right. Then we will recess until the morning, 10 A.M. I want the Board of Education record here then, and I want no further recurrence of a situation where you are not prepared to proceed.

MR. LEVIEN: All right.

THE COURT: The Court cannot be granting recesses of this kind repeatedly; so we will proceed in the morning, and there will be no further delays.

MR. LEVIEN: I cannot have the doctor Thursday.

THE COURT: I am not going to tolerate this. That is just what I was apprehensive of.

MR. LEVIEN: I told your secretary before that I can only get the doctor on Friday. He is in Fort Dix on Thursdays, and he says he absolutely can't come.

THE COURT: Have him here on Friday.

MR. LEVIEN: He will be here Friday.

THE COURT: Is there any reason why we cannot conclude this case this week?

MR. LEVIEN: I don't see why we can't.

MR. HEYMAN: The only thing is, as I indicated to Judge Klein when he made the assignment, I have to get my doctor, and I don't know when his doctor is available. I found out this morning that his doctor —

THE COURT: You proceed, and if his doctor is not here, we will take your doctors out of order.

MR. HEYMAN: I don't know if I want to put a doctor on. I have to listen to what his doctor's testimony is, your Honor, and then I will determine whether I am going to have a doctor testify. My doctor didn't examine this patient. She died two years ago.

THE COURT: All right, 10 o'clock tomorrow.

MR. HEYMAN: Thank you, your Honor.

(Trial recessed to Thursday, November 9, 1967, at 10:00 A.M.)

[Trial Continued]

MR. HEYMAN: . . .

Second, we had an understanding — Mr. Levien had informed the Court that his doctor would be here tomorrow at 2 o'clock. After great effort I reached my doctor, and I told him Friday at 2 o'clock, and he made plans. At about 9:30 last night Mr. Levien called me at home to tell me that his doctor is coming in today at 2 o'clock. I made efforts to reach my doctor, and I called him immediately after my conversation with Mr. Levien. He didn't call me back. I called at a quarter of nine this morning. His service took the message, and as of now I haven't heard from the doctor.

THE COURT: Well, you are not going to have a witness testify with regard to another witness's testimony in any event.

MR. HEYMAN: No, excepting I think I may have pointed out to your Honor that on this expert medical testimony, I don't think

I have the background to be able to cross examine unless I have this Dr. Kaplan at my side to indicate —

THE COURT: Then the City needs new counsel. Frankly, it is not the function of an expert witness to listen to the testimony of another expert and then in effect debate what he said. You may call an expert witness merely to testify to a hypothetical state of facts, and competent counsel will phrase the appropriate questions.

MR. HEYMAN: I have to do that depending —

THE COURT: You will have to do it.

MR. HEYMAN: Well, I will have to do it if the plaintiff establishes burden of proof. If I feel that the plaintiff has not established the burden of proof —

THE COURT: You are trying the case, not the Court.

MR. HEYMAN: Yes, I say —

THE COURT: And this case is going to be tried, let there be no mistake about it, continuously. I am not going to grant a recess so that you can prepare your case after the plaintiff presented his proof. That is not trial procedure.

MR. HEYMAN: Your Honor, I am ready with my case. It's only the medical that I am pointing out that I had my doctor arranged to come —

THE COURT: This is a medical case, period.

MR. HEYMAN: Yes.

THE COURT: Manifestly, there is no issue here but a medical question.

MR. HEYMAN: May we proceed then? I'd like to call the plaintiff.

MR. LEVIEN: Just a minute. If your Honor recalls, I said I had subpoenaed the Board of Education records, and they were to be here this morning. I subpoenaed them a couple of months ago in anticipation that they would be here, and the clerk brought them here, the Board of Education records; but I find that abstracted from those records are the medical records which were the things I wanted to introduce. Now I hear that Mr. Heyman, because of being a corporation counsel, got the medical records from the Board of Education.

THE COURT: All right. Are they here?

MR. HEYMAN: They are here, your Honor.

THE COURT: There will be no problem.

MR. HEYMAN: And Mr. Levien's statement that I abstracted them, he doesn't know procedure.

THE COURT: Come on, come on.

*   *   *

[Francis Ortelere, recalled]

MR. HEYMAN:

Q. You just stated that your wife handled all the money matters in the house; is that correct? **A.** Always. She was the business woman, yes.

Q. During this period that you testified that your wife had the breakdowns and all the other symptoms that you described — **A.** Yes.

Q. — on your direct testimony, who took care of the bills in the house such as your gas and light bill, your tax bills, and so forth? **A.** When the bills came in, if I'd see them, she's the only one had the checking account, she would make out the check. I'd stand right with her. She wouldn't let me have a checkbook.

Q. She handled all those matters? **A.** She made out the checks, yes.

Q. Who did the shopping for the house? **A.** I did.

Q. During this entire period you did? **A.** 15 months I did all the shopping.

Q. And who, for example, took care of the — did you have laundry going out? **A.** I did the laundry, the cooking, the housecleaning, and took care of her for 15 months.

Q. During this period, did you entertain friends at the house? **A.** No.

Q. You didn't entertain friends? **A.** No.

Q. Did your children visit you? **A.** Rarely.

Q. Rarely? **A.** My daughter, yes, because she's too far away. My son —

Q. No, I am just asking. I want to know. **A.** Now and then, yes.

Q. Now and then. Did your son also visit you? **A.** Now and then, yes.

Q. And do you have grandchildren? Do either of them have children? **A.** I have eight grandchildren.

Q. And did the children visit their grandparents, you and your wife? **A.** They would bring the children with them when they came, yes.

Q. And what was the relationship between you and your wife? Was it a pleasant and cordial, an intimate — **A.** I had 40 years the most happiest life a man could have.

Q. And what was the relationship between your wife and yourself and your children, also a cordial and intimate one? **A.** It was a very — I don't know how to express it.

Q. A happy one? **A.** A happy family, yes, all of us.

Q. During this period, and more particularly toward the end of 1964 and January of 1965 and February, did your wife visit any relatives or friends? **A.** At that time, let me think now — I'm not positive, but I do think I had her there for Christmas of '64. I'm not positive of that. My daughter can verify that. I am not sure.

Q. When you say you had her there, you mean at your daughter's home? **A.** I drove her to my daughter's home. I think I did, for Christmas of '64.

Q. Did you visit any other relatives or friends? **A.** No, never.

Q. During this period? **A.** Never, only my daughter.

Q. Only your daughter. Did your wife go to a beauty parlor? **A.** Never.

Q. Never went to a beauty parlor? **A.** Never in her life, never.

Q. What subject did your wife teach at school **A.** I don't know what she taught. She was a second grade teacher or third grade.

Q. In the public, elementary — **A.** Yes, in the grammar school.

Q. Right. Did your wife have any special interests or hobbies? **A.** Her main interest was school. That's all she lived for. That was her main interest.

Q. Did your wife do any drawing, painting? **A.** No, not in many — in late years, since —

Q. No, Mr. Ortelere, I am interested in this particular period. **A.** No, not in '64.

Q. Your wife didn't do any painting or drawing? **A.** No, never.

Q. Did she ever do painting or drawing? **A.** Well, she previously — this is back years ago — in her class she was a very good drawer. She could draw, yes.

Q. You stated yesterday that on February 10, 1965 — that's the day before you took your wife to the retirement board — she told you she wanted you to take her down to the retirement board? **A.** Correct.

Q. That's correct? **A.** Correct.

Q. Did she discuss with you on that day why she wanted to go down to the retirement board? **A.** She had said she wanted to go down about her retirement pension, and she was upset all that night, and I took here there, and that's all I know.

Q. Did you, just prior to February 10th — that is, February 9th or a few days before, or even a month or so before — discuss with your wife anything about her retirement? **A.** Never, because I didn't understand it. I never did.

Q. You never discussed it? **A.** No, sir.

Q. Did she discuss with you or tell you what her plans were? **A.** No.

Q. For retirement? **A.** No.

Q. Never discussed it? **A.** I never knew, no.

Q. Do you know, Mr. Ortelere, of your own knowledge, whether your wife spoke to either or both of your children regarding her plans for retirement? **A.** That I don't know. I don't think so.

* * *

Kay Frances Reville, 3011 Sheffield Drive, Norristown, Pennsylvania, called as a witness in behalf of the plaintiff having been first duly sworn, testified as follows:

Direct Examination by MR. LEVIEN:

Q. Mrs. Reville, you are the daughter of Grace Ortelere and Francis Ortelere? **A.** Yes.

Q. How old are you? **A.** I am 36.

Q. Are you married? **A.** Yes, I am.

Q. How many children do you have? **A.** Five.

* * *

By THE COURT: ...

Q. ... **A.** During Christmas week, whenever the children were around, mother normally would sit and read to the youngest two boys ... She failed to do this. She showed no interest in the children, and mother was usually very outgoing toward the children, and previous visits would get the older two aside, and she was teaching them to play pinochle. Well, she didn't bother with that either. Generally, she slept late; she put cotton in her ears so the children wouldn't bother her so she'd sleep late; and she really showed no interest in anything. She moped around the house, would drift off upstairs again to the room in the afternoon. I don't know if she napped or not, but she would disappear; and generally in any conversations we had, I did all the talking. Mother was very, very quiet. She complained — of course, she complained she didn't feel well. She complained of a pain in her neck and pressure in her ear; and she felt there was something wrong with her; and the doctor didn't know what was wrong with her, and she, a couple of times, she expressed this idea that she wasn't going to get over this, whatever this was; but mother felt there was something radically wrong; and generally she was sort of depressed. She was depressed. A very solemn visit, I would say it was. It was not usual, to say the least.

By MR. LEVIEN:

Q. Did she mention anything to you about her intention to retire from the school system?   **A.** Not then as much as probably the visit before in Thanksgiving. Christmas was a little hectic. Back in the fall she had mentioned retiring. Of course, she had, over the years, of course, a little bit talked about retiring, but in the fall she brought up the thought that possibly she was going to put me as a beneficiary with my understanding — she put this to me — with my understanding that this money would be my father's as long as he lived, so even if she named me a beneficiary she wanted dad to have this money as long as he lived. I said nothing. I commented nothing, because in conscience I couldn't. This is — I mean how can a person that might be left a beneficiary start telling her mother what to do. I just listened any time she said anything about pensions.

* * *

Q. When you saw your mother in the hospital after March 28, 1965, did she talk to you in any way about her retirement? **A.** Oh, yes, she was very anxious over it. She had told me she had gone to the psychiatrist again, and had gotten him to write a letter to someone, Board of Ed. or somebody. And the doctors had said that she was supposed to rest and not worry, and mother was very worried about this, and I offered to do anything I could to help. Exactly how I found out that the letter from the psychiatrist wasn't sufficient I am not sure. I must have — I made phone calls, I do know that. To exactly whom I don't remember. But I was told that the letter was not sufficient from Dr. D'Angelo, and while my mother was in the hospital I sent my husband over to see Dr. D'Angelo; and he wrote another letter which we mailed to — I am sure the Board of Ed.

Q. To the Teachers' Retirement Board?   A. Excuse me?

Q. To the Teachers' Retirement Board?   A. Yes. So many titles.

*   *   *

Ernani D'Angelo, 1250 Village Avenue, Baldwin, New York, called as a witness in behalf of the plaintiff, having been first duly sworn, testified as follows:

Direct Examination by MR. LEVIEN:

Q. Dr. D'Angelo, you are a physician duly licensed to practice in the State of New York?   A. I am.

Q. And when were you licensed?   A. 1930.

Q. Do you specialize in any field?   A. Psychiatry.

Q. How long have you been specializing in psychiatry? A. Since 1937.

Q. Do you have any degrees or certifications by the American Psychiatric — American Board of Psychiatrists?   A. Well, I graduated from Cornell Medical College in 1929; after interning I did general practice till 1937, and in 1937 I started in psychiatry. I put in eight years at Kings Park State Hospital where I received my training, full-time physician there; and since then I have been practicing in Jamaica doing nothing but psychiatry.

I am a qualified psychiatrist with the New York State Department of Mental Hygiene; I have a specialist's rating with the Workmen's Compensation Board; I am on the neuropsychiatric staff of the Queens General Hospital; I am a diplomate of the American Board of Psychiatry.

Q. Did you treat Mrs. Grace Ortelere?   A. Yes.

Q. At any time? When did she first come to you?   A. July 1st, 1964.

Q. Did she come to you alone or with somebody? **A.** With her husband. That is routine. I never see any patient alone. Always somebody accompanies them.

Q. And what did you find at that time? **A.** Well, at that time she was — the symptoms were — she was 59 years old. She had been complaining of agitation, depression, sleeplessness, poor appetite, loss of weight, confusion, difficulty in concentration, and depression was so severe that she didn't want to continue living the way she was. She said she'd rather be dead. Not that she wanted to commit suicide, but she said she'd rather be dead than go on suffering the way she was. I made diagnosis of a nervous breakdown. Her particular type was the involutional psychosis, melancholia type. That's the type — that is the diagnosis we give that particular type, after the change of life. Before the change of life we call that a manic depressive psychosis, depressed type.

Q. What treatment did you give her? **A.** Well, at that time there was also — although I didn't make a definite diagnosis there was a question in my mind that she probably had some hardening of the arteries of the brain, cerebral arteriosclerosis, and I made that — I had that impression. I didn't make that diagnosis at the time because of the confusion she was experiencing, and the difficulty in concentration; so I said that it was a possible CAS. That is cerebroarteriosclerosis. I prescribed shock therapy with tranquilizers and I gave her a series of twelve from July 1st to August 7th of 1964. Following that she did show some improvement, but she never recovered. I kept seeing her for consultations, or rather let's call them interviews once a month. She would tell me about her condition. She hoped that she could get back to work, school teaching, but she never did reach anything — never reached any improvement which would warrant my sending her back. At a time I was thinking of giving her some more shock therapy, but I didn't for two reasons: because, first of all, if it's a pure nervous breakdown such as an involutional psychosis is, usually a series of twelve shock treatments does the trick — not always but usually. And secondly, with the possibility of cerebral arteriosclerosis here, I didn't because naturally with a definite organic factor we don't usually give shock therapy; so for those two reasons I decided not to give her any more, and just see how she progressed, and followed her up.

Q. Did you see her in about December 1964 and January 1965?   **A.** I know I saw her at monthly intervals. The exact dates I don't have.

Q. And when you saw her did you observe her mental condition?   **A.** Well, she had shown some improvement, but she was still very sick. I mean there was the same symptoms there which were — although not as severe as when I first treated her — they kept her disabled as far as her work was concerned; and also as far as living any sort of a usual or average life, which of course she had done all the time before she got sick.

* * *

Q. I will repeat the question. Would you say from your observation of her that in February she had sufficient mental capacity to act with discretion in the ordinary affairs of life?   **A.** Well, due to her condition ever since I saw her, and if you want me, I will repeat the symptoms again, I would never consider her mentally incompetent where she could make a decision which would be rational, during no time that she was under my care.

MR. HEYMAN: Doctor would you repeat that? I didn't quite get the —

THE COURT: The reporter will read the last answer.

MR. HEYMAN: Would you read the last answer, please?

(The last answer was read.)

THE COURT: I take it you meant mentally competent?

THE WITNESS: Yes, naturally. The symptoms — I will go over them again.

MR. HEYMAN: Wait.

THE WITNESS: Mentally, she couldn't make a decision of any kind, actually, of any kind, small or large.

THE COURT: The answer as it was originally expressed apparently had a little ambiguity. The doctor said that there was no time when he would consider her to be mentally incompetent. I think it was a double negative that he went into.

THE WITNESS: Yes.

THE COURT: Inadvertently, it's manifest, and I think you recognize it from the total answer.

THE WITNESS: At no time since she was under my care was she ever mentally competent.

By THE COURT:

Q. Doctor, the Court is acquainted in a broad way with involutional melancholia, but perhaps for the record you could describe involutional melancholia as it existed in this patient. **A.** Yes, Involutional melancholia, I'd have to say generally what it is. It's a nervous breakdown following the change of life. Now, in her case it was characterized by agitation, depression, loss of appetite, loss of sleep, weakness, fatigue, some confusion, inability to concentrate, feeling so miserable that they don't care to continue to live, but not that she thought of suicide.

Q. Suicide frequently goes with it? **A.** Oh, yes, it can if the miseries get so strong, and they get no relief from therapy, then they quite often seek that as a relief. That's unfortunate, but it does happen. But today not too often with the therapies that we have.

Q. How does it affect the judgment processes, if that is a technically correct term? **A.** How does it? When you say the melancholia —

Q. How does the total situation? **A.** Well, first of all, they are not thinking rationally because they are feeling so miserable. All they can think of is their own miserable state. They feel sick all the time. They actually also feel, even though this may sound paradoxical, but it isn't, they feel that they are going out of their mind; but actually, they really never do completely go out of their mind. The mental cases that are out of their mind, they don't even know it. But with all those thoughts going on, they cannot think rationally. There is a distortion of everything. They also get all sorts of delusions that their — of their illness because they have gone to so many doctors, and they don't get any relief. Then they start thinking that this may be — anything they may read in the papers or some friend of theirs tells them, they will think they got it and that is the cause of their miseries. The only thing they are thinking of is how to get — how to find some relief from their symptoms. Now as a result of that, they have nothing left to think in any other manner. They can't think rationally, no matter what the situation is. They will even tell you, "I used to be able to think of anything and make any decision. Now," they say, "even getting up, I don't know whether I should get up or whether I should stay in bed." Or,

"I don't even know how to make a slice of toast any more." Everything is impossible to decide, and everything is too great an effort to even think of doing. They just don't have the effort, actually, because their nervous breakdown drains them of all their physical energies.

Q. Are they from time to time institutionalized as a result of the malady?   **A.** Well, at one time it was very common, but prior to — prior to tranquilizers and electric shock therapy. Now, very exceptional. Only where, let's say, they happen to be alone in the world, no relatives, and so forth, and they need to be hospitalized in order to receive therapy because there is nobody to take care of them. But I might say that I don't think I hospitalize a half a dozen a year any more, and I do quite a lot of this shock therapy. I probably have under my care — I probably treat maybe on the average at least ten a day, and if I hospitalize a half a dozen a year, that is a lot today. Previously they all had to go, practically, because we had to depend upon nature to heal the process. We don't know what the process is, but it's there; but today, as I say, very seldom do they hospitalize. I do it in the office. Some of them do it on an out-patient basis in a hospital. But that wouldn't be hospitalization. Or if they are too worried of suicide, where the family is afraid they may not be able to take care of them, then we hospitalize, but as I say, they are very rare today.

Direct Examination (continued) by MR. LEVIEN:

Q. Now, doctor, I show you this page from the medical record of the hospital.   **A.** See, they can't be made to concentrate on any real vital problems. They are so obsessed with their own miseries.

Q. Just a minute. This is a page from the medical record — I forget what exhibit number that is.

MR. HEYMAN: The medical record?

MR. LEVIEN: What exhibit is that?

THE COURT: Suppose we get the exhibit.

Q. This is from the exhibit. Exhibit 9. I ask you whether that gives you any information about her arteriosclerotic condition. **A.** Well, the impression here, it's an aneurism at the junction of the basal and posterior — and left posterior cerebral arteries. Now, an aneurism is an enlarging of the blood vessel at one point. In other words, it forms a bulb. It's due to a weakening of the wall, and that is always due to — well, it could be due to any type of pathology, any disease; but in her case it probably was due to cerebral arteriosclerosis, the hardening of the arteries. A lot of people think that when the arteries become hard, they become stronger. They become just actually weaker because it's a replacement with this calcium which makes the vessel wall brittle, and that is how a stroke comes. Eventually, the blood will force that breakoff, break through the vessel wall because it becomes hard and brittle like if you take a piece of round rubber tube, and you let it lie around for ten years, it loses its elasticity and becomes brittle. And of course, it easily breaks, and that is what happens in some individuals when they get hardening of the arteries, but instead of breaking, sometimes one of the walls, part of the wall may become weak and bulge; and we call that an aneurism, an out-pocketing, and that is what she has, which is indicative of an underlying cerebral arteriosclerosis. That means hardening of the arteries of the brain. "Cerebral" is brain.

Q. Would that arteriosclerosis arise overnight in one month or would it be — **A.** No, that is a gradual process always and it's progressive. It's gradual and progressive.

Q. From that exhibit would you say that Mrs. Ortelere had arteriosclerosis in February and in January of 1965? **A.** Years prior to this diagnosis, years. This takes years to form, an aneurism. The same way if a person gets a stroke. That hardening of the arteries has been forming for years and years. In other words, the vessel wall finally becomes weakened from the sclerotic process, and the pressure of the blood breaks it.

Q. Doctor, I show you this plaintiff's Exhibit 6 which it has been testified to, is in the handwriting of Grace Ortelere and was written about March 16, 1965. Will you look at it and tell us whether that gives any indication of her mental condition at that time? **A.** Yes, I would say it does. I mean it shows an individual who is possessed of many psychosomatic delusions. She's got a half a dozen illnesses in her imagination which do not exist, and had she come across some other terms, she probably would have thought she had those. Everything about this is irrational.

By THE COURT:

Q. The fact that that was written some time in March —
MR. LEVIEN: 16th.

Q. — would that reflect on her condition early in February?
A. Definitely. This doesn't come overnight. I said this is a process that's been going on ever since I observed her, and no doubt before that when she had to stop teaching; and even then it was gradually building up, because she could no longer concentrate on her work or handle the discipline of the children and keep the hours which are necessary for teaching, getting up, going to school, preparing for the next day. It was all too much for her.

MR. LEVIEN: Now I call on the defendant to produce the letter that Dr. D'Angelo sent to the retirement board on March 26, 1965.

(Document handed to the witness.)

By MR. LEVIEN:

Q. Is this a letter in your handwriting? **A.** That's right.

Q. Did you send that out on March 26? **A.** Yes.

Q. 1965? **A.** Yes, I did.

Q. At whose request did you send it out? **A.** Well, I believe it was — well, it had to be Mrs. Ortelere.

Q. She came to your office? **A.** I believe it was with her husband, yes.

MR. LEVIEN: I offer that in evidence now.

MR. HEYMAN: No objection.

THE COURT: All right, it will be received in evidence as plaintiff's Exhibit 15.

(Letter by Dr. D'Angelo dated March 26, 1965 received in evidence and marked plaintiff's Exhibit 15.)

MR. LEVIEN: I call on the defendant to produce the letter that Dr. D'Angelo sent to the retirement board on April 2, 1965.

MR. HEYMAN: Your Honor, may I interrupt at this time? You have the medical file of the Board of Education. Do you mind if I have it?

THE COURT: Surely. (File handed to Mr. Heyman.)

Q. Is that your letter in your handwriting? **A.** I read it [*sic*], yes.

Q. Did you send it out to the Teachers' Retirement Board?
A. That's right.

Q. And at this time Mrs. Ortelere was in the hospital. Do you know who asked you to send the letter? **A.** I think it was her nephew, I believe, or — I don't recall, nephew or husband. I don't know; one of them. I don't recall who came to me. Maybe it was her husband or nephew, I don't know.

MR. LEVIEN: I offer that in evidence.

A. I gave it to one of them anyhow because that's my letter.

MR. HEYMAN: No objection.

THE COURT: It will be received in evidence as plaintiff's Exhibit 16.

(Letter written by Dr. D'Angelo received in evidence, dated April 2, 1965, and marked plaintiff's Exhibit 16.)

Q. Would you say that a person in the condition that Grace Ortelere was in when you treated her, observed her, does have occasional lucid moments?

MR. HEYMAN: I object to that, your Honor. I think it's leading.

THE COURT: All right, objection sustained. Rephrase your question.

Q. Was a person in Mrs. Ortelere's condition as you observed it always mentally incompetent, or did she on occasion have a lucid moment?

MR. HEYMAN: I will object again, your Honor.

THE COURT: Objection overruled.

A. Now, when I say that cerebral arteriosclerosis — or when it is said; I don't say these things, it is a fact — that it does cause confusion and memory defects and everything that goes with those things, it is also a fact in cerebroarteriosclerosis that the condition is not always the same from day to day. In cerebral arteriosclerosis the reason the individual cannot think well and has lapses of forgetfulness and confusion is because due to the hardening of the arteries. There is also a shrinkage of the arteries. In other words, the rubber is replaced by the placques, and the arteries actually shrink. Therefore, the amount of blood that gets to the brain is diminished, and depending upon the diminution of the blood to the brain, so is the amount of forgetfulness and confusion apparent. Now, on some days these individuals do feel a little better than on others. The heart action is a little stronger, and therefore some more blood is forced through those arteries, those shrunken arteries, on certain days; so these individuals seem to be a lot better some days. They can think better; they are not so forgetful, but that is, of course, only temporary, because they happen to feel better and the heart action is a little stronger. Now, therefore, cerebral arteriosclerosis is also characterized by lucid intervals until, of course, it becomes very severe, and then it's complete forgetfulness and everything else. So they do have periods when they think clearer than others.

By THE COURT:

Q. How advanced was this patient in the latter part of your treatment? **A.** Well, actually I would say the condition — there is no way of my being scientific or mathematical about this. I'd say she had — it was medium, moderately advanced, let me put it that way. I can't say it was very severe. I can't say it was mild. But it was moderate. The cerebral arteriosclerosis. But you have got to remember here that is not the only cause of the confusion and forgetfulness. The fact that this woman was so sick with her emotional symptoms that she couldn't think about anything else. If you talked to her and she might answer, and she might not. All she wants to say is, "I got this, and I got this wrong, and help me out here." So it's like almost an absent-minded person, you might say, where —

Q. The symptoms, I suspect, are very similar to those of senility. **A.** Well, that's cerebral arteriosclerosis, yes, but she also had the emotional disorders with it. Senility is just where they become second childhood, where they don't have the emotional miseries with it. But she had it. She had both, and that was what really interfered with her concentration, and what I call making her — it made her irrational.

By MR. LEVIEN:

Q. Assuming that on February 11th Mrs. Ortelere was interviewed by a lady from the Teachers' Retirement Board, and she is told that if she chooses the maximum she will get $6,148 per year; if she chooses Option 1 she will get $5,247 per year, leaving a reserve of $70,925; if she chooses the Option 1 on an annuity she will get $5,762 per year, consisting of an annuity allowance and so forth — there is a lot of figures — do you think she was able to comprehend and make a decision in her condition on February 11th with all those figures being given to her? **A.** I would say no. . . .

Cross Examination by MR. HEYMAN:

Q. Doctor, do you keep records with reference to every patient that you treat? **A.** Yes, I do keep records, naturally.

Q. And did you keep a record of your treatment of Mrs. Ortelere from the time she came to you, as you testified on July 1, 1964? **A.** I have a record of the shock therapy.

Q. I am just asking you, Doctor. **A.** Yes. Well, I want to break it down.

Q. Doctor, I will ask you the questions, and if you just please answer them — **A.** I am trying to, but you won't let me. I said all I have is the shock treatment record.

Q. Doctor —

THE COURT: Counselor, I suggest that you don't admonish the witness. That is a function of the Court if it is necessary. Ask him questions.

MR. HEYMAN: Your Honor, would you ask the witness, please, to be responsive to my questions, so that I could proceed with my examination?

THE COURT: Proceed; ask your questions.

THE WITNESS: I am trying to, if you will give me a chance. I can't always say yes or no. I am just asking to talk; that's all.

Q. Doctor, all I wanted to know is whether you have your records here in connection with the treatment. **A.** I don't have them all here.

Q. You knew you were going to be called as a witness? **A.** That's right, that's right.

Q. And you didn't bring those records with you? **A.** No, because my secretary-nurse has been out a week — I mean a month. She's been very ill, and I haven't been able to find them, but I will find them, and if you want me to come back — not tomorrow — but I will find them and bring them to you. I don't have them now.

Q. You say you have part of the record? **A.** I have the shock treatment record, that's right, because that's in a separate file.

Q. Doctor, you indicated a sheet of paper that you said were the shock treatment records? **A.** That's right.

Q. May I take a look at them? **A.** Yes, you may.

Q. And, Doctor, is this sheet that you handed me with the name of Mrs. Grace Ortelere on top the actual, original record, or is this a copy from your record?   **A.** Original.

Q. This is the original record?   **A.** That's right, yes. I write it in day to day as she gets the therapy.

> MR. HEYMAN: I offer this in evidence, your Honor.
>
> THE COURT: All right. It will be received in evidence as defendant's Exhibit C.
>
> THE WITNESS: Will I get that back?
>
> THE COURT: Yes.
>
> MR. LEVIEN: No objection.
>
> (Record of Dr. D'Angelo received in evidence and marked Defendant's Exhibit C.)

Q. Now, Doctor, as you indicated, Defendant's Exhibit C in evidence, the paper you just handed me, merely contains the record of the shock treatments; is that correct?   **A.** That's right, yes. The diagnosis and the —

Q. And —   **A.** — the dates of the therapy.

Q. Right, and you also testified that you saw Mrs. Ortelere from August 7, 1964 right through, I believe, March of 1965 on a monthly consultation basis once a month; is that correct? **A.** That's right.

Q. And where do you keep those records, Doctor, of these consultations?   **A.** In her file.

Q. Do you keep it separate and distinct from the records that you have in connection with her shock treatments?   **A.** Oh, yes, that's in a separate file because I am always using that.

Q. You weren't using that, Doctor, in August, September, October, or November, or even December and January of 1965 because you said you finished the shock treatment on August 7, 1964; is that correct?   **A.** These are right next to my desk. They are always available to me, these, these papers. I have piles of them there right next to my desk. I just reach out to the year and the date if a patient comes back.

Q. But Doctor —   **A.** That is not a file. That's just the one plain sheet for the shock treatment record.

Q. Doctor, you are sure that Mrs. Ortelere came to you once a month thereafter; is that correct?   **A.** That's right.

Q. For consultation?   **A.** That's right.

Q. Do you know the last time that she came to you? **A.** I can't give you the date, but it was shortly before she died.

Q. Wasn't she in the hospital at that time, Doctor? **A.** That's right, shortly before she went into the hospital.

Q. Do you know when she entered the hospital? **A.** No, I don't know. I know that, as I found out now, to refresh my memory, she died in March of '65, the year after I treated her.

Q. No, she died on April 8, 1965. **A.** Well, April, March or April. I don't think that matters.

Q. And, Doctor, when she came to you for consultation, did she come alone? **A.** No, never.

Q. And isn't it accepted medical practice to make records of the dates that a patient visits you? **A.** I have them, and I will get the file.

Q. But you didn't bring them in court today? **A.** I couldn't find them I told you.

THE COURT: Counselor, I suggest that we have a medical witness here, and the Court is well acquainted with the rather frequent dereliction of people in that profession in keeping records; and in any event this witness does not have to be scolded. You may ask him the simple question as to whether he has records, but I suggest you refrain from raising your voice.

MR. HEYMAN: Your Honor, I wasn't scolding this witness. It's my manner of speaking. If in any way it indicates that, I am sorry.

THE COURT: The Court is sitting without a jury. It knows that some doctors are methodical in recordkeeping and some are not. Nonetheless, you may put that fact in evidence, and the Court will consider it appropriately.

Q. Doctor, would I be correct in saying that Mrs. Ortelere came to you for the first consultation after you finished the shock treatments about September of 1964? **A.** If that would be a month later, it would be.

Q. Yes. And do you recall, Doctor, whether you prescribed any medicine or medications for Mrs. Ortelere at that time? **A.** Well, I had her on tranquilizers.

Q. Pardon me? **A.** I had her on tranquilizers.

Q. Did you prescribe them at that time?   **A.** Yes, she'd been getting them all along.

Q. Could you give me the name?   **A.** Librium.

Q. Pardon me.   **A.** Librium.

Q. Was there any dosage to that, Doctor? **A.** Ten milligrams.

Q. Ten milligrams?   **A.** Ten mg. three times a day. She'd been taking that all along.

THE COURT: Is that a barbiturate?

THE WITNESS: No, no, it's a tranquilizer.

Q. And, Doctor, when she came the following month, did you also prescribe —   **A.** She continued on that throughout.

Q. In other words, you continued her on the same prescription, or did you prescribe —   **A.** Same prescription.

Q. Same prescription. From the first time that she came in September; is that correct?   **A.** That's right.

Q. What did you do, renew the prescription, Doctor?   **A.** It was a refillable prescription.

Q. So that she didn't need your further prescription to renew it; is that correct?   **A.** No, no, not for six months after that. The druggist calls and I send another one if — some of them call, some don't.

Q. But in Mrs. Ortelere's case, Doctor, did you then issue just one prescription and that continued throughout the next —   **A.** I might have issued another one, I don't know; but she continued to take the medication which is what is important.

Q. Well, Doctor, would your records indicate?   **A.** No, no, they wouldn't indicate whether I gave her one prescription or two prescriptions. It would indicate that she is on the Librium. I don't write down the dates I give a prescription.

Q. Don't you think that is important, Doctor?   **A.** No, definitely not. It's important that she gets the medication.

Q. But would it be important, Doctor, in connection with the necessity possibly of renewing or sometimes knowing exactly what you prescribed?   **A.** It's down there. What she's getting is down there, but you asked me if I put a note down every time I gave her another prescription for the same medicine.

Q. That's correct, yes.   **A.** Why should I?

Q. I am just asking you, Doctor.   **A.** I don't know why.

Q. I am just asking you whether you did.   **A.** I answered you ten times no. Why do you keep asking me?

Q. I am sorry, Doctor.   **A.** Don't you understand plain English when I say no?

Q. I am trying to —   **A.** Well —

Q. — understand, Doctor. I don't.   **A.** I am using plain one-syllable words.

Q. All right, I am sorry. Now, Doctor, in your direct examination you were describing involutional depression; is that correct? **A.** Involutional melancholia. The depression is one of the symptoms.

Q. Involutional melancholia?   **A.** Melancholia, that's right.

Q. Would that be the same as involutional psychosis? **A.** Well, involutional psychosis, melancholia type is the full name for involutional melancholia.

Q. I see. And when you were describing that, weren't you generalizing, Doctor, as to conditions that were symptoms involving that nature of sickness?   **A.** Well, I can generalize or I can be specific about Mrs. Ortelere. Which do you want to know?

Q. I asked you: weren't you generalizing?

THE COURT: The question and answer will speak for itself. We are not going to have this witness review and characterize his own testimony. Ask him a question with regard to any fact that you wish.

MR. HEYMAN: I was trying to obtain —

THE COURT: I will not allow the witness to characterize his own testimony, and when the Court speaks again, it will be heard out in full before you interrupt.

MR. HEYMAN: I am sorry.

Q. Doctor, does a person who has involutional melancholia necessarily be considered an incompetent person?   **A.** Not necessarily. If it's very mild, no. There are all degrees of involutional melancholia, just as there are all degrees of any medical illness.

Q. In Mrs. Ortelere's case what degree did she have?   **A.** Severe, severe.

Q. Doctor, I believe I heard you testify on direct examination that at no time, in answer to a question put to you by counsel for the plaintiff, at no time was she ever mentally competent. Is that the testimony you gave?   **A.** Generally speaking, for any length of time, yes.

Q. But later you did testify, in response to questions of counsel, that she had what you call lucid intervals?   **A.** They do. That is characteristic of cerebral arteriosclerosis. Some days there may be a day or even part of a day where they may have lucid intervals, that's right.

Q. Now you are talking generally. With reference to Mrs. Ortelere, did she have that Doctor?   **A.** Yes, she did have it.

Q. And would you know to the extent that she did have these lucid intervals?   **A.** No, no, I wouldn't know that. I do know one time she had it.

Q. When would that be Doctor?   **A.** When she wanted to change the — well, I don't know what you'd call it — she wanted to change her pension status from one to the other, that's all I know, because she realized she couldn't have been thinking right when she made her first choice. Now, then I say she was — she had a lucid interval.

Q. Doctor, I show you plaintiff's Exhibit 15 and ask you if that is the occasion that you say she had a lucid interval.   **A.** Yes, it would have to be, because she feels now that she made the wrong choice in her pension option, and had she been clearer mentally she would have chosen differently. I would say that she was — when I saw her at this time she was thinking clearly.

Q. Doctor, do you recall from looking at this record whether Mrs. Ortelere was at your office when you wrote that letter?   **A.** Yes, I would say — I wouldn't know now. Now, don't pin me down; I don't know. I couldn't say. I wouldn't recall now. I can't recall.

Q. But based on your statement that you just read, Doctor, you would say that Mrs. Ortelere in your opinion had a lucid interval at that time?   **A.** In making those statements, she had a lucid interval, definitely.

Q. She was acting rationally, in your opinion?   **A.** At that time, yes. She was thinking rationally then.

Q. And, Doctor —   **A.** Because she explained it to me very clearly then.

Q. Doctor, at the time Mrs. Ortelere had this lucid interval, did she show you the kind of application that she had filed? **A.** No, no, no, definitely not.

Q. Did you ever see the kind of application? **A.** Never, never.

Q. Doctor, did she discuss with you the fact that she was thinking about retiring either in December, January — December of 1964 or January of 1965? **A.** No, I wouldn't recall that. I wouldn't even ask that. When she retired would be her own affair, not mine. I don't recall anything like that. That's my answer.

Q. No, Doctor, I merely want to know whether she discussed it with you. **A.** Oh, retirement was definitely there. Retirement was definitely there, if that's what you mean. She was going to retire; that's all.

Q. No. Did she talk to you about it, Doctor? **A.** Yes.

Q. That is what I — **A.** Of course she did.

Q. She spoke to you about it? **A.** At times she did, yes, that's right.

Q. Was she rational? **A.** In fact, I told her she had to retire.

Q. Was she rational at the time that she discussed these? **A.** At times she was, yes.

Q. And would you know about when that was, Doctor? **A.** I wouldn't know. I couldn't tell you.

Q. Could you give us an approximate time, Doctor? Would it be December of 1964, January of 1965? **A.** Any time, because actually, after her — after I gave her the treatment, she didn't respond as a pure involutional melancholia would. Then, of course, the condition of retirement came up then, and it was always discussed one way or another, in one form or another.

Q. During those times that it was discussed one way or another, Doctor, was she rational? Did she understand what she was discussing with you? **A.** At times she would, and at times she wouldn't. It depended upon how miserable she felt. You got to understand that her — if she wasn't thinking straight, it was not only due to the hardening of the arteries; it was also due to the fact that she was suffering the tortures of hell as a result of her involutional melancholia, so that she couldn't think straight on anything really, although she could discuss things. She couldn't think straight. She never could as far as all the time I knew her regardless of the cause or regardless of sometimes she discussed her pension. That time she discussed it, and she said she made a big mistake because she wasn't thinking straight, if she was in her right mind she would never have made that choice. That is all I can impart to the Court, and I agree with her.

MR. HEYMAN: I move to strike the last statement out.

THE COURT: All right, strike it out.

Q. Doctor, on the basis of this letter — I don't know if I asked you this question — but on the basis of this plaintiff's Exhibit 15 in evidence, could you tell us whether on February 11, 1965, which is the date that Mrs. Ortelere signed the application, would she have been rational or irrational?   **A.** At that time I would say she was very irrational, on that date.

Q. On that specific date?   **A.** She had to be irrational, in my judgment.

Q. Doctor, is it not a fact that many persons with involutional —   **A.** Melancholia.

Q. — melancholia improve with treatment?   **A.** Yes, I would say 95 percent of my patients do; let me put it that way.

Q. And, Doctor, didn't you say that Mrs. Ortelere did improve somewhat with the treatment?   **A.** Slightly, yes, she did. She did improve as compared to her condition when she first came to my office.

Q. Yes, and the reason that you stopped the shock treatment was mainly because of her hardening of the arteries?   **A.** No, no, no.

Q. Is that what you said?   **A.** No, no, no.

Q. All right.   **A.** I said that I stopped it — first of all, that's about the amount that the average involutional melancholia needs. I give her a series. That's my own. Some may give ten, some may give fifteen, some give twenty; but I found out about a dozen treatments usually does the trick. Now, if it doesn't, then you look for other causes, and there was nothing here in her environment to make me think that it was a reaction — what we call a reaction to the environment, because her environment was an average type of environment; and then, in view of the confusion and poor concentration, I began to think that perhaps there's some cerebral arteriosclerosis here, for two reasons: First of all, she didn't respond the way they would where there is no situation involved. There was no situation here. Her life was an average school teacher's life. And secondly, she had this other difficulty, this confusion, inability to concentrate, and it bothered her.

Q. Doctor, did Mrs. Ortelere discuss with you around the end of the year, December of 1964 or January '65, her desire to resume her duties as a teacher?   **A.** She was thinking of it, yes. She thought of it, that's right.

Q. And at the time would you say that she was rational when she discussed that situation with you?   **A.** Well, she asked. She asked.

Q. What was your advice to her?   **A.** I didn't think she could do it.

Q. Did she give you a decision that she made with reference to whether she was going or not going to return?   **A.** I don't think so. I don't recall if she did. No, she wouldn't have gone without my — without asking me, because she was a very sick woman.

Q. Would any of your records indicate whether she had discussed this situation of resuming her teaching duties and what your advice to her was?   **A.** I remember it. I don't need to consult the record.

Q. I am just asking if your records would.   **A.** No, I don't think so. I don't think they —

Q. Would you make a note of a thing like that?   **A.** I don't think so, no. I doubt it very much.

Q. Doctor, was there a time in the course of your treatment of Mrs. Ortelere that you said to her, "You ought to go out more and do things?"   **A.** When you say go out more, let me put it this way: I do encourage my patients to go out for walks so that they don't shut themselves up too much. To that extent I might have said it.

Q. Did you also say to her, "Do things"?   **A.** No, I wouldn't say too much. In fact, I say just the opposite to my patients, to take it easy, light things, don't force themselves because, I mean, if they are not feeling well, I am not going to push them. You wouldn't let a patient with a broken leg run around the block. These people are sick. It's their nervous system, but they are sick.

Q. Doctor, would you recall whether or not Mrs. Ortelere discussed with you the redecoration of her home around that time, during the time that you were treating her?   **A.** She might have, yes, she might have. It's possible. I don't recall, no, but it's possible.

Q. Did she discuss with you anything about visiting friends or that she was playing cards?   **A.** I don't recall right offhand, but she might have. She might have.

Q. Doctor, would you consider or did you consider Mrs. Ortelere incapable or incompetent to manage her affairs during this entire period from the date that you commenced treatment up to, let's say, you issued that letter on March 26 of 1965?   **A.** I considered her incompetent all the time that I knew her, that she was under my care, and that would include any date you may mention.

Q. Under those circumstances, Doctor, did you suggest to any member of the family, Mr. Ortelere or someone else, that in view of that condition of Mrs. Ortelere, that she should be watched?   **A.** I never let her alone. I never let any of my patients alone.

Q. Did you suggest —   **A.** I suggest that she never be alone, that's routine with any of my patients, and I suggested it in this case, yes.

Q. Did you also suggest that she be watched with reference to any decisions or judgments that she may make?   **A.** No, no, no, not unless — not unless it was brought up to me.

Q. You merely indicated then, Doctor, as I take it, that she be watched physically?   **A.** That she not be alone, that she not be alone.

Q. Be alone?   **A.** Because a lot of them have suicidal tendencies, and in my early practice I had two patients commit suicide, and I learned.

Q. Doctor, in a situation where you feel a person is unable or incompetent to manage his or her own affairs, do you ever suggest that a committee be appointed for such a person?   **A.** No, not unless the family or relatives do.

Q. I didn't get that.   **A.** Only if the family or relatives ask me for my opinion do I give it, but I don't of my own accord, no.

Q. Even though you find — in your treatment you make a finding that a person is incapable of managing his own affairs, you never volunteer that?   **A.** That is a legal term. I am a doctor. If the family —

THE COURT: I must agree with the witness.

MR. HEYMAN: Pardon me?

THE COURT: I say the Court must agree with the witness. You wouldn't want to see him prosecuted for practicing law.

THE WITNESS: No, but it does come up.

Q. That is what I meant.   **A.** It does come up.

Q. Well, I didn't —   **A.** But it didn't come up here, if that's what you mean.

Q. I was just trying to find out whether in a situation of that kind you recommend for the patient's own —   **A.** If they ask me first, but I never do it of my own accord, no. It has come up many times.

Q. Doctor, do you know during the course of treatment whether Mrs. Ortelere managed the financial matters at her home?   **A.** I wouldn't know. I doubt it, but I don't know.

Q. If I tell you that the husband testified that Mrs. Ortelere —

THE COURT: Now, please, we are not going to have a comment on someone else's testimony. The witness said he has no knowledge of it. Proceed.

MR. HEYMAN: I think your Honor should permit me, may I respectfully suggest —

THE COURT: If you want to ask a hypothetical question you may, but you are not asking a hypothetical question. You are asking one witness to comment on another witness's testimony.

MR. HEYMAN: Your Honor, but the —

THE COURT: And I told you before that that will not be permitted.

MR. HEYMAN: But, your Honor, may I respectfully point out this is cross examination, and I think I should be allowed a little more leeway.

THE COURT: You can proceed to cross examine the witness but only within the law of evidence.

Q. Doctor, I show you defendant's Exhibit A in evidence, which is entitled "Final application for service retirement," and it's dated February 11, 1965, and ask you to look at that.   **A.** All right.

Q. Doctor, based on your treatment of Mrs. Ortelere, would you say that Mrs. Ortelere on that date, February 11, was of sufficient rational mental capacity to understand and sign such a form?   **A.** She could sign it, but she couldn't understand exactly what she was signing.

Q. Even though it's filled out in her own handwriting, Doctor?   **A.** That's right, that's right, she couldn't have had a rational grasp of the subject matter in this paper.

Q. Doctor, would it have been possible that at that time Mrs. Ortelere had what you call a lucid interval so that she —   **A.** Not the remotest possibility. She would never have signed such a document.

* * *

Miriam B. Clark, 140 Eighth Avenue, Brooklyn, New York, called as a witness in behalf of the defendant, having been first duly sworn, testified as follows:

Direct Examination by MR. HEYMAN:

Q. Dr. Clark, are you a physician duly licensed to practice medicine in the State of New York?   **A.** Yes.

Q. When were you admitted to such practice?   **A.** 1930.

Q. Are you still practicing to the present day, Doctor?   **A.** Yes.

Q. Are you employed by the Board of Education of the City of New York in the capacity of a doctor?   **A.** Yes.

Q. And are you a member of the medical board in that capacity of the Board of Education?   **A.** The medical division.

Q. Doctor, how long have you been so employed by the Board of Education?   **A.** Since May 15, 1939.

Q. Would you speak up a little?   **A.** Since May 15, 1939.

Q. Doctor, do you also practice medicine as a duly licensed physician?   **A.** Yes.

Q. In addition to your employment with the Board of Education?   **A.** Yes.

Q. Do you have any speciality in connection with your practice, Doctor?   **A.** Internal medicine.

Q. Doctor, in your capacity as a member of the medical division of the Board of Education, do you examine teachers or applicants for license and teachers who are returning from sick leave after an absence from their duties?   **A.** Yes.

Q. Doctor, do you remember examining a Mrs. Grace Ortelere at the Board of Education on February 2, 1965?   **A.** I do not remember her personally, but I can identify the notes that I made at the time of my examination.

Q. Doctor, does the Board of Education keep a file in the regular course of business that is called a medical file on each teacher who has to appear before the medical division? **A.** Yes.

Q. I show you this file and ask you if you can identify this as the file of Grace Ortelere of the medical division of the Board of Education. **A.** Yes.

Q. Doctor, will you refresh your recollection by looking through the file to know whether or not you did examine Grace Ortelere on February 2, 1965? **A.** This top sheet is my notes as to her examination on that day.

Q. Does that refresh your memory, Doctor? **A.** Yes.

Q. That you examined Mrs. Ortelere on that day? **A.** Yes, I know that I did, or I would not have made these notes.

Q. Doctor, where did you examine Mrs. Ortelere? **A.** At the Board of Education at 110 Livingston Street in the medical division.

Q. And do you remember, Doctor, whether Mrs. Ortelere was there alone or with anyone else? **A.** She was alone in my room, or I would have made a note as to that, which I did not do.

Q. Doctor, could you tell us about how long the examination of Mrs. Ortelere took on that day? **A.** I would judge from my notes that this must have been between a half and three-quarters of an hour.

Q. Could you tell us the purpose of the examination, Doctor? **A.** To determine whether she was in fit condition to return to teaching as of the beginning of that term.

Q. When you say the beginning of that term, Doctor, what term are you referring to? **A.** The term that began in February '65.

Q. Did you have with you at that time of the examination Mrs. Ortelere's medical file? **A.** Yes.

Q. Did you, prior to the examination review the file to see what was in it? **A.** Yes.

Q. Doctor, will you now tell us, if you can, what your examination consisted of at that time? **A.** Physical examination and an interview to try to determine her fitness to return, an interview as to what her health had been just preceding this time.

Q. Will you tell us, did you take a history from her?   **A.** Yes.

Q. Will you tell the Court what you ascertained from her as to the history?   **A.** I can only tell you from my notes. I wouldn't remember it. She had been absent since March 26, 1964 because of depression and nervousness. Her physician sent her to a psychiatrist. This depression and nervousness followed a heart attack had by her husband and his large losses in the stock market. At the present time, she said, her husband had recovered, and she had shaken off her worries concerning the stocks. I am quoting from my notes here. I questioned her as to what her treatment had been. She said that she had been treated by a psychiatrist, whose name I did not include here, until the late summer, when the psychiatrist told her to get out and do things, and that she has — she said she had not called him on the phone again, although he had requested her to do so. Then I questioned her as to how she was feeling at this time, February 2, '65. She said that she felt that she could return to school without any trouble. I questioned her as to what she had been doing recently to see whether she had been active or whether she had not been able to do things. She told me that she had had her house redecorated, that she shopped, that she had been seeing friends and playing cards, that she went and visited her daughter and her grandchildren, and that she had done some painting of pictures. From which I judged that she had apparently recovered from the depression with which the rest of this chart showed that she had suffered previously.

Q. Doctor, did you make any finding as to her condition to resume employment?   **A.** I have a note here that to me she appeared quite alert, by which I would mean that she answered my questions relatively and without any hesitation, and that she did not contradict herself. She didn't appear at all depressed. Neither did she appear euphoric — with her head in the clouds. She didn't claim that everything was perfect.

THE COURT: But you don't recall this yourself?

THE WITNESS: I am telling you from my notes. I do not recall her at all.

Q. Doctor, is it a practice to make notes in connection with every examination conducted by you and the other members of the medical division?   **A.** Yes.

Q. And do these notes become a regular part of the folder, medical file of the teacher? **A.** Yes.

Q. And this is the medical report or the notes that you took and formed part of the teacher's record? **A.** That's right.

Q. Doctor, what was your recommendation as a result of your examination and interview of Mrs. Ortelere at that time? **A.** I recommended she see her psychiatrist and ask him to send us a report, and I said at that time that I believed from my examination on that day that she was in fit condition for return to teaching.

Q. Doctor, did she appear rational to you at that time during the examination? **A.** Yes.

Q. Doctor, on the basis of this examination, could you give us an opinion as to whether or not — that is, in your opinion — Mrs. Ortelere would have become mentally unsound on February 11, 1965 nine days later? **A.** There was nothing —

> MR. LEVIEN: If your Honor please, I object to the question. This lady has testified she is an internist, she is not a psychiatrist.
>
> THE COURT: I will overrule the objection, but the Court has noted all those facts, you may be assured. Objection overruled.

Q. Would you answer the question, in your opinion. **A.** There was nothing in my examination on that day to make me suspect that anything — that any incompetence would occur by the 11th of February.

> THE COURT: Would it have altered your opinion if you had known that during July and August she had received twelve shock treatments?
>
> THE WITNESS: I knew that.

By THE COURT:

Q. Actually, Doctor, you wouldn't undertake yourself to really express an opinion as to mental competence, would you, in the medical sense? **A.** I would not make a final opinion — a final estimate. I would say that we get very used to examining teachers and forming opinions as to their fitness.

Q. But you are not a psychiatrist? **A.** We would not be the final decider.

* * *

Francis B. Ortelere, the plaintiff, recalled in rebuttal in his own behalf, having been previously sworn, testified further as follows:

Direct Examination by MR. LEVIEN:

Q. Mr. Ortelere, do you recall when you accompanied your wife to an examination at the Board of Education?   **A.** I did.

Q. On February 2nd?   **A.** I did.

Q. 1965?   **A.** I am a little doubt — I mean I don't — I am not saying that the doctor isn't correct, but as far as whether it was '64 or '65, that I have no recollection. But can I speak? . . . could I just talk to answer the doctor?

MR. LEVIEN: No, no, you have to answer questions.

THE WITNESS: Okay.

Q. Did your wife have anything to do with decorating your house?   **A.** The decorating the home I had done, and she was there. I called in the painters and the different people. Between the two of us we tried to select our — whatever we wanted. Then we come to get our carpeting, which we got wall to wall; and probably I can even find the man. We went to Allen Carpet in Jamaica, and we were trying to select carpeting, and she is telling the man her condition and about her shock treatment and all; and she says, "I am in no condition to pick out the rugs." So we selected some rug. It was delivered to the home, all laid. And after it was laid, she found out that it was not it; she didn't like it. So I had a lot of trouble. I had to have it all taken out and done over again, but I was with her; we selected it together; but after she got it she didn't want it.

Q. About when was this?   **A.** I don't remember dates. It might have been in — in '64. '64 was the year, yes sir.

Q. Did you have a heart attack in 1964?   **A.** Well, I will have to tell it. It's a story; I can't say yes. I had been out to a bachelor party with the fellows, and I got in late at night. I had too much to drink. I woke up at one o'clock short of breath, and I went to the window to get a breath of air. Immediately, she run to the phone, and she called the doctor. The doctor came in, and he examined me, maybe my heart was pumping fast; and he gave me some sort of a shot to put me to sleep. He made a report that I had a heart attack. The next day I woke up, I felt fine. I had three cardio — is it cardiographs or cardiograms — taken after that; and there is nothing wrong with my heart. She may have thought so, but there is nothing wrong with my heart. My stomach ulcers, yes.

Q. Did she do any painting? **A.** No, my wife didn't paint. She may have told — I am not saying she didn't tell the doctor. She may have told the doctor that, but she did not paint. Not that she couldn't; years ago she could.

Q. Did she play cards? **A.** Well, we had neighbors next door that lived there for thirty some-odd years, and when she was sick, going through this in '64, once in a while of an evening they'd come over and try to get her interested in playing pinochle, the four of us. She'd play for a while, and then she'd lose interest, and that she did once in a while, correct; but to go out, she never went out, which she told the doctor she did.

Q. Did she do shopping at that time? **A.** She never shopped. I did all the shopping and cooking.

MR. HEYMAN: Your Honor, I am going to object and move to strike it out on the same ground, that I wasn't permitted to ask their doctor questions to discredit their doctor. I don't think that this is proper redirect.

THE COURT: Objection overruled.

MR. LEVIEN: That is all.

THE WITNESS: You didn't have to ask me. I wanted to come.

THE COURT: Please, that is why you have ulcers. Sit down.

MR. LEVIEN: Frank, sit down.

THE COURT: Any cross examination? All right. You may step down.

(Witness excused.)

* * *

THE COURT: May I observe for the record . . . that the evidence of mental incompetency is very substantial. You have offered no really credible evidence to rebut it. I would suggest that if there is any legal issue that is involved, that that particularly be briefed; but we have a situation here where a woman obviously was seriously sick emotionally and mentally, and during that sickness retired. We have had a qualified psychiatrist give his opinion, and we have had no evidence to rebut it. However, the Court is reserving decision and invites you to submit anything that will guide the Court.

MR. HEYMAN: Thank you, your Honor.

[After this trial, Judge Murtagh issued the following opinion:]

ORTELERE v. TEACHERS' RETIREMENT BD.
Supreme Court of New York, Appellate Division 1968.
31 App.Div.2d 139, 295 N.Y.S.2d 506.

MURTAGH, J.

This is an action commenced by the surviving spouse of Grace W. Ortelere, a deceased pensioner, who for a period of thirty-seven years had been employed as a school teacher in the New York City Public School System.

On or about June 28, 1958, the decedent duly executed and filed with the defendant her "Selection of Benefits Under Option One," in which she named the plaintiff, her husband, as beneficiary.

Option One calls for the payment to the pensioner or her beneficiary, whoever survives, a sum of money which is less each month than would be paid if the duration of the pension was to be determined solely by the life of the pensioner.

The decedent died on April 8, 1965, having been absent from her teaching assignments from about March 26, 1964. From July 1, 1964, until her death the deceased was under the care of a psychiatrist, who testified that he treated and examined her up to the time of her death.

On February 11, 1965, the deceased, in the office of the Teachers' Retirement Board, located at 154 Nassau Street, New York, N.Y., executed a document wherein she changed her pension option from Option One, as heretofore described, to an option whereby she received the maximum monthly payment but which payments would only be made to her during her lifetime. At the time this document was executed there was, as is usual, no examination made of the pensioner to determine her mental capacity to understand what changes were being made and their various effects.

Sufficient has been shown to this court that, beginning sometime early in 1964 and until her death, the pensioner was under a severe mental incapacity and was on February 11, 1965, incapable of understanding and of acting with discretion.

The court finds that the decedent was still in the service of the City of New York as a public school teacher on April 8, 1965, the date of her death.

Any action taken by the decedent on February 11, 1965, in signing any documents is null and void and of no legal effect.

The plaintiff is granted judgment against the defendant for the amount of the reserve for the retirement allowance standing to the credit of the decedent at the time of her death on April 8, 1965, together with interest accrued thereon.

Submit order.

FURTHER QUESTIONS

1. Criticize Judge Breitel's statement that Mrs. Ortelere made a "foolhardy" choice of retirement plans.

2. Criticize Judge Breitel's assertion that "the system . . . should have known" of Mrs. Ortelere's illness. (Recall the UCC's "reason to know" test in its phrasing of the rule of *Hadley v. Baxendale*.) If a private insurance company handled the retirement scheme for the Board of Education would this case come out differently? What if the city had a separate "Insurance Department" which handled retirement and accident benefits for employees of all departments?

3. If the Board of Education had known Mrs. Ortelere was suffering from involutional melancholia and had at hand Judge Breitel's opinion about her incapacity, what would its proper course have been when Mrs. Ortelere came in to retire?

4. What should the Board of Education do to avoid future claims like that now pressed by Mr. Ortelere? Dr. D'Angelo testified that "I never see any patient alone. Always somebody accompanies them." Would this be a good practice for the Board of Education to adopt before it allows a change in retirement plans?

5. Judge Breitel says that "nothing less serious than a medically classified psychosis" will warrant invalidating a contract on the basis of mental illness. About this Zusman and Carnahan, the authors of a leading treatise, comment:

> Such a requirement can only foster a needless reliance upon functionally irrelevant psychiatric diagnostic categories. More important, it allows the legal process to be controlled by the psychiatric witness, since he alone can authoritatively classify the individual psychiatrically.[1]

Do you think Dr. D'Angelo was honest in his retrospective evaluation of Mrs. Ortelere's condition? Do you think he was accurate?[2]

---

1. J. Zusman and W. Carnahan, 1 Mental Health: New York Law and Practice 14-6.

2. If this latter question interests you as a general matter, you might see Ash, The Reliability of Psychiatric Diagnosis, 44 J.Abn. and Soc.Psych. 272 (1949) (estimating 64% reliability for diagnosis that patient falls into one of three major categories — psychosis, neurosis, personality disorder; emphasizing unreliability

6. Are there other reasons why Judge Breitel's limitation of this sort of claim of incapacity to "medically classified psychosis" is questionable? Why does Justice Breitel insist on it? Would you insist on it as an appellate judge?

In answering these questions you might bear in mind the deprecating comments of a writer, himself twice committed to an institution: "'[P]sychosis,' the antiseptic modern word that sends chills down the ravines of my friends' minds, has become so weakened (despite its impressive white-jacketed look) by narrow-minded, square, and fast-slipping ideological preconceptions that it must be held at arm's length, like a dead rat, for any cool understanding."[3] Consider also the comment in another context of a Professor of Law and Psychiatry:

> Even apart from the Szaszian mental-illness-is-a-myth group, there has been growing confusion in the mental health professions about which disorders are to be regarded as mental illness. Unless some clarity can be brought to the concept, everything which follows from it will [be] fatally infected with ambiguity.
>
> Obviously there is no reason for the facile equation of need for care with mental illness or insanity. It is easy to think of persons not mentally ill . . . but merely emotionally unbalanced or volatile, upset, tired, aggrieved, confused or physically impaired who would be helped by treatment.[4]

7. Would it vitiate the claims of Mrs. Ortelere's incapacity

(a) if she had consulted a lawyer before she went to the retirement board but then ignored the lawyer's advice, and the lawyer did nothing?

(b) if she brought a lawyer to the board but ignored the lawyer's advice, and the lawyer did nothing further?

8. What, do you think, in fact was the role of an attorney in Mrs. Ortelere's decision?

---

of more precise diagnosis), and Zubin, Classification of the Behavior Disorders, 18 Ann.Rev. of Psychol. 373 (1967) (taking a more optimistic view. Agreement over broad categories may be as high as 84%).

3. S. Krim, Views of a Nearsighted Cannonneer 120 (1961).

4. **A.** Stone, Mental Health and Law: A System in Transition 47 (1975).

9. What responsibility, if any, would you have as an attorney if you were consulted by Mrs. Ortelere and she told you first, that she wanted her contact with you kept confidential, and later that she intended to ignore your advice and select maximum retirement benefits?

10. In what respects, if any, was Mr. Ortelere's responsibility for his wife in this transaction different from the responsibility of a lawyer as suggested by your answers to the two previous questions? Did he adequately discharge his responsibilities? If not, is that relevant to his claim in this case? Suppose you were the judge and it were argued that:

> Mr. Ortelere and the board were at least equally at fault in not attending to Mrs. Ortelere's incompetence. Neither of them, therefore, has any better moral claim than the other. Neither makes a case that justice demands that the state intrude to restructure arrangements already made. The losses from Mrs. Ortelere's incapacity ought, consequently, to lie as they fall. Moreover if this case is decided for Mr. Ortelere, the most innocent of all parties will suffer — present contributors to the retirement fund.

How would you react to this as a judge?

11. Review Mr. Ortelere's testimony about the sales transactions entered into with Allen Carpet in Jamaica. Assume that all relevant papers and checks were signed only by Mrs. Ortelere and that though her husband was at the store and at the Ortelere home when the carpets were sold and delivered, he had no formal connection with the transaction. If Allen Carpet files an otherwise valid claim against Mrs. Ortelere's estate for the costs incurred in delivering and laying carpets she refused to accept, should the Estate executor pay the claim?

12. Earlier we asked whether courts, legislatures, or psychiatrists should frame the legal rule defining mental infirmity. Now that you've read the trial testimony in *Ortelere*, do you have any greater confidence that lawyers, judges, politicians or psychiatrists can draft a workable rule?

13. Given your present perceptions of the capability problems inherent in the undertaking, how would you phrase the laws as to the voidability of contracts on grounds of incapacity?

IX. ALLEN v. QUALITY FURNITURE

There was neither an appellate nor a trial court opinion in this case, which arose in the late 1960s. In place of such opinions, you may consider capability problems from another angle by studying the attached transcript of an intake interview between Ms. Allen and her attorney. Though based on the facts of a real "Allen v. Quality Furniture," this interview was simulated by the Legal Services Training Program in the mid-1970s as an instructional device. Susan Shapiro was selected to play the attorney role because of her skills as an interviewer. Ms. Allen was played by an actual legal aid client who had been instructed as to the facts of this case.

The entire interview (here substantially edited) ran almost two hours. As you read it, bear in mind that the ultimate judgment of a court is dependent on the initial capacity of a potential litigant to reach and to educate a lawyer. What does this transcript suggest about the capability problems that arise in the lawyer-client relationship?

SIMULATED INTERVIEW WITH MS. ALLEN

SHAPIRO: My name is Susan Shapiro, I'm one of the lawyers here. Would you like to take your coat off, you're going to be kind of cold when you go outside.

ALLEN: Yes, thank you.

Q. It still as windy as it was this morning? I haven't been out all day.

A. Well, it's okay, but it's kind of chilly.

Q. Mary Joyce Allen, right?

A. Yes.

Q. I have to ask you some questions about yourself, some vital statistics kinds of questions for our records.

A. Okay.

Q. Your address?   **A.** It's 2445 Memorial Drive, it's in the projects.

Q. 2445?   **A.** Yes.

Q. Is there an apartment number?   **A.** You just go up to like AG1.

Q. But if we were to send you a letter, we wouldn't need to put the apartment number?   **A.** Oh no.

Q. How old are you?   **A.** 29.

Q. And what's your marital status?   **A.** I'm divorced.

Q. And have any children?   **A.** Yes, there's Michael, Frank, and I have twins Shannon and Cheryl.

Q. And Michael's how old?   **A.** Michael is eight years old.

Q. And Frank?   **A.** Frank is six years old.

Q. And the twins?   **A.** They're four.

Q. That's a handful.   **A.** Yes.

Q. Anybody else live with you besides the four children?   **A.** Yeah, their grandmother.

Q. That's your mother?   **A.** Yes.

Q. Okay, now, are you employed?   **A.** Yes, I am.

Q. Where do you work?   **A.** At the Economy Laundry.

Q. Where is that located?   **A.** The Economy Laundry? It's right downtown.

Q. Downtown? That's some ways from where you live.   **A.** Yeah.

Q. What do you do there?   **A.** I'm a presser, at the laundry, but it's not too bad.

Q. No? How long have you been there?   **A.** This is the third year that I've been working there.

Q. What's your take-home pay, your net pay?   **A.** I make about $300 a month.

Q. That's after taxes and everything are taken out?   **A.** Yes, and that's for everything.

Q. I'm sorry to have to ask all these nosey questions, but part of this we need for our records, and as far as your income is concerned, the reason that I need to know that, as you probably know, the way legal services works ...   **A.** No, I just pass here on the weekends when I'm going shopping and I see the place and a lot of people always be in here. So I asked my neighbor did she know anything about it, and they had this announcement on television about going to legal services. So every-time I pass it, I always see it, so I just decided to come in and see what it was about. But I don't really know. I just know it's for poor people.

Q. The thing about the income is, we don't charge you anything at all, as long as you are eligible for our services, we can represent you, do whatever we can to help you with any legal problems that you have. We don't charge anything. But if you are not eligible for our services, then we can't represent you at all, we have to refer you to a lawyer in private practice. And the way that we have to decide whether you are eligible for our services is by what your income is. There is a guideline that our board of directors has adopted, that we just apply to everybody's income, wherever they get their income from, and that is we can represent you if your take-home pay is no more than $72.00 a week plus an allowance of $12.00 for each of your dependents. So as you can see you are well within our guidelines and there is certainly no problem about you being financially eligible for our services, but as I say that's why I have to ask all of this information.   **A.** Yes, but what about the man who said that he was going to have me pay all this money for something that I don't even know . . . he didn't say that's what he wanted, and now he's telling me he wants me to pay for that, so . . .

Q. Okay, let's get to that in a second. That's what you came in about today?   **A.** Yeah.

[Discussion about Ms. Allen's income continued here for about five more minutes.]

* * *

Q. Now, what's the problem?   **A.** Well, see this man, he came over my house one day when I was there with the kids. And he said he was going to sell me this food and he sold me the food and he sold me a freezer, but I didn't want a freezer. And he said that I have to pay for the freezer, when I called him to tell him that I didn't want the freezer because it wasn't working. And now he says that I have to pay all this money, but he told me that I could cancel it anytime that I got ready after a few months. Since I kept having so much trouble with the food and everything, I just told him to come get it and he told maybe he could work out something and nobody was home when he came but me, and I was trying to watch the kids and everything and it sounded like it was a bargain or something. And he said that my friend told him where I lived and I would probably be interested in it. So that's what happened.

Q. Okay. Have you gotten any court papers or any letters or anything about this? **A.** Well, I got this here thing, but I don't really know what it means. It have all this stuff on it.

COMMONWEALTH OF MASSACHUSETTS

THIRD DISTRICT COURT   DOCKET NO. 67332
OF EASTERN MIDDLESEX
MIDDLESEX, SS

QUALITY FURNITURE COMPANY, INC.,
A CORPORATION, PLAINTIFF   }   COMPLAINT
               vs.
MARY JOYCE ALLEN, DEFENDANT

1. On January 13, 1975, plaintiff and defendant for good and valuable consideration entered into a written contract, a copy of which is attached as Exhibit A.

2. Plaintiff has performed its obligations under the contract.

3. Defendant has failed since June 1, 1975 to pay plaintiff the agreed upon monthly installments of $30.20 and by the terms of the agreement now owes plaintiff the sum of $966.68.

WHEREFORE, plaintiff now demands judgment against defendant:

1. For the unpaid balance due and owing in the amount of $966.68, plus interest from June 1, 1975 until the date of judgment.

2. For attorney's fees in the sum of $175.00.

3. For the costs of the action.

4. For interest from the date of judgment until the unpaid balance on the aforesaid agreement is paid in full.

5. For such other relief as the Court deems just and proper.

WALLER, YOUNG & SAWYER
Attorneys for Quality Furniture Co., Inc.
131 First National Bank Bldg.
Boston, Mass.   By: /s/ _____
262-4160   RONALD A. MARSTEN
                          For the firm
                          September 3, 1975

EXHIBIT A*

Est. 1840
Reliable
Dependable
AAA Quality

QUALITY FURNITURE, INC.
188 Malcolm Street
Carson

Martin Axel
Owner

#93639   Retail Installment Contract and Security Agreement

QUALITY FURNITURE, INC. hereby agrees to sell and the undersigned Buyer or Buyers, jointly and severally, agree to purchase the following goods on the following terms:

Description of Goods: *1 Arctic Dream*

The undersigned (herein called Purchaser, whether one or more) purchases from *Quality Furniture, Inc.* (seller) and grants to *same* _____ a security interest in, subject to the terms and conditions hereof, the following described property:

PURCHASER'S NAME *Mary Joyce Allen*
PURCHASER'S ADDRESS *2445 Memorial Drive*

CITY *Carson*   STATE ___ ZIP *30306*

1. CASH PRICE	$ *840.00*
2. LESS: CASH DOWN PAYMENT	$ *---*
3. TRADE-IN	$ *--*
4. TOTAL DOWN PAYMENT	$ *0*
5. UNPAID BALANCE OF CASH PRICE	$ *840.00*
6. OTHER CHARGES:	
Acc. and Health Sys.	$ *32.40*
Credit report	$ *4.60*
7. AMOUNT FINANCED	$ *877.00*
8. FINANCE CHARGE	$ *210.48*
9. TOTAL OF PAYMENTS	$ *1,087.48*
10. DEFERRED PAYMENT PRICE (1+6+8)	$ *1,087.48*
11. ANNUAL PERCENTAGE RATE	$ *14.5*

QUANTITY   DESCRIPTION   AMOUNT

QUANTITY	DESCRIPTION	AMOUNT	
1	Arctic Dream		
1	Food cabinet		
1	Chaise lounge		
1	Kitch aura 8"		
4	Kitchen Chairs		
1	Kithcen Table		

Purchaser hereby agrees to pay to *Quality Furniture Co.* at their offices shown above the "TOTAL OF PAYMENTS" shown above in *36* monthly installments of $ *30.20* (final payment to be $ *30.48*) the first installment being payable *Feb 1st* , 19*72* , and all subsequent installments on the same day of each consecutive month until paid in full. The finance charge applies from *Jan. 13, 1972* . *Two payments authorized: $15.10 the 1st and 16th each month*

In the event that there shall be a default in the payment of any of the installments of this Agreement on the due date thereof, or a proceeding in bankruptcy, receivership or on solvency be instituted by or against the buyer or either of them, then the entire balance of this note shall immediately become due at the option of the holder thereof, without notice or demand, together with interest on each installment after maturity thereof, at the rate of eight percentum (8%) per annum: and the power of sale or repossession contained herein, shall become fully exercisable. Buyer agrees to pay Seller's reasonable attorneys fees in any suit on this contract.

SIGNED *Richard Owens*   DATE *Jan. 13, 1972* SIGNED *Mary Joyce Allen*

Notice to Buyer: You are entitled to a copy of the contract you sign. You have the right to pay in advance the unpaid balance of this contract and obtain a partial refund of the finance charge based on the "Rule of 78's".

*This is a mockup, not the actual contract. — RD/GW

ALLEN: It's from the courthouse, that's what the girl next door to me said. It was from the courthouse. And that I have to come to court because these people are suing me, but you don't sue poor people because they don't have anything to be suing for. And I don't even know what this is suing me for. He should be paying me because I'm the one that got this stuff and it's no good or anything. And I just came in here with that to see what could be done.

Q. Okay. Is Quality Furniture, are those the people that you dealt with about the food?   **A.** Yes, that's where I got the food from, Quality Furniture Company.

Q. Well, as I look at this quickly what it looks like is . . . . How long ago did you get this?   **A.** Let me see, that was around February sometime. And I got that because . . . . Yeah, it was February because it was about a month or so after my oldest son that's Michael Dwayne, and it was about a month or so after his birthday.

Q. That you got the papers from the court?   **A.** Oh no, I thought, no that was when the man came.

Q. How long ago did you get these court papers?   **A.** Oh that wasn't too long ago. I'd say recent. About two weeks or so.

Q. Okay. Do you remember the exact date?   **A.** No, I sure don't.

Q. You said about two weeks ago. Was it a week ago?   **A.** Yeah it was. . . .

Q. Did you get them at home or at work?   **A.** They came to my house. My mother, she usually gets the mail out and I come there from work and they was on the table right by the door, the mail. And I opened it up and that's what I saw, I saw this in there.

Q. This had come in the mail?   **A.** Yes, that come in the mail.

Q. What this looks like is a complaint that Quality Furniture has filed in court against you saying that you made an agreement, a monthly installment agreement to pay a certain amount $30.20 every month and that this was for a total amount of $1,087.48 and that you've made four payments.   **A.** But he didn't tell me that until I called on the telephone.

Q. Okay, I'm just telling you what it looks as if they are saying in this paper. That doesn't make it true, as far as I'm concerned, but that's what they're saying. And that you were supposed to make these installment payments and you stopped making them and that's why they're suing you for the whole balance that's left.   **A.** But, that's not what happened.

Q. Okay, let's go back to what happened. Now you say it was in February of this year?   **A.** Yeah, it was in February.

Q. Was it early or late in February?   **A.** I say about a month after Michael Dwayne's birthday. His birthday is the 15th of January, so I guess it was around that time in February.

Q. Around the middle of February?   **A.** Yeah. This man came.

Q. Did this man give his name and all?   **A.** Robert or Richard. I think it was Richard, but he never did give me his last name, that I can remember.

Q. Do you remember what he looked like?   **A.** He was a white man, he wasn't too tall, because I just saw him that one time.

Q. Did he come and knock on the door?   **A.** Yeah, he knocked on the door and it was just me and the twins and I'd say he was about medium height, he had like dark hair and was kind of bald up front.

Q. Glasses?   **A.** Well, I can't remember any glasses. I don't think he had any glasses. He was kind of heavy. And he just knocked on the door. And he was real friendly and everything. And he was talking about his furniture company.

Q. Did he know your name?   **A.** Yeah, he said he knew one of my neighbors.

Q. Who was that, did he say?   **A.** He said that he knew Bill Sparks.

Q. Is he a neighbor of yours?   **A.** Yes, he's a neighbor of mine. And he had on a suit. I don't know if he had a car or not because like I say, he just knocked on the door.

Q. And what did he say, besides that he knew your neighbor?   **A.** He said that my neighbor told him that I like to get bargains and everybody's always looking for bargains because everything is so high. And you just don't have much and you're trying to make it so when you think you got a good deal you go into it. He said it was quality, first rate and everything.

Q. What was?   **A.** His furniture company, for the food and freezer. So I said okay, because he said this was a real deal for saving money and everybody's trying to save money these days.

Because things are just so hard when you're trying to make it by yourself and you have kids and your mother and everything. So I said okay, I'll be interested in listening to what you have to say. So he said oh, well just call me Richard, and he said well, Mary, and everything and that's what happened.

Q. Well, what was it that he said, what did he have to offer, did he say, in so many words? **A.** Yeah. He —

Q. What? **A.** He was offering a means to save money buying food.

Q. How? **A.** That he said that his company bought food in large amounts, they bought a whole lot at one time, and he said when you buy things a whole lot at one time, you save money. And he said since they bought it a whole lot at one time they could sell it for low prices. And he told me that they could sell it for low prices, so he asked me how much did I pay for food and then he had this list with him that had all the food listed on it that you buy when you go to the supermarket. And I told him. He said what do you get when you go, and I told him everything that I got and he added it up and everything. And he said now with his company they have all this food and everything and I can get the same stuff for ten or twenty dollars cheaper each week, so then he told me that would be about forty or eighty dollars a month. And so I said that sounds good, and I was trying to keep my eyes on the twins and he just sounded very, very friendly and everything, so I said okay.

Q. You mentioned a freezer, where did the freezer come in? **A.** Well, see he said that if I get this food, the best way to keep the food would be in a freezer. And I said well, I don't have a freezer, but he said well, with this food you get a freezer. And he said something about the freezer is eight dollars a month, and if I wanted to keep the freezer, everything that I had paid towards the rental of the freezer would go towards buying the freezer.

Q. Now he said with the food you get a freezer, is that what he said? **A.** That's what he said.

Q. Did he also say something about renting the freezer? **A.** Well, he . . . maybe he didn't say rent straight out, but he said I'd get the freezer with the food and that if I didn't want to keep the freezer or if I wanted to buy the freezer, everything I had paid towards it, for keeping my food in it, would go towards the cost of it, and anytime I got ready to cancel, just tell him. And that's what I did and that's when I kept getting all these phone calls and these letters and everything. And it's just really something, because you have so many things to worry about and this man he just keeps calling, and sending letters and everything, so I can't afford to be paying them all that money, because I told them I didn't want it.

Q. Okay, well, I think there's something we can do, at the very least, right away, to make him stop calling. Let's get to that in a second. Going back to this freezer for a minute, did he say how much you would be paying his company for the food, after he went to this price list and showed you it would be less to get it from him?   **A.** Well, I had to pay him $52.00 every two weeks. That was around the beginning, like when I got my paycheck, the beginning of each month and the second week of each month. And I was never late. I always sent my money in on time, because they had this way that you pay with these coupons and stuff.

Q. Now, did you and he talk about how long this was going to continue?   **A.** Until I got ready to cancel, after a few months. He said all I had to do was just do it for a few months, and then after a few months he said I could cancel anytime after that few months time that you had to take it.

Q. And was he talking then about the food or about the freezer?   **A.** Well, just the food. He said anytime I didn't want the food, what would I do with the freezer?

Q. Okay, but what I need to know is what your conversation with him was, whether he was saying that you could cancel the freezer deal or the food deal or the whole deal in a few months.   **A.** Well, he said the freezer came with the food, so if I don't want the food, I don't want the freezer either.

Q. Let's see. These court papers that you got, attached to them is this thing called a retail installment contract and security agreement. Down here at the bottom it's signed by Richard Owens and then it says Mary Joyce Allen. Is that your signature?   **A.** Yes.

Q. Does this paper look at all familiar to you?   **A.** Well, he give me one of those, but I can't read so well, because I only went to the eighth grade. But it had all that language and numbers and everything, but then he explained it to me.

Q. He explained it?   **A.** Yeah.

Q. Can you remember what he said? When he was explaining this piece of paper do you remember what he said? **A.** He just said it would be a good bargain, I'd get top quality foods, and that I could cancel it when I got ready.

Q. Alright, fine. Did he say anything about a total of payments being $1,087 do you remember that figure at all? **A.** No, I don't. All I know is he just said pay the $52.00 and after a few months that I had to take it, if I wasn't happy, I could just cancel everything.

Q. Did he read you any language from this piece of paper at all when he was explaining? **A.** No. Because I didn't understand all those words. So he said he was just going to put it in lay, regular talk.

Q. Let me make sure I understand. What you're saying is that you did sign a piece of paper which you understood to be the agreement for this deal? **A.** For the food.

Q. And it might have looked something like this paper but you're not sure. So he went away and then what happened? **A.** My food came.

Q. How long afterwards? **A.** Right away. He said it would be right away.

Q. You mean the next few days? **A.** Yes. And everything came. And I never heard of the stuff that I got. But like the sugar and the flour and the rice, it was all sort of in good shape and everything. But it wasn't anything that I had heard of before. But he said it was all going to be top quality.

Q. How was it? **A.** That stuff was good but the canned goods were in bad shape.

Q. What was wrong with them? **A.** Well, some of them didn't have labels.

Q. No labels at all? **A.** No. Some, the labels were yellow. Didn't have any names in the canned food I used to get. And some of the cans were bent up.

Q. How about the stuff inside? What kind of quality was that? **A.** Well, like in the bent up cans, some of the stuff wasn't too good.

Q. Do you put in an order to tell them what to send you, like how much rice? **A.** No. They just said it was going to be enough for four months.

Q. And had the freezer come by this time, too? **A.** Yes, because it all came together. Because I couldn't have the food without the freezer.

Q. Oh, so the freezer came with the first order of stuff? Within a few days after this Richard was there? **A.** Yes.

Q. Okay. And did they bring the freezer in and put it up in your apartment? **A.** Yes.

Q. What did the freezer look like? Did it have a name on it? **A.** Yes. It just looked like a regular freezer.

Q. Did it look used, new? What did it look like when it first got there? **A.** It just looked like a freezer. It wasn't scratched up or anything.

Q. Is it an upright freezer like a refrigerator? **A.** No, it's just a regular freezer.

Q. Where's the door? **A.** It's on the top.

Q. So you bend over and open up the door? **A.** Yes.

Q. Sort of like a washing machine? **A.** Yes. Except that it has a bigger top than a washing machine.

Q. Right. Did it keep stuff frozen? **A.** Well, like I had to send for the man twice and I bought some ice cream and it didn't stay. It got soft.

Q. How long was the ice cream in the freezer? **A.** Less than a day.

Q. And it was soft? **A.** Yes.

Q. It was hard when you put it in? **A.** Yeah. The meat was soft. It wasn't frozen. Blood was running all over the freezer. So I just had to call the man to come to fix it because I can't be eating, my kids can't be eating food like that.

Q. Where did you call? **A.** I called this man Richard.

Q. You called him? **A.** At the Quality Furniture Company.

Q. He had left you his name or his number? **A.** Yes, he did on a little card.

Q. Do you still have that card? **A.** I don't know. I could go home and look around.

Q. You might have it at home? Okay. But you called him? **A.** Yeah. And he said it would be taken care of right away.

Q. Was it? **A.** Well, like the next day a man came.

Q. Were you home when he came? **A.** Yeah. And he messed around with the freezer and everything.

Q. Was it any better after that?   **A.** He had to come twice so I guess it wasn't. But I didn't notice it right away.

Q. But then you noticed it again, that it wasn't keeping stuff frozen?   **A.** Yes. And I had to go buy meat and everything I needed was supposed to be right there.

* * *

Q. Do you remember the day, or about the day, or the month that you first called him and told him that you wanted to cancel?   **A.** The fourth month. I guess that was around May.

Q. Do you think it was May?   **A.** Yeah.

Q. Do you remember was it early or late May?   **A.** Well, it was early in May because the food was supposed to last to May.

Q. Okay. And you called him and he said you could cancel the food but you had to keep paying for the freezer?   **A.** Right.

Q. And did he say anything about how much you owed for the freezer?   **A.** He told me I owed $1000 and something for a freezer. And then he told me I had to pay him for this freezer monthly, by the month, the same way I was paying for the food.

Q. Did he say how much?   **A.** He said about $30 for three years. Now I know that when he came to my house, he didn't tell me that. He told me that the freezer came with the food, and if I don't want the food, what am I going to do with the freezer? Why would I want the freezer if I don't have any food? That just doesn't make any sense. And I don't know why he did this, because he said that when I got ready to cancel, I could cancel.

Q. Okay. So you called and you said you wanted to cancel and he said well, you're still supposed to pay for the freezer?   **A.** Yeah. That's right. And I called him back and told him to come, I didn't want it.

Q. When did you call him back?   **A.** I called him back the same day. The first time I talked to him, I talked to him that morning, and then I called him back that afternoon. Because that just doesn't make any sense for him to tell me that when that's not what he told me in the first place.

Q. And what did he say the second time you called?   **A.** He said, calm down. I mean, when you're trying to make it and people are constantly trying to tell you what to do, it just doesn't make any sense. And I told him, what do you mean, calm down. He said, well, he's sure he can find some way to straighten this thing out. He would try and help me in the best way he could.

Q. That's what he said?   **A.** Yeah.

Q. Anything else?   **A.** No, that's all that he said. I just told him to come and get it because I was cancelling, to come get the freezer.

Q. Did he say he'd come and get it?   **A.** No, he didn't.

Q. Has he come and gotten it?   **A.** No, he just keeps sending me bills for the freezer and I told him that I didn't want that freezer because I didn't want the food. I was cancelling the order.

Q. Do you have any of the bills with you?   **A.** No.

Q. You might have some at home?   **A.** Well, like I told you, we had to send in those coupons with your money.

Q. Okay. So he hasn't come and the freezer's still there.   **A.** Right. And it's not working.

Q. It's not working at all?   **A.** Well, it's like a refrigerator.

Q. It doesn't keep things frozen?   **A.** No.

Q. Do you use it all?   **A.** I don't have anything to put in it. It's just sitting there.

Q. Okay. Taking up room?   **A.** Yeah.

Q. Now what have you heard from him, from Quality Furniture, from anybody there since that day you talked to him?   **A.** They just keep calling me, seven o'clock in the morning, eleven o'clock at night. They even called on my job. They called on my job and my boss told me not to be having that going on and messing up his work day. And now if they're going to keep calling me on my job and everything, then how am I supposed to support my kids? I have bills to pay, rent and stuff, and everything. And now they call me on my job and tell me, that's none of my boss's business for them to be telling everybody everything about my business because I told them that I didn't want it and they just keep on calling and sending all these letters and everything. And that just doesn't make any sense.

Q. Do you know how many times they called on your job? Did your boss tell you?   **A.** I think he said that if they ever do it again, I'd have to be fired. So I guess they must have called one time.

Q. How long ago was that, do you know?   **A.** That was about two weeks, I guess. I don't know. It might have been more. I just told him when the food ran out and the freezer wasn't working, I called him. That might have been a month or it might have been two weeks. And they called my job. All I know is these people, they just working on my nerves and everything and I just can't have this because it's just costing me too much money when I'm not getting nothing from it.

Q. I know. And I'm sorry to have to keep asking you for these details. It's just that some of them might matter, you know. And, also, I just want to know as much as I can possibly know about everything because they've already filed these court papers. And we have to answer the court papers. And there are certainly things we can say. A lot of things we can say in answer to the court papers. But, you know, in order to do that we have to know everything that I can possibly know. Not that it's a lot of fun to talk about but. Anyway, how many times have they called you? **A.** The last about two months, they must have called me a dozen times, ten, twelve times. Every time I turn around, the phone's ringing. I'm trying to get my rest so I can get up and go to work and they call me. I'm trying to get ready for work and they call me. And they're calling me when I'm trying to fix my kids' dinner or trying to get my kids ready for school. They just calling and calling and calling.

Q. Do they call early in the morning? **A.** They call seven o'clock in the morning, eleven o'clock at night, two o'clock, all day, all day. Just keep calling and calling and calling. And this is just getting on my nerves, because I told them I didn't want it and they keep sending all these letters and they have this lady calling me telling I have to pay this money, and what they're going to do.

Q. Is it always a lady? **A.** Yeah.

Q. What does she say they're going to do? **A.** They say I have to pay this money or they are going to destroy my credit rating. Now how are you going to get along? When you're not rich you have to have something to pay for things little by little. They're just making me a nervous wreck, because they can't be doing this, because after all that's not what they said, they said I could cancel it anytime I got ready.

Q. Well, also they're not supposed to call you. And besides this is not right or fair for them to call you, they also are not allowed by the law to call you and keep acting like that. And the first thing that I'll do, and I'll do that today, is write to them and simply say that you've come to us, that if they have anything else to say about this, or anything to ask, or anything to talk about they should get in touch with me and not you. And also, that they are not to call you any more, because they're upsetting you. They're disturbing. **A.** I can't . . . my nerves . . . I'm just a nervous wreck.

Q. But the other thing is that if they do call you anymore before they get this letter, say. Like if you go home and they call you tonight, what I would urge you to do, how you handle them of course is up to you, but what I would urge you to do and hope you would do, just tell them that you've got nothing to say to them, you've got nothing to talk to them about, you have a lawyer and your lawyer will deal for you. And just give them my name and give them my number and say goodbye and hang up. And there's no reason for you to discuss it with them any further.

* * *

Q. When was the last time you heard from them most recently? **A.** Well, this thing come in the mail.

Q. What else? **A.** Well, I just want to hurry up and get this thing because it's just making my nerves bad and I just have to keep running back and forth to the doctor and everything and I have to lose days from my job to come in here and everything just bothers me on my job and everything. I just have to get this thing taken care of.

Q. Have you had to go to the doctor since they started calling you? **A.** Yeah.

Q. Were you going to the doctor before that? **A.** Well, we went a couple of times, my kids and my mother. But after all this stuff started, my kids stayed sick. They wasn't eating right and it's cold outside and everything.

Q. What was wrong with you that you had to go to the doctor? **A.** My nerves are just so upset and the doctor gave me some medicine to calm my nerves down and that cost $7.50 a bottle and I have to keep getting it refilled. I mean, I'm just in the kitchen and knocking things around and had to take the twins to the doctor because I'm worried about everything and they just called me on the phone over at my girlfriend's house and I ran back to the house to look at the food and knocked the hot water off the stove and scalded my child. And I can't have these people upsetting my nerves like.

Q. Which child got scalded?   **A.** Cheryl, the twin.

Q. Did she have to go to the hospital?   **A.** Yeah. I had to take her to the doctor. That was about $40.

Q. Is she okay?   **A.** Well, it's coming along.

Q. How long ago did it happen?   **A.** It wasn't too long ago.

Q. Like two weeks?   **A.** Everything, all the months and the weeks are starting to run together. All this stuff is just making me a nervous wreck and my kids been sick, eating this food and I just don't want it anymore. And they just bother me. I mean, I have to work and support my kids and I have to get along on my job and they just keep bothering me and just upsetting me. And I just can't have it.

Q. Okay. Let me tell you what I'm going to try to do. First of all, as I say, I'm going to write to them and tell them to let you alone. If they want to bother somebody, they can bother me. They're not going to bother you anymore. And, please, if you hear from them, you tell them the same because, as you say, you can't have them calling you and bothering you. And, as I say, that's what you come here for. So I'll deal with them, okay. Secondly, now about your job. I would be glad to get in touch with them but I don't want to do that without asking you. Do you think it would make it better or worse? Do you want to wait and see if they bother you anymore or do you want me to call and try to talk to your employer?   **A.** No, because he just said he doesn't want nothing interrupting his office work.

Q. But let me suggest this. If there is any more problem, if he mentions it to you at all, tell him that you think this is a mix-up and that you're not paying this because you don't think you should have to and suggest to him that he call me if he has any questions, okay? And then if you feel at any time that it would help for me to talk to him, just let me know. And I'll call and talk to him. Now about the court papers. What they said here was that you owe them this money and they want a judgment against you for that amount, because you owe it, because you signed this contract promising to pay that.   **A.** But I didn't sign no papers to buy this freezer.

Q. I understand that. Well, we do have a problem because this is your signature at the bottom of this paper. I understand that that's what you understood and if we can't settle this out of court, then you'll have an opportunity to go on the witness stand and explain that that's what you meant to be signing. That you did not mean to be buying the freezer. But, as I say, you don't want the lawyer just to tell you the good things. You come to the lawyer to get the straight story even if it isn't all very pleasant. I think there are a lot of things we can do about it. No lawyer who is worth anything would promise you that you were going to win because you know that life and courts are just not that predictable. But I think that you have a good chance. And the first thing that we have to do is file papers in answer to these papers that you will sign, that we'll prepare that when they are prepared, you and I will sit down and talk about after work or on a Saturday or sometime that isn't going to take you off your job. And those papers will say, you know, generally the sorts of things we've been talking, that you did not intend to sign a contract to buy a freezer. That you did not intend to agree to buy a freezer. That you intended to enter into a deal to buy food and to rent a freezer while you were buying food. I'm going over this, so that if I say anything wrong, you'll correct me, right? Because this is what I'm going to be putting in your papers between now and the next time we talk. And you understood and were told by this man that you could cancel this deal at any time if you decided to cancel and you did and, in the meantime, they've been bothering you and making you nervous and making you sick and making you spill hot water and so forth. Okay. **A.** Well, I appreciate this.

Q. Well, there's nothing to appreciate, certainly not yet. I hope we can get it straightened out one way or another. In the meantime, do you have any question? **A.** No, I just want to get this thing over with. It's just too much.

FIRST QUESTIONS

1. As a leading practitioner and teacher once put it, in the interview the lawyer must teach the client and the client must teach the lawyer. The lawyer must be educated about the transactions and relationships in which she or he will intrude. In a critical sense the client must be taught how to be a client: ultimately, perhaps, how to testify, but in the short term, how to recall relevant facts and to participate in determining priorities (which issues should be contested, with what intensity, etc.). The success of this often repeated, but nonetheless remarkable, collaboration depends in significant measure on the rapport established between the participants.

How does Ms. Shapiro try to establish rapport here? Pick out one or two instances in which she falters in this respect. What suggestions would you offer to improve her performance? (Recall that Ms. Shapiro was selected to conduct this interview because she was considered an unusually able Legal Services Lawyer.)

2. What more would you like to know from Ms. Allen? How, if at all, could anything of further value be gained during this interview? (For example, what questions might have been asked that were not?)

3. What, precisely, is Ms. Allen's problem? By whom and at what stage in the interview was it decided what her problem was? Reconsider *Sullivan v. O'Connor* in this light. In what ways were Mrs. Sullivan's lawyers sensitive or insensitive to her problems?

4. Recall that psychiatric diagnoses, broadly defined, are wrong in between sixteen and thirty-six percent of all cases where they are made (see the discussion in regard to *Ortelere* in Chapter 8). What is your intuition about the accuracy of legal diagnoses in cases like Ms. Allen's? How much confidence do you have in your diagnosis? (Compare your analysis with others offered in class.)

5. Imagine interviewing Mrs. Ortelere. Imagine interviewing Mr. Ortelere. Imagine interviewing Alice Sullivan. If anything, these people would appear to offer you less help than Ms. Allen. How does a lawyer go about constructing a case in these circumstances? This obviously imposes a capability problem of concern to us. If the quality of advocacy depends on the qualities of a client (capacity to articulate, to organize information, to recall facts, to

appear credible, etc.) how does that skew the legal system? What does a lawyer do to counter that skewing?*

---

*If these questions interest you, you can readily find a large literature on interviewing skills. The following are especially recommended: David   A. Binder, Paul Bergman, Susan C. Price, Paul R. Tremblay, Lawyers as Counselors: A Client-Centered Approach (2d ed. 2004); Stefan H. Krieger & Richard K. Neumann, Jr., Essential Lawyering Skills: Interviewing, Counseling, Negotiating, and Persuasive Fact Analysis (2003); Robert M. Basteress & Joseph D. Harbaugh, Interviewing, Counseling, and Negotiation: Skills for Effective Representation (1990); Thomas L. Shaffer & James R. Elkins, Legal Interviewing and Counseling in a Nutshell (1997). Some useful older sources include R. Redmont, Attorney Personalities and Some Psychological Aspects of Legal Consultation 109 U.Pa. L.Rev. 972 (1961); V. Appel and R. Atta, The Attorney-Client Dyad — An Outsider's View 22 Oklahoma L.Rev. 243 (1969); and D. Rosenthal, Lawyer and Client: Who's in Charge? (1974).

SUPPLEMENTARY COMMENTS

[The *Allen* case was originally developed by Phil Schrag, then a staff attorney for the National Office for the Rights of the Indigent, now a professor at Georgetown Law School. In the following article,* Professor Schrag describes the circumstances surrounding his first interview with Mr. Allen[†] and subsequent events.]

> This is the Court of Chancery, which has its decaying houses and its blighted lands in every shire, which has its worn-out lunatic in every madhouse and its dead in every churchyard, which has its ruined suitor with his slipshod heels and threadbare dress borrowing and begging through the round of every man's acquaintance, which gives to monied might the means abundantly of wearying out the right, which so exhausts finances, patience, courage, hope, so overthrows the brain and breaks the heart, that there is not an honourable man among its practitioners who would not give — who does not often give — the warning, "Suffer any wrong that can be done you rather than come here!"
>
> — Charles Dickens, Bleak House

During 1968, I spent most of my time as a staff attorney of the National Office for the Rights of the Indigent (NORI), the poverty-law affiliate of the NAACP Legal Defense Fund, trying to bring test cases to challenge some unjust doctrines of consumer law. This article is a chronicle of my attempt.

*   *   *

New York has thousands of retail sellers operating so close to the margin that many will engage in any degree of chicanery to

---

*Reprinted with permission from Philip Schrag, Bleak House 1968: A Report on Consumer Test Litigation, 44 NYU L.Rev. 115 (1969).

[†]Note that the actual interview was with a man, not the "Ms. Allen" who appeared in the simulated Legal Services interview. Moreover, "Mr. Allen" is itself a pseudonym, as is "Quality Furniture." — RD/GW.

make a sale. Thousands of fraudulent or unconscionable sales are made every day; thousands of warranties are breached. Customers who complain are put off indefinitely. . . .

New York has a dozen finance companies which immediately buy up contracts signed by low-income consumers from the sellers. When a finance company buys a consumer contract, the buyer becomes a cipher in an IBM computer. The computer mails the buyer a coupon book and instructs him to mail to it one coupon each month along with his check or money order. With the coupon book, the buyer receives a notice that if he has any complaints about the goods he bought, he must notify the finance company of them within ten days or lose forever his claims and defenses. (I have never met a consumer who read the notice when he received it, nor have I met one who understood it when I read it to him.) If the buyer later has a problem (e. g., a leg falls off his table a month after he bought it), and calls the store, they tell him: "We sold your contract to the credit company — we have nothing to do with you any more." And if he calls the credit company, he is told: "All we do is collect your payments; we're not responsible for the quality of the merchandise."

As everywhere, buyers confronted with this kind of treatment often stop paying; they think this will force someone to pay attention to their complaint, or at least effect rough justice. But as soon as a payment is missed, the computer starts spitting out dunning letters, and even letters over the signature of the collection attorney threatening suit.

The consumer may then be informed that a suit has been commenced against him, but more often, the finance company's collection attorney fills in a standard form complaint and gives it to a process server or city marshal who destroys it and files a perjured affidavit of service; "sewer service," as it is called, is widespread. So a buyer first learns that a default judgment has been entered against him when his employer notifies him of a garnishment and warns him that more than one wage garnishment is cause for dismissal. It is at this point that the consumer typically visits Legal Aid, if he sees a lawyer at all. Thus, when the settlement process begins in New York, the Legal Aid lawyer has to try to reopen a default judgment and has to face a finance company considered by the law to be a bona fide purchaser, immune from any defenses.

One nice thing about NORI is that when you get mad about a problem, you are pretty free to take a whack at it. So, in December 1967, I decided to bring a series of consumer test cases to shake up the system, or at least to strengthen the bargaining power of the consumers' representatives. I set two goals to work towards: (1) abolishing the doctrine of the so-called holder-in-due-course of consumer paper, so that finance companies would be liable for the misdeeds of the sellers they dealt with and would police them, thereby reducing the volume of unfair dealings. Abolition of this doctrine would also give Legal Aid a more viable threat of contested litigation. (2) Experimenting with new devices for the resolution of consumer grievances, other than informal settlement, which might give more consumers better relief. Punitive damages against sellers was one alternative which came immediately to mind. I notified Legal Aid that I was willing to take two or three interesting cases from them, to litigate rather than to settle; it was not long before I had a consumer client.

II.

[The first client referred to Prof. Schrag was "Mr. Allen," who related essentially the facts which can be culled from the recreated interview in the first part of this chapter. Mr. Allen (note that in the recreated interview this role is played by Ms. Allen) acquired a freezer from "Richard," a salesman for "Quality Furniture," as a part of his participation in a food purchase program. When he cancelled the food portion of the program he found, to his surprise, that he was committed to paying $1087 over three years for the freezer. He made fourteen payments to a finance company (Budget Finance) before coming to Legal Aid. Note that the recreated interview describes Ms. Allen as a Massachusetts debtor who had defaulted but that in reality Mr. Allen was a New York buyer who had not defaulted on payments.]

I was very pleased to have a client who was in the rare position of not having defaulted, much less not having lost a default judgment. It seemed like a fine opportunity to test an affirmative strategy — suing rather than being sued. I told Mr. Allen that my organization was in the test-case business — and that if we represented him, his case might take a long time to litigate, although the potential payoff was great, for others as well as for himself. I said that if he preferred to try for a quick compromise settlement, I would find a good lawyer to represent him. He said he would stick with me, and we started to draft a complaint.

Among the advantages of bringing a suit rather than defending is the choice of venue. Budget Finance, which as far as I know does not engage in sewer service, gets its default judgments by bringing all of its suits in Queens, making it very inconvenient for defendants in Manhattan and the Bronx to appear. We chose to sue in Manhattan. More important, I decided to sue in state supreme court rather than in civil court. This had several advantages: I could ask for large amounts of damages; the judges were reputed to be more academically oriented and better in general; the West Publishing Company was more likely to print any decision I obtained; and I could appeal to the appellate division rather than to the appellate term. Of course, the federal district could would have been an even better forum. But, although there are a few theories under which federal causes of action may be said to lie to remedy consumer abuses (e. g., implying a tort from the mail fraud statute or the FTC Act), contract law is basically state law, and it is the state courts that must be looked to for reform.

The decision of whom to sue was easy — I decided to join as defendants the finance company which held the contract, the store for which Richard worked, and Richard, whose last name (Lewis) was discovered only after an extensive telephone conversation with his employer in which I pretended that I was a prospective customer. Having three defendants made it more likely that I would recover against at least one of them and gave me a statutory right to discovery against all of the principals, since they would all be parties.

For a first cause of action, we alleged that the contract was unconscionable under Section 2-302 of the Uniform Commercial Code, because the price charged — even the $840 cash price — was outrageously high. We demanded rescission, or at least reformation, of the price term. . . .

For a second cause of action, we alleged fraud — Richard's leading my client to believe that he was renting the freezer and his assurances that the food would last for four months. Further, I drew upon a 1961 case which held that punitive damages lay for fraud where the fraud could be shown to be the "basis" of a seller's business — a regular business practice. I knew from Mr. Allen's friend that Richard had made similar fraudulent representations to him, and I soon found out that he had made similar representations to other buyers. The 1961 case had gone almost unused and had never been applied in a case of sales to low-income consumers; this looked like a good opportunity to blaze a trail. In addition, a demand for punitive damages would make it impossible for Budget Finance to moot the case by returning my client's money. I therefore asked for $50,000.

As additional causes of action, I complained of several violations of New York's Retail Instalment Sales Act — the contract given Mr. Allen by Richard had no date, no seller's address, and omitted material terms negotiated orally (e. g., the freezer and food sales were on separate contracts, and neither contained the warranty that the food would last four months). In addition, the printing on the contract was in six-point type rather than the eight-point type required by the law. But all of these violations put together could not gain more for Mr. Allen than recoupment of the credit service charge — $235 — and he could get that only if Budget failed to "correct the violation" (whatever that means) within the meaning of Section 414(3) of the Personal Property Law within ten days of notification of the violation by the buyer.

There remained the issue of the holder in due course. Among the papers received by Mr. Allen with his coupon book was a document he had never read or tried to read — the notice which under New York law enables a credit company to become a bona fide purchaser of a consumer contract. It consisted of a single 125-word sentence, to wit:

> 1. If the within statement of your transaction with the seller is not correct in every respect; or 2. if the vehicle or goods described in or in an enclosure with this notice have not been delivered to you by the seller or are not now in your possession; or 3. if the seller has not fully performed all his agreements with you; you must notify the assignee in writing at the address indicated at right in [*sic*] or in an enclosure with this notice within ten days from the date of the mailing of this notice; otherwise, you will have no right to assert against the assignee any right of action or

defense arising out of the sale which you might otherwise have against the seller.

I had two possible attacks on Budget's status. One was to show that they had not acquired the contract "in good faith" and "without notice of a claim or defense." This would require proving a course of dealing between them and Quality Furniture or some other proof indicating they had knowledge of overreaching. Perhaps the price of $1087 for a freezer — apparent on the face of the contract — would be sufficient. The other strategy was to argue that despite Section 403 of the Personal Property Law, Section 9-206 of the Uniform Commercial Code left the court free to abolish holder-in-due-course status for all purchasers of consumer paper. I decided to allege all of these theories and to elect among them only after I had used discovery to learn more of the relations between the companies.

I instructed Mr. Allen to keep up his monthly payments, but to put them into a savings account rather than sending them to Budget. Then, in early December 1967, I hired a reputable process server and looked forward to an early confrontation with the issues.

January

I dimly hoped, of course, for a motion to dismiss or to strike part of my complaint. The essential issue in most civil test cases in federal court is resolved at an early stage, in litigation over the complaint. The issue to be resolved usually turns on whether or not the new cause of action being pushed by the plaintiff exists. A ruling on a motion to dismiss for failure to state a cause of action, and subsequent appeals, short-circuits months or years of pre-trial investigation, as well as the trial itself. But I owed it to my client to put all of his causes of action into the complaint; and most, if not all of them, were patently undismissable. Also, it was in my opponents' interest to avoid any decision for as long as possible — both to delay my case and to avoid any precedents. They decided to answer the complaint.

I first heard from Budget's collection attorney — how much would I settle for? In expectation of such an offer, I had discussed settlement with Mr. Allen, and we agreed that under no conditions would we accept a settlement that did not include some punitive damages. Such a settlement would have been so unusual that it could itself have been publicized and would have demonstrated that an aggressive complaint was enough to improve upon the settlement system. This was equally evident to Budget, so a settlement was out of the question. The collection attorney requested an extension of time to answer; he told me that Budget did not consider him capable of managing contested litigation. Although I was anxious to get on with the case, particularly in light of inevitable delays due to court congestion, I agreed to the extension, as it is the general custom to do so.

On January 10, I received Budget's answer from Bender, Segal, Parker & Lochinger, their Wall Street counsel. Budget denied or had no knowledge of most of the allegations in the complaint and claimed that, in any event, it was a holder in due course of the contract, having sent Mr. Allen a notice. Along with the answer came a notice to take the oral deposition of Mr. Allen on January 23.

I was annoyed, but not entirely surprised by this demand. Annoyed, because to save Mr. Allen the trouble of having to miss work to attend a deposition, I had put into the complaint just about every fact he had told me. Not surprised, because oral examination is a natural enough device to harass a plaintiff. But on the whole, I was not very upset. After all, Mr. Allen was just a man who bought a freezer. He had very little information to give them — certainly none that could hurt his case. He was extremely angry at what had been done to him — so his answers to their questions were likely to be damaging to them. And since he had so little to say, it would be all over in an hour or two — and then it would be my turn.

Along with Budget's answer and notice came the combined answer of Richard Lewis and Quality Furniture, who had hired the same lawyer, a sole practitioner named Alfred Stone, to represent them. (I later learned that Stone was one of the city's leading collection attorneys, and worked for several small finance companies as well as for Quality.) This was curious, because the joint answer denied an agency relationship between Lewis and the store; such a denial would be in the interest of the store but not of the salesman. My hunch is that the store agreed to hire the lawyer and gave the salesman a free ride. In any event, the agency relation was easy to prove, so I was more intrigued than concerned about the denial.

Their answer included a demand that I amend my complaint to add as a co-plaintiff and necessary party Mrs. Allen, whose name was on the contract. I had indeed overlooked this detail. I had no objection to doing so, except for the vague feeling that at some point, a defendant might demand to examine Mrs. Allen, as they would have a right to do if she were a party. A seller obtaining a wife's signature to a contract gets more than additional security — it gets an extra opportunity to make life difficult for the buyer if either side wishes to threaten litigation.

The day before Mr. Allen's examination began, I went over his case with him again. He had little to add that was not in his complaint, so I felt reasonably confident that the questioning would be brief.

We arrived at Bender, Segal's for the examination at 10:30, as required by the notice, but Bender, Segal kept us waiting until 11:00. Finally a young lawyer emerged into the waiting room and introduced himself as Jack Schwartz; he would conduct the examination in the conference room. Alfred Stone did not show up, and at 11:15 we began. Although the traditional New York practice is to object to every possible question, I had resolved not to object even to improper questions unless Mr. Allen felt really harassed; objections would take more time, and litigation over their propriety would delay the lawsuit and waste my time. Yet Schwartz's first questions almost provoked me, for he launched into an inquiry into Allen's finances — his earnings and that of his wife. But after a while, he got back on the track and asked about Mr. Allen's discussions with Richard. His questions covered every facet of the sale: how Allen knew who Richard was and whom he represented; who had made the referral; what his friend who referred him had said; what Richard had said about the food and the freezer; what Richard had shown him (the list of foods to be supplied, which Allen brought to the examination, as required); what papers Allen had signed; and what Allen had said when he called Richard to cancel. Schwartz's style of questioning was so detailed and so nearly repetitive (but not truly duplicative and therefore not objectionable) that the examination seemed hardly to be progressing. One brief sample:

Q. Did Mr. Lewis give you the freezer contract to look at during your discussion? **A.** Are you referring to giving it to me to read?

Q. Yes. **A.** No.

Q. Did you ask him to see it? **A.** No.

Q. Did he explain to you what its contents were? What it said? **A.** No.

Q. When was the first time that you saw it? **A.** I think that night.

Q. More specifically, when during the course of this discussion or conversation with Mr. Lewis did he first present you with or hand to you this document, or the original? **A.** I don't recall.

Q. Was it after he had done all his figuring on the yellow paper, as you testified before? **A.** Yes.

Q. Was it already filled in the way it is now? **A.** I don't recall.

Q. To your knowledge or to your recollection did Mr. Lewis fill in anything after he handed it to you? **A.** I don't recall. I was just asked to sign it.

Q. Did you ask any questions when he asked you to sign this? **A.** No.

Q. Had you already agreed to purchase the freezer? **A.** Purchase? No, rent.

Q. Is your signature on it? **A.** Yes.

Q. Is your wife's? **A.** Yes.

Q. Did you both sign that, the evening of your first visit from Mr. Lewis? **A.** I think so.

Q. At the time you signed it, were all of the writings now on it filled in? **A.** I don't recall.

Q. Did you read it before you signed it? **A.** No.

Q. Did your wife? **A.** No.

Q. Were you given an opportunity to do so? **A.** I don't understand you.

Q. Could you have read it? **A.** Could I have read it?

Q. Yes. **A.** Possibly.

Q. When you say possibly, what do you mean? **A.** I was just asked to sign it.

Q. Were you told you could not read it? **A.** No.

The examination became even more tedious as Schwartz began questioning Allen about each of the many papers that he had at some point received from Richard or Quality — forms to refer other customers, lists of groceries, invoices which came with the food, envelopes in which other papers had been placed, etc. When did Allen first see each paper? Where? Whose writing was on it? What had Allen scribbled on the back? When? What did Richard say about it? And so on.

Shortly after 1:00 P.M., Schwartz announced that he had much questioning left to do. Somewhat angry about the pace, but anxious to get the examination over with, we broke for lunch. After lunch, the same slow process was repeated: What had Mr. Allen signed on Richard's second visit? Had he read the papers? When was this visit? Who was present? What was said? Another hour passed. Mr. Allen began to get confused about all the papers; occasionally he contradicted himself. Still, objections would only prolong the examination, and the contradictions were about trivial details. Finally Schwartz concluded his questions about the transactions. Surely we must be finished.

* * *

But Schwartz had begun a whole new line of questions — and he began reading down the complaint, paragraph by paragraph, asking Mr. Allen about his legal claims: Just which part of Richard's statement was fraudulent? How do you know that the representations were false? What do you mean by an exorbitant price? Is that just a high price? High with relation to what? I constantly expected my client to say that he didn't know or understand, but each time, he attempted to explain the complaint I had drafted as best he could, even after some dialogue between Schwartz and myself about how the witness could not know such things.

And now it was 5:00 P.M., and although Mr. Allen had been answering questions for a full day, Schwartz announced that he had many more questions — that he had not even begun to ask about Mr. Allen's relation to Budget Finance. "Of course you are free to seek a protective order from the Court," he said, "but my questioning has been relevant and you will not win" (a forecast concurred in by neutral sources). Reluctantly, I agreed that if I did not seek such an order, I would produce Mr. Allen again after we both had the transcript of the first session.

Meanwhile, I had begun my investigation. On January 19, to lay the groundwork for an oral deposition, I served Richard Lewis's lawyer with a demand to see all of the documents which might lie in the background of the case: contracts between Lewis and Quality Furniture; agreements between Quality and Budget, invoices showing the price Quality paid for freezers, lists of other freezer customers (relevant because such customers were witnesses to the pattern of Lewis's selling techniques), etc. I demanded that these documents be produced in my office on February 1.

Early in January, a Harlem newspaper had carried some publicity about the institution of a consumers' test case, and as a result I received many requests for help from the community. From these, I selected three other cases, which I commenced in rapid succession while I awaited discovery in Allen:

Buenavidez v. Lewis: One request for help came from Salvador Buenavidez, a Bronx resident of Puerto Rican birth, who worked as a can inspector. He had also been victimized by Richard Lewis's freezer sales. The facts of his case were virtually identical to those of Mr. Allen's. I took his case because it would enable me, for very little extra investigative work, to bring a second action against Lewis, Quality, and Budget, in case the Allen suit was somehow mooted or in case I might wish to try some variation in strategy — a sort of controlled experiment. Initially, I modeled Mr. Buenavidez's complaint on that of Mr. Allen and demanded $50,000 damages. Budget followed with a parallel answer and a demand that he be orally examined — in February.

Collins v. Budget Finance: [Mrs. Collins had purchased apparently defective carpeting from a company which went out of business. Her $1200 debt was assigned to Budget Finance.]

Day v. Dependable Credit Corp.: Robert Day's problem combined those of Mr. Allen and Mrs. Collins. Mr. and Mrs. Day had bought a freezer and food plan from a door-to-door salesman. They were relatively satisfied with the food but had not realized until long after they signed the contract that $1163 was an outrageous price to pay for a freezer. Theirs was also an especially appealing test case because a few months after the sale to the Days, the Attorney General of New York had enjoined the company from selling freezers by means of fraud and at exorbitant prices. Ten weeks after being enjoined, the seller went bankrupt (presumably because no finance company wanted to come under the scrutiny of the state by buying paper from the seller). But Dependable Credit Corp., the finance company which bought the Days' contract, was enforcing it and $800,000 worth of other freezer contracts; the injunction was causing it no discomfort at all. This too seemed to be a good case in which to challenge the ability of finance companies to immunize themselves from claims. Once again I brought suit for punitive damages.

February

There were times during February and March when I felt as though I shared offices with Messrs. Bender, Segal, Parker & Lochinger. Their oral examinations of my clients seemed endless. Mr. Allen was brought back, and his testimony consumed a total of 247 pages. Mr. Buenavidez was examined, required to appear a second time, and brought back for still a third session; his testimony required 411 pages. Mrs. Collins's testimony took only one day, because compared with the purchasers of freezers and food, who had countless invoices, she had very few documents which could be gone over line by line. Hence Jack Schwartz could think of only 863 questions to ask her. When I joined Mrs. Allen as a party plaintiff, Budget's attorneys, as I feared they would, exercised their right to require her to be questioned: and she had to submit to a day of examination. Mrs. Buenavidez was similarly examined.

Any further quotation of the questioning would render this article too tedious to bear. Suffice it to say that I found myself continually apologizing to my clients for causing them to be subjected to the length and difficulty of the questioning; its infliction upon clients is a very real cost of making a test case out of a dispute which could be routinely settled in an hour — though such a settlement also has costs, which are, however, less tangible. Schwartz's questions continued to be very nearly repetitive, although he was careful never to ask precisely the same question a second time, unless the witness gave an ambiguous answer. The trouble was that my clients had great difficulty recalling precisely the events in a sale which had taken place two years earlier, and each minor uncertainty provided Schwartz with fuel for an additional half-hour of questioning. In two or three days of questioning, there were also inevitable self-contradictions; and these often occasioned an attempt by Schwartz to go over the same ground again, to "straighten it out."

Schwartz never ceased asking my clients to interpret the legal wording of their complaints and to interpret for him their allegations. I might have prevailed if I had objected to some of these questions, but I adopted the simpler response of permitting my client to answer after I had made a speech on the record that my client was not a lawyer and that we would not be bound by any legal interpretation he or she placed on the complaint.

These examinations became an enormous burden on my time and effectively precluded me from initiating any new cases. . . . (Of course, I received some satisfaction at the thought that whatever my time cost NORI, Bender, Segal would be billing Budget many, many times as much.) . . .

Meanwhile, I attempted to proceed with my side of the cases. On the morning of February 1, I expected Richard Lewis's attorney, Alfred Stone, to appear in my office with the documents I had demanded relating to Mr. Allen's case. But when no one arrived at the appointed hour, I called Mr. Stone. "Didn't you get my motion papers?" he asked. "I sent them out the day before yesterday." The making of a motion to prevent discovery stays the disclosure until the motion is decided.

The next day, I received Mr. Stone's motion papers. I noticed that although a movant may make his motion returnable in eight days, Mr. Stone had "noticed" his motion for February 18, nearly three weeks away, and had thus prolonged the period that my discovery was stayed, even if he lost his motion. For grounds, Mr. Stone argued that the notice served "does not specifically designate the documents to be produced, and furthermore the items demanded clearly indicate that the plaintiffs have embarked on a fishing expedition . . . ." This was surprising to me, since I thought my descriptions had been extraordinarily particular. In my papers, I pointed out how specific each of my descriptions was and that Mr. Stone had made no claim that he did not know what I was referring to. In addition, I explained the relevance of each category of papers I demanded to see to my theory of the case.

On February 18, I appeared in court, fully expecting to argue this motion so that I could get on with the case (having lost three weeks) and perhaps encourage the court to write a short opinion on the relevance of the documents I'd asked for, which might suggest some movement in the law. My first shock was the discovery that two hundred and fifty motions were scheduled to be heard that day and that this was an average calendar. My second shock was the sight of the courtroom; as the clerk called the calendar, he could hardly be heard over the hubbub, as dozens of attorneys engaged in last-minute negotiations. And after the clerk called, "Oyez oyez, all those with business for this honorable court, step forward and be heard," I received my third shock of the day: I stepped forward to announce myself ready for argument, and the judge said, "You should know we don't allow argument on discovery motions; submit your papers."

My fourth shock occurred later that day, when another lawyer informed me, in response to my story of what had occurred, that not only do the judges not allow argument, but that the docket is so crowded that they do not read the motion papers; the papers are usually read by someone from a pool of law assistants who writes a short decision to which the judge assigned to motions puts his name. And my fifth shock came three weeks later when, having waited all that time for some decision, the court ruled:

> Motion for a protective order vacating the notice of discovery and inspection is denied without prejudice to renewal upon proper papers, including a copy of the complaint, without which the court cannot determine the propriety of the items objected to, which defendants maintain go beyond the scope of the transaction involving plaintiff.

In other words, my adversary had lost because he had not filed enough papers (the complaint had been filed in the court clerk's office, but the motions judge and clerks evidently do not pull papers from their own court files — the complaint must also be annexed to motion papers). But in reality, since my adversary was free to start all over again, I had lost many hours in preparing papers and had lost six weeks' time.

Somewhat miffed, I decided to try a different approach. One reason for initially demanding the inspection of documents, rather than an oral examination of Richard Lewis, was that I had naively thought that such a strategy would enable me to begin my investigation more expeditiously. New York law provides that the plaintiff may not serve a demand for an oral examination within twenty days of service of the complaint without leave of the court — which leave, if forthcoming, inevitably requires more than the statutory twenty days. The purpose of this rule is to give a defendant an opportunity to obtain priority in taking a deposition. But the statutes contain no such twenty-day rule in the case of demands for inspection of documents. Therefore, I had served my abortive demand for inspection of documents within twenty days of my amended complaint, thinking that this would give me a head start in discovery.

By the time I "won" the motion, however, more than twenty days had passed, so I served a demand for an oral examination, requiring Richard Lewis to bring with him all of the documents I wanted to see.

Once again I was served with a motion for a protective order, staying discovery. The ground for Mr. Stone's motion was simply that the deposition of Mr. Allen, which Budget was taking, had been recessed indefinitely, and "it is elementary that the right of defendants to examine the plaintiffs has priority and the examination of the defendant may not go forward until the examination of the plaintiffs has been completed."

Once again I was furious at the delay (again, Mr. Stone gave me three weeks before the motion was submitted to the court) but convinced that this would be an easy victory, I answered his motion papers by pointing out that "priority of disclosure" is simply a shorthand for the twenty-day rule, and I had not transgressed the rule requiring a twenty-day lag between the service of the complaint and the service of a notice for an examination. I pointed out that at the rate we were going, the examination of Mr. Allen might take several sessions, spread out over a period of months, and it would delay the case if my right to discovery had to await defendants' completion of their discovery.

I had to wait until March 4 for this motion to be submitted to the court. . . .

On March 12, the court decided, as usual without opinion, Mr. Stone's motion to prevent me from examining Richard Lewis until the Allens had been fully examined:

Defendant Richard Lewis is directed to appear for examination ten days after the completion of the examination of the plaintiffs.

Stymied once again. However, there was still outstanding my demand for inspection of the documents, and Stone had not renewed his motion to preclude that discovery. So the next day I sent him by hand delivery a demand that he produce the documents on March 15.

No one appeared on March 15. Again I called Stone, and again he told me he had a motion in the mail. His renewed motion again complained that I had not described the documents with sufficient specificity, and also noted that the court had directed his client to appear for an examination some time in the future. "It is submitted that when such examinations are completed and the examination of the defendant Richard Lewis is had, the necessity of the production of the particular documents now sought to be produced will be more readily determinable and the plaintiffs will then be enabled to apply for the discovery and inspection of any documents which they specifically designate." This motion, also, was not returnable for three weeks, so I had to wait until April 8 to submit essentially the same arguments we had been through before. . . .

Meanwhile, I began my discovery in the case of Mrs. Collins. I waited until her deposition had been completed, to avoid another hassle over "priority," and then served Budget, on April 16, with about ninety interrogatories relating to their connections and course of dealing with the carpet seller, Buy-Well. I chose to use interrogatories rather than an oral deposition because I feared that on an oral examination, any individual officer or employee of Budget would disclaim knowledge of more than a small portion of Budget's operations, and I would have to take dozens of examinations to find out the facts. On the other hand, interrogatories would search the company's corporate knowledge and could always be followed up by depositions to learn more details. Following a leading form book, I addressed my questions to be answered by "Budget Finance Corp., by an officer or agent thereof." I asked many detailed questions about the knowledge Budget had of Buy-Well, such as "To the knowledge of any officer, director, or agent of Budget, did any of Buy-Well's incorporators have any prior business experience? Had any of them directed a business which had failed?" After serving the interrogatories, I sat back to wait, not so much for answers as for an expected motion to dismiss the questions. . . .

While I was waiting, the court ruled on Mr. Stone's third motion for a protective order in the Allen case:

> Motion for a protective order vacating the notice of discovery and inspection is granted without prejudice to plaintiffs' seeking such discovery after completion of the pending examinations, at which time the relevant documents will be specifically identified.

This was only a minor disappointment, because the end was in sight: on April 16, Bender, Segal completed questioning the Allens; and so, by the court's previous order, I had a right to examine Richard Lewis by April 26. Thus, on April 17, I called Mr. Stone and told him that the examinations were completed. But he took the position that the examinations of the Allens were not "completed" until the transcripts were typed and signed by the Allens.

I had no choice but to accept his interpretation, because it would take longer for me to make a motion to the court (on eight days' notice) to order the examination scheduled and to wait for the decision, than to wait for the transcripts and have my clients read and correct and sign them.

Towards the end of April, Bender, Segal moved to vacate all of my interrogatories in the Collins case.

They relied upon a variety of grounds, but most heavily on the claim that I was asking questions about Budget's "present knowledge" of Buy-Well's status and activities, whereas "the present knowledge of any of Budget's officers, directors, or agents is not material, because it is not in any way related to, or indicative of, the knowledge, if any, of the persons concerned at the relevant time." Bender, Segal listed by number several of my questions which supposedly indicated that I was asking questions about an irrelevant period of time. These included such questions as "To the knowledge of any officer, director or agent of Budget, what were Buy-Well's assets at the time of the assignment?"

I answered these contentions by arguing that we sought to demonstrate a continuing close relationship between Budget and Buy-Well, and all the relations between them were relevant to proving the existence of the course of dealing. Then I waited for May 9, when the motion would be submitted.

May

The Collins motion was indeed submitted to the court on May 9, but there was to be no decision that month, nor indeed until June 14. . . .

But in the Allen case, I expected real progress towards examining Richard Lewis. The transcripts of the examinations of the Allens were signed May 3, and I notified Mr. Stone of the event, saying that I expected to examine his client by May 13, in conformity with the court's order. He said he would talk to his client about a date and call me back. But by May 7, he had not called me back, so I called him again. He said he had not been able to reach his client who "didn't have a telephone," and he would call me in "a couple of days." Since that would take us almost to the tenth day after May 3, I sent him a hand-delivered letter notifying him that I would conduct the examination on May 13, at 10:00 A.M.

I hired a stenographer for the morning of the 13th, and this time I genuinely expected Stone and Lewis to appear. But they did not. And so, after waiting for fifteen minutes, I called Stone.

He said that he hadn't reached his client, that he thought his client might get in touch with him "any day now" and that he hadn't called me the day before because that "was a very hectic day for me."

I was extremely angry, both because I was getting nothing in return for having subjected my clients to questioning, and because I was getting no closer to testing the legal issues I had set out to challenge. So once again I went back to my typewriter, this time to write a motion to strike the answer of Richard Lewis for his failure to appear or alternatively to order him to appear and to pay the stenographer's bill and reasonable attorney's fees for the time I had to spend writing motions to make him appear.

Stone answered by saying that "we could not possibly communicate with our client . . . on such short notice. [Schrag is trying to have this court impose] costs on the defendant Lewis who had been completely unaware of these conversations between counsel and who is certainly not avoiding any examination. [We do not] understand the reasons for this apparent zeal on the part of the moving attorney . . . [T]here is no particular urgency to the proceedings herein." He concluded by requesting that the court merely fix a date and time for Lewis to be examined at the court house, which struck me as an odd request since the examining party is supposed to have his choice of where to conduct the examination.

June

On the third of June, my motion to punish Lewis was granted only to the extent of requiring Lewis to appear for examination on the 17th. No mention was made in the decision of my request for costs or counsel fees. The court set the court house as the place of examination. So by failing to appear within ten days as the court had earlier ordered, Stone was able both to delay the case by a month and four days and to have the examination switched from my office to the court house across the street from his office, with no penalty whatsoever.

But Stone and Lewis did appear on the 17th, and the examination must be reckoned a success. Lewis denied making any guarantees that the food would last four months but gave evidence going beyond my expectations about his close relationship with Budget Finance. He testified, for example, that when a customer gave him an order, he made the customer fill out a credit application (on a Budget form) which was then sent to the finance company. If Budget approved the credit, the customer was notified that the sale was final, but if Budget rejected the credit application, the customer was told the deal was off; Lewis made no effort to finance his sales except through Budget.

At noon, Stone flatly refused to come back after eating. He said he was a busy man with other things to do, nor could he come back to complete the examination during the next few weeks. I thought I had a right to insist on a continuation reasonably promptly, but given the inevitable month's delay between the making of a motion and its resolution, I had no way to enforce any demand for an earlier date. I therefore agreed to the setting of July 15 as an adjourned date. . . .

In June, also, the court finally ruled on Bender, Segal's motion to strike my Collins interrogatories; their motion was granted. One of the court's grounds had been relied upon by defendant: that many of the questions "contain no frame of reference as to time." That ruling was wrong, but at least I could feel that the court was trying to be rational. But the court's other ground, which had not been mentioned by defendant, was simply absurd: "Plaintiff does not expect a single witness to have the requisite degree of knowledge upon the matters sought to be disclosed and the requesting of a single person ["Budget, by an officer or agent thereof"] to furnish disclosure concerning the acts and personal knowledge of other officers and employees is onerous and oppressive." I had used that language only because I had copied it out of a form book, and it was supposed to be the proper way to search corporate knowledge. However, I had no opportunity to tell that to the court, since it came up with that ground on its own.

The court's objections did not seem insuperable, and I had no alternative but to start again, by serving a new set of interrogatories. I therefore redrafted my questions, inserting into each one a cumbersome phrase about the time period involved, so that they now read, e.g.,

> To the knowledge, as of the date of the assignment, of any persons who were then and are now officers, directors, or agents of Budget, what were Buy-Well's assets at the time of the assignment in question?

I readdressed the questions to "Budget, by such officers or agents thereof as have knowledge of the facts," shipped them off to Bender, Segal, and waited for the inevitable motion to strike — which duly came.

* * *

On July 15, I completed my examination of Richard Lewis. This second session was less successful than the first. I asked him about other customers to whom he had sold freezers, pointing out that these questions were relevant because I had to prove a pattern or practice of fraudulent dealings in order to collect punitive damages. But Stone directed Lewis not to answer these questions nor to reveal the names of other buyers, on the ground that they were not relevant to any valid action I might have. In addition, Lewis did not produce any of his business records, claiming that he had gone out of business shortly before my suit was instituted and had destroyed all his records at that time because he no longer needed them. I felt certain that he was not telling the truth but had no way to prove that he had not destroyed his records.

At the beginning of July, contemplating the completion of the examination of Richard Lewis on July 15, I served Stone with a notice to examine the president of Quality Furniture on July 16. I had not wanted to examine him earlier, because I assumed that information revealed by Lewis would be of help in questioning officers of Quality. But on the 15th, Stone again announced that he would not comply with my demand, and I was relegated to choosing between the adjourned date he offered me — August 13 — or moving to punish his client, a motion which, in the light of the history of the case, I felt no confidence about winning. I accepted his August 13 date.

August

But on August 9th, he wrote me:

Dear Sir:

Please be advised that our client Quality Furniture, Inc., has filed a petition in bankruptcy under chapter XI. Under the circumstances all proceedings against it are stayed until disposition of that proceeding. The examination scheduled for August 13th will therefore have to be delayed to some future date.

Ah, the regretful tone of his letter, Ah, the law. At this point I started thinking seriously about some other career.

A little research confirmed the fact that the federal bankruptcy court had indeed stayed all state court proceedings against Quality (to preserve the estate for the creditors) and that it was virtually impossible to have such a stay vacated. Yet this might delay my suits against them indefinitely.

With no particular plan in mind, however, I resolved to attend the first hearing in the case in federal bankruptcy court and do what I could for my clients. That hearing was set for August 27.

Meanwhile, I invented a tort. I served an amended complaint on behalf of Mr. and Mrs. Day, accusing Dependable Credit of engaging in a pattern and practice of purchasing unconscionable contracts, which on their face were exorbitant, and alleging that such conduct subjected them to liability for punitive damages. I hoped that this claim would seem so outrageous to them that they would move to dismiss, but they did not. They merely answered. So to provoke the issue, I served them with a notice to inspect all of the freezer contracts they had bought during the last three years. I knew they could not comply with this demand because they would have to fear that I would peruse the contracts to solicit new plaintiffs to sue them. Little did they know that I had my hands full with half a dozen cases. They had to object to the notice on the ground that my tort was unknown to the law. And they did, by a motion returnable August 23. They did me the favors of informing the court that this was an important test case and of arguing squarely on the merits rather than on some obscure technical ground. In my response, I too argued the merits, presenting the court with a somewhat academic analysis of the role of tort law in regulating merchant-consumer relations, quoting the Kerner Commission Report, and marshalling whatever legal and secondary support I could for my tort. At last, after seven months, this was test case litigation as I had imagined it as a law student. I expected to lose, but at least I would have an appealable decision, and I would be able to present an issue of some significance to an appellate court. I looked forward to September for a square ruling on the merits, one way or the other.

The next August event was a decision on Bender, Segal's motion to dismiss my second set of Collins interrogatories. Bender, Segal had argued once again that my questions were not specific enough in delineating the time period involved (I really could not imagine how to be more specific). I had pointed out to the court that the time period referred to was as specific as it could possibly be, that no one could have any doubt about what I was asking, and that I was asking only for corporate knowledge at the time of the assignment of Mrs. Collins' contract to Budget. And I noted that this time I had not addressed my questions to a single officer or agent, but rather to whatever employees knew the facts. The court ruled:

> Motion to strike is granted with leave to serve new and proper interrogatories. Although afforded an opportunity to submit proper interrogatories, the defects heretofore appearing in the original questions have not yet been cured.

End of decision. Not a hint of what was wrong, or how I could serve more proper questions. The next time I saw Jack Schwartz, my adversary at Bender, Segal, I expressed my astonishment at the fact that the court did not seem even to have read my arguments. "I'm not going to knock them when I win," he said. "But what do you expect when they have two hundred and fifty motions a day, and the judges don't even get near motion papers, but permit their cases to be decided by clerks and assistants who have had at best a third-rate legal education?"

Toward the end of August, I moved to compel Richard Lewis to reveal the names and addresses of his other freezer customers (which Stone had ordered him not to do at the examination), on the theory that they were essential witnesses to the pattern of his fraud. His attorney resisted my motion. Since he claimed to have destroyed his records, I did not really expect to obtain names, but I thought I might at least obtain a ruling, which would be something of a precedent, that such names and addresses were relevant and therefore discoverable.

August 27 — the first hearing on Quality's bankruptcy — turned out to be one of the more exciting days of the year. I arrived in the bankruptcy court a little early so as to hear some earlier case and get some idea of how the court worked, since I knew nothing whatever about bankruptcy. When I went into the hearing room, there were only three seats left, all in one row. I sat in the middle seat, and soon two gentlemen entered and sat on either side of me. Presently they began talking over me, and my mind snapped to attention when I heard one of them say "Quality." It developed from their conversation that one was Quality's bankruptcy lawyer and the other its treasurer, and they were talking about me. Evidently they did not know any more than I did what the status of my case was now that they had filed in bankruptcy. So far so good.

Quality's case was called by the bankruptcy referee, and the two men next to me and several others from around the room moved forward and sat at a big counsel table. The referee turned to the attorney for the chief creditor — the one with the largest claim — and announced that he would now hear nominations for members of the creditors' committee, which would supervise the operation of the store until it was either closed down in a full-fledged bankruptcy or reached a composition with unsecured creditors. "Whom do you nominate?" he asked.

With all the spontaneity of an obviously rigged election, the chief creditor nominated himself and several other people.

"Are there any other nominations?" asked the referee, in his best *pro forma* manner.

I figured it was now or never, and any forum for injecting an issue is better than no forum, so I stood up in the back of the room and announced, "I nominate Jack Greenberg."

The courtroom reacted like the audience in a movie wedding where the mysterious stranger runs into the church and objects to the vows. All eyes turned on me. The lawyers at the counsel table swiveled around to see who had spoken. The referee leaned forward, pointed at me and said, "Who are you? And who is Jack Greenberg?"

Edging ever so slowly into the aisle and forward, I explained that Jack Greenberg and I were Director-Counsel and Assistant Counsel of the NAACP Legal Defense Fund and that we represented consumers who were creditors of Quality in that they had pending in state court punitive damage claims against Quality for fraud in making sales. The referee was stumped by my unusual motion, and after some hesitation, he denied it, without giving any satisfactory reason. But clearly he felt badly about denying it, so he turned to Quality's lawyer and demanded to know about this alleged fraud.

Quality's bankruptcy counsel was, however, not its litigation counsel, and he had to admit he didn't know anything about the state court cases. This made the referee very angry.

The referee, unable to obtain any information from Quality, then turned to me and asked me the status of these cases, a question which I did not exactly seek to evade.

"Your honor," I said, "these cases were proceeding along in an orderly fashion, and the plaintiffs were systematically conducting discovery proceedings, when suddenly these proceedings were interrupted by your stay of all state court proceedings, which I hereby move to vacate."

General tumult at the counsel table, and Quality's lawyer rose to his feet violently asserting that this would jeopardize the estate, injure the creditors, and so forth, without quite explaining how. But the referee announced his inclination to grant my motion, whereupon the chief creditor claimed that he was a contributor to the Legal Defense Fund and would not object. "One of these days," said the referee to Quality's lawyer, "these people are going to inquire into all of the credit practices up in Harlem, aren't they?" "Yes, they are," said Quality's lawyer sheepishly.

Of course, nothing in the law is quite as simple as that: the referee instructed me to make my motion in writing, returnable September 17, and then it took him until September 30 to sign the order, so it took fully two months for me to get back to where I had been on August 9 when I was informed of the bankruptcy proceeding. And even then, the stay was vacated only as to my discovery, and I would have to apply for further relief (which I might not be granted) to go on the state court trial calendar.

September

At the beginning of September I left for a three-week vacation. I returned to find that I had won more little victories while I was away than during any comparable period while at work.

For one thing, the court had granted my motion to require Lewis to produce the names and addresses of his other customers. Unfortunately, it reached this decision without any opinion whatsoever, so the precedential value was limited. And, as I expected, even the immediate impact of the decision was slight. While I was still away, another NORI attorney interrogated Lewis (pursuant to the order) about his business records, but Lewis stuck to his story that "I never kept any books of account" and that "I threw away most of the things [records] that I had, being that I had no more any interest in the business. . . . What am I going to do with them? . . . Of course, to me it was garbage."

... [M]ost surprising, my motion to see all of Dependable Credit's contracts was granted. Unfortunately, although both sides had framed the issue on the motion in terms of a test of the existence of the tort of persistent unconscionability, the court's brief order in my favor was as cryptic as any that it had ever handed down against me:

> Motion for a protective order modifying notice of examination before trial is denied, and defendant, together with the records set forth in plaintiff's notice, is directed to appear for examination before trial at Special Term, Part II [the part of the court for *ex parte* motions] of this court at 10 A.M. September 26, 1968, at which time rulings with respect to the admissibility of the records may be obtained from the justice presiding at said Special Term.

It was difficult to fathom what this order meant. First, the court seems to have thought that I was seeking, and the credit company resisting, an examination before trial; actually, I had simply asked for copies of certain written documents. More puzzling, what did the court leave to the *ex parte* judge to decide? Surely, after having read our papers, which fully briefed the issue of the existence of a tort cause of action, it could not be passing the buck for deciding that rather complex and important issue to another judge to decide on the spot on the basis of five minutes of oral argument, without submission of briefs. Yet the court did mean to give the *ex parte* judge something to decide, and it avoided in its decision any mention of the underlying issue.

Inevitably, my adversary and I got into an argument on the telephone as to what the order meant. But since I had won the motion, I was in a stronger position, and I was able to persuade Dependable's lawyers that the court must be presumed to have acted rationally, and it therefore must have resolved the tort issue in my favor and left it open to Dependable only to resist disclosure of particular contracts on grounds of privilege, rather than relevance.

Accepting this interpretation, my adversary announced that he would appeal the decision to the January term of the appellate division, and since that appeal would give me a second chance to obtain an authoritative opinion on the existence of a tort remedy,

I was happy to consent to a stay of the disclosure until the appeal was decided.

My final effort in September was the drafting of a third set of interrogatories in the Collins case. A staff attorney older and wiser than I concluded that although the court had never said so either time, what it really found offensive in my first two sets of interrogatories was their sheer length — that ninety written questions was simply too much for the court, regardless of their relevance or of the equities. So I chopped them down to the nineteen most important questions, those which I considered to be most essentially directed to the evidence I would need to establish. Once again these questions sought to establish Budget's state of mind and knowledge of Buy-Well's affairs at the time it bought Mrs. Collins' contract. In addition, I asked Budget (as I had done before) to attach certain essential documents to its answers, such as copies "of all documents reflecting [the payment to Buy-Well for the Collins contract], including, but not limited to, cancelled checks and ledger sheets," and "copies of any credit reports on the plaintiff and any relevant memoranda and correspondence."

Budget's objection to these interrogatories was that they were "simply immaterial, irrelevant and unnecessary, because they seek information beyond the scope of any proper issues raised by the pleadings." So once again, I hoped that by demonstrating in detailed terms the relevance of each question to proving the connection between Budget and Buy-Well, I could at least get the court to say, in ruling the questions relevant, that a finance company could be shown to lack *bona fides* if it had sufficient knowledge of the fly-by-night character of the dealers it purchased contracts from. Of course, it would be six weeks before I got any decision at all.

October

Now the year was rushing to a close, and my activity became centered more and more around the case that had triggered all the others — Mr. Allen's freezer. On October 7, I sent Mr. Stone a copy of the freshly signed order of the federal court permitting my interrogation of Quality's officers to proceed. I asked him to select a date convenient for him so that he would not make a motion on the excuse that I had picked an impossible date. Not having heard from him, I called him a week later, and he said that he had not asked his client about a date, but he would do so the next week. Of course, the next week, when I called again, he said that he would not have time to contact his client until the following week. Having no choice but to set a date myself, I sent him a notice demanding examinations of Quality's president and treasurer on October 31, and requiring them to bring with them their lists, if they had any, of Lewis's other freezer customers.

As usual, at the last possible moment Stone served me with a motion (returnable three weeks hence) for a protective order, claiming that I had no right to examine both officers until I first demonstrated that one did not have all the requisite knowledge and that I was seeking the production of improper and irrelevant documents, such as the list of the other freezer customers. I pointed out that we had already been through the issue of the lists of customers and that the law of the case had been resolved in my favor.

November

Or so I thought. Without further explanation, the court in November permitted the examination to proceed (at the court house, as Stone had again requested), but my demand to see the customer lists was stricken "as improper." Since I didn't think that Quality would produce such lists in any event, I did not bother wasting six months on an appeal.

Shortly thereafter, the court struck my third set of Collins interrogatories. Once again, its reasoning made little contact with the questions asked or the facts in the record. According to the court:

> With respect to those portions of the interrogatories seeking detailed information as to the corporate makeup of the vendor, and the operation of its business, the business background of its principals, officers, and employees, the fact that the corporation is now dissolved, absent any other circumstances, does not create an obligation upon the defendant to procure these answers for plaintiff. The requirement that defendant reproduce quantities of books, records, documents and papers, bears [*sic*] the cost there-

of and furnish the same without charge to plaintiff, is oppressive and burdensome.

This decision was truly frustrating. I had not asked Budget to go out and "procure" anything; I simply wanted to know what it had known about Buy-Well. Nor had I relied, in my papers, on a theory having anything to do with the fact that Buy-Well was dissolved. I had just said that I was entitled to information in the possession of Budget. I had asked for the reproduction of a few pieces of paper, as I was entitled to do, but had not demanded copying of "quantities of books, records, documents and papers"; nor had I made any comments about the cost of reproduction. Growing doubts about my own ability to write plain English were allayed only by Jack Schwartz's mentioning once again (referring this time to the latest Collins decision) that I could not reasonably expect any closer attention to the facts from such an overworked court.

The court granted me permission to submit proper interrogatories to another judge, for approval by the court, so I drafted still a fourth set of questions. This fourth set (now down to seventeen questions) was very much like the third; I cut out demands for some of the papers to be duplicated, and now asked for copies of only nine pieces of paper. My motion papers stressed that I was not seeking to make Budget "procure" anything. Basically, the fourth set of interrogatories was a desperate attempt to get some judge, assistant, or clerk, seriously to read through the motion papers and render a reasoned decision, even if only to say that the information I sought was irrelevant. At least that order would be worth appealing.

Of course, Jack Schwartz used the court's inattention to the facts against me. He argued:

> In an artificial and contrived attempt to circumvent the ruling plaintiff now proffers identical questions with the explanation that the questions do not require Budget to "procure" information regarding a third party. Mr. Schrag has thus seized upon some pretended semantic distinction in an effort to avoid the clear and unmistakable intent of Mr. Justice B----'s decision. This attempt to render Justice B----'s decision a virtual nullity is itself an affront to this court.

As the year 1968 ran out, the court had not yet ruled on the fourth set of Collins interrogatories.

December

Although Quality's bankruptcy proceedings made a trial in the Allen and Buenavidez cases seem further off than ever, there was still precedent to be set along the way. At the urging of Susan Freiman, a young, brilliant Legal Aid attorney with a flair for bankruptcy law, I went back to the federal court on another scheduled date for a hearing in Quality's case, to renew my motion to place a defrauded consumers' representative on Quality's creditors' committee. Again the courtroom spectators were astonished when I stood up in the audience and made an oral motion — this time to add Shyleur Barrack, the director of the Harlem office of the Legal Aid Society, to the committee. Both the creditors' lawyer and Quality's lawyer objected violently. "We on the creditors' committee are concerned with real creditors' claims, with claims of merchants who have advanced money or goods to Quality. We're not concerned with claims of consumers."

"That's exactly the point he's trying to make," said the bankruptcy referee. "Since you are not looking out for his clients' interest, he wants to add someone to the committee who will do so. And it's my job to see to it that the creditors' committee has as broad a spectrum of representation as possible."

"Well then," said the creditors' lawyer, "the reason you can't grant his motion is that his clients haven't filed proofs of claim. And no one is a creditor in this proceeding unless they have filed a claim in this court."

The referee didn't even ask me whether I had filed the proofs or not. "We'll soon find out if they have," he said. And from under his desk he whisked out a telephone, dialed the clerk, ordered the file sent to him, and recessed the case for ten minutes.

In the back of the room, the creditors' lawyer and Quality's lawyer buzzed anxiously about the calling of their bluff. Miss Freiman and I, meanwhile, exchanged smug looks, for, months earlier, without knowing exactly why we did it, we had filed proofs of claim on behalf of Allen; Buenavidez; and a Legal Aid client who had bought a freezer from Richard Lewis, was being sued by Budget, and had made a claim against Quality.

When the case was called again and the referee pointed out that our clients seemed to be creditors within the letter of Chapter XI of the Bankruptcy Law, the creditors' and debtor's lawyers had run out of objections. The referee granted my motion, whereupon, as before, the objectors withdrew their objection "for the sake of peace."

That afternoon, in trying to assess what we had accomplished, we discovered that voting power on a creditors' committee is proportional to the dollar value of the claims a member represents. Since our punitive damage claims amounted to over $100,000, we represented the largest creditor, and were running the store.

The next week, we all went to the creditors' committee meeting: Barrack as a member, Miss Freiman and I as his special counsel. The members, lawyers for various creditors, had heard something of our success in court, but were nevertheless stunned by our physical presence in their midst; they had never seen anything like this, and simply didn't know what to make of us. "You're chasing a rainbow," one said to Miss Freiman.

"Perhaps there's a pot of gold at the end of it," she answered.

But when Quality's lawyer arrived, it became evident at once that we had come to participate in the last meeting of creditors, and to witness the end of a 133-year-old minor empire. Quality's owners simply could not reach a suitable arrangement with the creditors and were ready to consent to an adjudication of bankruptcy. The store would be closed down and sold at auction for the benefit of creditors.

But the consumers' representatives still had a role to play. We listened in silent amazement as the creditors decided not to close the store at once, but to obtain an adjudication of bankruptcy to take effect just before Christmas. Christmas sales would swell the pot which they would eventually divide; contracts for the merchandise sold would quickly be assigned to Budget for cash. No one mentioned the fact that each sale would involve express and implied warranties to consumers which would be meaningless because Quality would be out of business and Budget would claim to be a bona fide purchaser.

Back in court three days later, the creditors and Quality made a joint application for an adjudication of bankruptcy to take effect just before Christmas. Once again there was a stirring in the back of the court. "Before you sign that order, your Honor," said Miss Freiman in a tiny voice, "I think that there is something that you should know."

"What's that?" asked his Honor. And she told him about the warranties that would be valid for four years under the Uniform Commercial Code, or until Christmas, whichever came sooner.

"Are you suggesting that I close down the store at once?" he asked.

"I suppose I am," she said.

"So ordered," replied his Honor. And he ordered Quality's lawyer immediately to telephone the store and instruct the management to stop selling, to send home the employees, and to lock the door.

The lawyers for Quality and the creditors simply lost control over themselves. Flailing their arms, they demanded to know from Miss Freiman who she was and whom she thought she represented. "She doesn't represent any potential buyer; she has no standing to make a motion," yelled one of the lawyers. "I doubt she's even a lawyer."

But Miss Freiman, who did not represent a potential buyer, stood mute, and after the room was again calm, the referee said quietly, "I guess you gentlemen will simply have to accept her as the representative of the community."

III.
CONCLUSION

My involvement in the bankruptcy proceedings was one of the high and even humorous spots in what was otherwise a disillusioning year. Disillusioning because I learned how time-consuming and how costly test cases are, but most of all because I had thought that poverty lawyers and the judiciary — at least in the North — would be partners in reforming the law as quickly as possible. I learned, instead, that the lower state courts — on which so much really depends — are neither friendly nor hostile to law reform. Instead, they are totally indifferent.[*]

---

[*]In 1975, however, the FTC did adopt a regulation requiring consumer credit contracts to state prominently that they are "subject to all claims and defenses which the debtor could assert against" the original seller. See 16 C.F.R. 433.2.

In recent years, as the problems of the poor have shifted from those of racial discrimination to those of an imbalance of economic power, the legal questions of burning importance to the poor have undergone a corresponding shift from constitutional issues to rights under state law. As the law of consumer protection, landlord-tenant relations, and the family become foci for law reform efforts, state court test litigation becomes more and more important. Yet to the extent New York's practice and procedure is typical, the state courts have made an expeditious resolution of a novel issue all but impossible. . . .

IV.
EPILOGUE

I finished writing this history on New Year's Day, 1969, and, on the theory that any twelve-month period is representative of a continuous process, I had not intended to bring it up to date in galley proofs. But recent events have changed my mind.

In the Allen case, it seems unlikely that I will be able either to have the facts tried or to obtain recovery for my client. The federal court is moving toward hearing claims against the bankrupt and distributing its assets, but the Bankruptcy Act permits only tort claims based on negligence to be proved and allowed in bankruptcy proceedings; for historical reasons, intentional torts are not provable in bankruptcy, so I may not be able to have my case heard in the federal forum. (Of course, my clients' claims will not be discharged in bankruptcy, but since Quality is not planning to reopen its doors, undischarged claims will be worthless.) The claims cannot be proved in state court in time to participate as judgment claims in the bankruptcy proceeding, because, even if there were no further delays whatsoever in the state court, it would be over a year before the cases could work their way to the top of the calendar. And delays such as those reported in this article are virtually inevitable.

As for Collins, the Court finally ordered Budget Finance to answer my interrogatories. But Budget answered more than half of the questions by stating:

Budget is unable to answer this question through its present officers, agents or employees or as a result of examination of its files.

The Day case was decided by the appellate division early in February. In that appeal, I had sought to sustain the lower court's denial to Dependable of a protective order by arguing that a pattern or practice of financing contracts that were on their face unconscionable was tortious. I made plain in my brief that I was relying for the relief demanded upon tort theory, not upon the Uniform Commercial Code:

> We do not dispute appellant's argument that the Uniform Commercial Code does not provide for damages in the case of an unconscionable sale. Respondents do not look to the Code for the damages they demand. Rather they rely upon the common law doctrine that "the infliction of intentional harm, resulting in damage, without legal excuses or justification" is tortious. Penn-Ohio Steel Corp. v. Allis-Chalmers Mfg. Co., 7 App.Div.2d 441, 443, 184 N.Y.S.2d 58 (1st Dept. 1959). Respondents refer to the traditional doctrines of unconscionability for guidelines as to wrongful conduct; they refer to tort law for their remedy. . . . Unconscionability is a tort [as well as a contract defense] where it is a regular and knowing practice.

In its short opinion unanimously reversing the decision of the lower court, the appellate division ignored the allegations of the complaint and the theory of my brief:

> The plaintiffs seek to recover punitive damages from defendant asserting a complaint based on Uniform Commercial Code Section 2-302 in that plaintiffs were induced to buy a refrigerator freezer at an "unconscionable" price within the meaning of the said statute. . . . Section 2-302 of the Uniform Commercial Code does not provide any damages to a party who enters into an unconscionable contract. . . . The documents called for under the notice of inspection are neither material nor necessary to plaintiff's [*sic*] cause of action. . . .

FURTHER QUESTIONS

1. In an omitted portion of this article Professor Schrag comments that when consumers are represented by lawyers their creditors almost invariably settle potential cases with "little consideration of their merits." Other commentators have made the same point. This suggests that the structure of representation for the poor is more important than the substance of the law. If so, is Schrag putting enormous energy into dealing with the wrong problem? How, other than by allocating a large influx of funds to budgets for legal services, might you increase the availability of lawyers for indigent consumers? Is the failure of representation a common difficulty in other circumstances? Is this an intractable capability problem?

2. Why are bankruptcy proceedings so expeditious while State Supreme Court proceedings so languorous? Why not simply submit cases like *Allen* to a referee at the outset and then have all parties and witnesses express their views directly to him or her? Would capability problems be more or less oppressive in this context?

3. Schrag suggests that he had an advantage in the *Allen* case because Mr. Allen had not defaulted. Schrag's litigation stance was, however, remedial. Is there any way other than by litigation to take prophylactic measures so as to reduce the number of instances in which contracts like these are signed and assigned? (Be as imaginative as you can be in constructing alternatives.) What capability problems do these alternatives encounter?

4. This account of *Allen v. Quality Furniture* should bring home the critical point that capability problems are not problems for everyone. Often they are exploited. One litigant's frustration is another's satisfaction. Try to think of particular instances in which if you represented a client like Mr. Allen you would use capability problems to your own advantage. Would the use of such problems be ethical? Would the failure to take advantage of such problems be ethical?

INDEX

Prepared by Geoffrey R. Watson